CH00840958

NETTLES AND CREAM

NETTLES AND CREAM

John Calver

ATHENA PRESS
LONDON

NETTLES AND CREAM
Copyright © John Calver 2005

All Rights Reserved

No part of this book may be reproduced in any form
by photocopying or by any electronic or mechanical means,
including information storage or retrieval systems,
without permission in writing from both the copyright
owner and the publisher of this book.

ISBN 1 84401 471 1

First Published 2005
ATHENA PRESS
Queen's House, 2 Holly Road
Twickenham TW1 4EG
United Kingdom

Printed for Athena Press

To Flora

Acknowledgements

Thanks to:

Val and Pauline Wrycraft for transferring the manuscript from longhand.

A Childs for the family trees.

M J Everett for continuous assistance in every way.

M and Barry Mason for half a lifetime of friendship and assistance.

Jim and Robert Macaulay for all work done on the farm and good advice.

Yvonne, Elizabeth and the late P Brunning for a long friendship and help.

Don Fisher for friendship and cooperation.

C M Simmons and son for help during difficult coal trade times.

The family of the late Percy Smith Blacksmith.

Eric and Pam March for unfailing friendship and help.

Preface

Someone said: Nettles and Cream – more of the former, not a lot of cream. Maybe it was so. But if we had no nettles, the cream would not have been so sweet.

My roots are deep in Wrabnesss as you will see, with both my parents' families spending their working lives there. The cream from the beginning, the environment that we lived in. I had boyhood friends; we were in a world of imagination. Inanimate objects could become anything we fancied. Having myopia, I was able to see and study very small things, and was able to draw and paint in watercolours, and later make small items from wood. There was the bonus of living things all around us, with farm animals, chickens, ducks on the pond, cats and dogs, garden flowers and orchards.

I enjoyed my school days and didn't want to leave, but leaving coincided with the beginning of the war in 1939. I had no option but to go into my father's retail coal business – a rough, hard job. There were compensations for there were many interesting people in the villages that we called on.

After a longish wait, I married Flora. We were childhood sweethearts, cream indeed. She helped me and everyone all the time. Good days. We had laughter in our lives especially when we became involved with village entertainments.

Nettles were poking their stings through as you will see later in the story, but I guess they are in everyone's life.

I called no man master and did not become a millionaire but we survived reasonably well. I always considered that if your needs are supplied, your wants are not as important.

John Calver

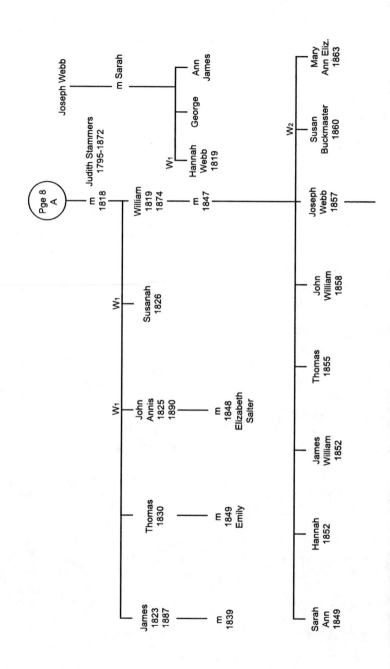

Pge 8 A

Joseph Webb — m Sarah

W1
Hannah Webb 1819 — George — Ann James

Judith Stammers 1795-1872

m 1818

William 1819 1874

m 1847

W2
Susan Buckmaster 1860 — Mary Ann Eliz. 1863

Joseph Webb 1857

John William 1858

Thomas 1855

James William 1852

Hannah 1852

Sarah Ann 1849

W1
Susanah 1826

W1
John Annis 1825 1890 — m 1848 Elizabeth Salter

Thomas 1830 — m 1849 Emily

James 1823 1887 — m 1839

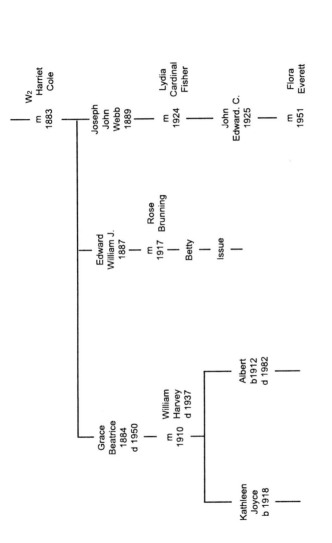

W₂
Harriet
Cole

m
1883

Joseph
John
Webb
1889

Lydia
Cardinal
Fisher

m
1924

John
Edward. C.
1925

Flora
Everett

m
1951

Rose
Brunning

Edward
William J.
1887

m
1917

Betty

Issue

Grace
Beatrice
1884
d 1950

William
Harvey
d 1937

m
1910

Albert
b 1912
d 1982

Kathleen
Joyce
b 1918

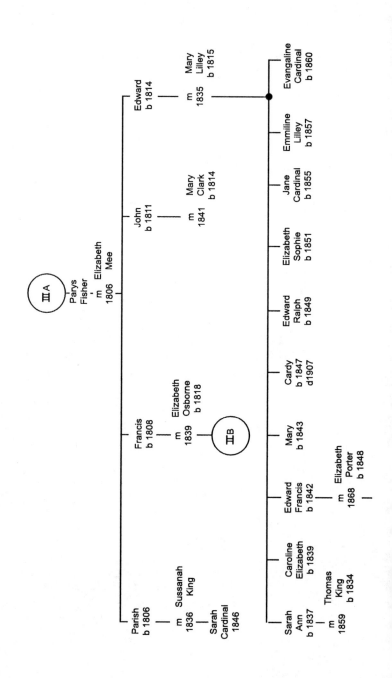

IIIA

Parys Fisher — m 1806 — Elizabeth Mee

Parish b 1806 — m 1836 — Sussanah King / Sarah Cardinal 1846

Francis b 1808 — m 1839 — Elizabeth Osborne b 1818

IIB

John b 1811 — m 1841 — Mary Clark b 1814

Edward b 1814 — m 1835 — Mary Lilley b 1815

Sarah Ann b 1837 — m 1859 — Thomas King b 1834

Caroline Elizabeth b 1839

Edward Francis b 1842 — m 1868 — Elizabeth Porter b 1848

Mary b 1843

Cardy b 1847 d 1907

Edward Ralph b 1849

Elizabeth Sophie b 1851

Jane Cardinal b 1855

Emmiline Lilley b 1857

Evangaline Cardinal b 1860

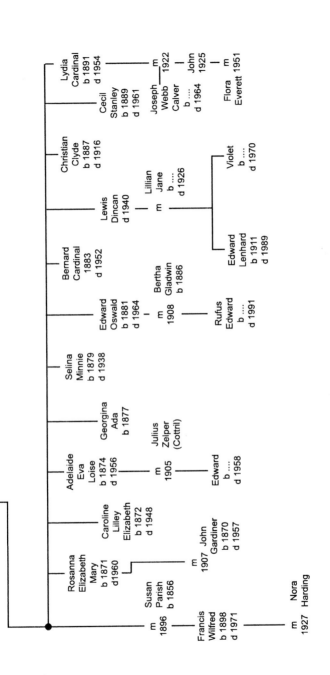

Chapter One

Wrabness is a small Essex village on high ground on the south bank of the River Stour. Its extent is about 1100 acres.

The sandy shore is about three-quarters of a mile in length, and is in this day and age a very popular spot when the sun shines and the affluent society spend their holidays in the assortment of chalets and caravans that abound.

The river laps at the base of the cliffs, gradually eroding them. How far out into the river did they jut 1000 years ago? There is no doubt that in those far-off days there was a satisfactory landing facility for those fellows we call Vikings, for what better spots could you find for smuggling and trading or claiming certain areas?

When William of Normandy came over the sea in the conquest of these islands, Wrabness was recorded in the Domesday Survey as 'Being held by St Edmund'. It consisted of:

1 Manor and 5 Hides of Land
6 Villeins
8 Cottars
6 Serfs
3 ploughs on the demesne
6 ploughs belonging to the men

There is one meadow – one mill, one salt pan.

There are 2 colts, 30 swine, 200 sheep and five hives of bees.

It is worth six pounds.

The little church of All Saints stands overlooking the river just south-east of the ness or promontory that give the village part of its unusual name. Whether the Saxons laid its very first foundations in unknown, but that the Norman builders' hands were busy here is certain. This is observed from a few fragments of the original arch showing above the new south door. Across the nave is the real evidence.

This is the door leading into the vestry (which was built in

1908, when the building was enlarged). You do not, of course, get a chance to see the simple pleasing lines of the arch behind unless you are signing the marriage register. If one was thus engaged, one would not be expected to be drooling about architecture. However, here it is, pure Norman, with single round columns capped with cushion capitals, and surely stone brought from France, for there is no stone in the part of Essex resembling this. I should think the date is between 1100 and 1160, and the door hung there was of course the north door.

When Johannes, or John the Chaplin, whose name is the first of the long list of incumbents, dated 1220, was taking the service the building was very small, and *The Monuments of North-East Essex* tells us: 'The walls are if septaria – rubble and brick with limestone dressings...the Nave was built in the early 12th Century. Early in the 14th Century the Chancel was rebuilt.'

An extract from the Parish Records tell us that AD 1697 on Thursday morning (about the appearance of day) after the celebration of the Holy Sacrament in the Chancel on Easter Sunday, immediately the whole roof of it fell flat to the ground, together with the fore wall to within two or three feet of the foundation, which being ripped up about a foot under the chancel door there lies across it a 'gravestone upon which is to be seen a large patee cross at length. This summer if was erected firm and strong and afterwards it was ceilled'.

'The walls wainscoted, the communion table devoutly railed, the floor new paved and three convenient seats now built of all which there was none before.'

Again to quote *The Monuments of North-East Essex*, 'The roof of the East parts of the nave is of late 15th Century date, and of simple hammer beam type with moulded main timbers: the spandrels of the braces below the hammer beams are carved with foliage.'

In the porch on the west wall is a coffin top of Purbeck marble with a foliated cross upon a Calvary. (This is now fitted into the south porch wall.) To quote further from that source: 'The early 12th Century north doorway with a round arch of two plain orders, enclosing a rubble tympanum supported by a segmented arch: the jambs have each a free shaft with cushion capital and a chamfered abacus continued round the inner order.' There is also a font with an octagonal bowl and panelled sides, each carved with an evangelistic symbol or a seated saint, all defaced etc., fifteenth century. Further investigation show that the panels could be representing:

N side St John, NE side an Eagle
E side St Mark, SE side a Winged Lion
S side St Luke, SW side a Winged Ox
W side St Matthew, NW side an Angel.
From the church records we learn that:

Anno 1700 in December the Churchyard was planted round with young ash trees and the parsonage house being ready to drop and did in part fall down, was this year pulled down to the ground and erected again three rooms of a floor, three story high…together with a kitchen or brew house a Dairy and Dairy chamber not adjoining the head house.

Before alterations at the church there was a gallery across the west end of the church.

I have read that the stone tower collapsed and that it contained five bells. I doubt if such a humble building would have had a tower and surely not with five bells.

The call to attend service is now tolled upon a solitary bell housed in an ivy-clad structure of open oak studwork in the south-west of the churchyard. This structure has since been rebuilt using some of the original timbers to great success.

Without the ivy I imagine it would collapse. When this was built is difficult to say. The woodwork is probably seventeenth century.

The hall or mansion house (now rebuilt) stands a little way east from the church, as we see in Morant's *History of Essex*, and just previously 'Wrabness Hall'; and Denballs and the two Manors in this Parish.

From *The Monuments of North-East Essex* again we learn that:

Wrabness Hall, 120 yards E of the Church, is of two storeys, timber framed & plastered, the roofs covered with slate. The E wing of the house was built in the 15th Century and the W wing was added or rebuilt in the 16th Century.

Before and after the conquest, the Parish belonged to the Abbey of St Edmundsbury in Suffolk. Under the Abbey it was held by the Le Blund family who 'paid 10 marks a year to the cellarer of the Monastery'.

The Le Blunds were descendants from Robert Le Blund or (Blong), who fought beside the Conqueror.

Eventually the Manors of Wrabness were presented to a convent at Bruisyard in Suffolk and afterward bought by Sir John Hinde, a rich citizen of London. At the time of his decease in 1418 he 'held the manor of Wrabness with a seawater mill'.

He was Sheriff in 1381 and Lord Mayor in 1391. He had two sons; both became Sheriffs of Essex and one inherited our village in 1456.

It later went to the Ayloffs, whose ancestors were Portreeves of London when Edward the Confessor was King, so the family were here before the Normans controlled the land.

In 1686 the village was sold to Sir Thomas Davell, who was Member of Parliament for Harwich on several occasions. A relative of Sir Thomas, Daniel Burr, eventually inherited the lands of Wrabness and in time they were purchased by Lewes Peake Garland. In 1722 he married the daughter of Major General Serring Talbot and Wrabness remained in this family for many years. The Manor of Denballs was held in the mid-sixteenth century by Christopher Roydon, through the marriage of his only daughter to John Lucas, who was shot by his captors after gallantly defending Colchester against the Puritans.

One noteworthy gentleman who served the village well was the Rev. Robert Richie who died in 1728. He was rector here for 27 years and vicar of Ramsey for 48. He is known through the fact that he presented his remarkable collection of books on alchemy to the library at Colchester Castle. He appears to have been a very charitable fellow for upon his tomb in the north-west corner of the graveyard these words are inscribed.

A father of the Orphan, a helper of the friendless, a preventor of strife and one that spend his life in acts of charity and beneficence.

Between 1837 and 1891, the Rev. Patrick Fenn was the

incumbent here and Anthony Cox Fenn held the position after him until 1910.

It is worth noting that at the first official census in 1801 there were 27 houses, 37 families and 162 people living in this village. The number had increased to 261 fifty years later and to 300 in 1901. *White's Directory of Essex* for 1848 records that:

Mary Cook was shopkeeper; John Fisher was shopkeeper.
Richard Johnson was shopkeeper and beer house owner; John Lawrence Parish Clerk.
John Paskell, wheelwright etc.
John Sherman, blacksmith and beer house owner; Nathan Taylor, victualler Wheatsheaf
Aaron Chisnol
John Chisnall
Benjamin Clark
Stephen Lott – Dimbols, Edward Fisher
Francis Richardson – The Hall, William Robinson.
Rev. Fenn M.A. has 50 acres of Glebe and a good residence built in 1840 at a cost of £1300.

The same source records in 1863,
Some of the above names and in addition:

Francis Fisher – machine owner
Israel Hamm – shoemaker
Joseph Johnson – shoemaker
John Johnson – tailor
William Bland – stationmaster, trains several times a day to all parts (Branch Harwich to Manningtree opened in 1854).

By 1866 we see there are four Fishers farming in Wrabness.

By 1886, Joseph Calver is landlord of the Black Boy Inn but the Fishers are less numerous, with E Fisher only.

By 1890, The School is noted: built in 1872, enlarged in 1875 for 50 children, average attendance 31. Miss Laura Ashford, headmistress.

John Potter – shopkeeper 1902–1912 – Sub-Post Office Joseph Calver, shopkeeper 1914–1912.

Harriet Calver – shopkeeper 1916–1932.

Grace Harvey (née Calver) – shopkeeper 1932–1950; Albert Harvey – shopkeeper 1950. 1888, Pillar Box closes at 5.30 in winter 6.30 summer. This was opposite Dimbols Farm.

Prior to 1840, Wrabness received service via un official local post of Manningtree, cost one penny per letter.

The terminal point of the post from Manningtree was the postman's hut on Primrose Hill before the opening of the Sub-Post Office.

This Hill was in existence in the first decade of the twentieth century. From the Parish Records:

In 1821 on 5th Dec., Joseph Ship, male age 16, was bound to James Howard as an apprentice to the trade of fisherman at Mistley for five years.

The premium was £25.00. The overseers were then, John and Francis Richardson. The lot of an apprentice was binding as an indenture I have stated. This does not apply to Joseph above but to one Mark Mayhew (not of Wrabness) and... During the term the faid apprentice has faid Master faithfully shall serve, his secrets keep, his lawful commands everywhere glad by do: he shall do no damage to his faid master, nor fee it to be done of others, but that he, to the utmost of his power, shall let, or forthwith give warning to his faid master of the same: he shall not waft the goods of his faid master, or lend them unlawfully to any:

He shall not commit Fornication, nor Contract Matrimony within the said term: he shall not play at Cards, Dice, tables or any other unlawful games, where by the said master may have any lofs: with his own goods or others, during the said Term, without licence of his faid master, he shall neither buy or fell: he shall not haunt Taverns or Playhouses, nor abfent himself from the said Master's Service Day or Night unlawfully, but in all things as a faithfull apprentice he shall behave himself towards his said Master, and all his during the said term... The Master...by the best means that he can, shall teach and instruct or cause to be instructed finding unto his said apprentice, Meat, Drink, Apparel, lodgings and all other Niceffaries according to the custom of the city...

The lads do not appear to have enjoyed much freedom but the lot of the workers then was not far removed from the serfs who had been tied to the land throughout the centuries.

The old record of the apprentices gives further detail of three other boys between 1823 and 1829 who were all tied to the fishing trade in Harwich. In 1825 the name Fisher appears as overseer, and in 1843 he is recorded as a surveyor *for* the village. In the Highway Rate Book of that year he was farming land with an annual value of £95, upon which the rate to be collected was £2 7s 9d. The rate was 6d in the £.

It is interesting to read in a paragraph at the end of the assessment that 'the persons numbered from 46–69 are excused by the Magistrate from the payment of the poor rate on account of their poverty, and do solicite they may be excused *from* the payment of the surveyors rate *for* the same reason'.

The annual value of these cottages was between £1 and £2 10s and the rate in proportion 6d to 1s 3d. Their living conditions were not very lush, I fear, for their occupants were given exemption for the duration of the book till 1856. In beautiful handwriting we see the names such as:

    Abraham Ham
    Stephen Lott
    Isaac Jennings,
    Nathan Taylor.

Stephen Lott then occupied Dimbols, which was assessed at £142 5s.

In 1850, widow Porter's house was £1 and rate due 2d.

Francis Richardson occupied Wrabness Hall and was to pay £3 7s 2d and 10d on the Wharf in the receipt and payment book, it is recorded in 1847.

    4th October Journey to Thorpe for having rate signed 4s
    4th October Journey to Thorpe for attending Revising Barrister 5s
    22nd December Journey to Manningtree for attending auditor 3s

Stephen Lott, Churchwarden, signed his name as overseer, as did Aron Chisnell but Benjamin Clarke is designated by his mark X.

Edward Fisher was my grandfather. I did not know him, for he died four years before I was born. Some of the jigsaw puzzle is from memory of uncles telling the snippets to me as a small boy onwards until I reached the age of 45. This grandfather was my mother's father and he was born in 1842. He took part in the building of the single line railway from Manningtree to Harwich. Brick carrying was among the activities that he was involved in, and the bridge that today still spans Wheatsheaf Lane, although it has been repaired periodically, probably has many of the original bricks in it. I assume bridges were widened when railways were upgraded to take an up and down line, although there does not seem to be any evidence of this on the several bridges around this locality.

1854 was the date that the railway was extended from Manningtree to Harwich, so my grandfather would have been twelve years old. He witnessed the disappearance of wagons over the end of the rail, as soil was brought to fill the valleys, and there were reputed to be several such casualties near the bridge. Westward of this the line goes up a fair gradient, and one assumes that the breaking systems of rolling stock was not very efficient.

Some of the original sleepers from the single track make up a coal shed to this day (about 1960) at one of the farms he owned (It is called Fishers Farm on our OS map of about 1875.) These pieces of wood are a semicircle, i.e. a long cut centrally along its length, and had two hole chairs fixed to the flat side. This holding was one of 20 acres and the house is ancient. I had the privilege of doing some renovating there a few years ago and studied its construction briefly. Originally it was a small cottage with a downstairs room about 15' x 16'. This was warmed by a fireplace with a 9' hearth with the large oak lintel spanning it. The iron bar from hanging pots is still there with a sliding shackle in remarkable condition. The bridging joist across the room is of oak and 10" square; the common joists are 5" x 4" and all are adzed to shape.

The adjoining rooms have beams of smaller size and show the marks of the pit saw, and are of later date. In one of the bedrooms a priests hiding hole near the chimney was discovered. The bottom plates of the old place were laid on a foundation of roughly laid stones including pieces of septaria with no bonding. I introduced a damp course under here and found that the foundation was not dug into the ground at all. The walls were of wattle and daub, and while the wattle – of hazel – was reduced to powder. The oak crosspieces upon which the sticks were tied with bark thongs was a sound as ever. The house was enlarged lengthways and along the back an out-shot built, probably in the nineteenth century.

It has a floor of black and red quarry tiles. It housed a long pine table until recently, which was made to Grandfather's order. Whether he started a family before he acquired it, or did so with the intention of having several members to sit around it, I do not know. But a large family arrived fairly quickly.

To map out the chronology of his movements in the farming world is difficult, for all the informants have departed. There is a two-page indenture dated Michaelmas 1888, with details of the various fields that Edward wished to purchase, and the two gentlemen (they are described as gentlemen) in the names of David and William Mustard, who were willing to advance the sum of £400 for the purpose. The near perfect copybook penmanship goes on:

'And all that messuage or tenement known and distinguished by the following description (namely) The Barn Pightle' (Pightle or Pyghtle meant usually a three-sided enclosure of grass into which the cows and calves would be collected before nightfall near to the house) *'containing one acre three roods twenty-one perches.'*

The Old Barn field containing one acre two roods and six perches. He appears to have arrived at about 28 acres in all *'and that by equal half-yearly payments of interest at the rate of four pounds per cent was to be paid on 29th March and 29th September'.*

On a map headed 'A plan of the Manor and Parish of Wrabness accurately Delineated AD 1797 by John Prickett, Surveyor, Middlesex' some buildings are shown, but the work is devoted to the naming of each field and enclosure; some of the names just mentioned in the indenture appear, but they are not in any adjacent group to make up a farm. The old map is quite unusual; there are names some of which tell their own story. Decoy Pond is pronounced locally 'Kypens', and some of the fields conjure thoughts of very different and difficult types of land.

This village is made up with very mixed soil, and the Clay Collins still has its name, and is very much a problem in wet winters – especially if there is an absence of frost: 'I doubt, master, if we'll be able to drill on that owd bit a clay now tha's got as late as this.'

'Well, bor, you'll hat'a put the press on and have an extra loss on.'

On the Smyth drills the press was an iron bar with a hinge in the centre applied across the wooden levers held downwards with hooks to force the coulters into the soil. Drilling corn like this was sometimes referred to a 'puddling it in' and was often a bad start for the wheat and a good one for weeds, especially mayweed.

It was a gloomy prospect to walk to work over the footpaths, most of which have disappeared, and feed the horses before it was daylight.

The comb sack was about your shoulders and if it started to rain, you'd be hanging back to make up your mind what was best to do. 'It rain in the hosspond, master.'

'Well, you oun't go ploughing in there, so come on let's be hearing from ye.'

The fields mentioned on the map are now for the most part very much enlarged. North of my present smallholding, six fields now are turned into one of about 50 acres. To the west, Temple Field is still as it was, by reason of the deep brook parting it from its neighbour; but the eight acres called The Upper Lands, and the nine acres called The Hangings, are all into one. The cart path up to the nine acres up which I used to stroll when a boy with the long grass brushing my knees has disappeared. Blue cornflowers grew here, and I have gathered these with pink and white campion to make a pretty bouquet for my Ma, many times.

The old stage coach road to Manningtree along the river is shown, and the mile stone mark at the w. end of Wall Lane is LXIV. I assume that this route was used because it was quite flat and cut off several steep hills that were encountered on the normal highway to Bradfield.

Grandfather was farming 40 acres at Shipps Farm at the turn of the twentieth century.

It must have been a poor old spot on which to earn a living at that time. One field, which could have easily become a sandpit would rarely produce a crop of corn unless it rained frequently, and to the west the clay fields on the hill appear.

The old house was single story, with gable-end roof of pantiles and tarred weatherboard wall. It stood end on to the road, and through my childhood eyes looked lofty and unfriendly. The usual brick floors prevailed, but it had the benefit of quite high bedrooms as opposed to the usual lean-to type. The Quach below the sandy field was a delightful spot, with willows trees in abundance, a lot of undergrowth and a bubbling stream. Pheasants and partridge and rabbits were always in residence, and often were shot to provide a cheap and tasty meal. Frogs lived there too.

I haven't seen a frog for years. I suppose modern methods of farming have destroyed them.

Across the road from here was (and still is) Spring Cottage, so called because of a bubbling little spring in the ditch at the front of the house, which had a small brick enclosure built round it at some time, just big enough to dip a bucket in. Clear water continuously filled the little well, and the surplus spilled over the edge into the ditch. The supply was only about two feet below ground level and never receded to the driest year. The only snag to its purity would be when some small rodent fell in, and its body's presence was not noticed until it had become a bit unpleasant.

'Didn't you see that owd mouse in there Rosie? What a set-out! Now we shan't know whether tha's alright or not.'

The cottage was now of two lets and belonged to Grandfather from about 1900. Each let had one large room on the ground floor and two bedrooms above. Access to which was by a staircase of which each thread was a 'winder'. There was little furniture in these little rooms, for it was very difficult to get any up there.

Subsequently an out-shot was built along the back, and this served as the kitchen. The back doors were just 5' high. There was one window of the smallest dimensions and an earth floor, contributing to crippling arthritis and tuberculosis. In houses of this type large families were reared for many decades.

Among the few documents that I have is one dated 1st July 1895. It runs to six pages of perfect copybook hand and is a lease of New House Farm from 'Barnes Wimbush Esq. to Edward Fisher here in after designated the Lessee'. It ran for seven years:

The Lessor reserves for himself all trees and underwood with liberty for his agents or workmen with or without horses carts and carriages at all times to fell and carry way the trees and underwood hereby reserved.

He also reserved rabbits and game for himself and 'liberty to enter on the said premises to view the condition thereof'. The farm consisted of 52 acres and 12 perches, with all fields set out in the usual way, viz. the eleven acres; 12acres, 3 rood, 28 perches; Pear-tree and Rickfield, 13a, 3r, 31p, and so on. The rent was to be £80 per annum, and the first payment fell due on the 24th December.

'Well, I 'spect that'll hetta be paid, but tha's a bit of a tight, un just afore Christmas.'

In the 23 paragraphs that the document contains most of them all informed the Lessee of what he was *not* to do. The Lessor did give Grandfather the right to 'peaceable enjoy the said premises during the said term, without any lawful interruption from the farmer'. Should it have read 'unlawful'?

The house at this farm still stands in much the same form as then, being of red brick and two stories. In the lean-to attics one has a lovely view of the western reaches of the River Stour, and the sunsets there are very lovely. There is also the corn barn and the stockyards behind, sheltered from the north and north-east winds. As with many outlying farm buildings (the farm now is worked with another), these days they are slowly falling into decay. An interesting feature of the house was that during the 1930s it was let to two families who had to share the long kitchen along the back which contained one large stone sink. So if tempers became frayed, the washday problems would not be lessened. One back door served both families and a call from the elder gentleman that, 'You can put the blacksmith on together' meant everyone was present as far as he was concerned.

Edward Fisher seated left; standing, Lydia, Lily, Rosana; below seated, unknown, Bertha with son; seated on right, Grandfather's second wife Susan, circa 1915

Lydia Fisher, circa 1911

Lydia

Uncle Lewis

Cecil Fisher

Lydia Fisher, left, and sister, Lily

My grandfather also rented Priory Farm from around 1906, which comprised 114 acres of arable, 5 of pasture and 7 of coppice. He in fact was farming most of the southern parts of the village then. The family that he sired numbered around ten.

There was Rosie, who was born in 1872, Adelaide Eva Loise, Minnie Selina, Lewis, Bernard, Edward, Christian, Cecil and Lydia Cardinal who arrived in 1891. Lydia was my mother. Her mother died in 1894, aged forty-six. After producing all those babies and perhaps one or two of which I have no knowledge, she must have been worn out. Rosie married John. He was a very short stubby man and rather inarticulate; when one addressed him his replies were punctuated by 'Yis, yis' and regular clearings of the throat. On their wedding day he temporarily lost sight of his bride and was heard to say, 'I wonder where she be, I mustn't loose her now.'.

There was a stillborn baby, eventually, but nothing thereafter. 'A rare set-out that was,' so I was told. John worked as odd hand on various farms in the vicinity. He never attained any elevation at all in his eight-four years. Chopping out beet, swedes carting and filling muck, brushing out ditches, were his tasks, and of course the threshing machine, at which he was always taking off the chaff.

Adelaide was the typical Victorian aunt, who would retain her composure if the roof collapsed all around her. She married a haberdasher who unfortunately had the surname Zipler. He was suspected of German connection, and I think was the subject of ridicule during and after the hostilities of 1914–1918, in which he took no part. They rented shops at different times at Witham and around, selling drapery and allied items, with very little success. 'You see,' she told me once, 'we took the shop over in…nearly all the stock was bad' (meaning out of fashion) 'and we carried it forward and never sold hardly any of it.'

Now Aunt Lilley remained a spinster, and I think she should have joined a nunnery. She was very pious. She seldom laughed. There was always a family problem with her piety. She gave me a prayer book when I was ten years old and said she would like to see me go to church more often, a hope which was not fulfilled, I fear. She was twenty-one when her mother died, and she consequently mothered this family of hungry lads and men and heard all the complaints of all and sundry. She was a splendid cook, but I think the clock was her enemy, for often 'the dinner was too hot to eat and generally late' – so said an uncle; and Father always bade us to 'come back as soon as you have swallowed your dinner.'

Sister Minnie also was unmarried; I think most of her early days were spent in service at large houses in Southend and similar coastal resorts.

She eventually became housekeeper to an architect. She was very sedate and precise and always dressed immaculately.

Of the brothers, Lewis and Edward married. Bernard, Christian and Cecil did not; Lydia of course did. I consider that their father was a hard taskmaster and as is often the case with old family businesses the brothers did not often agree among themselves or with their father. These was a degree of craftiness in some of them, and bouts of silence when something was amiss, often going on for days on end.

Grandfather married Susan Parish in 1896 and another brother arrived in 1898. Grandfather fancied himself as a local gent, and often went off in his pony and cart to his various friends of similar circumstances. He appreciated being made welcome with large amounts of food and was partial to Scotch. He was engaged in farming about 150 acres at this time, and how successfully is questionable, for when one of the farms he rented came up for sale he 'just stood by at the auction and couldn't utter a word', said Cecil, on one occasion of regret. An ancient looking trade card with an art nouveau book advertised 'E Fisher & sons, Potato Merchants'.

One consignment of 5 cwt. were duly delivered to Mistley. A complaint followed that they were 'the dirtiest spuds that had ever been seen'. 'Better have them back,' says a wise proprietor, 'send one of the lads'.

Cecil was sent off to collect them. On arrival home they were tipped out on the floor of a cart lodge and several buckets of water thrown over them. After a short drying period they were bagged up and delivered a second time. When the time was due for them to be paid for, the client declared his complete satisfaction with the fresh delivery, which were not only clean but of much better quality and size.

Years of depression in farming up to 1900 probably did not help the industry greatly. After a wet autumn with wheat 'puddled in', charlock and poppies were numerous. Some control of weeds was effected by horse hoeing, with small hoes cutting in between the corn. 'I am half shy of it going round the farm; we couldn't win with the weather, so much agin us.' To think that 12 sacks of wheat was considered a good crop, and often it was less!

The price was about 41s per quarter, i.e. 2 sacks of 18 stones, and a sample was taken to the Corn Exchange in a black velvet bag in order to show the grain to the best advantage.

In the early years of the twentieth century my mother was attending the village school and was caned by a very stern master for something she was not guilty of. This caused her father to organise for her education at a private school in Dovercourt, under Miss Foster. Here she was brought up on parsing and analysing, as follows:

The	Def article
Cricketers	Mas. gen. nom case
Had	Trans verb. 3 person plur num
"	Act voice indic mood past tense
"	Irregular
a	Indef article
Pleasant	Qual adj qualifying trip
Trip	Com Noun Sin Num 3 per
"	Neuter gen objective case

All this was written in large copperplate handwriting, and shorthand, music, long division sums and composition were in the curriculum.

A large proportion of the lessons are marked with a capital E in red ink, which I consider denoted 'excellent'. The school fees were one guinea per quarter, with exercise books extra. The costs were drawing book, 3d, rubber 1 d, 3 exercise books at 3d each. Quarter totals were around £1 4s to £1 7s, and were paid in most cases in about two months.

One account has black edge around it, indicating the loss of one of the teachers' family in 1902. Lydia was turned out from here with a sound schooling and always wrote very legibly and never altered her well-taught methods. I wondered why she didn't take up teaching; perhaps her father could not afford the fees. A poetry book dated 1902, in which many poems are duly marked 'learnt and inwardly digested', is prefaced by the following:

> It is important that the process of acquiring the art of reading – not as a mechanical art, merely, but as an accomplishment – should be rendered to the pupil as pleasing and attractively as possible. It is necessary, also, that this reading should be of such a nature as imperceptibly to impress him with a sense of a true and beautiful style, thus becoming to him a source of intellectual pleasure, by gratifying a taste which it serves to create. And, more obviously still, it is of the utmost consequence in educational work, that the heart should be addressed as well as the intellect and that the development of the moral affections should go on together with the culture of the mind. It has therefore been the aim of the Editor of this volume to present such a selection as will make the work a really useful auxiliary to the teacher who recognises the importance of the principals referred to, and is desirous of carrying them into effect in the daily works of the school.

The first poem in the volume is entitled 'Little Jim' and begins:

> The cottage was a thatched one
> The outside old and mean
> Yet everything within the cot
> Was wondrous neat and clean.
>
> The night was dark and stormy
> The wind was howling wild
> A patient mother knelt beside
> The deathbed of her child.

The poem goes on for another thirteen verses to tell us of the tragic end of the little fellow. Other poems, such as 'The Wreck', 'The Graves of the Household', 'I remember – I remember' and 'Never give up', were duly learned and marked. One which seems to capture scenes of country lanes entitled 'Golden Harvest Time'

is contained in a little book of written verse in my mother's hand
of 1899.

Softly sighs the morning breeze
Stealing through the yellow corn,
Through the wealth of glowing poppies
Shining with the dew of morn.

Casting ripples on the water
Softly wooing lily leaves
Softly waving rye and barley
Standing by in golden sheaves.

Gently singing round fair children
On a wagon load of corn –
Who hath crowned their little sister
Harvest Queen this lovely morn?

Twining poppies' ruddy blossoms
Mid the glitter of her hair,
Where the golden sunbeams gather
Leaving all their glory there.

Swaying ruddy fruit and golden
That the lovely summer brings,
Bearing over rocky passes
Early song the skylark sings.

Wafting over wood and meadow
Silver clouds of thistledown
Teasing ringlets of a maiden
Who has lovely eyes of brown.

Wooing forth the dainty blushes
On each pretty dimpled cheek
Where had rested white of lilies
Roses now play hide and seek.

Till her lover, passing onward
Through the fields of golden corn
Stays to kiss the lips the wind has
On this lovely summer morn.

It paints a rather loving picture; I doubt if many of the workers on farms saw harvest through the poet's eyes. Probably not; more likely it was a plod from morn till night, scything, binding, stooking, carting, stacking, thatching. Only recently I said to some gentlemen who had been engaged in farm work all their lives, 'I'd love to have just two days on the old-fashioned harvest.'

Their immediate reaction was, 'You're welcome!' One of them remarked, 'I wouldn't have those days back for a pension! Forking uphill from the bully hole was damned hard work. Some of those wheat sheaves weighed a hundredweight.'

So there you are, but who would not like to meet his lover in the midst of skylarks and thistledown? Not quite so much of the latter in 1975; deep cultivations and chemical sprays have helped to get rid of them. But with an unkind spring, as we have had this year, several fields of poppies have been visible.

Further with the book of verse. 'How to Behave' commences:

Banging the door

'Tis not polite to bang the door
When from the room you go.
It should be closed quite quietly
As most of you will know.

A very instructive set of lines entitled *Sitting Well* goes thus:

Now, chairs were meant for use as seat
And not for exercise
In twists and turns and wriggles round,
So sit still, I advise.

When Others Talk

'Tis very rude to interrupt
When others talk or read
Unless there's great necessity,
So this rule mind you heed.

At Table

It is not nice to see a child
Eat in an ugly way
Take great big bites and scatter crumbs
Or with his food to play
Nor should he grease his hands at all
Nor spill his milk or tea,
Nor smear the jam across his face
Such things should never be.

I beg your pardon

When children do not hear what's said
They never should shout 'What?'
'I beg your pardon' they must say
And listen on the spot.

On the back cover of the little book there appears an advisement for pen nibs: 'They come as a boon and a blessing to men – The Pickwick, The Owl and the Waverley Pen'. There is a Pickwickian-style gentleman holding and peering through a magnifying glass to make sure that the information on a signpost with four arms with the name of the various nibs upon them is correct. The 'Flying Dutchman' nib is claimed to write 200 words with one dip of ink, which would be held in reserve in a kind of hood on its top.

On a recent programme on TV, when an extended investigation into education was being thrashed out, it was pointed out that in infant schools it is common for there to be a 50 per cent failure in teaching children to read. The reply from one of the lady experts was, 'Yes, but in many schools children are taught equally important things – how to move, for instance.'

My ma was eight years old when she started to write in her book of poems and the script is perfectly readable.

Winter evenings were partly spent singing popular songs round the piano. Lydia was a popular pianist and Herman Spinks' 'In the shadows' was often requested. Grandfather stated without fear of contradiction that 'Killarney's Lakes and Dells' was good enough to be played and sung in any church in the kingdom.

The Priory Farm was the hub of the family for several years, and there Aunt Lilly worked and slaved, for years on end, cooking hams in large boilers, or preparing and cooking game, pork, rabbits or hares, baking bread in the brick oven, making butter, washing, ironing, mending and cutting down worn garments to fit younger members of the household.

Her brothers were all large strong lads, and when I first remember them they would have been 35–45 years old and were strong muscle-men, with chests 44" at a minimum. Long days of work in the fields made their arms like iron girders. Bernard was the one who appealed to me. He was a handyman and always mending items that were broken, especially if they were of wood. He was a schemer. If the weather was bad, he was to be found in the workshop. His favourite tool was the draw knife. Axe handles were a challenge, and he would preserve a piece of ash with a fine grain and try to engineer the grain to run naturally along the curves. He also had been a brewer of home-brewed beer, which sustained them during harvest particularly but also generally. Mangold and parsnip wine were also made; with the beet the later into the year this could be done. The more mellow were the beet, then the stronger the wine. They were used to feed the cows and bullocks in the winter and stored in clamps, covered with straw and earthed up. They would be harvested in the late autumn, and if the frosts were not too severe some would keep until May. Whitsun was a favourite time to make the potent brew, in Bernard's opinion. The effect upon the senses of one who imbibed to many tumblers of this was deadening. The next morning one was heard to say 'I fare whole this morning.'

To drown their sorrows, sometimes a party of two or three would be carried on into the night. I was told of two vases that were borrowed off the drawing room mantelshelf to be used by the participants when they thought that the time had come for a long drink!

Chapter Two

In the Parish Council Minute Book beginning in March 1895, it is apparent that there was a need for allotment gardens. Anthony Cox Fenn, who was the Rector of this village from 1891 to 1909, was the Chairman of the Council. The minutes state that 'All parishioners interested are invited to attend'. He would at once proceed to state that the portion of land he was prepared to let for allotment purposes was that par of the Glebe known as Forefield onto Station Road, and that the rent would be 4d per rod, per year, to be charged from Michaelmas 1894 and paid in half-yearly instalments. A charge of one shilling be required of each allotment holder on his taking possession, to go towards meeting the expenses incurred in enclosing the ground.

> Some present objected to the rent... The chairman put it to the Council whether they considered 4d a Rod to be a fair and reasonable charge and obtained their unanimous opinion that it was... He then put the same question to the electors present, asking for a show of hands, whereupon 13 were held up as agreeing to its being fair and reasonable rent.

It goes on and eventually lists those who wished to add to their intake of vegetables.

1.	James Smith	30 Rods
2.	William Cole	20 Rods
3.	Peter Cole	40 Rods
4.	Ephraim Catchpole	40 Rods

...and so on, making 20 applicants in all, including

Miss Fanny Canty	10 Rods
Israel Ham	10 Rods

Miss Canty was a schoolmistress and is listed as receiving the sum of £4 4s 4d per month in 1895. The last mentioned gentleman was the village shoemaker who lived along the main Harwich road in a weatherboard cottage. It is still there, although modernised. I have the windows that used to be in the bedroom dormers and the pair measure 3' x 2', illustrating the poor ventilation afforded – only one could have been opened – during the summertime.

When his son, Alfred, who worked for my father during the 1920s, passed on, we moved his few sticks of furniture. Among them was a small oak coffer, plain and functional, and an oak bureau, which was very broken and was disregarded. I have still the coffer and it is in use. If I had the bureau now it would have been restored. From what I remember of the handles of the drawers, it was late Georgian. I said that Israel was the shoemaker. He was actually a cordwainer. I kept the nippers that were his, and they were in The Bygones department.

The hammer head part used to knock in tacks and is very worn down; it must have knocked in thousands. He always had Mondays off to go and purchase leather. When a customer tapped on his door he was told to, 'Oop the door and come in.' I think a pair of boots costs a week's wages, but they lasted a long time; they were full of hobnails and the heels were shod like a horse's hoof. They had a lot of hard wear walking to work and following a pair of horses, but someone considered it was worthy of a few lines:

> Hurrah for the Ploughman's life!
> To wake with the rising sun
> And follow with glee o'er the furrowed lea
> The plough, till his course is run.
>
> They may talk of a life mid the ocean's strife
> Or the town of jollity,
> But give me pure air and the fields so fair
> A ploughman's life for me!

Two newspaper cuttings in 1982 from the '75 Years Ago' series, for 1907:

A gun was discharged in the dark outside Wrabness Wheatsheaf Inn. Some of the shot lodged in the wrist and clothing of Cecil Fisher of Priory Farm. The man with the gun said he had suffered some annoyance from some of the young men earlier in the evening.

And around October of the same year,

An enjoyable harvest home was held at Wrabness Priory, when Edward Fisher invited his tenants and harvest men to a substantial repast. The genial host presided over an attendance of 24 guests being supported by Mr Herbert Garnham (The farmer at Dimbols) in the vice chair. Toast and song followed the repast, Miss Lydia Fisher and Miss Gladwin accompanying on the piano. At the close hearty cheers were given to Mr and Mrs Fisher and Family.

Let us return to the allotments, or the Garden Field, as it was known by the participants. Two councillors were allocated the task 'to measure off and apportion the allotments and produce a plan of the ground and holdings to which they were to affix the name of each applicant'. They apparently sorted out on which side of the field they lived, and gave 'to each the plot nearest and most conveniently situated for his holding'.

All the valiant fellows seemed happy with the arrangement, and all paid the shilling and were given the number of their plot. It appears that Grandfather Fisher was one of the two overseers of the Parish for on 25th March 1895. They were directed to pay to Rev. Anthony Cox Fenn £1 7s 7d from the poor rate to meet the expenses of the Parish Council meetings. It is also recorded that Chairman be requested to write to the owners of Henry Howard's house, calling his attention to the fact that the house was in a very dilapidated condition and that the Council desired him to take steps to have this house – his property – put into a more tenantable and more comfortable state of repair. The unsanitary condition of the ditch at the rear of Marshall's house was concerning the unfortunate few who lived nearby. In October of that year most of the allotment holders were present and paid their rent. Several of them stated that they were satisfied with their holdings and had no fault to find. In time one or two holders had to give up their plots but there was quick application from another parishioner to take them over. It does appear that Peter Cole had left his plot, XXII, in an unsatisfactory condition of cultivation. When the chairman wound up the last meeting of the council (before re-election) he congratulated the members for the courtesy they had shown him during his year in office, and congratulated them on the fact that nearly all they attempted they had been able to accomplish, and if they had not done any great amount of good they certainly had done no one any harm.

Our Rector was undoubtedly a good man for all mention of him is charitable. His Rectory was (and still is) a pleasant house, with a Georgian front. His garden and lawns were very well kept, with resident gardeners to attend them, I was assured by my father during the Second World War. "This place is a disgrace these days. The Rev. Fenn would have this altered if he was here."

One poor old lady by the name of Maria Scarfe, who lived along in a two-roomed bungalow not far from the Rectory, earned a few coppers picking stones and helping to scrub the school. Walter Spalding, one of the last and the oldest actual parishioner born here, told me 'of Ria' that if she woke up and it was bright moonlight, she didn't know but what it was daybreak, and used to go up to the school, may have been 3 or 4 a.m. Poor people had no clock. In order to have a drink of tea, she was obliged to go to the Rectory to collect used tea leaves which were emptied from the pot onto the grating to the drain. She said she had 'the master funny farins at times'. She was allowed 1s 6d per week from the overseers for coal in 1895. Many were attending the school at about this time, and where they all lived conjures up ideas of much overcrowding. There are about 28 houses shown on an OS map for 1872, excluding the farms and Rectory.

In 1876 the Rate Books are interesting. On the Priory Farms of 135 acres, the gross rateable value was £174, and with the rate at 8d in the pound, the amount was £5 16s per year. On the Wheatsheaf Inn, 33 poles was charged at 8s, and our beloved Rector's house and land of 58 acres brought in the sum of £14 6s 4d.

Twenty years later items paid out are recorded as follows:

W Porter & M Scarfe	Scrubbing school	3s 6d
J Calver	Soda and soap	2s 3d
James Smith	Emptying closets	1s 6d
Archibald Paskell	Repairs to locks	4s 1s
J Calver	Brooms	1s 10d
W Rowland	Trimming hedge	1s
Smith and Scarfe	Cleaning school	3s
T Rowland	Sweeping down walls	- 6d
AC Fenn	Two bundles of straw	1s
Ellen Blake	Coal	11s 7d
M Munsley	One dozen pen holders	1s
J Porter	Framing four pictures	8s

The date was 10th May 1897, and a meeting of all Parishioners had been convened to take place in the schoolroom, to determine as to what should be done to commemorate Queen Victoria's Jubilee. The meeting was well attended, and various resolutions were unanimously carried.

One proposition from Mr F Richardson was that 22nd June be observed as a holiday, and that employers of labour pay for the day and that a good substantial meal of meat and pudding be provided for all parishioners who cared to come and partake of it, and that sport and games be got up for the amusement of the people. A committee was formed to collect from the parish and also from landowners and others outside the Parish. Our worthy chairman requested 'those who were willing and able to attend a thanksgiving service at the church on that date at eleven o'clock.'

The sum of £25 8s 3d was collected, and it was most revealing to see what it was expended on. There was:

118¾ lb. Beef at 9d/lb.
39 lb. Mutton at 10d/lb.
3 Hams, £1 9s 4d
36 gal. Ale, £2 2s
18 gals Porter, £1 1s
2 Bottles Irish Whiskey, 7s
1 oz. best Scotch Snuff, 6d

32 doz. Mineral Water, £1 1s 4d – 1½d each
1 Bushel of Nuts, 10s
21 lb. Sweets, 5s 3d
1 lb. best shag tobacco, 4s
10 lb. butter, 10s
5 lb. tea, 10s

Etc. etc. The list concluded with fireworks 10s, to come to the tidy sum of £25 19s.

Three pages in the minute book are given to the description of the Royal Day. The day was pleasantly and happily observed and we had the proverbial Queen's weather – a bright and beautiful day. All employers of labour kindly and generously fell in with the arrangements and gave the day as far as possible as a holiday. I wonder if these was slight dissention from the rule. I am sure I can hear, 'Well, I'll give 'em half the day, but they ought to come in and feed and water the hosses – I should hev thought – and them pigs will want a bit of fodder.'

However, the Reverend continues, after the service at the church all repaired to the churchyard gate, where there was awaiting them four wagons besides two or three private vehicles. They were quickly filled and started in a procession round the parish, adding greatly to the holiday tone of the day.

By 12.30 p.m., the Rectory lawn was safely reached and everything was in readiness for the creature comforts of the parishioners, and they were soon busy replenishing the needs of the inner man with the good old honest English fare of Roast Beef and Plum Pudding – not that they were the only eatables to be had. There was boiled as well as roast beef, and legs and shoulders of mutton from sheep that had been grazed in the parish, and which were fit to set before a king. The diners were well waited on by a large body of willing helpers, and it was a pleasure to see how quickly the carvers carved and the waiters ran and all wants were supplied. There then followed a little interval of rest when the pipe and fragrant weed were allowed to reign whilst the good Queen and her doings were discussed.

Sports were indulged in at four o'clock, and at five o'clock tea was announced. This was no hurried meal, but one at which chat and laughter and pleasant fun found place together with the cups that cheers but not inebriates. Sports again occupied the evening 'until it was nearly dark', when prizes were presented to the winners. I would have thought that a good number of the company were too full of good and drink to run very hard or far. Forks, spades, rakes, hoes, scythes, braces (very useful on such days), and brush and comb, scissors and box iron and heater, and the inevitable frying pan, were the prizes that were competed for. A jubilee rocket signalled the firing of a 21-gun salute by the churchwardens, and the grounds were illuminated by a number of coloured lights. This ended a most pleasant and happy day, and one which no doubt found a place in the memory for many years to come: God save the Queen. How many young ladies were paired up with their future husbands on that balmy day, I wonder. Wandering home in the twilight with the crickets chirping and a warm breeze through the trees was enough to turn a young man's fancy…

The celebration of King Edward VII's Coronation followed fairly soon in the scheme of things, and at a meeting of the PC in April 1902 it was decided that 'the day, 26th June, should be celebrated on similar lines to what was done on the occasion of the late Queen's Jubilee of blessed memory'. Who could disagree with that? I ask you. I should imagine that the receivers of the fare hoped that the Royal Family would continue to provide reasons for such days of merriment. £27 6s 2d was subscribed by the folks and landowners this time. The amounts of food and drink were of similar quantity to that found necessary previously, and it is interesting to note that beef and mutton were now both 9d per lb., and Grandfather was held responsible for obtaining 162 lb. of it. Mr SB Storr was to supply 50 quarters of bread costing £1 0s 10d. The two publicans, Mr Gladwin of the Wheatsheaf and Mr Wells at the Black Boy, were commissioned to supply ale, porter, tobacco etc. The account of the Coronation takes a rather unexpected turn. The so-called Coronation Festivities were carried out as planned, except that owing to the sudden and unexpected illness of the King (who had to undergo a severe operation for appendicitis) the service at the church, instead of being of a festive nature, assumed the aspect of devotion and intercession for the King. There were no gay decorations of flags in the village or the Rectory, and no procession of wagons. At midday all hearts were comforted and cheered by the news brought by train that the King was doing well and that it was his desire that the day should be kept as a holiday, and the festivities should be on through out the land.

At one o'clock some 250 out of the population of 300 of the parish assembled at the Rectory, and a meal and sports were enjoyed, in one assumes a similar manner to the one five years before. There was a balance in hand of £2 15s 1d, and after several suggestions as to how best it could be spent, it was decided that in November of that year a Parish Tea should be provided. Our valiant Rector was charged with the job of obtaining sufficient supplies. A gramophone was considered as being an interesting addition to the entertainment for the period after the tea.

There was no further mention of the tea or the entertainment, so whether it was carried out I do not know. It appears that 1903 was not too kind to the allotment holders and other agriculturists, for mention is made that 'great complaints were made about the potato crop being poor after so exceptionally wet a season'.

Some holders of plots are reported as only paying one quarter's rent; perhaps they put too many pennies into the celebration fund. At most PC meetings there were complaints about the foul state of ditches, and the sanitary officer was often being asked to come to inspect them. I do not imagine he could do anything to assist, apart from tell the occupiers to clean them out, which I very much doubt if they did. Seventy-three years later we still have some problems with ditches being used to receive unsanitary effluent, and complaints are considered by the PC of the day with about the same ineffective results. In 1904, Grandfather Fisher made out a nomination paper and was accepted as a councillor; at this point I will mention that my father's father, Joseph Webb Calver, was nominated as an overseer. So both my grandparents were looking after the poor. I regret to make continued reference to the subject, but later in that year mention is made of the cesspit at the back of Joseph's shop, and Mr Cook, the sanitary officer, was asked to intervene and 'consider its offensive condition'.

I can who well imagine the remarks that Joseph used at this

juncture: 'I know I'm not,' says he. 'If the best they can b— well do is to find fault with my drains they can get on with their council muck. Don't do any good anyway. Can you tell me what they've achieved, that interfering dominating crowd?'

He did not appear to remain as an overseer very long, for in the following year his name is superseded. Joseph was the son of William, who was a master on the old sailing ships. I have the punishment log of one vessel, the *Avoca*, called after a village in Ireland at the meeting of the waters of twin rivers. This ship was registered at Newcastle in 1870 and was 270 tonnes. The log tells us of the activities of some of the crew on a voyage to Bahia in South America, and it may serve to show that the strain of Calvers was strong and dominant.

In the copy of the pages of the log, some pages are missing, and the first indication of the crew being insubordinate is on Tuesday 22nd February 1870, at Bahia. Allen McLean refused to go in the boat to fetch the Captain on board, signed by the master and William Thomas Finch Mate (as was each entry). On Saturday 5th March: Allen McLean refused to moor the boat to both master and mate; and on 7th, the same fellow refused to go and sleep in the sugar-laden lighter to see that she came to no harm, according to the rule of the port. He is in trouble again the next day, when he was ordered to go with the boat to bring the Captain on board, but he would not go till he had washed in his own time; and he used abusive language to the Captain when coming off with the boat – for which offences Captain took him before the consul and had him imprisoned the following day. The next entry is on Monday 14th March at Bahia. The Captain went to the jail to see if McLean would come out and go on board to do his duty, but this rather hostile crew member answered 'that he would stop his time and that not one goddam farthing of his wages should be stopped for expenses'. He is next visited by the Captain on 27th, and in answer to the same request as before Melean said the 'Captain was a bloody rough' and struck him in the eye.

At this William then went with the Sergeant of the jail to acquaint the consul with the occurrence, for which offence our offending seaman and was put in irons! At about the same time

John Dohorty, of similar temperament and opinion as McLean, was due to have shore leave until 6 p.m. He broke the terms of his leave by not returning until fourteen hours later. There is no punishment recorded for this transgression, but a fine of 6s was levied upon him, which may have been the greater of the five evils. All within a day or so it is logged that

> John Doherty went ashore with the boat, without leave, leaving the boy to do his duty, the boatswain in the boat having charge of her. At 7 p.m. the Captain had to scull the boat off the ship himself. Cook and boatswain away drinking. Sent boat on shore again to look for them but could only find boatswain. Geo Cook, AB, refused to fetch the Capt and was absent without leave and when he returned again he again refused to go in the boat and fetch the Cap on board when he would not, nor did not till he had something to eat or in his own time.

However, on 24th March at 3.30 p.m. JD came on board from a shore boat intoxicated and not fit for his duty went and lay down in the carpenter's room till 6 p.m. 'Ship under sailing orders since 22nd inst.'

By 24th May our worthies had arrived at Queenstown, and our troublesome sailor 'answered to both the above written statements that it was quite right'. In the column of the log which is headed 'Fine or Forfeiture inflicted', there is no entry. There is no further information in the book. I am sure our Captain was a very dominant man, and when my father used to shout we all took notice; he could be heard from a mile away, and I can hear Captain William ordering JD to do to his duty in the very same style. Unfortunately, William and two of his sons fell victim to yellow fever in 1872 and died in Paraiba in South America.

From 1884 to 1891, my grandfather was landlord of the Black Boy Inn. There was a very good trade at that time satisfying the thirst and appetite of horsemen loading and unloading barges on the river, at what is described as Cunningford Loading on the map previously referred to. There were posts in the river when I was younger where the barges were made fast. Access to the river was via Stone Lane, and then about a quarter of a mile west. This area was known as 'The Hard' among the men using it.

49

E Fisher was one of the surveyors of the village in 1898, and is recorded as charging the sum of five shilling for 'Repairs to Hardway'. On shore, David Ship was employed in filling ruts and putting in stone, and the charge on the parish was 2s per day. For providing transport with horse and cart, 7s 6d per day was levied. On the same page we see for A & CH Paskell, Blacksmith: repair of tools 2s 6d, and to William Paskell, 'To supply and erection of direction post, £1 5s'.

At low tide horses and wagons would be able to get close enough to the vessels and unload London muck and export trussed hay. This was trussed (a truss would now be called a bale) by local hay tyers/tiers who with a large cutting knife with a blade about 24" long, and a wooden handle across the top held with both hands, cut vertical sections out of a stack of stuver. This a mixture of grass and clover, which through warming up after stacking was a dark brown colour and smelt lovely and sweet, and was good food for horses, and cattle. The trusses were tied with straw ropes twizzled up with a wimble from a stack of loose straw.

The method was to draw some straw from the stack and twist round the hook on the wimble, which was turned while the operator walked backwards. The slabs of stuver were put into a press before tying.

The Black Boy had posts outside with iron pipes between them and iron rings fixed upon them to allow horses to be tied up, while their operators ate bread and cheese and downed their pints. Sam Boast (Boost) used to supply bread with a pony and baker's cart as transport. There was more beer spilled on the floor in here during one day than is drunk in the week now, said my father in the 1930s. He told of one of the old lads who used to have a plough spud (a flat, spade-like device for cleaning the breast about 4" across on a wooden handle), and when the landlord was absent from the bar, he would push the spud over the counter to the shelf at the back where small change was thrown and manage to manipulate some onto the blade to buy more booze.

My father was born at the pub in 1890, and spent many hours therein until arthritis became his master. Grandfather Joseph must have earned a few pounds at the pub because he managed to buy four acres of land opposite and built a row of four terraced houses.

One of these was used as a general stores, and eventually also as the post office from about 1914. Joseph was quite an enterprising fellow. He had a delivery of coal which was not of very good quality. 'I'll have something better than this, I know,' he said, and so saying put pen to paper and ordered a wagon of the splendid stuff to arrive at Wrabness Station. As there was more contained in the wagon than he needed, he started to sell some and established himself as a coal merchant. He stored this in an open-fronted shed within the bounds of his four acres. Also nearby was built a gable-end shed of timber upon a brick foundation to make a stable for the cob and shelter a trap, to which to he was harnessed; and the copper house, where pigs that were fattened on the premises were killed, scalded to remove the bristles, and cut up to be sold fresh or put into brine to preserve.

The old shed measured about 20' x 10' and was pulled down in 1960. The corrugated iron was all rusted but some of the timber was still quite sound. Behind this, on the south side was a lean-to glasshouse were cucumbers were grown and about one acre of various fruit trees and currant and gooseberry bushes grew. There was a group of pear trees of five varieties. One was Pitmaston Duchess, the juiciest pear I have ever met. It was bright yellow when ripe, and as it was peeled the juice ran down your fingers. Father told me that when his brother and sister had one it was divided into three to be shared. One of the stewing variety was splendid standby in the winter. They would keep until March if gathered carefully in October. They needed cooking for about four hours and turned out red and delicious. I doubt if anyone would have the time and patience to see to them now. Apple trees of all descriptions, and Victoria plums, a walnut tree and hazel stubs completed the little holding. The shop would have all the various items mentioned on sale as the season progressed, apart from the coal, which was sold in 1 cwt. and 1/2 cwt. bags. Flour was stored loose in a hutch and scooped out and weighed as required. I remember the fusty smell issuing from it when the floor was becoming visible; it was never thoroughly cleaned and I guess there were weevils in the cracks. Sugar was also stored in a similar manner and dispensed into tough blue paper bags. Behind the counter was a projecting metal peg on which the marble sealing in the contents of the ginger beer bottle was pushed downward to provide thirsty boys with a beverage for the price of about 1½d. This was codswollop.

Someone called 'Rodney Dod' assisted in cutting up a pig, and when the opportunity presented itself took one of its kidneys. 'Well, tha's a rum 'un,' says Joseph. 'Never knew a pig with one kidney afore.' For a long time after the lad was chastised by his mates: 'Rodney killed a pig with one kidney.'

My father and his brother, Ted, worked for their father, and were engaged in looking after the orchard, digging and hoeing, cleaning out and feeding pigs, unloading coal from the station and delivering it round the village.

When the need arose the trap was used to collect a lady or gent from the train to take him or her to relative or friend at farm or private house. This was a vehicle open to the elements, and if the weather was wet or cold, or both, the journey was unpleasant. A large waterproof rug was provided for placing over the customer's knees. Father was not at all pleased when it rained heavily and the drops from My Lady's umbrella dripped down his neck during the journey! Likewise, he was not particularly happy if he had been delivering coal or cleaning out the pigs and was not allowed sufficient time to clean himself up to be presentable to his fare. At some time in the early years of the century – perhaps 1908 – Joseph Sr. hired about 40 acres of land to south-west, namely Merchants Farm. This was about three miles away as the crow flies. The two brothers were directed to 'get to work' on this holding, and they were also informed, if they were short of money, 'Don't come crying to me!'

My father dared not ask for any cash from his father, but resorted to begging a few shillings from his mother, Harriet, many times. The journey to the farm was made via footpaths, cutting by half the journey by road. The paths were of course made for such use when men had to walk several miles to work.

One old lad who worked for Grandfather Joseph slept under a hedge near the duck decoy that existed near where the 'Red Barn' was. His name was Rowland, nicknamed 'Sprouts'. My father and a mate set fire to his 'bed' one day, and thereafter the poor old man was given leave to sleep in the stable at the coal yard, where he survived with a meal now and then from his employer for several years.

In 1906 the PC was discussing a continuation school to take place in the evenings, and it was proposed that two ladies should serve on the committee that was to supervise the arrangements. Miss Fenn and Miss E Garnham were unanimously elected. 'It was further unanimously agreed that Reading, Writing, Arithmetic and English were the chosen subjects. Mr Robinson and Grandfather Fisher were in agreement that 'poultry work should be taken as a special subject'.

Mr Lightfoot, the schoolmaster, was assisting with the continuation classes: rough carpentry for the men and lads, and sick nursing for the women. I wonder how rough carpentry was taught. I would say either carpentry was properly learnt or not at all, for there was always an adequate supply of poor craftsmen; perhaps they were shown how to make hen coops or rabbit hutches. My father had leather hinges to allow the door to open, and a large padlock – not a great deal of security if the intending thief owned a knife. Until about thirty years ago, the school was still used for the purpose for which it was built just over a century ago. It has two rooms, for infants and seniors.

Ninety children attended here in my parents' school days; now I think there are under twenty. The enterprising authorities organised a penny bank, and the entries are worth mentioning. Sixty members of the classes were listed in the ledger as savers. The 4d interest seems to be the set amount and was paid in most cases irrespective of the amount in total. In January 1902, Lydia Fisher commenced the account with 7s 6d to her credit; 6d was paid in during January, 6d in March, 5d in April, 1d September. No interest was allowed, and the 9s was withdrawn. Joseph Calver started off with 1s 10d, and from April to September paid in 12s. Cecil Fisher began with 9s 5d and added 1s 6d during the year. Our Rector's daughter, Christine, had £1 3s 5d at the commencement and accumulated a further 1s 10d plus 4d interest.

Martha Gosling, who added to her starting balance of 6s 8d with regular payments of 2d from April to November, gained interest of 4d to total 7s. She made no withdrawals, paid in 7s 6d during the next year, and was quite well off with £1 3s 8d in December 1904.

The four sons in the Storr family – John, George, Leonard and Claude – regularly saved £1 13s 3d during that year. It would seem some of the working families were able to do better than the landowners, and others.

In 1906 passengers were still liable to injury if they used the trains. The carriages were much higher than the platform and a certain Miss White slipped between it and the train and very nearly met with a nasty accident. Four years later the position was unaltered, and the railway company was reluctant to improve the platform, as the traffic was very light.

Steps were later provided 'to enable the old and infirm passengers to alight from or join the trains' (the height of platform was 2' above rail level).

In 1907 a meeting of the PC was summoned for seven o'clock. 'I went up to the schoolroom but no one came to it,' writes the Chairman. This is repeated as the next entry six months later. The old fellow's handwriting has by now deteriorated considerably and in 1910 we find that the well-loved and agreeable Rector has passed away.

In 1911 we were under the leadership of Mr W Garnham, H Garnham, Leonard Robinson and E Fisher, with the schoolmaster as clerk. The Rector was E Miller, and it is worth recording that the Coronation of George V was to be sorted out, and our new Reverend stated his pleasure at assisting, but he would not countenance any intoxicants on his meadow. It goes on:

Councillor Fisher considered Wrabness to be a very steady village. The last coronation passed off most pleasantly and he was sure this one would too (Applause). Everyone present considered that celebrations similar to the previous ones would be perfectly suitable. The Rector said he could not conscientiously assist under these conditions; he would rather cut off his right arm than allow drink to be brought to his meadow.

At a meeting nine days later, Grandfather Edward is presiding over a 'numerous attendance' and amid more applause

> announced he would lend his meadow for the Coronation Dinner, Tea and Sports. The village again was scoured for cash and £21 19s 5d was forthcoming. The food required was in similar proportions, with beef and mutton still 9d per pound. Decorated wagons were to be given prizes of £1, 3s and 2s.

It is interesting that the Co-op Society are now among the traders benefiting from the purchasers. They provided the prizes of 'Coronation cups – mugs, braces, stocking, figs, teapots, and a cruet.

Spades, forks, pitchforks, and hedge hooks were also to be competed for. There was a credit balance of 5s 4½d, which 'was unanimously handed to Mrs Fisher for her untiring efforts'. Grandfather had married again several years before.

22nd June 1911 is recorded in the minute book in large bold handwriting and is outlined in red ink. The village folks were conveyed at midday round the village in three decorated wagons to the Coronation Field opposite the Priory Farm. At dusk the prizes were handed to the winners by Mrs Fisher, amid much applause, after which Mr Lightfoot proposed a hearty vote of thanks to Grandfather, without whom there would probably have been no village celebration.

Mr W Garnham said that under such a good lead the gathering could not have been more successful. Edward responded, 'No one could cast a single slur upon the day's proceeding…and they showed that Wrabness was what he had always considered it to be, viz. a model village.' Among other things he thanked the committee and their friends who for three nights had worked well in fixing up the tent.

This was a structure of long poles lashed together with rope and covered with stack cloths. So everyone, with the possible exception of the Rector, went on their way home to their cottages well filled with booze, meat, plum duff, and well smoked into the bargain. Three postcards illustrate the proceedings.

Coronation of George V, 1911

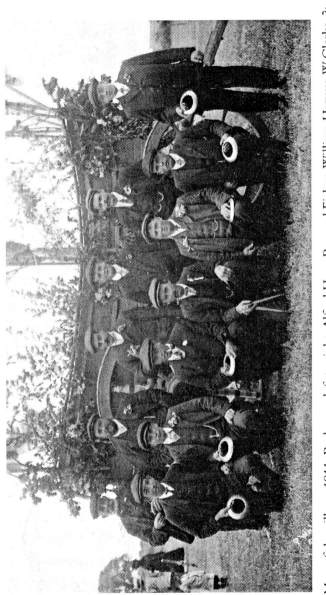

Men of the village, 1911. Back row, left to right: Alfred Haw, Bernard Fisher, William Harvey, W Clarke, ?; front row: first four unknown, Cecil Fisher, my father Joseph and standing B Lungley

Arriving for Coronation, 1911

Chapter Three

In 1911 my Uncle Christian was probably not too pleased with working for his father at menial farm work for very little money.

'Well you get your keep, young man, don't forget,' he was told. But he embarked from these shores for Australia. I have a photo of him working out there clearing scrubland in clouds of dust, and another of him with mates round the camp fire with billy can over the sticks. I think the various uncles would have been aged between 34 and 27, and just right for the army when hostilities broke out in that year. Christian joined up in the Australian forces. Bernard and Lewis joined up, but Cecil and Edward JR escaped. My father served from 1916 to 1918.

> Against heroic wrong
> Unconscious of her fate
> Exalts our new imperial song,
> And still we make our ancient boast
> At home or by the battle's hearth
> We venture furthest, dare the most
> The chosen valour of the earth.

> Our doom is written thus
> So may our souls find grace;
> Empire is the gift of us
> The genius of the race
> In empire, winning for the world
> A nobler power and place
> Establishing our ancient boast
> That freedom lights their genial hearth
> Who venture furthest dare the most
> And are the valour of the Earth.

Who fall in Britain's wars
How fortunate are they,
Sepulchred as conquerors
In Britain's memory.
And those who mourn,
How sweet their tears,
How proud their glorious dead,
They boast, who shone upon the battle's hearth –
Who ventured furthest, dared the most
And were the valour of the earth.
No sacrifice shall tame
No terror daunt our will
Destiny's immortal dim
Our conquering arms fulfil
Redeem the earth for man and make
While women dry their tears and run
To feed the battle's glowing hearth
With husband, brother, lover, son
The chosen valour of the earth.

A thousand years of war
In front of Britain's throng
Empire Britain battled for
Against heroic wrong;
The sword that won must guard and beat
The measure of her song
While Britons make their ancient boast
By every battle's glowing hearth
Who venture furthest, dare the most
The chosen valour of the earth.

I have one page of a letter written home from Christie, and he says:

Yes, I am a rolling stone all right, but the worst of it is I am not gathering too much moss. I am getting 10s a day of eight hours. I can save about two pounds a week, but we have had a bit of lost time lately through rain, so it's brought the average down a bit. We are having some lovely weather here now; it's more like summer than winter, and I think the rain is just about over. The crops around here a looking very good as it is new country just opened up. Yes, I think it would do Cecil a world of good to be away from home, for a year or two. In fact I think everyone ought to leave home for a bit. They would be appreciated more when they come back. No, I haven't found a young lady yet. They don't trouble me much out here. I suppose I shall find someone when I come home. I suppose you will be soon be looking for someone shortly. If you find a decent one don't do like I did and lose it.

With the usual kindly references to all at home, the letter is concluded. He was in active service in July 1916, for I have a field postcard, where he informed Miss Fisher at Ships Farm by crossing out the sentences not required, thus: 'I am quite well, I have received your letter.' His signature on the bottom was all that was allowed.

I fear that, as with so many thousands at that time in our history, nothing more can have been heard of him. To further quote from a letter of 1st November 1916, from someone who knew him by the name of John Phillips,

I would not give up hope; men are every day turning up after their friends have given up all hope of seeing them again. I have no clear recollection of seeing him on the 19th July [the actual date of the field postcard]. *I shall never forget that date, but I remember seeing and speaking to him the previous evening when he had toothache. Otherwise he was in good health; the army life seemed to suit him. He was very stout, almost as broad as he was long. He carried about with him a pocketbook full of old letters and photos. He showed me a photo of his home, I remember it distinctly, so that there should have been no difficulty in identifying him if he was taken to one of our dressing stations. He also had a good identification disc on. I have come across a man who would not let his friends know for a long time that he was wounded. He had lost a leg and felt it so much that he would not write himself or let anyone else. That was a terrible fight we had. The latest account I have heard puts the losses of the 32 Battn. (ours) at 700 killed and wounded out of 850 who took part in the attack. I can quite believe it, for the losses of other battalions were heavier. I was a brave fight. I did not see a man hang back. I was hit by shrapnel as soon as I got over the parapet. About thirteen wounds, and I lost my speech. I have now recovered it but I have to undergo another operation to remove another piece of shrapnel, but that is nothing. This is a splendid hospital with good doctors and nurses. I wish Christie was here. If I do hear anything of him I will write you at once good or bad news.*

I guess Christie was among those 700 probably blown to pieces. I have a note on an envelope in Mother's hand:

Letter sent to War Office 27th August 1918. No news. I should have abandoned hope very soon after the battle.

However, I doubt if the folks at home had much idea of the conditions prevailing at the front.

My mother was issued with a Permit Book in October 1916 allowing her to enter Harwich Special Military Area for the purpose of shopping. Her occupation was household duties and farm work, and it was necessary to fill in a section station if you had any male relatives in arms for or against His Majesty; and there are listed three brothers, all labelled 'For', of course. The permit was extended until 1919, and without it she wouldn't be allowed into the town.

I have another letter written to Grandfather from a brother in East London in 1915. He is not in very good health and says:

I feel rather nervous driving at night in the fog, since the town has to be kept dark, sometimes we can hardly see ourselves, it is extremely dangerous. Accidents are always happening, when the last raid was made on London about three weeks ago by the German Hell Hounds, they were very near to us. I had just got home when we heard the first bomb explode. It shook me as I sat in my chair and in a few seconds we saw the infernal machine passing over; it was quite a warfare, with the guns firing from the Tower of London and other places. There were many people killed and injured; I hope the next time they come they will stop in the sea and have a bath until all their sins are washed away. 'Love your enemies.'

If anyone whosoever they might be should say they loved such enemies as these, in my opinion they would be telling a confounded lie. If anyone cannot be won over by kindness, frightfulness will never do it...

The greedy Kaiser at their head is without doubt the biggest hypocrite that ever lived – having been so religious; as it was once stated that he said, 'The Lord Jesus Christ first, and himself next'. He goes on for another page, with his opinions of the German leader, and then mentions Nurse Cavell's brutal murder and says,

I hope the day is near at hand when all those who are capable of doing such fiendish work will be swept off the face of the earth with the besom of destruction, for they have made lies their refuge and under falsehood they have hid themselves…and I trust that God will dispose, and will not the Judge of all the earth do right?

One of the brothers came home from the hostilities with mechanical things in mind, and somewhere around 1918 a Titan tractor was purchased. It did not prove to be a very great success, for it was in the barn at Foxes Farm for many years, ignored. From what I heard of it, starting was a hazard, with a long crank handle to swing it. It was not much more manoeuvrable than a traction engine, and for ploughing you needed a wide headland. A plough accompanied it, and was relegated to a hedge until an acetylene torch cut it into moveable pieces about thirty years later.

On 19th July 1919, our village celebrated the peace that had at long last come about, and as previously a 'capital meal of bread and butter, ham, beef, sausage rolls, salad, cake, buns, tarts, tea and fruit was enjoyed, but there was an absence of beer and porter, for this was held on the Rectory lawn and Mr Miller was still Rector. Potted meat is mentioned in the list of items that were surplus: 'Unheard of stuff, don't think much to it'. I am sure these words rippled under the tablecloths by someone remembering past events. Two hundred and fifty folk were catered for, and £34 16s was contributed by villages and landowners.

Grandfather Joseph died in 1914 and the Post Office and General Store were run by his wife and her daughter, Aunt Grace. The coal trade was still just ticking over, I believe, the Calvers were not alone in selling coal.

W Robinson of Foxes Farm was in the coal trade. He supplied Mrs Cave at the Gate House 2 tons 12 cwt. at £2 per ton in 1918. Mrs Garrett purchased 5 cwt. and was charged 8s 6d – obviously discount for large quantities. Grandfather Edward was also selling coal; I imagine competition was quite fierce, but of course this was the only method most people had for cooking their food, apart from wood, and they used several hundredweight weekly.

So at the start of the second decade of the twentieth century we have the Fishers at the Firs, Foxes and Butlers Farms; but in 1921 Grandfather died aged 79, and the will that he left was to prove to be a trial for its executors for many years.

The cottage I mentioned before (Spring Cottage) was bequeathed to Aunts Rose and Lily. Foxes went to Bernard, Butlers to Lewis. Priory was leased and not part of the estate. Uncle Lewis and Bernard and Lily were executors, and they were required to pay his wife £300 within one year, and Lily £300 in two years. Rose was to receive £200 in three years, Adelaide £200 in four years, Minnie £200 in five years, Cecil £200 in six years and Lydia £200 in seven years. So poor old Bernard had a rope round his neck and 'one chuck would break it' – for there just wasn't any money in the bank! Foxes Farm consisted of 59 acres, Butlers of 35 acres. The Firs had been bequeathed to his wife, and the passage reads

> upon Foxes Farm I here by charge ALL the legacies herein before bequeathed to my said wife and children and until all the same shall be discharged. I empower my Trustees to raise sufficient money by Mortgage of such farm to discharge such of the same as shall be in arrear and I declare that no mortgage shall be bound to ascertain whether such money is required for the purpose aforesaid.

In those days 59 acres was worth about £15 per acre – what an impossible task! My father and Lydia must have been acquainted when the will was read, for the solicitor said before commencing, 'Is there anyone here that any member of the family considers should be absent?'

'Yes, there is,' retorted Cecil, 'Joe Calver!'

With slight surprise, Joe replied, 'Oh well, if that's the case I'll soon clear off.' He did not stay another moment.

So the family took up its various new residences, and Bernard, Cecil and Lily and Lydia went to Foxes, to survive as best as they could. My father and his brother were in partnership during the second decade. The turnover from farming at Clays Farm, Wix (Merchants had been given up) and delivery of coal during 1920 was £1430, and in 1921 £1640; the balance at the bank at the end of this year was £221. Joseph was looking for somewhere to settle down and marry, and in 1921 the holding, where I am writing these notes, came up for sale.

Joseph Calver, Sr

Harriet Calver

Aunt Grace, Joseph, Albert, circa 1915

William Harvey, husband of Grace Calver

Ted Calver in his younger days

Instructions to Soldier.

1. You will produce this book whenever you require an advance of cash on account.

2. You will give a receipt, on the acquittance roll of the Officer paying you, for all cash advances made to you. The Officer making the payment will sign the corresponding entry in this book on the page for Cash Payments.

3. You will make no entries in this book, except to sign your name on pages 3 and 5.

4. **When you have been placed under orders for active service (and not before)** you may make your will, if you so desire, on page 13.

5. Should you lose your book you will at once report the loss to your Commanding Officer. A new book will be obtained, if possible, from the Paymaster, but it must be understood that no pay can be issued in respect of the period before the date on which you report your loss, until you are finally settled with.

REMEMBER—

1. Never speak about naval or military matters **in public** or to any **stranger.**

2. The enemy wants **information** about everything naval or military; your ship, regiment, or battery; your movements and supplies.

3. He tries to obtain this through **spies,** who may be bar loungers, prostitutes, shopkeepers or business men, or dressed as clergymen, officers, soldiers, or sailors.

4. If you talk of naval or military matters to **any stranger** or in public places you may help the enemy.

5. If the enemy is without information, he is like a blind man. His **success** against us depends on **information.** If you keep him in the dark you help to win our battles.

In every game you play you try to keep from your opponent what you are going to do next, so as to surprise him. It is the same in war.

(A946) W. W. & Sons. 1 746: 1,000m. P.P.Ltd. 3/16

Extract from Joseph's army pay book

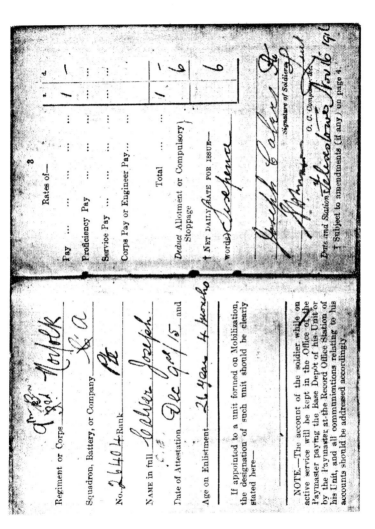

Extract from Joseph's army pay book

Tele.: No. 124 Chelmsford.

ESSEX AGRICULTURAL EXECUTIVE COMMITTEE.

ALL COMMUNICATIONS TO BE
ADDRESSED TO
" THE SECRETARY."
AND NOT TO INDIVIDUALS.

INSTITUTE OF AGRICULTURE,

CHELMSFORD, 13th June, 191 8

GCH/CAM.

Dear Madam,

Pte. J. Calver - 260408.

Your application for the services of the above
man have received the careful consideration of my Committee
who are unable under the circumstances to recommend that
leave should be granted to the above man.

I regret that I am therefore unable to
assist you in this matter.

Yours faithfully,

G. O Laurence

for Secretary.

Mrs. Calver,
Krabness, Tendring,
Essex.

Harriet's attempts to release Joseph (letter)

AN ATTRACTIVE AND WELL-EQUIPPED

SMALL HOLDING,

KNOWN AS

"Domine Farm,"

Situate in the Parish of Wrabness, on the Main Road from Harwich to Manningtree, about 6½ miles from the former and 6 miles from the latter.

IT COMPRISES:—

A Double-Tenement Cottage,

Timber built, with plain tiled roof. One Tenement has—Living Room, with Small Room adjoining; Kitchen, with brick oven, sink, and copper; Pantry; and Two Bedrooms; and is let to Mr. W. Gooding at **£4 per Annum**. The other Tenement has—Living Room, with four cupboards; Kitchen, with range and sink; and One Bedroom; and has been unoccupied since the death of the late owner.

A Substantial and Conveniently Arranged

SET OF FARM PREMISES,

Including Large timber-built and slated Corn Barn; brick, timber, and tiled Stable for **3 Horses**; Horse Yard, with timber-built and tiled Shed; brick and timber-built and tiled Cart Lodge; and

Two Enclosures of Productive Arable Land,

Suitable for a **Market Garden**, and in excellent heart and condition, having been in the occupation of the late Mr. Robinson for many years.

It comprises Ord. No. 157 and part of No. 159, and has an Area by the Ordnance Survey (1897 edition) of

15 Acres   3 Roods   15 Poles,

Or thereabouts.

There are also VALUABLE ROAD FRONTAGES of about 190 ft. to the Harwich to Manningtree Main Road, and about 780 ft. to the road leading from the Main Road to Wrabness Village.

TENURE   ...   .   **FREEHOLD.**

Land Tax paid, 1921, 5s. 3d.   Tithe Rent-charge paid, 1921, £6 3s. 6d.

POSSESSION WILL BE GIVEN ON SEPTEMBER 29th, 1921.

The Purchaser shall pay, in addition to the purchase-money, the usual Tenant-Right Valuation, according to the custom of the County of Essex.

CONDITIONS OF SALE.

I. The property is sold subject to the conditions following, and to the conditions known as "the National Conditions of Sale" (a print of which can be seen at the office of the vendors' solicitors and will be produced at the auction), so far as such latter conditions are not inconsistent with the conditions following.

II. The day for the completion of the purchase shall be the 29th day of September, 1921.

III. The expression "the office of the vendor's solicitor" in the National Conditions of Sale shall mean the office at Manningtree of Messrs. WARD & WARD.

IV. The vendors are selling as personal representatives and trustees.

V. The title shall commence with an indenture of conveyance dated the 4th day of July, 1868, and no earlier or other title shall be required or enquired into.

VI. In case interest shall become payable on the balance of purchase-money, the same shall be calculated at the rate of 6 per cent.

These Particulars may be had of the Solicitors, Messrs. WARD & WARD, Manningtree; and of the AUCTIONEERS, 26, Princes Street, Ipswich.

Small holding poster

Lydia, JC, Joseph, circa 1930

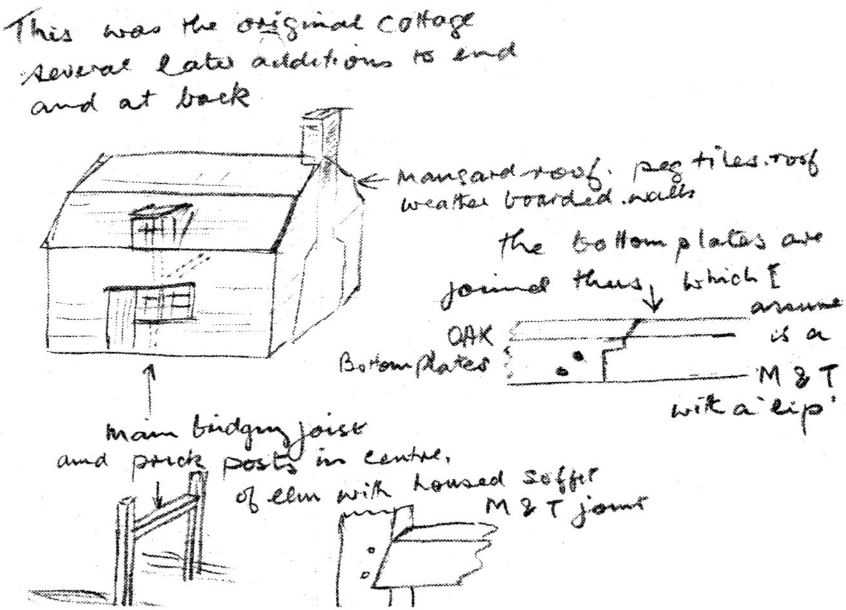

This was the original cottage
several later additions to East
and back

mansard roof; peg tiles roof
weather boarded walls

The bottom plates are
joined thus, which I
assume is a
M & T
with a 'cip'

OAK
bottom plates

main bridging joist
and principal posts in centre,
of elm with housed soffit
M & T joint

This was the original cottage

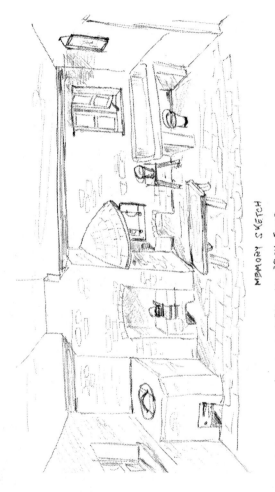

MEMORY SKETCH

KITCHEN AT DOMINE FARM WITH BRICK FLOOR

COPPER.   BACKSTOCK   STONE SINK

                    PIG STOOL   INTO CHIMNEY

SIZE approx 12 × 9 ft the CURVED HOOD over OVEN took SMOKE UP

Kitchen at Domine Farm

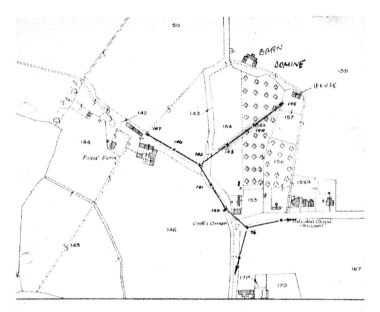

WRABNESS. L

Map of Wrabness

BRICK OVEN DOOR.
freestanding on feet wrot iron

Brick oven door

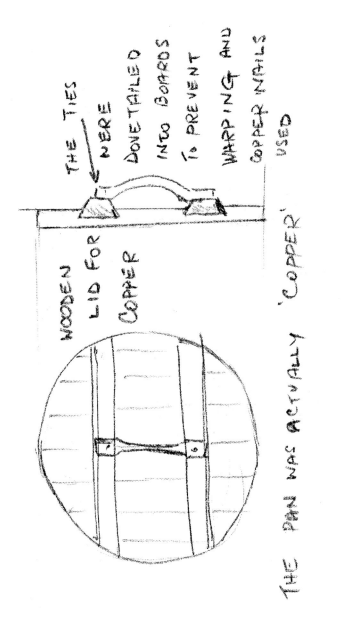

THE TIES WERE DOVETAILED INTO BOARDS TO PREVENT WARPING AND COPPER NAILS USED

WOODEN LID FOR COPPER

THE PAN WAS ACTUALLY 'COPPER'

Wooden lid for copper

Joseph, circa 1923

Joseph Calver, circa 1922

John Calver, Jackie Coogan cap, 1932

John Calver, circa 1946

The particulars on the auctioneers' pamphlet mentioned in manorial survey 1564 are:

> An attractive and well-equipped small holding known as Domine Farm, it comprises a double tenement cottage, timber built with plain tiled roof. One tenement has living rooms with small room adjoining: kitchen with brick oven sink and copper, pantry and two bedrooms, and is let to W Gooding at £4 per annum. The other tenement has living room with four cupboards, kitchen with range and sink and one bedroom. A substantial and conveniently arranged set of farm premises with large timber built and slated corn barn, brick timber and tiled stable for three horses. Horse yard with timber built and tiled shed and tiled cart lodge. The land is in excellent heart, having been in the occupation of the late W Robinson for many years and extended to 15 acres, 3 roods and 15 poles. Tithe rent charge £6 3s 6d; to be sold at the Corn Exchange, Colchester, on Saturday 23rd July 1921.

So Joseph, having first confirmed that his bride-to-be would like to live there, went off and became the highest bidder for this great estate. He did not get a bargain; it cost him £1000. This was a high figure for those times. He paid £400 and had a mortgage for the remainder. The house was of weatherboard painted slate grey with a mansard roof. It was of elm, studs, beams and floor joist, with an oak plate on brick footings. There was dry rot, here and there. The studs were nogged in with red bricks, grouted with a clay daub, and lime plastered all over inside. The weatherboards were originally elm, and were much patched with softwood pieces. Mice had no difficulty in getting inside, and the sparrows and starlings built under the tiles. The floors, with one exception, were of hard brick laid directly upon a sandy loamy mixture. The farm buildings were fair, but rats had taken their toll on the woodwork. On the map of field names previously referred to a barn is shown on this same spot. The buildings are near the highway and the cottage away up the drive tucked away in the trees, one of which is a yew tree – probably planted when the house was built in 1828, according to recent opinion. The tree was estimated to be 177 years old in 2005 by David Bethany. The house was built long before 1828.

So, for better or worse, my parents wed in the church in June 1922. I have one of the little invitation cards with the impressed ivy leaves around the edges. The reception was held at Foxes, and Joseph considered that Cecil ate more meat than everyone else put together; in fact, 'he had never seen such a guts'. They went off to relatives in London for a week's honeymoon. It was the only holiday they ever had together. An account from Tom Frasers of Ipswich is worth mentioning. It lists:

1 pair satin walnut toilets £14 (this was a dressing table and washstand with marble top).
4' 6" brass and iron bedstead with spring mattress £5 12s 6d
7 Piece suit in Moquette £19 19s. This included a sofa and two armchairs.
Brass Fender 19s 6d
12' x 9' Tapestry carpet £5 5s

From Crane Bros at Harwich, they purchased, among other items, a pudding basin, 6½d; 1 enamel pail, 5s 6d; 1 tin tray, 1s 6d; 2 flat irons, 3s 5d; a pie dish, 1s; a tin kettle, 1s 3½d; 2 bone spoons, 9d (these are still used for boiled eggs). At the bottom of the invoice is printed a notice about a 1/2 gallon of varnish stain which will give two coats on a floor 11' square – 6s for a floor covering!

So there we were, all settled down in a country cottage. Just what a lot of folk dream about… When the sun shone you had flies by the hundred. There was a concentrated effort to catch as many as possible – on those sticky strips that unrolled when they were hung on a nail and pulled downwards. They caught some but there were still hundreds in every room about the house.

You'd find the pesky flies. They buzzed and never seemed to stop and…until they died…on mirrors, edges of doors, on the picture frames, they did just that. They had a fair amount of encouragement at the back of Domine; in fact the first thing you saw was the lavatory. The yew tree was possibly planted there to keep it cool. It was a noble structure of studwork in pine, all about 5' x 4' with a tiled roof, just like a large sentry box. There was a brick-lined pit which was emptied when it was thought to be full enough.

Father did not approve of this operation so he boarded the pit over and had a large bucket instead, which was attended to far more frequently. Then there was the seat: a large, smooth, kindly piece of pine 1¼" thick. It was so comfortable, you could meditate in there. You could plan the next move in there. You could escape there, as Joseph did one day when Mr Skilton, who came round village with a travelling shop, wished to present his account. There he stayed secure within its studwork and weatherboards, with the door securely hanked on the inside to a staple big enough to hold a horse.

I think there were workmen who specialised in constructing these establishments. Perhaps they were called 'loo wrights' or 'privy wrights'. Near to the yew was a plum tree – black gages, we called them. It had a trunk that my arms would not encircle, and those plums were lovely. The tree was large and accessible with a ladder, so most of them fell on the ground and washed and eaten either raw or cooked. Chickens roamed around, so washing was essential. There was an orchard nearby and the owner's sows used to enjoy them.

The sows should not have trespassed, but the boundary was chicken wire netting – not really a substantial fence for the purpose. The garden had a profusion of fruit trees with an espalier apple tree growing a soft sweet codling. A young visitor was told not to pick any of these. This proved rather a trial but was overcome by walking along the tree and taking a bite out of those that were of a convenient height. 'Well, what about that!' someone probably said. 'Well, we can't git onto her cause she e'nt picked none.' Most of the trees were large and old. There are now only two remaining. One was called by us boys the 'Umbrella Tree' for it was just like an umbrella, with its branches touching the ground. There was a large greengage and a Blenhiem orange. These have all but disappeared.

The house had two front doors; one was jammed shut through movement of the frame. The other was rarely opened and it was kept securely closed with an iron bar which was pushed into a mortise in one of the large upright posts, forming the main frame of the house. A very sure method. These faced south and led into the garden. When first built, one of these doors was the only access to the house. It was just 25' x 15'. The downstairs room was one-third larder, two-thirds living space. 'Enough room for a cow and calf,' someone said. Cupboards occupied the chimney corners, and above were two bedrooms. The one at the top of the stairs had just enough room for a single bed. If you fell out of bed there was little to prevent you falling downstairs. A rough-hewn newel post with a rail nailed thereto was the only protection.

There was a hook hanging from a chain in the chimney to support the cooking pot. The wood fire was not allowed to go out in bad weather. There does not appear to be any remnants of an oven being attached. At some date not recorded an addition of the second tenement was built, which consisted of just one room up and one down. At the back, the north, in the early nineteenth century a dairy was built; this is shown on a map when the holding was sold in 1850. It measures about 8' 6" square inside. To the north was a small lattice of horizontal slats – a window with a shutter that was removable. In a housekeeper's receipt book of 1817 instruction is given as follows. In the conduct of a dairy:

A dairy house ought to be so situated that the windows or lattices face north and it should at all times be kept perfectly cool and clean. Lattices are preferable to glazed lights as they admit a free circulation of air, and if glazed lights open they admit a free circulation of air; and if much air draws in, oiled paper may be pasted over the lattice or a frame constructed so as to fly backwards and forwards at pleasure. Dairies cannot be kept too clean in summer; they ought therefore to be erected if possible near a spring of running water.

If a pump can be fixed in the place or stream of water conveyed through, it will tend to preserve a continual freshness and purity of the air. The floor should be neatly paved with red brick of smooth stone and laid with a proper descent so that no water may stagnate it. The utensils of the dairy should all be made of wood. [The wood of the horse chestnut tree was used for making these. It was white naturally, and as far as I know is of little use for any other purpose.] Lead, copper and brass are poisonous and cast iron gives a disagreeable taste to the production of the dairy. Well-glazed pans are ideal. The well-known effects of the poison of lead are bodily debility palsy and death! Wooden vessels can be kept perfectly clean with good care and washing and scalding them with salt and water.

At the corner in the north-west of our new-shaped house, a kitchen for brewing was built. This contained a copper of about 15 gallon capacity, a stone sink a small fireplace with what I've given to understand was called a backstock. This consisted of two raised brickwork stumps on either side with a iron grate and bars. Onto this chimney was a quarter-circle dome of brickwork, and under this was a brick oven. The ash, dust and smoke was caught by the dome and carried into the chimney. The water supply was a well about 20' from the back door. This usually dried up in the summer and we then had to carry water from the well at the farm buildings. The sink water dribbled from a pipe into a hole about 12' away from the dairy window – so much for health and hygiene. On a brick at the back of the kitchen we can see 'MG 1843'. Who MG was I've no idea; perhaps it was Martha Gosling or perhaps the builder. Eventually in the later years of the nineteenth century the house acquired another kitchen in the north-east corner, fitted with stone sink and backstock fireplace.

Living in these isolated spots is not very commendable in bad winters – even in 1983; but in 1843 they were much worse. Let us consider it. A pig must have been essential. Its meat was used completely. The fat was consumed and was necessary for survival. Rabbits were always around, and although the poorer classes were denied them by the owners of farms, on this holding one would imagine rabbits would not be covered by this rule. Chickens would have been around and, as today, were very useful. Geese, perhaps, would be kept; they provided down and feathers. According to our housekeeper's recipes, goose feathers were particularly valuable; these birds were unmercifully plucked five times a year in some countries. The first operation is performed at Lady Day for feathers and quills, and is repeated four times between then and Michaelmas for feathers only.

They should be 13 or 14 weeks old before they are subject to this operation. Ducks were also part of the habitat. Pork could be salted and hung for winter use. Bullaces were put into earthenware jars, tied over with linen and cooked slowly in the oven after baking was complete.

These were used as dessert in pies and as an antidote to sore throats, for they were sharp and syrupy. Tallow candles would have lit the dark evenings. The wood yard would have been filled with faggots and bavins (bundles of sticks tied for the oven) and with tree top wood (spray) before the weather turned to cold. The kitchen garden would have been all important, and provided soft fruits and vegetables. Perhaps it doesn't look too bad, in fact even slightly appealing, but you had to scrap about all day long to survive – just about the same as the birds do from morn to night.

On the conveyance previously mentioned, calf pens and pigsties are shown along the roadway from the house to the barn. It shows much industry, and in times of war farming was more prosperous; I dare say the occupants lived a little more graciously. Perhaps the wife and mother was proud of the little establishment with its whitewashed walls and ceilings and scrubbed brick floors. Today the roadway is tarmacked. We have a motor vehicle, and we have mains water and electricity; but sometimes in the winter when the better winds blow from the north-east it is not very appealing.

Foxes Farm was a short walk from here – six minutes in fact, down the roadway, past the barn, over the highway, over the style, and along the side of the Pyghtle. At some time in the summer of 1924, Aunt Lily made the journey from there to visit Lydia. Conversation between the two sisters can only be imagined, for Lydia had to tell her the joyous news that she was with child. Poor Lily was shattered, and on the way home past the barn found Joseph and attacked him with, 'What have you done to my sister?'

I should imagine that he told her! They never did see eye to eye, and this was the last straw. After a difficult confinement in January 1925, Lydia was the proud owner of a son. Dr Brea, who was well liked, told Joseph that it would be inadvisable to have further children. Although things had not turned out as well as they might. He told Alfred Ham, who worked here then, 'Well, Al, you know where I'm go to, don't you?'

'Ha, ha! You've a boy – I think I do,' he replied, and Joseph walked off to the Wheatsheaf Inn. He went in and probably stayed there for the remainder of the day, and half the night perhaps. We had the service of a midwife who stayed three weeks.

Alfred Ham, centre, Joseph, right

'She was a woman I disliked.' So my ma said. I had an early introduction to farm activities, for before she left took me down to see the threshing machine at work. Obviously I do not recall this.

Uncle Edward (Fisher's) wife wrote:

Dear Lydia,

I feel I must write and congratulate you on the birth of a son. We were all delighted to hear the news and we all trust he will grow up to be a comfort to you both.

Has he got blue eyes and is he fat? I must come and see him soon. Rather cold for the little stranger, he did not pick a very warm time. Trust you are feeling fairly under the circumstances, and hope you will have a good recovery.

Love, Bertha

PS: only a baby small never at rest. Small but how dear to us – God knoweth best.

I was a troublesome child. I always ate too quickly (and still do); I like my own way (and still do). The slightest noise woke me. The grandfather clock was the worst offender. Mother used to try to cover it up with a blanket, which can't have helped much for you couldn't see what time of day it was, and its effect on the noise was negligible. No one thought of removing the bell! On one of the frequent visits to Foxes (which were daily, for we had our milk in a quart can with a lid), Uncle Cecil took a good look at me and said, 'Do you think he'll rally?'

We were never without a cat. Mother brought one here called Toots when she moved. He was about ten years old and settled down all right; he lived for about eight more years. I recall him waiting for us near the stile when we came home from Foxes. As I grew up, I pushed him around in my pushchair in the house and garden.

There was large cockerel that followed me all round the farm. He was a beauty with colourful tail feathers flopping about. The hens went all around the farm and laid eggs in all sorts of odd places. They went to bed in a hen house on wheels that stood under the yew tree. Father brought this at the Suffolk Show in about 1930; he told the vendors that he wanted the one he saw on the showground, to which there was a little doubt expressed. He said, 'Well, if you don't let me have that one I shan't buy one at all.'

So he put his mark with a knife thus xx on the side and that was that. The hen house is still with us. Although now used as a garden shed, so whether it was made especially for the show I do not know, but it was very well made. When the chickens rattled their perches at night Mother said they were sorting out their sheets. Beetles we called 'butterwitches' or 'buzzy witches' used to collide with the wire netting in the twilight. We do not seem to hear them now.

The first time I was allowed to collect the milk on my own, I climbed the stile all right on the way out, but when I returned with the one and a half pints, the stile could not be surmounted so I walked back from whence I came and round by the road home. It did not occur to me to stand the can down and them climb over. We had butter from the same source, and according to a newspaper cutting in 1925 butter was in short supply. The retail price was going up by 1 penny a pound, making 2s 1d for New Zealand and 2s 2d for Danish. In 1921 in July the farm wage was 56s 1d and by Sept had dropped to 41s 4½d. Buy December 1933 the wage was 30s 9d for a week of 48¼ hours.

Domine was always well stocked with pigs. Bullocks were fattened in the winter. Two horses occupied the stable; one was used on the coal van and sometimes unloading rail wagons into stock using a tumbrel. The coal business was small, and probably only handling 7–10 tons weekly. Alfred was always around and was very kind to me. He had a white beard, wore a muffler around his neck and trousers tied below his knees. These were known as 'joskins'; they prevented wear on the knee of the trouser when bending. He had many a pint of home-brewed beer in the back kitchen. When Father used to ask him if he wanted a drink he would some times reply, 'Ha, ha, Joe boy, that's two words for yourself, and one for me.' And afterwards, 'Ha, ha, I can feel it doing my old belly good!'

Jim Garret, who lived next door to Alfred, was chief ganger on the railway here. He walked to work and home at midday for his 'bait' or dinner, as most folk described it then. He really marched along the road, his hobnailed boots crunching the stones along the road. The distance was about one mile each way. I recall him saying, when all the batters were cut each summer time with a scythe, 'When you sweat the dampness keep you cool.' On Sundays he would come down through the gardens which adjoined ours to help Father 'forder' or straw up the cattle yard and tidy up the sleeping quarters of the pigs. Very little money changed hands. There was not a lot of it around. A kind of barter system prevailed. A pint or two of beer, a few eggs, plums, apples, mangolds to make wine, or a bundle of straw for the potato clamp sufficed.

Chapter Four

I began my education at the village Church of England school when five years old, and was usually late. Miss Kindrid was very kind to me and understanding. I was rather poor at studies for I had near sight (myopia), and couldn't read the writing on the blackboard. Until I was whisked into hospital with appendicitis, no one discovered that spectacles would remedy my education. We spent two years in the infants' room and were then upgraded to the tender care of Miss Tippins. I excelled at drawing and often had examples of my efforts shown to the class by her. 'This is how I want you to do it,' she would say. We had Horlicks made with hot water only. Those in the class who looked as if they needed it had cod liver oil and malt at the appropriate time on certain days. This was dispensed by one teaspoon, each child licking it after its predecessor with no wipe in between. I think Miss T supplied this out of her own pocket. She wore a brown gymslip and plimsolls for country dancing. She would have her gramophone on a chair in the playground churning our traditional tunes, and I recall the words that went with one were:

> If all the world were paper
> And all the sea was ink,
> If all the trees were bread and cheese
> What should we have to drink?

Whether these were correct ones I never discovered. The gramophone seemed to run down fairly frequently and she would charge towards it and rewind it very vigorously. One day some boys were talking in class and she halted proceedings. 'Come out to the front, whoever is talking,' she commanded. One honest lad, Gordon, walked out and Miss T shook him well – 'to shake some sense into you' – and pushed him into the entrance porch. When she considered he had been there long enough she opened the classroom door and called him back but her request went unheeded. Shortly afterward, Gordon turned up accompanied by his grandmother. The shaking had caused the top button of his shirt collar to pop off. His guardian stormed and demanded that Miss T sew the button back on!

If it were not done she would keep him at home until it was. I don't remember the outcome. Miss T did try very hard to keep law and order: 'Do this slowly and carefully,' she would press.

'Good, better, best, never let it rest till the good is better and the better best' was a motto. Everyone had to set this out in 1" capitals and fill in with Indian ink. I had the distinction of doing a 'Speak No Evil, Hear no Evil, Think no Evil'. The capital letters were illuminated and filled in with gold paint. I got great praise for this. It was framed and present to me when I left. I hung it in our living room. I don't know if Father noticed it. It didn't seem to make much difference to his language.

Both the schoolmistresses cycled in from Mistley every day, weather permitting; they were never late. There was a wicker invalid chair which was stored at Dimbols Farm for the use of anyone who was infirm. News would be left at the school for two trustworthy boys to collect and deliver this to the needy person. It was steered by a single wheel in front with a long iron rod with a T-handle. One day I and Fred were to do the honours. I sat and steered Fred pushed, we gathered speed down the hill from Dimbols. I failed to negotiate the corner, and into the ditch we went.

At Christmas we had to perform a concert in the village hall or the school. I disliked these and more so then usual one year when five or six of us were to dress up as pixies from the stock of clothes from the 'prop box'.

There was nothing in there to fit me. Rosie T produced a pair of her own blue bloomers for me to wear – oh dear, the humiliation! The boys ragged me unmercifully. I hated her, the concert and everything, until it was all over. I had also to recite; my poetic contribution was:

These are my two drops of rain
Floating down the window pane

I am waiting her to see
Which the winning one will be:
Both of them have different names –
One is John and one is James.

I went on to tell those who were listening that if James reached the winning spot at the bottom of the pane the sun would surely shine and small boys would be able to play with their toys in the garden. The last line was, 'Look, I told you – there's the sun.' I couldn't get to that point quickly enough. I pointed upwards, but not in the direction of the red bulb glowing on the back of the stage.

'You should have pointed to that!' I was told. 'I put it up there especially for your act.'

I made no reply, but just looked at my toes and 'got off'. No one had told me that the bulb was exclusively for me. I do not recall anyone telling me that I was any good, or that I wasn't, so I assumed that I wasn't.

We had to write down the Lord's Prayer from memory. I tried to look over Walter's shoulder: *Are Father*, he'd begun, so I did the same. Rosie didn't give us a lot of credit for that, or for the remainder. She had favourites. Once we had a oral exam by a inspector. Most of the questions were Scripture. I didn't shine very much, and at the end of it the inspector asked our teacher who she thought should have certificates. She said she thought Barbara had answered very well. In fact Barbara didn't do as well an anyone else, but she was current favourite.

There were casualties. Once, in a skipping session, Dick Garratt – who was paired with a rather shorter partner – came down, and being rather closer than he should have been to her cracked his chin on her head. He had his tongue out and of course his teeth cut through his tongue. He yelled and was walked home. The wound was stitched and he recovered.

Dick Joughin was being harassed by one of he bigger boys. So one fine morning his older brother, who was training at Holbrook School, was to be seen at the school gate. The offender was pointed out and Theodore simply ran round the playground, tripped him up and brought him crashing down onto his knees.

That was an end of the matter. He was simply humiliated. We continued here until we were eleven, and then continued our education of Parkeston Elementary School.

Chapter Five: Flora's Story

(Flora was to become my wife much later)
College Farm, Great Blakenham, Suffolk, stood about two miles from the main road. It consisted of three houses. The larger one, detached, was occupied by Uncle Harry Everett; the smaller semi-detached house by Granny on the one side and Charles on the other. Between them was situated the brick-built outhouses with a central bake house with wash house at either end.

Water was from a well in the yard with covered windlass to convey the wooden bucket holding about 12 gallons down the eighty or so feet of its depth. There were the usual set of farm buildings to serve the stabling of eighteen horses, with a piggery and bullock yards. The little community was to a great extend self-supporting, with large vegetable gardens, a supply of rabbits, hen's eggs and the occasional pheasant. The annual show at Ipswich was an occasion to remember lovely produce from the gardens, scrubbed potatoes, carrots and the like, homemade bread, jam, pickles, baskets of wild flowers, all stacked onto a wagon for the five-mile journey. The journey was sometimes made on foot by a mother with perambulator and a babe or two when there was a need for provisions such as flour and fruit, or for items that could not be purchased at the village.

In 1928 the owner of the lands sold out to the Government for the training of foreign immigrants in the arts of farming. They lived in Bareham workhouse. The brothers Everett were given the chance to stay. Two of them did, but Charles had decided to 'go abroad'. He saw an advert in the *East Anglian* for a horseman for a Mr Barrow of Roydon Hall, Ramsey. He came on the train with his wife, Sara, and daughter, Daisy, to be met at Wrabness by car. No. 3, Chapel Cottages, was the house going with the job, which was looked at before going to the farm. The cottages are a terraced row of four lets with three bedrooms, two very small, two downstairs, and a small scullery apiece. They were not in a very

Sisters Flora and Daisy

Milk delivery van, Flora on the left

Flora at Dimbols

Flora, 1958

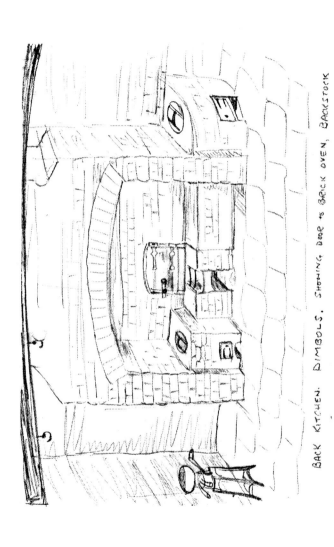

BACK KITCHEN. DIMBOLS. SHOWING DOOR TO BRICK OVEN, BACKSTOCK

Back kitchen, Dimbols

The arrangement of farm buildings and pond were nearby, Blakenham, Suffolk

good state of decoration. Charles accepted the job. He did not relish the journey to the farm, a distance of one and a half miles.

Back at Blakenham the news was met with disbelief. Tears flowed, friend and relatives arrived in considerable number. The village, in common with many communities then, was made up with families that had intermarried for generations. They considered that Charles was going to the other side of the world.

On the appointed day the motor van turn up and all the household chattels, garden tools and pea sticks were loaded up. It was a great upset, Granny ran along by side of the van waving her hankie and as it gathered speed ran on behind. Flora thought she was coming with them and worried that she would be tired when they arrived in Wrabness.

The various items were arranged in the house and out. Outside the back door was a little neat heap of kindling wood and shovel of coal to light the fire. This was a sharing time – a lovely gesture from a kindly Welsh family who had moved into No. 1 a year before the slump in the coal industry had brought them to Essex. The mother had died before, and the father, five brothers and one male lodger, looked after by sister Florence (sixteen), made up the family. There were difficulties with the cooking range at No.1. Florence was offered the use of the stove in No. 2, which was empty, so she had to journey to and fro to cook meals.

No. 2 was to be occupied, and the new tenants came to look around and couldn't understand why the smell of cooking was so prevalent. A new range arrived for No. 1, and stood in the yard for several days in the rain before Mr Fordham, a local builder, could fit it. So this created the extra work of cleaning off rust before blackening it. The governor called at No. 3 the morning following to see how the Everetts were getting on.

'We're not getting on at all,' said Sara in no uncertain terms. 'Look at the filthy state of this place' He was shown the state of the shelves, the stairs and paintwork. He had to agree it was not very palatable. 'Perhaps No. 4 is in better shape, ma'am.' The two parties had a look around. It was agreed to be in passable order. So up came everything. The two girls helped by dragging cardboard boxes full of various items from one house to another. When it was all accomplished, they sat down and cried and cried. So they settled down as best they could in the end house of the row.

'Granny' Seager, the dumpy postman who called with a letter from home within a few days of their arrival, comforted everyone by saying, 'Don't bother to unpack, ma'am. You won't be here long – nobody stays here any longer than a few weeks.' The postman cycled in all weathers from Manningtree and would bring medicine from the doctor's for a few pence per bottle.

Flora was seven years old and went to the village school. She had an arrangement with my mother, when I needed to have my hand held on the way to our place of learning. If Mother and I had gone a stone was placed on our gate post to indicate our early start, and vice versa if Flora had gone first. Occasionally she would be presented with 6d for the saving of Mother's time and energy.

Jim Garratt's garden was extensive. In fact the plot is marked on the old field name map as a separate plot and was probably a marked gardener's holding. Flora's father had a large plot of garden there, along with another neighbour. He would take his daughters along when the weather was suitable and sit them down on his coat. As the plot was hired they were bid to, 'Sit down there, together. Don't wander about and get into mischief. This here ain't my property.'

The hedge parting our property from Jim's had a tall paled gate through which I used to peer and say a meek 'Hello' to the girls. I had something in my hand, Flora tells me, and used to keep fumbling with it and rarely looked up. 'We couldn't get you to talk,' said she.

Charles was horseman at Roydon Hall and took part in the breaking-in of horses. He was to kind to them, so his mates told him. This was his nature – quiet and tolerant. At harvest time, Sara and the girls used to walk the one and a half miles to take 'beaver' (the afternoon break) to him, and they would all sit down 'under the stack' and eat together. The meal was cold bacon sandwiches, harvest cake and tea in bottles wrapped in newspaper. The cakes were made with yeast or lard and plenty of fruit. After the meal, Chas was pestered to give the girls a ride, and they would be put up on the trace horse when the empty wagon went off for another load of sheaves. Mother would tell him, 'You are worse than they are. Now you be careful, mawthers, we don't want any more trouble.' While the girls were thus occupied, the various wives who had been on a similar mission would exchange gossip of the day's events. A few yards down the road from Chapel Cottages was the Methodist Chapel. It was full to capacity on Sunday.

Flora: We went to Sunday School in the 'School Room' at 10 a.m., and immediately this ended had to go into the Chapel Room and join the morning service. Then, School Room again at 2.15 for another hour. We were allowed to go for a walk after this if the weather was suitable. If we grizzled about going to Sunday School, the threat from Mother was, 'If you don't go to chapel, I shan't let you go for a walk.' At 6.15 we went to evening service.

The annual anniversary service was heralded as the great event of the year. We practised for this for weeks before learning duets and recitations. Violin solos and community singing fitted the bill. The building was packed. One of the regular worshippers, a Mr Brown, always gave me a sweet. One of his favourites got most of the remainder in the bag. Another favourite who was never offered any insisted on sitting in her place one morning…surely Mr Brown would not notice the move. But he did, and apart from a slight hesitation his favourite got her usual prize. There was a pinching and hair-pulling episode after this. Quite a lot of mirth crept in, one of the hymns with the chorus beginning 'At the cross, at the cross' had the remaining lines substituted by:

> Where the Major lost his hoss
> And the sly old devil ran away
> When he heard the German guns
> He was eating currant buns…

The words were not heard above the louder voices – or we hoped they were not, for one anniversary I had a smart new frock and Daisy had one identical. Mrs Taylor made them. She loaned us four buttons, two on each frock, and said, 'I would like them back, Mrs Everett, when you're done with them.'

All dressed for the occasion, I proceeded to the chapel door and tripped, grazing my arm. Back to the house, and Mother put

Vaseline on the wound and swathed it in a strip of sheet. Going back to the chapel I met N.

'I'm not standing near you with your arm all bound up,' said she.

'I couldn't help it,' I protested.

'Of course, she couldn't help falling over,' said another.

'She hasn't hurt herself half enough,' said N, with spite.

My recitation was, 'If you have sunshine in your heart, don't keep it, pass it round', and earned more sarcastic remarks from N. 'Huh, she's got some sunshine in her heart.'

On Sunday, Bob Gosling came with the news of a tragic fire at a children's home in London. He was moved to tears. We had an extra hymn that day: 'Around the throne of God in Heaven'.

Mr Durrant's wife was confined to a wheelchair, and we always tried to get into chapel before she arrived pushed by her husband. If they arrived as we were going out we would hang back. I didn't like to see him carry her in. They always came in all weathers.

Behind Jim Garratt's house was a lean-to roughly made with rail sleepers covered with tarpaulin and several coats of tar. My sister, Jim's daughter, Clara, and son, Dick, and I used to play in there. There was a section at the far end where they stored kindling wood and logs parted with a couple of boards and some sacks hanging in front. This was our house. We had a potted meat jar with a few flowers and Clara's mother would provide us with a cup of cocoa, strong, and with a little sugar, and bread and margarine, Dick used to sneeze all over us. It was like an earthquake. We would try to push him out and he didn't appreciate this and would splutter out something like, 'I'll tell my mudder of you.' He had an impediment in his speech but was very kindly. Our toys were few. A small rag doll with a china face or a small bundle of cloth tied in various places to make a head etc., a skipping rope and an iron hoop formed the basis of our pastimes.

In winter evenings we were sent to bed quite soon after tea to be out of Mother's way. She was always at work packing tomorrows 'grub' bags for Father and two brothers, who were also working at the farm, mending clothes, darning socks, cleaning and cooking. She very rarely went out. Accidents sometimes happened on the farms. Our Welsh neighbours had a brother run over by the wheel of a loaded wagon. His ambulance was a tumbril – nice treatment for injuries that proved fatal. One day, Dad had become trapped between the cart shafts and a spirity horse, injuring his ribs. Mother wanted to rub him with embrocation oils, we called it, but he was in agony and couldn't bear her to touch him. He couldn't bear his clothes to be pulled off. After several weeks he returned to work. There was no money from his employer; we survived on the Blue Club sickness benefit and the Foresters' Friendly Society. About one year later, in January, we all had the flu and Dad tried to keep going. He developed pneumonia, but insisted on keeping up; he even went out to draw a bucket of water from the well at the back of the houses. The next day he died, aged forty-nine. He looked like an old man. He was worked to death. The doctor, who had seen him at about 9 a.m. that day, admitted, 'I didn't think he was as ill as he was.'

Granny came from 'home' to help. Father's body was brought down the stairs into the front room. Corpses were often kept in their homes until the funeral. Mother didn't consider that Daisy and I should witness this, but Granny said, 'Let 'em be that won't hurt 'em to see.' Father's funeral was at Great Blakenham. The bill for this and the journey was £7. He was taken 'home', for mother thought we would be returning there.

We continued to live at Chapel Cottages because my brothers were still working at Roydon Hall. One day one of them brought a box of Shredded Wheat home from the farm. These had recently become a new and easy form of breakfast food. 'We're not eating that rubbish,' said Mother – and put them on the copper fire!' 'Up the copper hole' was the term. Two years later, my brothers were becoming involved in matrimony, and this meant that my mother and my sister and I would be under pressure to move. In October 1934 I caught scarlet fever and was whisked off to the isolation hospital with two other lads who had fallen prey to this. I spent seven weeks and three days in there. It was like a concentration camp. My brothers came to see me a few times, but Mother didn't come at all. Visitors spoke to us through the windows (closed), and the beds were turned round for this.

My bed was usually not moved. Treatment was negligible; injections were given to lower the fever, and we had plenty of fluids. The final episode at the hospital was being given a bath in strong disinfectant, which was the most unpleasant bath I've ever had. Who was coming to collect me? I had no idea. On the appointed day the parson of our village, Rev. Wade Evans, came to take me home in his car. At one corner he said, 'Are we on the right road – what did the sign say?'

'This house *To Let*,' said my sister.

Mother was present and when we were nearly home she said, 'We're not going back to Chapel Cottages, you know.'

I was speechless. Why hadn't I been told before? 'Where are we going, then?' I blurted out.

'To David Marshall's thatched cottage,' I was told.

This cottage was one of the relics of the seventeenth century. It had two lets. The north side adjoined the road. It had a stable door (i.e. two doors, one top, one bottom) about 5' high. The floors were brick damp and mouldy. There was a long kind of kitchen lit by a small window. It was alive with mice; they were into everything. There was a primitive kitchen range under the open chimney where the soot could fall into the fry pan. The water supply was a well just outside the stable door. Lighting was of course by candles and oil lamps. The roof was thatched and full of sparrows' nests. When we entered the old shack my heart sank. One thing that took my eye was the fitted corner cupboard.

I opened the door and there were some stale cakes on the shelf. I was so thin and hungry I started to eat them. 'You mustn't eat them – they've been there for days,' said Mother.

I was so hungry I didn't heed her and she stood and surveyed my appearance dumfounded. In the cupboard was a jar of marmalade without a cover. When we were about to dig in for a spoonful I noticed that the side of the jar was covered in pieces of mouse fur.

I became mousetrap setter. One morning I found the culprit – a very sticky mouse. We caught dozens. I used to hang them under the yew tree, a rather nicely clipped specimen. Someone called it 'mouse house' once.

The doctor called soon after I returned home and said, 'Feed her up well.' Mother now received 18s a week; 5s of this was allowance for me, and 3s for my sister. The rent was 4s per week. We had a very plain and often meatless diet: dumplings made with baking powder, turnips, cauliflowers and cabbage. The farm nearby grew vegetables and for a few pence we purchased these items. Sometimes we had water sop – pieces of bread with pepper and salt and a little butter with hot water poured over. I was glad to get to bed sometimes to get away from the unhappy surroundings. Sometimes when I got there I couldn't sleep for worrying about what would happen on the morrow.

Christmas 1934 drew near and suddenly we were overwhelmed be food. A hamper arrived by the carriers, Legget and Dyer. This was from Blakenham, containing among many jars and fruit a chicken. Mr Porter, father of eight children, was a regular attender of the chapel. He was the last person one would have expected to have been able to afford to give us a chicken, but this he did: a large cockerel. Mother, not expecting anyone to send or give us a bird had ordered one from John's father. This also arrived free of charge. So there we were with three chickens and no cold store. They were rich to me, and I was soon sick of the scent or the sight of chicken carcasses.

At the hospital I was told not to go near smelly drains for fear in reinfection. This, believe it or not, was not problem at 'Thatch'. There was no drain; there was no sink. All the water used was carried out in a bowl or bucket and thrown on the garden. Next to us in the other let lived a cowman, Fred, and his wife. He was a fine upright man who worked hard and was as strong as a lion. He used to depart for work at a very early hour. He was a good neighbour and helped us with the garden when possible. We were sometimes asked in to listen to the gramophone and have a little jig around. Emily, his wife, was very demure and pleasant. After they moved from here a year or two later we were all very upset to hear that she had died in confinement; poor Fred just could not take it in and was heartbroken. It was very sad.

Miss King, known as 'Aunt Tot', who lived nearby and did a little domestic work for Mrs Marshall, would visit us some times. She would toddle up the fifty yards of highway, tap on the door and say, 'Hello, Mrs Everett. I was just hanging on. Weren't quite time to go to Mrs Marshall's, so I thought I'd give ee a look.' Then, her voice now going more squeaky, she'd say, 'Don't know what's gooin' on over the road – the nurse bin there twice yisty.'

'Step inside, Miss K.'

'Well, so I will…mustn't stop though.'

Further investigation… 'Did I see your brother call on ye the day afore yistyday?'

'Well,' said Mother, hesitating, 'Yes, he did Miss K.'

'Uh-huh, I thought that was him. Everything all right, I suppose?'

She hadn't time to stay for a cup of tea, although she might as well have done so, for it was easily fifteen minutes later when she made her way back to Mrs Marshall's.

I went back to school after the Christmas holidays. This was in Parkeston, where we had an annual party. It ended rather late in the evening. My Aunt Nazey, who lived in the street, was up at ours having Sunday tea, bread and butter, celery, bread and jam. The matter of my staying with her on the night of the party was discussed. Sara didn't think that this was a very good idea. 'No gal of mine is going to a do like that all them mawthers there; what one don't think of the other will.'

I looked at my aunt. She retorted, 'Why, let the girl come, she'll be all right. She can stop 'long me; do her good, that. What she wants is a little change.'

After more toing and froing Mother said with reluctance that I could go. 'Do you bring any trouble home here, I'll chop you legs orf.'

I went to school on the Friday of the party with my nightdress in a paper bag – no flannel and soap in a plastic zip bag then. The assembly room was used for the party and great excitement prevailed; we played all the party games.

There was a lot of noise outside. It was dark and unwelcoming. One impish lad said, 'Come and sit next to me.' I was disinclined. Someone else took up the offer and sat on four drawing pins placed points upwards. I left the party and ran to my aunt's house.

Meals with her were a little bit organised: 'Don't pick up your plate to eat, don't wipe it with a piece of bread, dear. You shouldn't want to go to the toilet during a meal.' All this was said in the nicest possible way.

I was expected home by midday on Saturday and caught the appropriate train. I felt quite important. I had been away for a night! Mother's greeting was not especially encouraging; something needed doing – sticks to chop, or the potty required empting.

In the spring of 1935 I left school. My testimonial told whoever was interested that I had reached Standard VII. It stated that 'She is a quiet girl who has plodded along with a fair amount of success in most subjects. She is strictly honest, diligent and trustworthy and I am sure will serve any employer well.' It was signed 'Frank Thurlow – Headmaster'.

A week before I left, we heard of a vacancy at Dimbols Farm for a maid. Mother sent me up with a note. I tapped on the back door of the farmhouse and was met by one of the two maiden ladies. They, with Mr E Garnham and his wife and daughter, occupied the establishment.

'Please, my mother has sent you a letter,' I said.

She snatched the envelope and snapped, 'Wait, I'll see if there is an answer.' She was about to shut the door but my feet had found their way onto the step. She paused and snapped again, 'Don't stand on the doorstep!' Then she slammed the door shut.

I wandered across the yard to admire the rabbits, but she opened the door, and said, 'I told you to stand near the door. There is no answer – I'll come and see your mother.'

I went home and hoped I wouldn't be accepted. I told Mother what she had said.

'I do hope they will want you – we could do with the money,' said Ma.

A few days later Miss Nellie came to see us. She was accompanied by a relative who was staying at Dimbols. I hadn't seen her before; she was tall and impressive, with pleasant manners. I said to myself, I would like to work for you; but the sight of the short impatient impetuous old maid who had seen me at the door made me shrink away. She met my Ma with, 'Can we come in? I want a word with your mother on her own.'

I disappeared down the garden and wandered about briefly. I was summoned to go back and Ma said, 'Miss Garnham has decided to give you the job, and you are to start at a quarter to eight in the morning.'

My wages were to be 3s 6d per week. This lasted for seven months. Mother's allowance for me was reduced to nil. So my sister's allowance of 3s went up to 5s. Thus we were 6d per week better off! So I left school on Friday afternoon and started work the next morning and worked till noon. I was given 6d, which I was allowed to keep. I put it in my handbag and carried it around the afternoon. I felt rich.

On the following Monday, I began to find out what this seven-bedroom farmhouse was like. It was lighted by oil lamps and heated by coal. I peeled potatoes and cleaned several pairs of shoes, and was told how to scald the milk pails. There were several cows, and milk was delivered in the village daily. The family consisted of Miss Elizabeth, Miss Nellie, Edgar Garnham and his wife, Gwen, and their daughter, Coralie.

In the early days of my employ the cowshed floors were straw on muck, and the milking was accomplished in fairly unhygienic conditions. After a year or two, the MMB decreed that a concrete floor with a gully for swilling down had to be provided. The cows came in in batches of four and their necks were secured by a hinged piece of wood fixed at the top by a pin. While the cows were confined and being milked, they were fed a mixture of crushed oats, chaff and maize flatches. This latter was named 'kositos' and was quite palatable, and often I've had a mouthful to chew.

There were two cowmen. One milked in the shed just mentioned and the other in a much smaller one that held only one cow. They started work at 5.30 a.m., seven days a week. The oats were crushed at Frank Fisher's mill at The Firs, and Candy, one of the cowmen, used to take four or five 12-stone sacks of whole oats to there and bring the crushed one back.

They had now become eight sacks, and much lighter. His conveyance was horse and tumbril. He sat upon the old cart and often appeared to be nodding off. The horse knew the way. There were few motors through the lane then.

The bull was kept in a separate pew. A heavy construction of iron pipes and cast iron posts were necessary. An old wagon stood in the middle of the cow yard; it had a load of straw upon it and had been there many years. Grass grew from it and chickens laid their eggs in nooks and crannies on it. The MMB decreed that is should be moved. Soon after I went to work there it was also deemed necessary to have a cooler for the milk. This was installed, and where the milk separator was set a frame of wood was built and a tank to supply a head of water for the cooler was put aloft upon it. The water was pumped up into it, by hand pump, from a well in the back yard. The cowman had this job (later it became one of my chores). There was a float fixed to a string with a weight attached. As the water rose, the weight descended down the side of the tank. Sometimes the pump operator would be 'miles away' in thought, and 'Stop, stop!' would be the call, for water would flood over onto the kitchen floor.

Mr Garnham delivered the milk from a motorcycle and sidecar in the early days. Later a large Austin car was purchased and used for the job. This was a square old tub and christened 'The Hearse' – this was before the milk bottle days. The car carried a galvanised churn, and delivery to the houses made by means of a smaller also galvanised can with a hinged lid, and the milk was allocated out with a measure into the customer's jug. Two measures were carried – a half pint and one pint. These had a lead stamped seal to verify they had the amount they should have. Surplus cream was separated with a hand-driven separator. It had two spouts – skim milk issued from one, and cream from the other. This was made into butter or cream cheese. Some cream was sold in little waxed paper pots and cost, according to size, 3d, 6d and 1s. The separator was another hard task; at first I was not expected to turn the handle. It needed two hands to start with, and its internal conical discs were revolved round at high speed. There were twenty of these. Cleanliness was essential. They were first washed in cold water, then warmer water, with a detergent cleaner which ruined your hands. They were then scalded with boiling water wiped up while still hot and then put together again in the cast iron casing.

When butter was made cream was put into the churn, and you had to keep up a steady rhythm and you must not stop turning that handle. Eventually the butter would start to form and 'lump around the churn'. You could inspect at this stage through a little glass peephole in the lid; also gas was released by pressing a valve. It was then worked in the 'butter worker'. This was a long wooden trough about 18" wide and 36" long, on legs. It had a serrated wooden roller which was pushed along the trough over the butter to squeeze the buttermilk out. This was used for cooking and was especially good for scones.

We used the brick oven about once in two weeks. I dreaded this day. Miss Nellie Garnham came into her own on these occasions. In the back yard were countless faggots and bundles of sticks about 3' long also known as bavins, which stood on end. Each time we used the oven, the three or four required were to be found in the 'buttery' (an old pantiled shed in the back yard) put in there to keep very dry. These were replenished from stock each time: 'You've got time to put some faggots in the dry' was the snapped command. To operate the oven a faggot was pushed into the open oven, lit with paper and match, and when burned through another one introduced.

The smoke went up the chimney. This also served to take the smoke from the coppers. Ashes were raked into the back stock grate. When the cavernous oven was hot, the ready prepared dough loaves were slid in on the peel, a long handled tool with a thin wooden blade at the business end. The doors were then closed and baking day was under way. Cakes of various sorts were put in later. In season, stewing pears would be peeled and cut into slices, put into earthenware jars with cloves and covered with a piece of brown paper, and slowly cooked therein, and when chickens were plucked for the table, the feathers were stored, and were baked to purify them for filling pillows and cushions.

Miss Nellie was a tartar to work for and frightening to be in close proximity to. She stamped her feet in temper and frustration if I didn't do exactly what she thought I should do. Monday morning was washday. We kept the wash blue in one half of a coconut shell. I had to get this and to do so had to climb three steps to where it was stored. One day I wasn't quick enough. She stormed past me grabbed the shell and threw it on the stone floor, smashing it into several pieces. She said with venom, 'Did that frighten you? If it didn't, it should have done!'

On another occasion I was too slow passing cakes to her to put in the oven, and she shouted, 'Come on, come on! Make haste, or else I'll put you in next!'

I raced to the back door, stumbled over the step and collided with Ernie Pratchet, the Co-op baker, who called occasionally.

'Whatever is the matter?' said he, surprised.

'That old woman's going to put me in the brick oven!' I said tearfully.

'Why, don't be silly,' he said. 'She can't do that. Come on back indoors.'

I crept behind him and he addressed the old demon. 'What do you mean by upsetting this girl like this?'

'You get on with your business, you duzzy fool!' she snapped.

More words passed between them, but none of them helped me much. I sure the baker saved me from the brick oven. My lunch was a cup of milk warmed by standing it with its saucer on top in a hand bowl of hot water taken from the copper. With it were two pieces of bread and butter left from the breakfast table, turned up at the edges, and on Sundays a rock cake was the supplement to the milk. I sat on the steps leading to the cellar door, embarrassed at showing my knees.

Part of my culinary apprenticeship was not very satisfying. One morning Nellie went to Dovercourt and left me to make a semolina pudding. The direction was: 'Using the double cooker with milk, bring to the boil, then stir in the semolina till it thickens.' I did this, then turned out the flame of the paraffin stove that it was heated upon. There was my undoing. It should have been cooked for a further twenty minutes. Another telling-off. I also cut the heads off the asparagus and the knobs off the Jerusalem artichokes. Frequently on a Saturday afternoon, about half an hour before I was due to knock off work, Madam would produce a 1/2 lb. of sausages and say, 'You might make a few sausage rolls before you go.'

I was scrubbing the doorstep one cold morning and stubbed by finger against the doorpost. I got to me feet and nursed my hurt.

'Do you think I shall lose my nail?' I said to Aunt N, with concern.

'If you don't, you ought to,' she retorted, with her usual venom.

On another occasion while washing up I ran my finger against a carving knife that was standing upright in the sink on a rubber mat. I cut it badly and it bled profusely. 'Should I have it stitched?' I enquired.

'Oh, it's nothing much, it'll be all right,' I was told.

It was bandaged for days and constantly wet and took ages healing up. I fell over on the back yard outside one day and landed on my back upon an uneven brick that formed the surface of the yard. I was hurt and could not ride my cycle and lost my sense of taste and smell for several months.

Mrs Barker was employed on a part-time basis for menial tasks. One of these was whitewashing. She would cover her head, wear wellingtons and a mackintosh, and slop whitewash over the walls and made a shocking mess. Her glasses would be covered with it and she had to frequently stop to clean them. Cleaning the place up afterwards was really hard work, for the floors were covered white.

Miss Elizabeth (Aunt Libby or Lib) was a much milder lady. She was 'involved' in ironing with the old box iron. The hot 'bit' within lumped around with every movement. 'Haven't you finished ironing yet, Lib? It sounds like Joe Calver fillin' beets!' (This meant mangolds being harvested in a tumbril.) Libby cleaned silver, dusted and polished, laid the table and was always busy. I must mention their mother, who died in 1922 and had had to manage the farm since her husband, Caleb, died in 1873, aged 44. This hard taskmaster was nick named 'Old Mother Damstick'. She carried an ebony walking stick, and if someone was not doing whatever it was that she thought they should be, would threaten them thus: 'I'll take a damn stick to you!'

Hens and perhaps other feathered beings sometimes were rendered lifeless by one savage swing of this stick to their necks.

There was an episode when my employers started breeding Norwich Terriers. I loved them. A basket of pups was delightful. When first born they stumbled and snuffled over one another, and as they grew up I used to assist the veterinary surgeon to shorten their tails. He would feel along the tail with his large thumb nail for a joint and nip off the end with his cutter. I didn't care for this job much. Later, a lovely old boxer turned up. He was the best dog that anyone could have owned. He was named Bill. He would take and empty jam jar, hold it in between his front paws and lick it absolutely clean with his capable tongue. He would accompany me to the front door if the bell rang. He would have probably licked the visitors, but his appearance was formidable. He was encouraged to sit at the piano on a chair, with a pipe in his mouth and a scarf round his neck and thump on the keys with his front paws.

One job I liked more than any was taking the three terriers Hannah, Flackie and Jamie, and Bill down the meadow to roam round Brakey Grove for the last half-hour of the day. Bill had a limp one day. I lifted his front paw. It felt decidedly hot. He had a thorn in his pad. I carefully drew it out with my fingers, and while I was so engaged he closed his slobbery jaws round my wrist in a gesture of 'Don't you hurt me too much'. He licked me and was really grateful – the gratitude went on for several minutes. He was chastised by a relative of the family once. He got tired of this and simply jumped up at him, pushing him over on the lawn and stood over him with one paw resting on his chest.

My wages rose from 3s 6d to 5s a week after about seven months, and continued at this rate for about a year; then, with pressure applied via a reluctant request from a frightened servant, I was given 9s a week. This remained the norm for a long time. I had to provide a pinafore; there was nothing forthcoming for free.

I had to help with mealtimes. I had to carry dishes of food to the dining room. I stayed to lunch and was allowed a portion of whatever was on the menu. I had to exit back to the kitchen, and when the bell rang I went back to the dining room to receive my portion from the corner of the dinner wagon. This bell would ring again very soon and the same procedure applied for the pudding. I complained to Mother; she said she was treated similarly and didn't think I was badly treated.

I graduated to riding a cycle. A second-hand machine was purchased from a neighbour for 4s which was paid for at 1s per week. I had now been on the milk round for a year or so with Mrs

Gwen driving. I recall one Sunday, 3rd September 1939. Arthur Goddard who farmed Poplar Hall called frequently and on this day he said to me as I was washing milk utensils, 'You know what we've got to do now, don't you? Put our backs into it! Good day to you!' I muttered that I thought I had been doing that for the past several years.

Soon, the army arrived and were in evidence all around the village. They needed milk, and I delivered to the gun sites and searchlight stations. One of these searchlights was situated opposite the house on the meadow overlooking Brakey Grove. The granary was sleeping quarters for some of the soldiers during the day, and some were to be found there trying to come to terms with the aftermath of injections. I had to go up there for corn for the chickens and disliked this, but they were very little trouble. They were soon moved to houses in the village that were commandeered for the military. Dimbols became a billet for three officers and their batmen. They took over the best kitchen to cook their food. I was relegated to the back kitchen once again. I liked this less than ever, and asked to go home to dinner. I didn't really win, for when I got home there were jobs to do and my dinner hour was very short.

When the army arrived my life did seem to take on a slightly rosier character. It may have been a feeling of security. Sometimes the lads would 'take the mickey', to the detriment of Aunt Nellie. On one occasion a lance corporal scooped her up round the waist, carried her through the kitchen along the hall, and dropped her near the front door. She was always scuttling about, and he thought he would help her along a bit.

'Put me down! Put me down, you duzzy fool!' she protested. This caused great amusement. She did not see the funny side of anything, and especially this.

Finally I was paid £2 19s 11d per week. I would give back the one penny from the £3 laid on the table. This was the highest wage I ever received.

A tragic event happened one morning on the site opposite. The soldiers were apparently practising with hand grenades, and one that was thrown from inside the hut hit the door frame and bounced back inside. The pin had been withdrawn and the explosion wrecked the leg of one of the occupants. I was requested to get a blanket and a pillow for the injured party. I obliged and soon after was criticised from Mrs Gwen for bringing the wrong ones. 'Why couldn't you have brought one from the back bedroom? That was all the thanks that I got.

The Home Guard was being formed/recruited, and Edgar Garnham joined. He was quickly made up to Major. He was driven round the various local groups by his wife. It was all rather like *Dad's Army*. He supervised the drills in the neighbourhood. The phone was the most useful part of the equipment. When they were on duty I sometimes went back in the evenings to answer it and take messages. A red alert had to be made note of, with time of happening. Sometimes I had to go over to the searchlight with the information. On other occasions messages did not need to go anywhere and were sometimes contradicted soon after they were received, and no one knew what was supposed to be going on.

The milk round was occupying much of my time, and I had been learning to drive under supervision of Gwen. I had my first licence in 1941; we did not have to pass a driving test under war conditions. We now had the very latest delivery van vehicle – an Austin Seven van. Among the many orders made in emergency, we were not allowed to start until 7.30 a.m., for the blackouts was enforced and the headlights of vehicles were 90 per cent obscured. Milk was rationed to two and a half pints per person per week. If there was a surplus produced it was put into a 5 gallon churn, taken to the station, and taken to Ware, Herts, by train. Sometimes it had turned sour before it arrived and was returned to Wrabness. It smelled pretty horrid sometimes. When possible it was turned into cream cheese. It was poured into a muslin sheet about 2' square over a large basin. The liquid ran through. The corners of the square were taken together, tied, and hung on a tree, and the outside of the bag scraped with a knife every day. The bag had to be changed three times before the cheese 'made', otherwise the outside became caked and the cheese would go bad. They took about seven days to make. Washing these 'bags' was a rotten job. They had to be scrubbed to get rid of the residue. The cheese was pressed out and cut with a cake cutter and sold at 6d and 1s.

Fowls were a constant feature. We usually had about 100 laying hens. Sales to customers were restricted to one egg per person per week, on coupons from the ration book. The surplus eggs were collected by the egg packing station weekly. Servicemen on leave had special coupons and were allowed eggs, milk etc. Powdered dried egg was available in tins in addition to the whole egg ration. Customers resisted this; it was a poor substitute for the real thing, but there was nothing much to eat sometimes and we sold quite a lot of it. Some particular ladies would not accept a bent or damaged tin, and now and again arguments cropped up: 'You know I don't want a tin like that! I'll bet Mrs So-and-so didn't have one like that,' etc. When mixed with water and milk it was useful in cooking, and it could be scrambled and eaten on toast.

We were still selling milk 'loose' (i.e. not in bottles). 'Stand away from the doorsteps, Miss Everett, I don't want any milk sploshed on my step when I've just whitened it,' was the request of one customer. I had various girls to help occasionally. One vitriolic old dear confronted me about this one morning. 'I don't want that bit of a gal comin' to my door. You went next door, and they had more than I did.'

With the measuring method, I used to put the pint or whatever into their jug and tip in a little extra afterward. I guess my helper didn't do this. This customer was really horrid to me and I left in tears.

We were short of milk now and again. The round was always split in two parts. Under these circumstances the second round was the difficult one, for towards the end of it the white liquid was almost gone. On one of these days I said to my employer, 'I just can't face the second round, Mrs Garnham.'

'Don't be ridiculous! Of course you're going,' snapped the dear lady; and of course I went.

We were expected or obliged to do some kind of work to help the war effort. My sister joined the WRNS. I went into the WLA. We had breeches, green woollen jumpers, stout shoes, a brown felt hat, brown overalls and a brown overcoat, a sort of mink. A badge was standard equipment. A green armband was embellished with red triangles, one of which was added for each six months' service. I felt really dressed for the part I was playing. The rig saved my own clothes, and they were all good quality.

On the milk round we collected potato peelings and any other edible peelings for feeding the pigs. This was put into sandbags and carried on the front mudguards of the van. It was boiled up in a copper before feeding to them. There were also pails of surplus food from the cookhouses at the Gate House and other sites. Sometimes in hot weather maggots were present. My employer on some occasions picked up orange peel from the roadside. This was put into the marmalade that she managed to make. Oranges and bananas were available for children. It's amazing that such fruits ever got to this country with the hostilities going on. 'Isn't it a pity that we can't use banana skins,' said Gwen. We used to make a 'banana spread' by mashing parsnips and mixing it with banana essence and milk. It was quite acceptable. There were occasionally a perk from the cooks in the best kitchen. One of the helpers was given some dripping one day. It was put in her cycle basket. The weather was warm, a cat jumped up and managed to tip the container and a small amount of fat found its way onto the path. Needless to say, Gwen had to come along and see this. More 'errs' and 'arrs' were forthcoming.

One of the officers had a batman resident there, called Jack, who became friendly with me. I felt slightly sorry for him and darned his socks and did small things to make his life more pleasant. He was heard to say there was an unpleasant smell in the house. There was a cellar of ancient origin beneath the best kitchen floor. The scent was coming from a well in the cellar. Jack volunteered to clear it. He worked with buckets for some hours – and was it foul! It hadn't been cleaned for years. He took a bath afterward and sat in the sun behind a hedge to relax. Dolly, another casual assistant, who disliked Jack, came along with a bucket of water and tipped it over him. He did not like this one little bit. 'If I get near you I'll break your bloody neck,' said he with emphasis.

'You'll have to catch me first,' she retorted.

I think her bicycle suffered at a slightly later date.

My mother didn't like Jack at all. I simply felt sorry for him. 'It's a pity Dolly didn't drown him,' she said. He went overseas eventually. He was taken prisoner in Italy soon afterwards. Before he left, he asked me to keep in touch with his mother at Clacton-on-Sea. I had only one field card while he was a prisoner. I wrote and told his mother of the happenings. She could not read or write. I said to John Minns one days that I was going to see her on my day off.

'Good God!' said he. 'They lock people like you up over there.'

'I think there's a turning near the post office – do you know it?' I asked.

'God forsaken hole! You'll wish you'd never have gone,' he replied.

I went over on a Monday by bus. The previous night there had been an air raid and there was quite a lot of damage and confusion. The house where the old lady lived was one of several on the outskirts and very basic. She wore a man's cap and was illiterate. She was grateful for my visit.

As the war progressed Jack was released, I received a card with various words crossed out, and those remaining told me that he was back in England. He afterward wrote to say that Civvy Street was in sight. I showed the cowman the card.

'Don't tell you much – not very romantic,' said he.

My employer said, 'Don't keep him on a piece of string – make up your mind what you want to do.'

The days went by quickly, and Jack came to see me at the farm. He looked very thin. We shook hands and exchanged a few pleasantries. It seemed a bit of a cool meeting. I was putting milk through the cooler. My attention to this was distracted.

'Come on, come on! Where's the next bucket?' called the cowman.

'All right, I'm coming,' said I.

I returned the vessel and my slightly irritated workmate met me with, 'I shall have to take a back seat now, then.'

'You never had a front one,' said I firmly.

My friend hung about until I knocked off, and we cycled home together. My family was living in Hope Cottages in Rectory Road now. We went indoors.

'Mother, Jack's home,' I announced.

'Oh,' she said. 'We haven't got much to make use of – you can't stay here long.'

He was allowed to stay and slept in the back bedroom for a couple of nights.

My sister didn't like him. Mother said, 'We can't have this sort of nonsense going on.'

He made no effort to bring any food and spent quite a bit of time at the Black Boy Inn. I was getting into a dreadful muddle. I was glad he had survived the prison camp, but I didn't love him. I suffered all sorts of adverse comments from the family. We went for a walk together. I brought a bunch of wild flowers home.

'Aren't they lovely?' said Mother. She turned to Jack and said, 'Do you like them?'

'You can't eat flowers,' he replied.

This annoyed her. 'Does your mother want you?' she said.

'I've got six weeks of leave,' he replied.

We went on the train to Dovercourt to catch a bus for Clacton. Who should have been on the station going the same way but our neighbour, John Calver! I wished the ground would swallow me up. We did speak, but what was said is gone from my memory. He had brought me gifts he had made from wood and had kept in touch, off and on, during the war, and called some evenings for a chat. At Clacton we went to the pictures and I slept at his sister's.

When we returned to Wrabness, Mother asked me, 'Did he pay your fare and the pictures?'

I had to say he did not. I said that he had best return to his mother's for a few days. I had to write to him, and that letter took a bit of putting together. I made several attempts, tore it up and started again. In it I said, 'It would be best if we parted, for it would not work. We could still be friends, but I do not want to get to serious.'

His reply was waiting for me one day soon when I went home to dinner. It was lengthy. I read it and put it in my overall pocket. 'What did he say?' asked Ma.

He could see I was being ruled by my family; I felt completely dominated. 'He will not be bothering you anymore,' I said.

'You'd have rued the day if you got married to him,' she replied.

'Who said anything about getting married?' I said, with feeling.

She said soon after, 'I didn't keep you from seeing him. Put me in the workhouse, and then you can do as you like!'

Chapter Six: John Resumes the Story

I never really go on very well with my father. He was always shouting at me or somebody or something, and as I grew up spent quite a lot of time over at Foxes Farm.

The land is for the most part light and hungry. There are clay patches and these are tough and do not ever seem to produce a good crop. The farmhouse was (and still is) ancient; it is thatched and had no lean-tos upstairs, which is surprising for it doesn't look high enough. It had a front door which was rarely opened because if it was, you needed a hammer to get it shut again. It had a paled wood fence out the back, and this was the way in, up the path from the horse pond into the back yard where stood a semi-rotary pump which drew water from a spring near the pond. The delivery pipe was an upside-down U-pipe with a coupling joint at the top.

This was moveable in order to turn it upward to pour water in to prime the pump, and whilst in this position the cowman would place his left hand over the outlet and work the pump with his other, and this would cause a spray of water to be directed wherever he fancied. If any young folks happened to be just coming near at the right moment the spray would cool them down, to the great amusement of the operator.

The back door of the old house was just opposite the pump and to the left was the door to the dairy. This was an out-shot and under a wad of thatch, 20" thick. To the back of the house was the orchard with a walnut tree, Victoria and large black diamond plums, and several sorts of apples and a tall pear tree. This was all enclosed by iron hurdles on wheels (not all wheels complete) and beyond this was about 1½ acres of meadow with an elm fence around it. On here stood two cow houses built of railway sleepers with a corrugated iron roof and an ancient sack hanging across the doorways to keep the place dark and to deter the flies from entering.

Uncle Cecil was the cow keeper. He was a large fellow with a 46" chest and was about 5' 10" in height. His voice was deep, and of Essex origin. He was quick to rise to an excited state, and was sarcastic, crafty and evasive as the occasion demanded. He always wore a trilby hat encrusted with grease and dirt. His trousers were held up by 2" wire nails pushed through the cloth and across the brace ends where the buttons once were.

He had three cows; one was a Jersey and gave a lot of excellent quality milk.

He reared calves to perfection. Most of his working day was spent looking after them. The cows had to climb up a ramp of muck when they went into the sheds to be milked. When it rained, and for most of the winter, outside became a quagmire. I never knew him to clean them out.

The amount of straw used was frugal in an attempt to put off the evil day. I once said, 'I should think it's about time you got the tumbril out.'

'Oh, would je?' he retorted.

'What would happen when the cows' backs touch the roof?' I ventured.

'Well, you look, I shall heighten the roof!'

He would put the best milk into fleet cream pans about 18" in diameter and when the cream on top had ripened he would use a skimmer to take it off.

This was made into butter by churning by hand. The shelves in the dairy were wide planks supported on rude posts and the floor was of brick. The scrub brush was rarely used.

My Uncle Cecil took delight in frightening me by making moaning noises into a pail with a kind of hood on its top. The lattice window had a piece of perforated zinc tacked over it and inside, hinged at the top, was a kind of shutter which could be let down. It was supported by a piece of cord from the ceiling. My curiosity got the better of me one day, and as I stood on an upturned pail to investigate the cord, *wham!* – down went the shutter, covering a pan of cream with a layer of ancient dust. I hustled away from there and dared not return for several days. When I did, Cecil caught me by the ear and roared, 'You little sod! You'd better keep away from her if you can't leave things alone.'

Aunt Lily usually made the butter with a churn and butter worker. There were many frustrations.

An addition to his income was catching rabbits. He shot them, netted ferreted and set gin traps and snares. I have seen a terrified rabbit in a gin trap and gone back to the farm to tell him.

'That won't hurt for a little longer... Why the hell couldn't you have killed and brought it home? You're a proper fool.'

They were hulked (eviscerated) immediately and 'hurdled' – a knife blade was pushed behind the tendon in the back leg and the other foot pushed through. When he had ten or so and a few pounds of butter he would catch the Eastern National Bus and take them to Harwich for sale. The process of keeping blowflies off them was tiresome. The thatch of the dairy did keep it cool, and this was the usual store for them. Occasionally Mother and I were on the same bus as he. On one hot day the butter was put in the luggage rack, together with a pair of hobnail boots to be taken in for repair. As the bus rounded a bend, his wares slid out of their niche and fell among the passengers. The conductor suggested that he left them at the back of the bus.

A slightly subdued Cecil said, 'Well, yes, but things might get covered with dust comin' in the back door.'

Cochran's Pork Butchers was a port of call for us and Cecil. He would buy 2 lb. of the 'best pork sausages in town, they know just how much cayenne to put in.' Mutton was consumed regularly at Foxes. It was usually in a stew. Pieces of fat floated on top and this was consumed with gusto. Aunt Lily invited me to say to such a meal – and that fat! I would have been sick had I eaten it.

Cecil had a lurcher dog called Smoker, who spent his non-active time in a large box turned on its side to act as a kennel, rather exposed to the weather. He was well fed and did no harm. He accompanied Cecil on all hunting expeditions and would clear a field gate with ease. He would leap up and down in the corn each leap covering 4' or 5'. He was in his element and was a very faithful old lad. The fox was an unwelcome visitor and used to take rabbits from traps and snares. Cecil was one day determined to catch the villain. He suspended two chickens heads from a stick about 2' off the ground and placed several gins around in a circle, with a light camouflage of grass completing the scene; but in the morning, needless to say, the heads were gone and the traps still all set.

In the old house were remnants of furniture and chairs from many years ago but nothing of any great appeal. A large pine table covered with brown American cloth stood in the centre of the kitchen. There were four wooden chairs, a large pine dresser with two drawers and doors under, and a cabinet with a carved cupboard door and six drawers. A black kitchen range was the means of cooking; there was always a large kettle of water upon its top. The usual oil lamp stood in readiness on the table. This was an 'Aladdin' and gave a lovely light from its incandescent mantle. There were other things on the table keeping it company: a pile of newspapers; several letters, some years old; various pieces of crockery left from the previous meal. Under the solitary small window was a stone sink with lots of bits of soap in a dish on the sill, a shaving brush, cut-throat razor and a strop nearby. Face flannels were old pieces of woollen underwear.

To the right-hand side of the sink was a small looking-glass. Uncle Bernard, who was about the same build as Cecil, had a beard, which he used to clip with a long pair of scissors. He also kept his hair in trim with them. While he was thusly engaged in front of the mirror Cecil would come up behind him and pull faces and stick out his tongue.

Aunt Lily was usually sitting in the kitchen in shabby clothes and shoes.

When she did go outside the door she wore a high crowned hat. She rarely saw the funny side of anything, and maintained a serious look. Cecil and her were always talking of the state of their finances and of the way they had been treated, and Bernard was always being pulled to bits because he had paid very little of the legacies from their father's will. If he happened to enter the room while this was going on there was a sudden silence. He rarely talked with them, or they to him. He didn't often go into the house unless to sleep. In the winter, of necessity, he had to in the cold evenings. Cecil and he slept in single beds in the smaller of the two bedrooms. There was a passage of about 3' between the beds. At the top of the stairs was a large chest of drawers with a

Rear view of Foxes Farm House

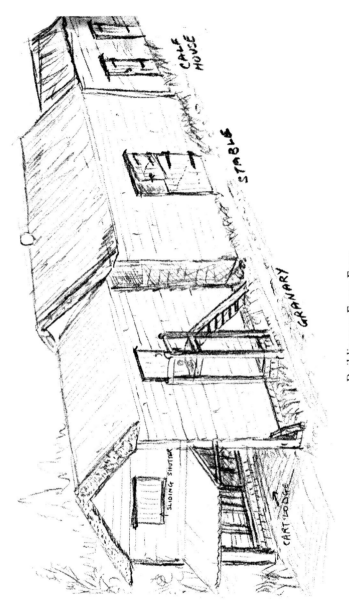

Buildings at Foxes Farm

Watercolour of arial view

china dish on top with collar studs buttons and odd cartridges for the three types of guns they possessed. A Victorian engraving of Charles Dickens' empty chair helped to make the scene nice and dreary; fluff and dust covered everything. The bottom rail of the small window had been missing for ages, and in the autumn leaves from the walnut tree would find their way onto the beds.

Bernard had a spell of seven days in bed with gout once, and when his sister asked if he needed anything did not reply. She took him the odd cups of tea and he did not utter a word. He did drink it, and probably had the odd piece of food, although told me he did not have 'nuthin for the whole week'. When he could hobble downstairs he plunged his still swollen and inflamed foot into a bucket of cold water! He dropped a heavy object onto a big toe once and did not take his sock off to see what damage he had done. Some time later when he did have to remove it, his toenail came off in the sock! Such were the yarns he would always tell.

The back house, as I mentioned, was a wooden shed about 12' square with a brick chimney and copper. There was a small grate and loose iron bars across to stand a kettle or other vessel on. The fuel was wood. About half the smoke went up the chimney and the other into the shed. The copper had a huge pile of old clothes on it when Bern made wine or beer he would throw them 'up a corner' and some would get mixed up with his feet. They were all replaced on the copper afterwards. In this establishment Bern had his own meals, which he prepared himself. His diet was tinned fish, corned beef, kippers and bloaters cooked on a gridiron over the sticks. The oil dropped out and made a sizzling smelly fire. In the early 1930s, electricity was being brought to the village. B wasn't going to have it in his place. He could boil a kettle in three minutes over sticks, and electric couldn't better that. I have seen him take a handful of shallots from the drawer of the washstand with its marble top, which served as a table. He would peel one and would pop it in his mouth and crunch it up while preparing the others to eat with bread and cheese.

His light was a candle or a hurricane lamp. In the winter the long dark evenings were made more interesting by walking over the footpath to the Wheatsheaf, where he would sit over a pint for long periods saying very little. Sometimes if the mood was more jovial he would tell yarns of years ago, and if he said something that he considered laughable he would chuckle and his whole being would oscillate.

Next to the back house was a corrugated iron shed where casks of wine were stored. At the back were his collection of corned beef tins. They were tapered and would fit into each other; when one was empty it would be pushed into the last one. They were not washed out. They resembled a tin snake, for he had curved them in various ways to I would think 15' long.

Mother and I would sometimes go and visit them in the evening and while Ma was in the house, I would sit for an hour or more in the smokey old shed listening to Bernard yarning about things past and present. 'Wo, hello, Jack,' he would greet me. 'Long years ago…' was usually the prelude to a story:

'Old Bot Lawrence and me were gittin' mangles (mangolds) off down by the Quach when the tumbril wheel fell to bits. "What shall us do?" says Bot. "Well, mend it, I s'pose."

'I had some wire in my dungaree pocket, so I wired it up. That lasted like that for a couple of years.' Then came a few minutes' pause.

'Do you know, Jack, how to scare owd hins?'

'No,' I said.

'Well, you want to flack a bag… When we were threshing once and I was clearin' up there were several owd hins about – might ha' bin a dozen or so. I picked up a bag and flacked it, well you never did see how they flew! Some went over the drum, some went over the barn, and some we never did see na more.' And then: 'I was rolling with two hosses once down the other side of the grove when I fell off in front of it. The roller went right over me up the back of me legs and back and struck the back of my head. Old Bot was there brushing a ditch, and he say, "Bunny, you orrite? You look suffin' white!"

'I said, "Yes, I might tell you I feel white."

Bern did all the ploughing with a pair of horses, and drilling corn was a job he took great pride in. Whoever was behind the drill had to be careful to shut off the seed just as the coulters went over the headland previously planted. It was not always easy to see the wheeling mark. The idea was to avoid a bunch of corn where the drill stopped. 'That want to dringle out,' was the instruction. When on a hill, he had to keep the seed box level by turning the cranked handle at the back of the box. Bern would be steering the drill at the front and guiding the horses with line reins. 'When you're drilling on the side of a hill you must steer a few inches to the inside or outside of your wheeling, otherwise you'll soon be as bent as a crooked stick.'

'How do you know how many inches to allow?' said I.

'Well, that depends on the steepness of the hill – your instinct will tell you how far,' said he.

I said earlier he was a schemer a handyman. He was really a craftsman.

He would always have sharp tools. When an axe or hook, spokeshave or chisel needed sharpening, this operation required the turning of the grindstone, and I often came in for this job. He would 'put the brakes on' sometimes when something was blunt. After grinding he would sit with a whetstone to hone up the tools to perfection.

'I've heard tell that years ago in foreign parts to tell when a sword was sharp they would hand up a silk cushion and draw the sharp edge across and cut it in two,' he was pleased to tell me. In the old shack he could have been a man from the Stone Age getting weapons ready for the hunt. He excelled with the spokeshave.

A cart shaft to be renewed was just 'a bit of fun'. A speciality was the wooden connecting rod of a self-binder. I'm sure if one broke he was glad of the opportunity to cut out and chamfer up a new one. 'Wanta nice bit of ash for that job, Jack,' he told me one day. 'I used to like a machine to need repairs, for this meant a bike ride to Colchester to Joslins for a spare bit. Once I went up there and left my bike near the window of the house with a spotted china dog on the sill. Joslins hadn't got just what I wanted unless I waited. So I went into the Castle Inn for a drink.

'When I came out, got the bits, and went to get me bike, I couldn't find it 'cos all the windows had a spotted dog in it!'

I was amazed to see him drill holes in iron with a geared breast drill. I tried my hand at this. 'You want to give it all you've got, Jack,' he advised.

The workshop was in the old granary. There was a bench and tools and a sliding shutter to close an open window. When this was opened you looked out over the pond overhung by willows and elms. A few ducks and moorhens would be present. The scene hadn't changed for centuries. On sunny days it was idyllic. In the winter it was fascinating when the overhanging trees were covered with hoarfrost. The ducks would lay their eggs in the roots of the old trees. Bernard had a dessert spoon fixed to a long stick to extract the eggs from inaccessible spots. 'They'll make me a dinner, Jack. Do you like duck eggs?' I didn't think I did. 'You don't know wha's good, boy!'

Among the treasures up those granary steps was a rusty sword with a blade of considerable length. That sword… I couldn't resist it! I walked over there one day, and seeing no one around brought it home. My mother advised a speedy return. 'Oh, let me keep it!' said I; but alas, I had to return it accompanied by Ma, who had to tell Cecil about my deeds.

'I knew he'd got it,' said he with elation, staring at me with that wicked eye.

After a pause I said, 'How did you know?'

'I knew,' he replied.

'How?' I repeated.

'I'll give you the topnuss slap of the skull if you een't careful,' he warned. So I withdrew.

Cecil was very fond of 'peeking', i.e. hiding in a shed or under cover of bushes and observing something going on.

The three sizes of guns owned by them were 12 bore, .410 and the 9 mm garden gun. The latter had a hexagonal barrel and a solid breech block that lifted up to allow a cartridge into the breech. This could be used with a cartridge with small shot for sparrows or rat shooting, or with a lead bullet only. The former had a paper case from the copper end, the bullet was mounted into the copper without the case. Bernard used to put a penny on a gatepost, pace thirty yards or so and without difficulty hit it with the bullet. I had said, 'Could I use it?'

'Well, I s'pose you can,' said he. 'You want to get your target sitting on the front sight.'

I tried several sparrow targets without a kill. But one evening atop the granary, a blackbird was singing beautifully. I took aim and bang. I retrieved its broken body and was ashamed of myself. I went home and told Ma, 'I've shot a singing bird.' I think I shed a tear, and she said, 'There's not a lot you can do now – you'll learn, my boy.'

I think this episode rather spoiled my sporting instincts. A little later I was about 10' away from a rabbit and could not bring myself to shoot it. It sat there and looked at me.

There were always cats around; about ten, in fact, was an average number. One or two of them would have a paw mutilated from being caught in a gin trap. Bernard liked cats, and they were always around at mealtimes. When he returned from working in the fields about 3.30 p.m. there would be a line of cats waiting for him from halfway down the path from the house to the pond. The elder ones would be first to greet him and the kittens, less venturous, would be nearer the house. 'Owd cats like company Jack,' he explained.

I recall one very young mother who had two kittens and had no idea about feeding them. They just starved to death. I found them in the cart lodge under the granary. They hadn't been fed, and when I touched them they let out pathetic screams. I pursued the matter and eventually followed their mother as she went to them. Their callings went unheeded. She rubbed her head on nearby pieces of wood, purring. I tried to encourage her to feed them, but to no avail. I told Bern about it. 'Oh, ar,' he murmured. 'There's plenty of owd cats about.'

He was cruel sometimes, and would lift a cat off the ground onto his lap by its ear. I protested once.

'You make too much fuss boy. That owd cat must like me doing that or that would keep out of me way.'

He would place an empty fish tin out for them to lick out; this would be the large size of can. In the need to get the total amount from the bottom of the can the poor old cat would get its head stuck and would not know what to do or which way to go. Bern would laugh at this at length, and not remove the can until he felt in the mind. He hustled one once and it went straight into the wall and became fixed more firmly. He would get sardine oil and rub over a cat's mouth and face to be amused at the washing which went on for half an hour or so. If a cat died no one bothered to bury it. I was shocked to see the remains of one at the back of the granary. Its ivory teeth were turned towards the sky and left an impression on my memory. Cecil used to feed them regularly on bread and milk. One day he charged out of the back door and stood on a kitten and killed it instantly. He was truly upset. 'Poor little old kitten,' was all he could say for several minutes.

Dug into the bank near the pond was a copper hastily created and used to boil potatoes for pig food. They kept a sow or two and one large crossbred specimen always would put its snout into a bucket of food before B could get to its trough. 'I'll settle that old bugger,' said he. So he took half a bucket of boiling potatoes to the troublesome animal and it received a scalded nose and mouth. He said, 'Your father was very soft towards his pigs – I'm not with mine.'

For most of my boyhood days I had Harold as a friend. He came from a large family in the village. He was a loyal companion and used to come over to Foxes sometimes. We would go to the copper and take a cold potato and I'd get some salt from off the kitchen dresser and have a little feast. He liked them more that I for I was not as hungry as he was. At Domine, we two played ceaselessly. Down the roadway to the barn were four old willow trees that had had been pollarded for many years previously, and the trunks were about 4' in diameter. The centres of these were all rotted away. We made a floor in two of them with dirt and bricks. These were our 'lighthouses'. We made model wireless sets from two blocks of wood, fixed together. The bottom piece was the 'receiver' and had the tops of sauce bottles for the tuning knobs. The top block had a piece of perforated zinc tacked on as the 'speakers'. We imagined all sorts of messages coming in on them. Sometimes they would be of hostile enemies, and we would go off and man the ditch, which was the trench between us and them. Our guns were of wood, just as well – but we did have a cap pistol. An old metal pipe was a field gun.

Under the granary at Foxes stood the old Titan tractor which was a constant lure to play with. You sat on the iron seat at the back between the traction engine-size wheels. The top of the two large cylinders were covered with an array of equipment that constituted carburettor, magneto, oil pump, etc. We were fascinated by all this. Why not make one of our own. So we got an orange box, two cycle wheels and two iron hurdle wheels for the basic machine. An old grease tin was fixed to the front to represent the cooling tank (on the Titan it held about 25 gallons of water) and we put various pieces of pipe and odd-shaped items on top for the other essential equipment.

Another orange box with a wheel or two hung around the sides made the threshing drum, and the straw pitcher was a length of wood propped up. This 'tackle' was situated on a grassy bank away from possible interference from grown-ups. To various booming and burring noises that we made, this pair of boys threshed imaginary stacks of corn. We developed a scheme of building stacks; kneeling down we had a beet-topping hook in front of us. Pushed onto the ground with our chests with both hands holding a portion of dry grass, it was cut in the centre. These little bundles were laid round as we used to build a stack to represent sheaves. Father was quite congratulatory about the stacks. We made circular ones about 2' high. But alas, the hens that roamed everywhere found them interesting and scratched them to bits.

One interested friend said, 'Where is the gear lever on the tractor?' This was soon remedied by pushing a long bolt into the ground of the back of 'tractor'. A toy farm evolved round this nucleus. We made pigsties from short pieces of wood and used large stones for the animals.

To the south of the house and garden, Father planted ten Bramley and six Cox's orange and two spice apple trees, enclosing the site in with 6' high wire netting. He bought a hen house to house 100 hens. This was a type of house with elevated droppings boards with perches above. The object was to keep the hens indoors if the weather was bad. Otherwise they were on free range. Mother was told 'that the hens were living out of the farm and the money for eggs sold was for housekeeping.' She was also told, 'It's about time that son of yours did something instead of playing about all day.'

I was about ten years old now. The eggs were collected every

Friday by Alfred Neal, market gardener and greengrocer. He drove a pony trap.

Sometimes members of his family were riding with him. He put the eggs into a large hamper with straw in the bottom. He had a round of calls and there seemed to be hundreds of eggs in it. He also bought any apples that we had to spare. What sort of income this activity brought in, I can't say. I think eggs were about shilling a dozen.

Our house was similar to many others in the 1930s. It was devoid of amenity and in need of new things. There was never any spare cash for renewing furnishings. We had carpet in the main room, which was Axminster, and although worn threadbare in places was still looking reasonable. This was laid upon a brick floor with newspaper under it. Without a carpet cleaner, dirt was trodden in and helped to wear it. Mother never had any assistance to take it up so it stayed where it was. Our table was similar to the one at Foxes, with a pile of newspapers on one end. It always had plenty of good plain food upon it. We had a 'front room' or sitting room, with an Edwardian-type sofa, two easy chairs and four dining chairs, and a piano; but Father rarely went in there. I spent some time in there but it was not used much.

The butcher called twice a week and Father gave him a standing order for a joint at the weekend – generally beef and stewing meat on Wednesday. The butcher's name was Bud King. He came by pony and closed-in cart sometimes he was a bit tiddly and would be a bit unsteady on his feet. He would repeat, 'Stand still, owd pony,' while he attempted to cut a joint.

Father was not very fair at home sometimes. He worked very hard and seemed to prefer bread and cheese and beer at about 12 noon. He would be engaged in delivering and unloading coal for several days a week. His sister, who you recall kept the village shop and post office, used to supply him with half a loaf of bread and a large piece of cheese, and into the Black Boy Inn he would be settled for an hour or so. I remember with clarity him coming in at about 1.45 to dinner, which was ready at one o'clock and announcing to Mother, 'Put my b— dinner in the oven, I don't want it now!' Then he slammed out again. Often good meals were spoiled in this way. If he was feeling a bit full he would take a bottle of Yorkshire relish, tip it up and have a swig. What good it did was a mystery.

I was not very enthusiastic about cleaning out the hen houses. I was accosted one morning with, 'Goo to hell if I know anything about you! All you want to do is play about or be making a fuss of an old cat. When I was your age I was working all day.'

I looked down my nose and as soon as possible was out of his sight in one of the lighthouses, or up among the huge branches of the horse chestnut tree growing to the east side of the house. Us two lads poking about under there one day found the rusty remains of a short-barrelled pistol. What a find! I got to work with saw and spokeshave and shaped up a piece of wood to form the butt and fixed it where I considered if should have been. This was a treasured possession, and the envy of one or two lads.

On sunny day Harold came down to play and Mother said, 'Hello, Harold. I wonder if you could come and clean out the hen's houses once a week. They are in rather a mess and I'll pay you 2s for the first week and then 1s each week afterward. Get chaff from the barn and put it on the floors and boards after you've cleaned them out.'

Harold jumped at the chance. A shilling was a handy sum to have in your hand. He came regularly for about three years, and after he outgrew the job it was passed on to younger brothers, who worked just as well as he did.

Us two lads were with Bernard one harvest time. He was riding the self-binder and said to me, 'Jack, goo back to the barn and get me the oil can.'

I made off and brought back the can and was rewarded with a penny. Harold saw my riches and walked behind the clattering binder for several rounds of the field to be sure to get the reward for the next item needed from afar. But alas, nothing required. Cecil was always present toward the end of the cutting of a field with his double 12 bore. It paid to keep behind him at this stage, for he took little heed of who was between him and his rabbit. There would be several boys and sometimes girls in a harvest field. Some were armed with sticks to kill a rabbit in the last pieces of standing corn. If Cecil was near to anyone who caught a rabbit he would take it away from the protesting boy.

Anyone was glad of a rabbit in those days. 'Poor man's food'. On another occasion Bern was working in a distant field and he said, 'Jack, goo back to the barn and bring me the footprint.'

I had no idea what he meant by this, but made off. I went to his tool department, but just did not know what I was looking for. Cecil was around, so I said, 'Uncle Bernard wants the footprint.'

'Ow, do he?'

'Do you know where it is?' said I.

'No...and if I did I shouldn't tell You.' He laughed, and when I said, 'Oh, go on, tell me where it is?' he mockingly said, 'Oh, tell me where it is, oh, tell me where it is! Hey ho, hey ho, tell me where it is!'

I was defeated. I trudged back over several acres to tell Bern that I couldn't find it. He was silent. I followed meekly behind him back to the farm to see him pick up a wrench which had the trademark 'FOOTPRINT', which of course lay on top of everything else in the heap of tools.

I found Cecil after this, and he said, 'What did Smasher say to you?' (Smasher was the name given to B by him.) 'Nothing,' said I.

'He's finished with you, mate.'

'I'll bet he hasn't! He'll speak to me again – and if he doesn't it will be your fault,' I said angrily. I punched him in the chest. We often had mock fights, but he was a bit put out this time, and retaliated with a quick punch that knocked me so that I fell and hit my head on the pear tree. 'Don't knock the pear tree down!' he mocked. I arose almost in tears, and he said, 'What a sap-skull fool you are, to be sure! Fancy blaring.' I blubbed a bit. 'Ow, don't blare, you'll be a biggest fool that I ever did see.'

The sun shone on but harvest was slow to progress; one of the best horses was not well. I don't think Bern was very interested in horses' welfare. Cecil had knowledge of some cures for ailments in his cows. 'That hoss has probably got a cowd,' said he. 'He should give it a bran mash and then a bit of stewed linseed.'

There was not rapport between them. These remarks were addressed to brother Edward, and Lewis who had turned up. A short conference brought forth, 'Why not try and use the Titan?'

Bernard thought it a poor idea, for when it was put away it was not going very well. There was one in our midst, namely Wallace (Tartar) Marshall. He had spent some time in the London Police Force as a driver of motors, and was considered knowledgeable enough to try to get the old machine working after fifteen years of inactivity.

'Oh yes, of course we would have to have that article to poke his snout in,' complained Cecil; for Wallace did not shine, in his opinion. However Wallace was asked, and he jumped at the idea. The cumbersome monster was pulled out of the cart lodge by a horse. Several gallons of water was poured into the cooling tank. Petrol was obtained and while the corn waited to be cut, to the delight of Harold and me, the uncles attempted to start the wheels turning. One after another, with the exception of Cecil, they were on the wrong side of the spark and the 24" crank threw them backward. 'Too far advanced,' said Wallace, about a dozen times, and could seemingly do nothing to correct it. One by one the men disappeared to a less dangerous pursuit.

Uncle Frank, who had used this elephantine horseless carriage when it was last in service, had heard of the problems. He was not involved with farming and was on holiday from his employment and came to the rescue. He knew that by moving a toothed fibre coupling the proper number of notches you could retard or advance the magneto without much difficulty; but he was not sure which way.

Wallace was gleaning information, and thought he could work it out. He offered advice; Frank didn't answer. The operation was carried out. The cranking process had to be attempted again to find out whether the fresh position was correct. 'I'm not touching the b— thing,' said someone. Wallace volunteered and gave it a swing or two; nothing happened. Bernard grabbed the crank and with his usual terrific surge of strength turned the engine two or three revolutions, and it burst into life with a deafening roar.

Frank climbed onto the seat and shunted the old machine about but didn't like the rumbling noises coming from within, and considered a bearing was worn. So it was silenced, and various spanners were used to expose two half-shell bearings, and two replacements pieces were brought from a shelf in a shed. They were not fitting very well, and files were brought into play.

Frank couldn't think quite why it was being difficult. So he went off up the lane on his crutches (he had lost a leg in a motor cycle accident several years ago), to hunt around on other shelves and came back with two more replacements that dropped into place perfectly. This had taken up two more precious days, and tempers were getting frayed. Bernard had made up a short pole for the binder in the meantime; no one ever gave him any credit for such jobs. So to the harvest. They had a field of oats in Temple Field previously cut round with scythe, and the stuff thus cut being tied into sheaves by hand. Us boys sometimes made 'bends' to tie them, while an uncle with a brushing hook would gather sufficient to make a sheaf.

The trouble was there were not enough gear ratios on the tractor to enable it to go slow enough. The speed was such that the back driving chain driving the canvas, knife and all the other clattering machinery flew off. Bernard who was riding the binder hollered to Frank to stop – to no avail, such was the noise of the Titan. Bernard used a stick to crash onto the sheet metal of the binder; still to no avail. Harold was quick off the mark and ran on ahead and signalled Frank to stop. With several trials they found the speed could not be lowered, and it needed a sort of figure of eight on the corners, making it necessary to move sheaves off the ends on every corner to avoid running over them with the large wheels. So after losing about a week of good weather they were still at square one; the old horse dolly appeared to be improving and was pressed into service, and eventually the corn was cut, traved or stooked and carted to the stack yard and thatched, and the old slog of preparation for the next year's harvest got under way.

Wallace Marshall's father, David, was a dealer in live and dead stock, and lived at the former Methodist Chapel. The house was built across the back of the building, and at one time was the village post office. He had a ginger beard and wore a hard hat. He used to go to Ipswich Market on Tuesdays, and us lads used to love to go there and see the treasures that he bought. 'I'll furnish your house for a guinea,' he would claim. This was possible if you could tolerate the poor quality of some of the items. Bernard bought an American wall clock there for 1s (it's still going well).

He sold a grandfather clock for 5s, wheeled in on a barrow over a mile, and didn't charge delivery. Several of the village lads would not stop playing a piano that he had stood outside. David was getting very angry. 'I'll stop you, you buggers!' he said (twice), and came round with a large hammer and smashed the movement and keys to matchwood.

He had a portable steam engine once for 30s. He kept pigs at the back of the house in very rough conditions. If any baby pigs died or were laid on by their mothers, he would throw them into the copper with the potatoes, to help feed the survivors. He also sold corn and pig meal, and this was stored in the chapel room in among various items of furniture, beds, books, etc. The windows hung with old cobwebs, festooned with dust from the provender. Father used to go to Ipswich sometimes and told me he had known David to sell a cow for a few pence profit: 'Small profits, quick returns.' 'I'm a gooing after me dinner, Jo,' he announced, and out of curiosity Father followed him to see where he dined; for he never went into a pub. He went into a cafe and had two pennyworth of peas, and that was his meal. His wife, Dinah, a large lady, used to sit in an armchair with lace shawl and cuffs and considered she was a duchess. Some people almost considered it a privilege to be asked in to see her. I could never understand why, because she always seemed dominant and aggressive to me. She was reputed to be a good cook, but Aunt Lily used to call her an old boaster.

'Morning, David,' Father said at 8.30 a.m. 'How's your wife?'

'Bit tetchy, bit tetchy,' he replied.

Father and he were discussing a deal and Dinah appeared at a window. 'David,' she called. 'David!' she then shouted, but he took little notice, so she bellowed again.

'All right, all right,' he said, walking toward the house.

She continued, 'Your b— letters are here, and your b— breakfast is ready. If you don't come in now I'll chuck it at you!'

Father and I left him to his fate, and he considered that 8.30 in the morning was not a good time to visit him.

When fireworks time came round, the lads used to terrorise David. Bangers would be placed in letterboxes, keyholes, and on window sills. He would come out of the door with a lantern to pursue one of the young tormentors who had been detailed to run in a certain direction. The route would be lined with the others of the gang hidden in a hedge, each with a firework, which was lit and dropped behind poor old David, who then swore and threatened them with the iron bar that he carried. As the torment proceeded he would be out of his mind for he was never able to catch anyone or really know who they were. It all seemed a bit unfair, because he was really quite a harmless old man and never interfered with anyone. My ma was not very keen on fireworks, and never had but a few. I could not see to get around in the dark and usually stayed indoors. One fine November, however, Cecil was in the mind for a little fun. Up on Hilly Field some long way from all the thatched roofs, there was a small straw stack from a crop threshed in the field. Mother and I went over to see the folks after tea. Cecil had a few fireworks, including two quite large ones; he took his gun also. He lit the straw all round and then set off the bangers. He fired his gun several times into the air and between each shot ran around like a wild man yelling at the fire. As the fire died down he took a fork and threw the embers of the fire into air. It was all quite spectacular. He was reprimanded by his sisters for making such a lot of noise. 'We could hear you in here with the door shut.' To which the reply was a high-pitched whistle of contempt.

The dark evenings that were spent at home were occupied mostly with a pencil or watercolours and a drawing book. In my early years I cut out endlessly pictures of traction engines, barn machinery and illustrations of gear used on the farms from the *Implement and Machinery Review*. These were played with as 'models' on the table – rather a flat land, but I never tired of them I loved pictures of trees and included them in the scene. The drawings that came later on were of all sorts of steam and railway engines of large proportions and of battles fought with large guns. The battles were influenced by my looking at copies of *With the Flag to Pretoria*, the catalogue of the Boer War, which were in abundance at Foxes.

Some of the pictures were horrific, and I doubt if they helped me get to sleep sometimes. Toys were handed down from the Calver side of the family. There was a model steam engine, a large

Meccano set and a small model railway on a circular track with engine and three wagons. The model farm animals, which were made of lead then, were lovely. I slowly built up a collection around a farmhouse and buildings. There were horses, wagons, tumbrils and other items faithfully reproduced. The model traction engines that are sold these days for £1000 plus would have found a place in my collection. I would have never left off playing with them.

The highways and lanes were made up then with coal tar and shingle laid on a hard core of larger stones rolled in with a 10-ton steamroller. The tar was heated in a horse-drawn boiler heated by a coal fire. With its funnel at front, it looked like Stephenson's *Rocket*. Tar was carried in wooden barrels holding about 20 gallons. They were hoisted on top of the boiler and the bung taken out and the tar poured into it. Near the school one day one of these old things caught fire. It was drawn by a horse and the poor old nag got scorched, for the operators tried to get the blazing inferno as far from the school as they could. Harold and I had to try our hand at making one of these. Once more old orange box was brought in to make the body. But we mended the garden path with water as tar and earth as stones, and dragged an old grease tin full of stones over it to the accompaniment of puffing noises to imitate the roller. I don't think the effect of this operation on my parents' shoes was appreciated.

Another little episode that got us into hot water was our attempt to get off the ground. There appeared about 25 pieces of matchboard, 5" wide and about 6' long thrown just inside Domine gate. Harold and I looked these over and we thought what a nice aeroplane could be made from them. So into the barn we carried several pieces; I was getting quite handy with a draw knife. So one piece was shaved to a blunt point from about halfway down to make the fuselage. The wings were about nailed on top and had their corners cut off and rounded. One board was cut to make the wheel struts, and another to make the tail and rudder. We got on so well making it that we had another go and had one each. They were a bit heavy, but we attempted to get them up into the horse chestnut tree and perch them in its branches. But there we were stuck. There was a big ivy bush under the old tree and we hid them under this. Father was eight pieces of wood short of the total that he had paid for, and went off on his cycle to have a word with whoever had brought them. Over teatime he was rather irate but did not say a word. The 'planes' were discovered fairly soon, and I slid off to Foxes to escape and was hustled up to bed fairly soon for a night or two.

My poor ma was always having to listen to Father's opinion of me and sometimes she was in tears. She rarely went out, except to Lloyds Bank at Harwich and to do some shopping. Looking back, it seems strange that with the other five days in the week, Saturday was the one that the week's takings had to be paid in to the bank. We left here on the 11.30 bus to get there with about two minutes to spare before it closed at 12 noon. I recall going through the alley next to Harwich Church and wanting to stop and look at the gravestones. If there was a grave with a raised top made of brick with a brick or stone portion missing, it had a fascination for me. I tried to imagine what was to be seen within. Mother tried to hurry me along. She was as thin as a rake, her teeth were in a bad state, and her feet were badly deformed with corns and bunions. The constant battle of life at Domine was wearing her down. 'He thinks more of those pigs than he does me,' she said, and would sit and gaze into space in deep thought for minutes on end. She and I always got on well, and I think I began to see how difficult life had become. 'Tears are blessings, let them flow / They make life completer / When the brow is clear again / Then the smile is sweeter.'

Father used to spend practically every evening at the Wheatsheaf and turn up home at 10.30–11.00 a.m. and slam most of the doors when he arrived. Mother and I were often in bed, and his presence upstairs usually was met by Mother's silence. They never seemed to have much happy time together. I suppose the alcohol was an escape route. The coal trade was competitive. 'Not enough chimney pots,' he used to say.

Somewhere around 1934 he bought a 1 ton Morris lorry and my cousin Albert learned to drive it. Father bought two small coal rounds off two of his competitors in Wix and Great Oakley, and made weekly deliveries. Householders cooked by coal and threshing engines used steam coal. Some farmers would buy a rail wagon direct for a factor such as T Moy, and would unload it with their own labour. Father didn't think a lot of this, but if he had supplied the fuel he would have to wait months for his money in a good many cases. He had high sides made for the lorry and a long tailgate and began to transport pigs to Colchester and Ipswich Markets, and sometimes bullocks. David Marshall would walk down here and say, 'Jo, I've bought two cows at old so-and-so's. Can you get them for me – give you a crown?'

'Can't do it for a crown, David.' So they probably agreed for a extra shilling.

Once on a journey a bullock's feet broke through the lorry floor and they stopped at a farm along the road home and begged a piece of wood to patch up over the holes. Father used to say, 'Hard work was never paid for.'

Mr Nunn at Wix owned the village store. I didn't know him, but I've heard several stories of him. A customer once went into the shop to buy some pills. On his asking for these Mr Nunn said, 'Ain't old Spooner got any?' Spooner was a competitor.

The customer, taken aback, said, 'If that's your attitude, stick them up your arse!'

Mr Nunn called to his baker, William Burgess, 'William!'

'Yes, Mr Nunn,' said he.

'I've found a new way of takin' pills. Somebody jest come here and told me to stick them up me arse.'

On another occasion a lady required a new chamber pot. 'What size do you require, marm?'

'What will fit your arse will fit mine,' was the reply.

He had quite a large coal round, and one of his sons, Jack, would be engaged in delivering it. He would stop at the nearest pub and spend the takings on treating his friends. I mentioned the baker. There was quite a busy bakery, carried on from the Manor House Stores, and lovely bread it was. The baker's horse-drawn trap finished up in the pond opposite the White Hart on more than one occasion.

Douglas Nunn also owned several sets of threshing tackle, and the arrival of one of these at Domine caused a commotion. We usually had two corn stacks – one of wheat, one of oats and barley. There was not a lot of room for the stacks and it was very cramped when the tackle arrived. The threshing drum was pulled into place alongside the stack and then the straw elevator commonly called the pitcher, which had been uncoupled before, had to be drawn past the drum and pushed under the back of it. One spot in the yard had been the site of a muck hill for ages, and on one occasion the engine dropped in and stayed there fore most of the day. Efforts to get the clumsy old thing out with jacks and chunks of wood and the spuds fixed to the wheels were interspersed with, 'I told you not to go on there, Satan!' This was Fred 'Satan' Payne, one of several engine drivers who were great characters. They arrived about 6 a.m. to get up steam for a 7 a.m. start. Some cycled, some walked miles to get to the farms all over the district. One memorable day was when the driver attending here had forgotten to cover the top of his funnel or chimney when leaving for home at the end of the day's work. So of course his fire had drawn up during the night and was out in the morning. This meant a late start to the accompaniment of Joseph's, 'Well, I'll goo to hell if I know anything about it. Bloody men standin' about here for hours... When will that bloody thing be hot enough?' When the wheels began to turn it was time for breakfast. 'Christ Almighty! Bin standin' about here since and now stopped for breakfast. I wish the b— thing would fly afire and the b— stacks with it!'

'I'll git a gun a shoot myself, that's what I'll do,' said Father. 'Never change a good mind, Joe,' said someone, which didn't seem to help the situation a lot.

Johny Gardiner would always be taking off the chaff. The chaff box in our case was always at the side of the corn stack, and a dustier spot was impossible to imagine. He was cursed if it got blocked up, for each bag when full had to be carried into the barn, and if you took few seconds to long in this operation the machine didn't wait for you. I was fascinated by all the wheels and belts – none of them guarded. Along the side near the chaff box were shakers delivering thistle heads and other weed seeds. Further long under the elevator was the 'caving' – short bits of straw that had to be kept clear with a rake in order that it in turn didn't block up. The two strongest men would be taking off the corn in those awful 4-bushel sacks and weighing 12 stone of oats, 16 stone of barley and 18 stone of wheat. They were wound up high enough to carry on someone's shoulders on a very insecure sack lifter that had a doubtful ratchet, and sometimes it would slip and allow the sack to come down to the ground with a crash.

Forking onto the drum was not too bad a job until you got below the level of its top and the rats had cut the strings of the sheaves, making it difficult to collect on a fork. At the bottom of the stack sometimes we had to gather up all the short bits and pieces onto an opened beet pulp bag, put the corners together, put one prong of the fork into them and hoist it onto the drum. At this stage the bottom was alive with mice and usually a few rats, and those men available grabbed a thatching peg and tried to kill the vermin. Later on it was obligatory to put wire netting around the stack before commencing work to capture them.

In the 1930s there were often six or so young men following the machine from farm to farm, hoping for a few days' work. Some of them were turned away. Father did not like to tell them they were not needed. One afternoon the local fishmonger called, and Satan bought bloaters and cooked them on his coal shovel in the firebox. Some of the lads had some and Father brought some home-brewed beer and they had a kind of afternoon tea. There was a little rustic humour and sarcasm, and it ended another dusty hard job for this day.

Bernard was to be found in his low garden. This was a kind of delta formed by the stream that had cut out a deep ditch north south through Foxes Farm. The place was a kind of bog. It must have been 75 x 30 yards and was surrounded by willow trees and grew high nettles. Further investigation showed raised cultivated beds that Bernard had created, and on which he grew fine marrows and runner beans by the barrow load. He never took any money for them and gave away no end. He presented me with a large yellow marrow once with my name neatly marked upon it when it was growing. I was amazed and inquired how did it come about. 'It grew like that,' was the short and of course accurate reply.

I went with him back to his shack. He went in and had a large piece of fruit cake brought back from Colchester. He cut two slices and we both tucked into it with pleasure. 'I've brought you a present, Jack,' said he, and gave me a paper parcel. I eagerly undid the string to find a small frying pan from Woolworths. I stared at it and said, 'Thank you,' and he chuckled a bit and said, 'I thought it might come in handy.'

He went across the yard into the house with a fair-sized piece of cake and slid it across the table to Lily and said, 'Here you are,' and went out again. She was rather taken aback, pushed it to one side and didn't appear to appreciate the gesture.

I went off to find him, he had gone to feed the horses, and I found him in the lobby where the corn hutch was. He perched upon its top and started to spin yarns. He chuckled and said, 'David Marshall say bugger Thorpe, Dick King say bugger pork.' He repeated it complete and expected me to laugh but I couldn't see much in it. I reckon now that David had had an unfortunate day at Thorpe Market and the butcher's pork was not very profitable. The fact that there was a rhyme probably was the crowning reason for amusement. He continued, 'I was ploughing the other day down past yours and I fared the master tired. I thought I'd have a "downer". As I sat down near the oak tree, there was a wagon and horses comin' down past Dimbols. When I woke up that was jest gooin' past me: I jumped up and fared the master lot better.' (Time taken by the wagon, perhaps three minutes.) He went on, 'When I was good deal younger some on us went to Mistley one evening. We had a few drinks at the Thorne. As we came home, we stopped at as many field gates as we could find, took 'em orf their hinges, then just stood them up so as when somebody come to open 'em they fell over afront on 'em. Three ladders had to come down from stacks; one we carried about half a mile and hid it in a spinney. Another time – you know the signpost at the Gatehouse corner?' (This was a three-way sign with *Harwich* painted on one arm.) 'We pulled this up took it to the top of Butler's Lane, dug a hole and pointed the Harwich arm down to Butler's Farm. There was now and then a steam lorry about. We sat and watched in the barn for some time, and there come one puffin' along towards Harwich. The driver pulled up when he saw the sign and turned down the lane. When he realised he was wrong he couldn't back out because of the bends and had to go on to the farm. He spent the next hour or so down there, 'cause that was as wet as the devil, and he got stuck.

David Marshall wearing top hat

'Howsomever, the police got the hear about it, and when it was dark we had to go and retrieve the post. "What shall us do?" says one. "We'll drop it into old Al Hams' well," said another.

'So that is what we did. Alfred stood near his gate next morning, and I was off down to Little Hales to plough. Little Hales was the name of a field.

'"Ha, ha, Bunny!" said Al. "Had a bit of a job to get me bucket down the well this morning. So I stopped and had a look. Well, whoever could've dropped that in there? I says. I suspect that you know a little bit about that, Bunny!"

'"Why no, Al, I don't know nothin' about that… Shall I help you get it out?"

'"Well, that fared to be in there rather tight, that was!" he said. "If we can get it out it will do quite nicely in my grate." So I tied up the horses and lent him a hand to get it out. After the day's work about 3 p.m. I went off home and see Al at his gate. "Ha, ha, made a nice bit of kindling, Bunny."

'He slid off the corn hutch and had a peek out of the stable door. No one was about, and after a short pause he was telling me, "We used to have a laugh when just about twilight time two on us would get a piece of string across the road and hold each end behind a tree, and when a pony trap come along we would just drop the string far enough to tip off the old fella's hat!"'

Cecil was never a very early riser. I arrived over at Foxes one morning at about 10 a.m. and he had just arrived on the ground floor. He hadn't shaved for a week and he smelt of stale perspiration as usual. He had yet to milk the cows and they were reminding him quite frequently. He did stay a moment for a large cup of tea, which he swallowed in one long drink. He consumed as enormous amount of tea, which was strong. His teapot was never cold. I have the spoon which he stirred many gallons. It is worn flat at the tip. He put on his boots and went out without tying the laces. He proceeded to milk one of the cows and I chivvied him because he was late in rising. 'You'll get a cut of the skull if you keep that up – you fool. You'd do more good if you go and grind me up a bushel of beets.'

So I condescended and went off to the turnip house and cleaned and sliced up in the turnip cutter a bushel of mangold and swede. Harold found me, and he had a few pieces of swede and considered this good food. I pushed the bushel skip full to the cow house in a barrow. I had another go at Cecil about being late, and Harold spoke about his untied laces dragging in the muck, and we were both told to clear off; and as the language was rather crude we went.

It was several months before I knew why he was late on that particular day. Father got to hear and I overheard him telling Mother. At Dimbols cows were kept; in fact the owners supplied milk to the village, and they had a bull permanently on the farm locked up in an iron-framed pen. Cecil knew where the key was hung, and to avoid paying a stud fee he set off at about midnight with his cow and led her through the fields where possible to the bull pen. He unlocked the gate and got her served and thence home about three hours later.

In the house at Foxes, although everything was rough and ready, dusty, cobwebby and unloved and unpolished, food was rather a different matter. Cecil was really a very good cook, and very fussy. I witnessed a 'hare celebration' once. He had caught a nice hare and it had hung for the necessary period and this was the day for preparing it. He began in mid-morning. He needed no book of reference on how to jug it. His sister had to keep out of his way, and by teatime all was ready. If there was a tiny speck of fur (fleck) on any part he would holler as if he expected it to jump off of its own accord.

'Have you ever had hare, boy?' he asked.

I said I hadn't.

'Well, sit down and have some.'

It all smelt delicious; we sat down to jugged hare and redcurrant jelly, potatoes and cauliflower. I had a large plateful. His was bigger. On the other side of the table sat John Gardiner; his wife, Rosie, was visiting Lily and was in the front room. John was not invited to join in the feast and Cecil did not speak to him until we were halfway through: 'Smell nice, don't it, Johnie?' – to which he was compelled to agree!

So a whole day was spent in seeing to the cows and calves and the preparation and eating of a hare. Cecil was fond of a flutter on the horses and could put a few shillings on with the publican. He would slip indoors and switch on the radio. Yes, they had a receiver with the apparatus in a box and the speaker on top all decorated in fretwork. He'd listen to important races. On one occasion he was full of expectations but despite turning and twiddling the knobs and, 'Wha' wha's amiss a you?' It failed to convey the hoped-for winner. He later learned that Bernard had removed one of the valves.

These incidents were just part of their way of life, and the farm ticked over; but had they worked together, it would surely have been to its and their advantage. I have seen Bernard using a thistle hook taking about half a drag of corn at a time, and it took an hour to go across an 11-acre field once. 'Can't think where they all come from! When we drilled it there worn't a sign of any.'

When the corn was harvested you needed a fork to stook or trave it, for the sheaves especially barley were full of those prickly weeds. There was no fertiliser used, and some of the light parts there was nothing in the land to grow a crop. 'This land want a shower of shit and a shower of rain once a fortnight,' said Bern. Sugar beet and mangolds and swedes were grown, and in the case of beet the seed was natural and used to send up several plants which had to be chopped out to leave single plants – not a very pleasant job unless you were good at it. Sometimes in the growing time if the weather was tiresome and the weeds rampant, Bernard would run a horse hoe down the rows and them across them. The hoe was rigged with hoes suitable adjusted, and after they had gone across the rows the crop looked rather bare. I think this job was done in desperation. Sow thistle, cat's tail and wire weed were hopeless to control, and awful weeds to hand hoe. It took a week to chop an acre. Now with rubbed seed and spaced planting, one acre can be gone through in a day. The horse hoe's penetration of the soil depended on the amount of weight the operator could put on the handles. The horse was led by another man or boy or driven from behind with reins.

I first met Aunt Adelaide at Foxes when I was about ten years of age. She had come from Witham, where she and her husband were in the haberdashery trade, to see Bernard about the payment of some of the money to which she was entitled under her father's will. There had been a real old kafuffle (argument), I assumed, because when I went into the house with Mother the atmosphere was very 'rigid'. Aunt Lily was more serious than ever. Cecil was convincing Adelaide that Bernard was the 'biggest fool he had ever known, and if he hadn't have grown wheat on such and such a field, the income would have been much better,' and when I was going to help him with the hay. 'What do you think he was doing? Boring a hole in a piece of iron – no earthly good. There he was, the best part of a lovely morning, and when he'd done it that worn't any use.'

Adelaide had been paid £110 of her just entitlement in the year I was born and there was no more forthcoming in 1935. Needless to say, Bernard was nowhere to be seen. After the original debate, he had probably cleared off to the Wheatsheaf to sit in silence for several hours on end. I guess the problem stayed as it was and life chuntered on.

A few years later, Mother and I were making the usual journey across the footpath to see the folk and as we traversed in a southerly direction we constantly turned round to witness the aurora borealis. The date was 27th January 1938. The bars and shafts of reddish light glowed and then died away. It was awe-inspiring and a bit frightening. Upon entering the kitchen I excitedly told those present about the phenomenon. Cecil was finishing his meal with the third cup of tea, and did his best to frighten me more by saying, 'The red streaks were a volcano erupting upcountry, and to be careful on the way home cause you might get a crack on the skull from the falling embers.'

I went to find Bernard. He was in his shack. 'Hello, Jack,' says he.

'Hello, Uncle, how are you?'

'Medium,' was his reply.

'Have you seen the lights in the sky?' said I.

'What lights?' he questioned.

'Why, out here!' I exclaimed.

I went into the yard, and through the trees they made the place eerie. He came out and looked. 'Why, they'll be the northern lights. Tha's the sun shining on ice crystals.'

We went back into the kippery, smoky shack and sat down. He was full of stars, space, light years, comets and distances of heavenly bodies from the earth. I said, 'If space ends what is on the other side?' And he said he thought this was beyond comprehension. He talked of the evolution of man from the apes and I was fixed to my seat – a box with a Hessian bag for a cushion – almost afraid to move. The weather would change tomorrow, for the wind was backing from the north-west, and just before dark there was a 'bar of cloud from the school bridge to the Priory', roughly north-east to south-west, and Bernard said, 'If you ever see that, Jack, you can take a bet on the weather changing.'

The evening had disappeared in a matter of a few minutes, or so it seemed, for Mother opened the door and said, 'It's nearly nine o'clock.'

So off we went, with this boy chattering about all the things he had been told. She wasn't very impressed for she thought all such things were best left undiscussed. I thought that it was all very revealing, and was sure that what I was told helped my education, or the thoughts helped anyway. One day when the sun shone, several lads and lassies and Harold and I were sliding down a straw stack in the stack yard. Cecil saw us and went indoors after his 'smoke pole'. He approached us from the cover of the barn and fired a shot just over the heads of those on the top of the stack. Everyone scattered, and one or two mothers walked down to Foxes to ask him what he meant by this action. His reply was, 'What the hell do they want to come playing about down here for? Next time I shan't be so careful!'

The police were mentioned, and Cecil said, 'I don't care a bugger about the police, nor about you! You're trespassing here, anyhow, so if I were you together I'd just git up the lane and stay there… Lot of old women snuffling about,' he muttered. He still had his gun handy and marched off with it under his arm, cocksure of his dominant position.

I filtered back and nothing more was said about the stacks. 'Goo and grind me up some beet,' I was told, without any odd remarks. I did as he asked. He had been busy with a scythe and in sharpening it with a short piece of carborundum had badly cut his thumb, and I think the incident had sobered him up, for the cut was deep. 'Phil Garlic is about,' said he.

I was not following his line of reason and said, 'What are you talking about?'

'Why, you sap-skull, him up there!' he said, pointing to the sun. He continued, 'Do you know Humpty Twisler was up the road?'

I looked at him more curiously than before. 'Where and what is Humpty Twisler?' I asked.

'If you goo up to the Priory Farm you'll see him.'

So I went over the footpath toward the farm, as he suggested, and there saw a huge machine on caterpillar tracks with rotating tines at the rear churning the soil quite deeply as it traversed the field. Several lads were present, and I was told this was a Gyrotiller. On my return to Foxes, I saw Cecil and said, 'Cor, that's a huge machine! I'd like to drive it.' I then queried his reason for the name he had given it.

'Well' said he, 'the driver is humpty backed, and he drive a twisler!'

The footpath was the 'main road' to the Wheatsheaf, where my father, Bernard, Cecil and Bert Clarke would walk to cut off a long walk round by road. Cecil would leave home ten minutes before closing time and demand a drink at the last minute. 'If you'd have been working as hard as I have today, you'd be late,' he would tell the landlady. Bert Clarke was another character. He was a bachelor and would work for short periods for a farmer and then would spend his earnings on beer. He had little to eat while on these sessions. On his way home through Foxes he would relieve himself just anywhere and had not thought for anyone, near or far.

Father was his lifelong pal, and I have seen Joseph lend him £1 many times when £1 would buy quite a lot of food and beer. When Bert died, Father was the only person apart from a few members of his family at his funeral. Bert was worth £2 7s in the school penny bank in 1907. Bert's father, Nanty, lived opposite the Black Boy Inn. He was a tall, thin fellow, and an ardent worshipper alternatively at the Methodist chapel and at church. At the conclusion of each hymn and at other times during the service when the congregation sang 'Amen', he would intone the finale after everyone else. He had his prayer and hymn book in one hand, and the music to accompany it in the other. Through some trivial disagreement he would switch from church to chapel, and on certain days in summer would hurry home from his place of worship, to stand in his garden wearing a white smock and large brimmed hat. He had bees, and seemed to like to show off by tending them. One bright Sunday morning when the bees were active, just before he arrived home one or two of the equally active lads enjoying a pint skipped across the road, and with a long pole tipped a hive over. Nanty's reaction can be imagined when he strutted into this garden. Among his claims was one to have driven a traction engine until the flywheel was worn as thin as a sixpence!

In 1936, when eleven years old, like all of us were who had reached that age, I was upgraded to Parkeston Elementary School. We went by LNER train, drawn by a dirty little tank engine, from here at 8.30 a.m. and come home to lunch (dinner it was then), go back to school at 1.30 and be home again at 4.30. There were no school dinners then; some pupils took sandwiches. Harold was a year older than I, and I asked him lots of questions about the new venue and of the lads and lassies who attended there. He said there was Big Jim, Tulley Day and Dinkum. It all sounded formidable, and I felt on that first day as if I was going into the unknown.

It turned out to be the best thing that had happened to me. We were taught technical drawing, science and art, in addition to the usual items, and the most important one to me was woodwork. Sport was well to the fore and there was a good-size playing field. Each class member was chosen according to capability to be a member of a house: they were Albert, Edward, Patrick and David. I was of little use in sport, and did not take part in football. Cricket was beyond me, for I could never catch a ball. Woodwork lessons were the highlight of the week for me, and were over too quickly. There was a dozen benches with two lads per bench. We had jack plane, tenon saw, three chisels, hammer, marking gauge, square and marking knife. We learnt the details of annular rings, and how to select the face side and face edge of timber, and how to set out small pieces of work with the marking knife. I soon mastered mortise and tenon and dovetail joints, and made footstools, trinket boxes, towel rails, coat hangers. I usually had a B+ or B- mark for most jobs. There was a grindstone with a water trough beneath turned by hand. Dick Garret was not really bright at woodwork. He was using a plane and it was not cutting thick enough shavings, so he encouraged it to improve its performance by tapping out the iron. Of course, the hammer blow was too heavy, and the shavings were now too thick, so he took his hammer and gave the cutting edge a clout, and took a piece out as big a half a sixpence. So far the next two lessons Dick was turning the stone with the master putting as much weight on as he could to remove the big gap.

Mr Colt was the master's name, and he was a bit abrupt with some of the boys, especially if they were not too adept. 'Don't cut a piece of timber between two stools – you'll break your miserable neck!' he'd say.

The bone glue we used, which was heated in a double boiler, was cracked up in a shallow box and resembled toffee. Many unwitting girls were led to believe this was what it was and soon found the difference when they put it in their mouths.

Science lessons were quite interesting. We learned the theory of magnetism, with iron filings performing tricks on a piece of paper when the magnet passed underneath. 'Like poles repel, unlike attract,' was the rule of thumb. We made simple electric motors and electromagnets.

The headmaster, Frank Thurlow, took us for science. We learned basic chemical symbols, and one little rhyme which helped us to remember two of these was:

Poor old Brown is dead and gone
We ne'er shall see him more –
For what he drank for H_2O
Was H_2SO_4!

On one occasion Frank made chlorine gas and took a nose full and nearly gassed himself. I don't recall any lessons in first aid, which should have been a precaution before teaching us to make poisons. We were asked to take a metal can to school that could be firmly bunged up to demonstrate atmospheric pressure when water in the vessel was boiled. When it was considered that the steam had dispelled the air, the seal was banged in. Cooling water was applied to the outside of the can and the vacuum thus caused the atmospheric pressure to crumple it. I volunteered a can and at lunch time passed Father on his cycle. The can was hanging on my handlebars. During the science lesson the can didn't conform to the experiment and I brought it back uncrumpled. The first thing Joseph said was, 'What were you taking my linseed oil can to school for? I'll have you know that I haven't got oil for them to use!' I did my best to explain the procedure of the lesson to him. 'Lot of nonsense! If that's what you go to school for, I'm dammed if I know what good it will do. I'll tell you one thing, and that isn't two – science will kill us all in time.'

Incidentally, the can still contains linseed oil. Technical drawing was quite easy for me, and isometric drawing was accomplished with ease. The whole school congregated for Assembly first thing each day. One of Mr Thurlow's favourite hymns was 'Ye blessed angels bright', accompanied on the piano. One morning we had a lesson in how not to brag. One of the lads from this village had said many times, in the hearing of the Head, that he could play the piano. On this particular morning the usual pianist was absent and our young artist was asked to fill the vacancy. He had to oblige. He sat there, struck a few notes, each attempt was interspersed by the Head's, 'He'll be all right in a minute.' But he could not read music at all, and he had to go back to his place crestfallen, and the hymn was sung unaccompanied.

The journey home from the station in the winter months in the dark was a problem to me. I just couldn't see. I had a lamp on my cycle which did nothing to assist my knowledge of where I was. Why I rode in these conditions is now a mystery to me. I regularly went into the ditch and especially the one on the sharp bend at the bottom of Dimbols Farm, and twisted my handlebars to all sorts of angles. If I heard anyone walking, I didn't know which side of the road they were on and sometimes caused amusement and sometimes a few curses. I headed straight for Flora, who was going home one evening. I think she was almost in the ditch herself as I mounted the grass. 'You want to look where you're going... Oh, it's you!' said she. Sometimes Mother attempted to walk to meet me but the journey was too arduous.

What us lads got up to in the train going to and from should not be written down. At Wrabness Station one porter, Bert Andrews, who was an excellent gardener and brought the station many first-class prizes, was often after our blood: 'Bert, Bert, dirty shirt' and 'Big Bonce Bertie, Dirty Shirty' was written on posters that were in evidence around the waiting area. I recall the watercolour painted headings on these they were very attractive. One advertised Ullswater as the place of your dreams. This was prefixed with a large 'B'. Sometimes we delayed going to the station until the train was within 100 yards of the platform, and then made a rush to the down side over the foot crossing and jumped into the last compartment while Bert was further up the platform.

One day, however, I guess he had had a word with the guard and the train did not start until our harassed porter had found us tyrants and entered our compartment. A few slaps round the head and threat of, 'I'll see your father about you,' quietened things down for a few days. One of our number was really a hard case. As the train went under bridges electric light bulbs would be hurled through an opened window at the brickwork. The word 'TOILET' would have its 'I' removed by scratching out with a knife blade, to read 'TO LET'. The warning over the doors, 'It is dangerous for passengers to put their heads out of the carriage windows' was altered. The leather strap used to pull up the sliding glass panel of the doors was cut off and thrown out, the armrests were slashed, and on one day of rampage a razor blade in a holder which was obtained especially for the purpose for a few pence, was used to cut two slits all the way along the seat backs. This caused two railway police officers to come to the school, and all the Wrabness children were commanded to the Assembly Room. We all said we knew nothing of these incidents, and after half an hour of questions we were allowed back to the classrooms. I think this episode did a little good, for things quietened down on our journeys to and fro. The ringleader mentioned before was a real daredevil. He would stand on a 20-gallon empty oil drum and walk it along the road. He would ride round the village sitting on the handlebars of his cycle, and walk along the parapet of the bridge across the railway. The last I heard of him he was a police sergeant.

With the knowledge of woodwork now sinking in, I made use

of the kitchen table as a bench and bought a few tools from Woolworths store. Most of these were 6d each part. I remember the hand drill of three parts, the handle, the chuck, and the bevel gear wheel; the chuck was able to accommodate a 1/4" drill and it was quite well made. I made rough models of farm tractors, and steam engines. One was of Stephenson's *Rocket* and was quite respectable. The wheels were cut out in plywood and were quite realistic. I didn't get much credit from Father for this.

"Bout time you made something useful,' was the usual response.

I was always in my element when Bert Fordham, the local builder, came to do any jobs around the house and buildings. One or two jobs that he did are still to be seen today. He was a good craftsman and I tried to assist or get in the way whenever I could. He occasionally had to patch up rotten weatherboards on the house. I learned to use the sliding bevel here. He had difficulty finding a fixing sometimes, for the studs were as rotten as the boards. 'I could make a carpenter out of you,' he said once in Father's hearing – to which there was a 'Ha!' in reply.

Over at Foxes, there dwelt a savage cockerel who was a peril to all who walked up the path to the back door. He would accost whoever attempted the journey with his spurs, and defied everyone. I armed myself with a hazel stick and when I visited the folks there I used to do battle with him. 'Battle' may sound exaggerated, but he did fight with me. I caught him under the back of his head and 'downed' him. I went indoors and saw Aunt Lily. I told her about this aggravation and she agreed that the bird was a trial. He had actually drawn blood on Cecil's leg and would have to be killed. 'I think I've saved him the job,' said I. We had a look outside, but he was not where I'd left him. I ventured to the spot, but he came up behind me and had another go at me! I had no weapon now, and ran the way I was going and out of the gate and up the granary steps. He left me and slowly went back to the hens.

Bernard saw the latter stages of this episode and laughed. 'Well there, Jack, never seen anyone run away from an oud cockerel afore!'

'He chased me and tried to stick his spurs into my leg,' I

retorted. 'I bet you'd run if he did it to you – does he come after you?'

'If he did I shan't take any notice of him,' he said with derision, and went into the stable, chuckling at my expense.

I was poking around the garden at Foxes one day when a car drew up at the gate. From it stepped the driver and Uncle Cecil. With a great deal of difficulty they were removing an invalid Aunt Minnie from the back seat. They carried her into the house and put her to bed upstairs. I went in eventually and there was a gloomy silence and I was told to be off home. Mother had told me a day or two before of her sister's dilemma. Lily had been informed by letter that Minnie had had a stroke. She was fifty-four years of age, Lily sixty-five. So a poor old lady, who was work-worn and tired out, had to accept the task of sick-nursing her sister, who was paralysed down her left side. Mother went over to help whenever she could, but Father did not think she should spend much time over at Foxes. He said, 'There's plenty of work to be done here if you like to do it.'

The doctor (Dr Bree) called in every week, but there was little he could do to help. I used to visit her regularly every Sunday morning; no one told me I should. I just went. She was always pleased to see me and was able to talk fairly well and her memory was very good. She was very ladylike and rather lovely. She tried to take comfort in the fact that the fingers of her paralysed hand were closed up after she had slept, and slowly opened out after she woke.

Surely they might come back into use again, because they did move; but this hope never materialised. She told me she had seen a ghost when she worked in service in a large house in Southend. In this house she slept in the nether regions and one of the other maids who slept nearby used to take a poker to her room because she was always afraid of the noises after midnight. Aunt Minnie had been at the house about fourteen days when one night she was awakened to see 'the tall, stately figure of a lady as a ghostly form wearing a white gown' standing at the foot of her bed. On the following night she saw the same apparition at the right-hand corner of the bed foot, and on the third night the vision appeared at her right-hand side, halfway along the side of the bed. She was compelled to tell her employers, of the happening and gave them notice. They were not surprised to hear about the ghost, for everyone who slept in that room had been disturbed by similar apparitions. It seemed that there was a continuous stream of maids taking the job and the spirit sending them away. She told me this story with such vividness that to this day it seems real.

A fire was lighted and kept going during the day and part of the night in the bedroom during most of the winter of 1936. One day the floor joists caught fire and the stricken invalid shouted as best she could and somehow drew attention to the fact. Uncle Cecil dealt with it before much damage had been caused. It was thought too risky to have fires after this; perhaps the shock brought on Minnie's pneumonia.

Bernard had ground coffee in stout aluminium foil packets. With these he made a long tube and fixed it to a kettle spout, containing water, kept boiling on an oil stove to conduct steam toward the invalid's face to assist her breathing. Somehow she recovered from this and was nursed by a very weary sister, Lily, who now had developed a severely ulcerated leg. How she dragged up and down the stairs with all the attendant problems of an inconvenient house was amazing. I recall one Sunday Aunt Minnie had had a herring for breakfast and when I visited her she had a little heap of bones on her plate. Each one had been sucked separately. Her general condition deteriorated and she developed pleurisy. The doctor on his usual visit gave her what was described as 'a draught', which was supposed to put her into oblivion. In the evening after she had been watched for about six hours and her watchers were wondering what was happening.

She slowly came to life and screamed out, 'Where am I? Where am I?'

Cecil was nearby and shouted, 'Foxes! Foxes!'

The doctor had to come again, and she was encouraged to swallow another draught. She didn't recover from this one, and was pronounced dead by the doctor quite late that evening. The undertaker came along and did the necessary, and she was laid out in her coffin in the bedroom. I was asked if I would like to see her and replied that I didn't quite know. Bernard said, 'She never did you any harm when she was alive and she certainly won't now.'

So I went with my ma and looked at the little old lady. She looked lovely. 'She is asleep and out of pain,' said Lydia.

It was all very sad. The bedroom was dusty and uncared for. The double bed that Lily slept in, if she ever slept, and the area to the side of the sickbed, were in a grubby state. The only shining pieces was the decorative brass knobs on the bedstead. These in this era fetch all manner of sums of money, but then only a few shillings. Decay and gloominess were everywhere; clothes unwashed, old grey stockings, and dark coloured dresses.

On the day of the funeral, poor Lily just sat and said very little. Bernard had a bottle of sherry or something similar for a little gathering afterward, and he wanted to open it before they all left, but the cork was in tight and the corkscrew was nowhere to be found.

'Where did you least use it, Cis?'

'I en't sin it for years,' Cecil replied. 'Whisky bottles don't need a corkscrew.' So it remained corked.

My father came to the funeral and, seeing Lily's broken look, offered to stay with her. She tearfully replied, 'No, thank you, I've got a few jobs to do… I've got to make up the fire.'

The taxis were all just moving off out of the yard when Cecil, in the first car, made a sudden decision that he needed a scarf. He stopped the proceedings by letting himself out of the car and blundered back to the house. 'Worn't quite ready… That was Smasher's (Bernard's) fault, humbuggin' about after that bottle.'

There was a little joviality when they returned from the church. I think, having seen the hopelessness of Minnie's case, they agreed 'it was a happy release'.

The cork was still proving a frustration. Nowhere could they find the implement to alleviate the difficulty. Bernard took the problem with him up to the granary and found a long screw which he drove into the cork and tried to pull it out, but of course it pulled its way out crumbling the cork in the process. So now he worried it out with any suitable tool on his bench. His arrival back in the house was preceded by, 'I'll bet I know wa's happened to that – in the time his bin, he's had time to drink that!'

He would have probably have done just that, but that crumbly cork had deposited part of itself into the liquid within, and now it would have to be strained – but through what? The little party was assembled in the large front room, with the exception of Lily. Conversation was sparse. Uncle Lewis and Uncle Edward both had troubles of their own. Their smallholding were not bringing in much cash. Father could converse with them, for ours was much the same. He was always a trifle envious of Cecil, who at the expense of everyone else seemed to contrive to have a few pound notes tucked away. In the ensuing period Bern was trying vainly to find a piece of muslin. Lily was muttering in the background about the evils of drink. She was very sure everything would have been a lot better than it was, had everyone not been of the opinion that a peep at the world through rose-coloured glasses helped.

She thought it was wicked. Her opinion was not shared by Bernard, who apart from ignoring her remarks was now victoriously preparing to pour the contents of his precious bottle through a rather stained tea-strainer. This had been thoroughly sterilised by wiping it out on a grubby tea cloth. The operation was to be performed upon the kitchen table just opposite Lily's chair. She could stand it no longer, and with as much outward disgust as she could muster, got up and in so doing moved the tablecloth. This happened to coincide with the initial trial run of the wine pouring, and alas – most of the contents of the stemmed glass were spilt! No word passed between them.

Lily's disappearance up to the bedroom helped the straining process, and at last those who needed some of the remaining liquid partook and refilled. This definitely eased the springs and loosened the tongues of the men, whose conversation had now got onto happenings of years ago.

'Do you remember Fred Howard? He said in the Sheaf once, "When you follow me to the church, take enow drink for one all round and stop before you git there and have a drink." "Why afore?" someone said. "Well, I shan't be with you when you come back."

Bernard laughed jocularly and went on, 'Owd Dick Draggon the thatcher would call at the Sheaf when he had just started thatchin' the corn stacks at Dimbols, and have a fill up a beer and say, "that they knew him well enough to trust him until he was paid when he'd finished the job". He would work all day and drink beer all evening and at the end of about fourteen days would settle the account and perhaps have 10s left in his pocket and go to the next farm as happy as a cricket.'

Father had left by now, and Bernard suggested a drop of his home-made wine, and from the account told me by Lily, a few days later, 'They should have been ashamed of themselves.' She was rather biased, and really there was little harm done.

I visited Bernard at midday on a Sunday soon after, and he was getting dressed up for the Wheatsheaf. He was vigorously shaking a pair of socks. 'Hello, Jack,' he said. 'How do you wash your socks? I do mine in cold water, and when they are dry I shake the dust out of them.' He was wearing a red handkerchief around his neck, 'Just to camouflage a dutty spot.' He wore short rubber boots with laces and they had built-in shine which suited him very well. He simply held them, already on his feet, under the pump and washed them clean. He brushed his coat with a wire brush lit his pipe and strutted off along the footpath to have a pint of 'Higgledy-piggledy, boiled to buggery, good water spoilt'! Sometimes he whistled and sometimes tried to sing:

'You may not be an angel
For angels are so few,
But until the day that one comes along
I'll only think of you.'

This was the only song I ever knew him to give any attention. Who he had in mind when he got to the last line, I've no idea. I drifted into the kitchen and was allowed to stay. Cecil was encouraging the kitchen fire to brighten up, and had thrust a poker into the fire to lift the embers and allow air to draw it up. The end 4" of the poker was glowing red. When he drew it out, he then thrust its hot point under the stove and brought the knob to rest on the fender. A cat that was resting beneath the range felt its heat and rushed out in between Cecil's legs. 'Why that ole cat is allus underneath there – where are you, puss? Hope I dint hurt it!'

A deep-seated discussion was ensuing between Cecil and his sister. Aunt Minnie had for several years looked after an architect at Danbury.

There were a number of gold sovereigns at large. How they

came to know of them, I cannot be sure, but a visit to the gentlemen in question was called for 'without delay'. Lily did not think she could make the journey. 'We can have a taxi,' said Cecil.

'Be cheaper to go by bus,' said his sister.

'But there's all that messin' about, changin' here and changin there, and bein' jostled about by a lot of strangers.' After a pause, he added, glancing in my direction 'And another thing – can't stop for a drink on the way! Where's the address of this architect fella?'

Lily said it was on the mantelshelf. Now, to find anything upon that shelf was a real work of art. As one faced it there was on the left hand a candlestick with enough wax in its dish to make a candle, and a dozen spent matches mixed in. I mentioned this once and Cecil said, 'Well, you see, you sap, when we get short of candles I tip it out, roll it into the right size and the old matches make the wick!'

Next to the candlestick were a score or so of envelopes. These contained anything from family letters to court summons for unpaid tithe demands. Most of them were a dark brown at the edges, some more than others, depending upon how long they had been there. There was a sort of filing system here: 'You know the new ones by their colour.' Then there was the only little glint of a shine that could be seen; this radiated from that part of the tin that contained the tea.

This was regularly polished by the action of fingers in its frequent journeys from its resting place to the table and back again. Near to it was a packet containing a delicacy used to bolster the flavour of the usual 'Doctor's China tea'. This had its foil lining sometimes carefully rolled up, and at other times hastily muddled into a crumpled mess. Then there were newspaper cuttings – or tearings, would be a more apt description – mixed with more envelopes and dust; a box of 12 bore and .410 cartridges – 'They'll keep nice and dry up there.' Then there was a large pincushion with pins from 1" to 6", the latter of course for keeping hats on; two or three reels of thread or cotton, with needles projecting from their centres holes, and a couple of empty reels long since run out of sewing material; and a packet of matches – the most necessary part of the whole collection. Above all these items Cecil had pinned cut-out pictures of beauties which had appeared in the 'News of the

World'. Lily frowned on these but as they were put up there by her favourite brother she said nothing aloud about their presence. Lastly, to complete the scene there was a large alarm clock with two bells on top that did not keep very accurate time. But time was not important; the cows told you when it was time for tea.

However, to return to the gold, Cecil had decided to take a taxi in its quest. A letter had to be written to RW Hooks, who provided these luxuries, and on the appointed day Cecil made an effort to be ready for a start at 8.30 a.m. On such a day he would have risen early and cleaned his brown boots, put a better cutting edge on his cut-throat razor than usual, and attacked his beard. It wasn't really a beard, just a stubble that was cut off when time allowed or when it had become uncomfortable. His teeth were rubbed with a toothbrush the bristles of which were so soft and worm down that it would have been better employed to polishing brass. His hair brushed with a brush the bristles of which just protruded from the mass of hair and fluff embedded in their roots. He would have put on a clean shirt and endeavoured to place a tie around its collar. It did not tie into a very smart knot because of the many creases at the spot selected. His best trilby hat and respectable mac would have been brushed – if a brush could be found. His appearance would have been fairly good compared with the day before, and would be completed with a cigar. These were only used for high days. He did have a few cigarettes. The brand was Double TT – about 4d for twenty. I would sometimes pester him for a smoke. He would carefully cut one into two and give me half. One day I said, 'Why can't I have a whole one? You get two ends when you cut them.'

This detail should not have been disclosed, because after this he didn't give me any at all.

The taxi arrived' at the appointed time, and after a last-minute flurry of activity, which included the airing of his mac lining and a scarf in front of the kitchen fire, he was off. Lily stayed at home. I never really knew all the details of what happened at Danbury. I did hear that on one of two more visits by Cecil there was a court appearance by the parties concerned, and eventually he returned victoriously with the sovereigns.

Shortly afterward the 'architect fella' was reported as deceased. 'There,' said Cecil, 'tha's a good job I went over there an' got

171

them when I did… If I han't ha' done, some of his people would ha' had 'em – then we shouldn't her ever sin 'em again.'

I was present one day when Mother, Lily and Cecil were discussing the next move, which was the collection of a few pieces of furniture and effects from Danbury. How could they be brought home? The only answer was a coach. This was arranged from the same place as the taxi. On a quiet, pleasantly warm day in June 1938, the four of us set off. The coach was about a 26-seater and we sat dotted about in what seemed to be a large area to me. On the way through Mistley, Cecil said, 'They'll say there worn't many went on that outing.' As soon as the clock showed that 10.30 a.m. had been passed, he hailed the driver to stop at the next pub. The request was readily carried out and we pulled up very soon. Cecil invited the driver into the bar and the pair were requested by Lily, 'Not to be in there too long.' She grumbled about pubs and their contents, and about the people who lowered their status to serve behind the bar – 'Very common' – and wicked were words often used. The two men emerged with four pint bottles of beer which were hastily pushed out of sight and the journey continued.

We found the site under Cecil's direction and an odder place I had never seen. An architect! There was no palatial country house, not even a bungalow but two wooden sheds on a piece of land of about three-quarters of an acre. The grass was knee-deep, and thick. The paths were uncut and difficult to find. The sheds were some distance apart. We entered one of them and there in we found a dressing table and chest of drawers and a small marble-topped washstand, both painted white. Across one end of the building was a raised form with 2" slats which had served as a bed. There were all the items one would expect to find in a bedroom, all quite tidy, and appeared undisturbed. The other larger building was a kind of living room with a small pine table and odd chairs and a writing slope without drawers. On this there were various papers and so on, and in a small tool chest some extremely good quality carpenter's tools: marking and cutting gouges of brass and ebony; steel planes; measuring equipment such as would have been used by craftsman. What was to be done?

'Well, we've come to take it home,' said someone, and we

started to pack the moveable items into the coach. The chest of drawers etc. were put in the gangway in the centre of the coach; smaller items were put on seats and in the racks. The bottles of beer were visited quite often. When lunch time came round, sandwiches were handed round. After a good deal of effort tea was made with water boiled on a double-burner 'Beatrice' oil stove. By about 3 p.m. all was loaded and we set off home again.

When we reached Foxes there was a rush to make some tea. 'Let's have a cup of real tea for a change,' said Cecil.

The bus driver was getting a bit tired of the day's events and didn't mince his words. 'Where do you want this stuff put? I want to get to my tea!'

'Oh, blast him!' said Cecil. 'I'll tell him in a minute – I don't know where the hell to put it.'

Eventually the whole lot was carried up and put into the granary. The driver looked suspiciously at the steps leading up to it. He was worried and told everyone so.

'They're all right, mate,' said Cecil. 'Last for years... Bloody fuss to make!' he muttered, out of earshot.

A few days latter I nipped up to the collection unseen and searched about and found the tools, and a folder full of plans and set squares. I took one or two of the less important items to Cecil and said, 'Could I have these, Uncle?'

He looked them over and then at me. 'What have you been doing up there, you young sod?'

'Nothing – only having a look.'

'Put them back! I shall sell them later to pay for the bus,' said he.

I jumped in with, 'I'll buy them off you!'

'*You?*' he hollered. 'You couldn't buy one of the screws! You een't got a pound to your name.'

'How much do you want, then?' said I.

'Ow, bugger off!' he said, and so I did just that – but not far. I headed for home, but when I was out of Cecil's sight I hid behind the stable in the mass of elder bushes. I crept back up to granary and hid my selection of items under some old sacks.

Soon after this he wanted some help. He had a Planet hoe, a small frame with two long handles on two wheels, and three or so

L-holes on the frame at the back. He wanted Harold and me to pull this gadget up and down between the rows of mangolds, using a strong stick as a whippletree roped onto the hoe, with him pressing on the handles. Of all the methods used to clean up beet! We thought this would be quite good fun, and pulled as hard as we could. My thoughts of the tools in the granary were very near. We arrived at the top of the field. I sat down on the brew.

'What, are you tired ariddy, mate?' jeered Cecil.

'No,' I replied, 'but I'm not doing anymore work until you let me have the things I asked for.'

'You little sod!' he hollered.

'Well, we're not working here for nothing. You pay Harold, and give me the tools.'

Cecil considered this for a minute and said, 'No, I'm dammed if I will. I'll push the hoe myself.' So he untied the ropes and off he went for a few yards.

These hoes were intended to be used with a push-pull motion. He went some way down the fields and found it was not as easy as when we pulled it.

Harold was not very pleased with me, for he had hoped to get a few shillings for his work, and said he would go back and help again. As it so happened a new family had moved into the old Ships Farmhouse in Wheatsheaf Lane, which was not far away from where we were. One of the sons, a great strong fellow who stuttered, came on the scene. He asked us what had we been doing. We told him. He collected up the stick and rope and hurried down to Cecil.

'W-would y-ou l-like me to help you, mister?' said the newcomer.

Without any hesitation he was put into harness and was like a young cob. He pulled he contraption like mad. When Cecil and his new slave returned to the top of the field where we were, he stuck a long tongue out at us, and feeling rather beaten, we ambled homeward.

I returned a few days later and Bernard was around the yard. He was needing someone to turn the grindstone and I readily obliged. He had a cutting knife (used on straw and haystacks to cut them into manageable sections) and a hedging hook to sharpen. He examined the hook. 'Somebody – no names, Jack – has used this on the chopping block. You only need chop a few sticks to gap a hook. There's little bits of grit on the faggot ends.'

I turned and turned he had a gallon drum of water with a tap that trickled ('drindel' was their word for it) its contents onto the stone as lubricant. This was filled several times before the required edge was obtained. 'I think tha's enow, Jack,' said Bern, with a pleasant look in my direction.

I talked about tools for woodwork, and was getting interested in lathe work. He had not used his old lathe for a long time and we went into the barn to see if it was usable. There was a pile of old sacks in the little lean-to where it was resting. I soon cleared these out. The wood-framed relic was one of his making. It had a heavy cast iron driving wheel worked by a foot treadle. The headstock had a wooden pulley with three speeds. The tailstock was a screw from the top of a mangle press. The driving belt was missing. Where was it?

'I don't know where it is, Jack. Gone back onto the set of harness that I took it off, I reckon. It was made from two lengths of top latch of the top o' the harness.'

I hunted about but could not find anything suitable. He found a gauge and flat skew chisel used for turning; they were blunt of course. So back to the grindstone. I turned it with fresh enthusiasm, and we soon had them sharpened up. I ventured to say, 'What are you going to do with them?'

He replied with a smile, 'You can have them if you like.'

'Cor, thank you, Uncle. That's lovely!' (They are still in use today.) I was quite bucked now, and mentioned the items from Danbury.

'Don't know anything about 'em. Where are they? said he.

I strode rapidly up the granary steps, followed by him. He was a little amused at my having hidden them. He looked them over. 'They're good quality, Jack. If I were you I'd take them home and say nothing more about them to anybody.'

I was delighted and took five or so items home and wrapped them in a piece of sack. I never mentioned them to Cecil and he didn't to me either. I hunted around our barn and eventually found some pieces of leather strap and fixed them together with bifurcated rivets, put on a buckle on one end, punched several holes in the opposite end and trotted off to Foxes.

With a bit of 'kiltering' I got it round the wheels of the old lathe and had a go at turning. The first effort was a piece of ash I found on the firewood heap. The gauge dug in and the work whizzed past my nose. I had a lot to learn.

One of the lads in the village had an airgun for sale, and I was interested. The price as 1s 6d. I thought this was rather dear so he and I tossed a penny: heads it was 1s 6d, tails 1s. It fell to me for a shilling. I had not had an airgun before. I paid the purchase price and took it home. I dropped it into the ditch near the gate on the road at home and went up to the house to see if Father was about. He was absent; Mother did not want to see the new acquisition. I had about 60 or so slug (pellets) all in the price, and had several shots at a target and was reasonably accurate.

I was potshotting one day and, fool that I was, aimed at a hen, pulled the trigger and hit the poor innocent victim on the side of the head at the edge of her eye. She spun round and didn't know what to do next. I ran after her, caught and carried her into the house.

'Now what have you done?' said Mother. I told her. 'What a senseless thing to do!' We shall have to keep this from Joseph's eyes.'

So the hen was put into a cardboard box with some straw and kept in an unused bedroom in amongst old newspapers and clothes. She was fed and watered. We washed the wound and it healed up. After about three weeks, we introduced her back to the hen run. The others didn't like the look of her and there were scuffles for a few hours. Our injured fowl had lost the sight of one eye and didn't come off very well. She survived, however, and Father could not understand why 'that owd hin had got her head held askew.' He was never told the reason. He never knew I had the gun. When he was up at the pub during winter evenings, I would take a cycle lamp and light up the sparrows sleeping under the eves of the house and shoot them. I got several like this. It never seemed to make any difference to their numbers. There were dozens in the hen runs and round the pigsties at feeding time.

After my previous episodes with shooting, I restricted my

shots to sparrows, considering them a pest. We always had two or three cats living here. One of them, a common tabby, would come outside when she saw me pick up the airgun and follow me in the hope of getting a fat sparrow. There was a .410 gun in the kitchen with a longer barrel than usual. I played around with this. We had quite cheap cartridges for it.

The brand was Trent. I found the percussion cap could be pushed out of an empty case quite easily. I flattened out the pin dent and put one of the pink 'caps' used in cap guns in, then the star shaped anvil, and replaced the assembly back into the cartridge. I then put about 50 'caps' into the case, put in a wad of paper and then a few airgun pellets in, and sealed the end with another wad. It caused quite an explosion, sufficient to break a jam jar at a few yards' range. There was a snag to this episode. The 'caps' were of poor quality explosive and they turned the .410 very rusty, and in a very few weeks it was in a bad state. 'What the hell have you been doing to this gun, young man?' I was asked. I avoided the inquiry as usual.

I attempted to clean up the bore with a piece of rag on the end of a wire but the rag was too plump and the wire pulled away. I was in a muddle. I had to tell Father, and there were several swear words. 'You'd better take it down to Smithy's.'

Percy Smith was our blacksmith, who had his shop at the crossroads. I did as I was instructed, and our very able smith took a length of 5/16" rod, heated one end in the fire, and burnt out the piece of cloth. He inspected the inside of the barrel, and was curious about the pits and rust. He sawed a slot in the end of the rod and slipped a piece of emery cloth into the slot and turned it into a wad. He then put a little oil on and worked it up and down the bore with a circular movement and improved its appearance considerably. Percy advised me, 'Keep it oiled, but before you use it clean it out with a dry wad. You've mucked up a good gun, me boy.'

I left the shop, not forgetting to say, 'Thank you, don't tell my Dad what I told you, will you.'

I hadn't finished with ballistics yet. I had read about the Lee Enfield rifle and the soft-nosed lead bullets used by the Boers in the Boer War books. These bullets flattened out when they hit their target. I had to have a try at making bullets. I got two pieces of hardish wood about 3/4" square, and a couple of inches long put them together in the vice and bored a 7/16" hole in the join, so I had a half in each piece of wood. I parted them, tidied them up and now I had a mould. I melted some lead and poured it into it. The next move was to take out the shot from a .410 cartridge, and place the bullet in its place. I found a piece of 4" x 4" wood around the barn; it was from the corner of a square bullock feeding manager. I stood it up near the corner of the stable. I walked up towards the house a distance of about 50 yards, loaded the gun, took aim and pulled the trigger. The old gun kicked like a donkey. The recoil snapped it open. The imprinted letters stamped in the brass end of the cartridge were flattened out completely. I inspected the target, a little shaken. I hit it just left of centre. I looked at the back. It had gone right through and into the corner of the woodwork of the stable. The hole was extended to about 3/4" and I imagined its effect on the human body. My readings of the war and the pictures of it seemed all the more horrific.

Chapter Seven

With several firsts in art, woodwork, science and composition to my credit, I left school in April 1939. Frank Thurlow gave me a good testimonial, which would have got me an introduction to any employer. When I arrived home carrying my document, Father wanted to see it, and after reading it he said, 'Well, I want some wood chopped for the copper I'm brewing tomorrow. Now perhaps we can get some work out of you...great louts going to school!'

Brewing beer was quite a performance. Father used to rise at 3 a.m. The kitchen was filled with a long stool (called a pig stool) with a large wooden tub upon it with a large wooden tap driven into a hole near the bottom. A woven basket in the shape of pear was used to strain the liquor from the steeped malt. Another smaller tub stood nearby for receiving liquor as the process continued. The recipe was to 1 bushel of malt allow 4 buckets of water, and 1½ lb. of hops to each bushel. The copper held 20 gallons; this was water brought from the well at the barn, which was carried in a bath held between Father and me, and a bucket held by each of us in the other hand. The copper was brought to boiling and one bucket of hot and one of cold was put into the large tub. The appropriate amount of malt was introduced steadily and stirred gently; this stood for four hours. The resulting liquor was taken via the tap into the copper, the hops added and simmered for a further four hours. This brew was then taken from the copper, put through a sieve back into the large tub, from which the malt grains had been removed. Yeast was added, and covered over with sacks slung across pieces of wood for I think a further four hours. Mangold or other root wines were made by boiling and about 3 lb. sugar to each gallon of water.

Back to the wood chopping. In the chicken run around a large plum tree a small 'spinney' of suckers had grown. I had helped Father to dig these up and this was to be chopped at the block for the copper. They had several thorns about them and were not very easy to deal with, but with perseverance I got through it.

The beer was stored in barrels in the back kitchen, usually 3 of 9 gallon size. Eventually with time, some would be ageing and would become sharp and very thirst-quenching and potent.

I overheard Father talking to a rep for one of the coal factors he bought from. 'What are you going to put him to, Joe?'

A very definite answer was forthcoming. 'He's got to earn his living the same as I've had to!'

Around this era, some of the German Navy visited Harwich and the same gentleman remarked to Father that he had seen some of the personnel and that they 'Were the hell of a lot of good-looking chaps.'

Joseph retorted, 'I never saw a good-looking German. You'll see what they'll do for us afore long.'

I did various jobs about the farm in the ensuing weeks. I went up to David Marshall's and bought a large kitchen cabinet for a pound. I got it home in sections on a barrow. It was made of soft white pine. I knocked it into pieces and made five hen coops. They were all different sizes but of the same pattern with paled fronts and the centre one protruding through the roof to slide up and down to allow the entrance of a hen. They were used for discouraging broody hens from sitting on one clutch of eggs. When used for the former purpose, four or five hens would be pushed in to make conditions as uncomfortable as possible for sitting. When a broody was shut up in a nest box in the chicken house for a few days until she was sitting tight, when you deliberately disturbed her she would resent the interference, and squawk at you. A few china eggs would be introduced under her to attempt to get her used to the idea. A small hollow would be made in the ground and coop placed over it. The idea was for a little moisture to keep the eggs on the damp side. The chosen hen would be put in the coop at nightfall and the 13 eggs would be carefully pushed under her. She would be encouraged to come off the nest for food and drink and a 'bask in the dust of one of the many shallow holes scraped all over the chicken run.

Sometimes if neglected a hen would become lousy and stand up off the eggs. Another snag arose occasionally if she decided to give up sitting, usually when 14 or so days of the 21 had been accomplished. There was always a cockerel running with the hens and we frequently used our own eggs. Sometimes sittings would be brought from elsewhere, Anconas and Black Leghorns were favourite. The Anconas were black with white speckles. They were very good layers, and some of them lived for seven or eight years. I was pleased with my efforts, and got a little praise. Father thought I should have more chickens to look after and brought a foster-mother. This would house about 50 day-old chicks. It was a difficult job to keep the temperature at the right value, and I fear that they often got too hot.

On the field next to Domine, which was three acres of fruit trees, in various stages of neglect, stood an old shepherd's hut. This belonged to Mr Thornally, and we bought it for 30s. It was mounted on large cast iron wheels. We had to jack it up to free the wheels, and towed it home with a horse. This was to make another hen house. It was my job to alter it by putting in perches and cutting a pop-hole and putting a hinged board for walking up and down to the door. Some of the weatherboard was rotten, so I replaced this. I was as happy as a cricket. Father gave me 5s a week, and I saved as much as I could and cycled to Dovercourt to buy a small tenon saw, a chisel, a hammer, and so on, when I had the cash. Bert Clarke once saw my small collection of tools and said, 'You're wasting your money, boy.'

I answered very definitely, 'You spend your money on beer – I'll buy tools. I'll have these in years to come, yours is gone.'

Father said, 'Well, Bert, I reckon he's about right there.'

I kept away from the coal yard as much as possible. Father tried to teach me how to plough out potatoes, with one old horse. I didn't get on very well. I pulled too hard on the reins and the horse would be in the wrong row. We always had about 1½ acres of mangolds for feeding to the four or five steers that were fattened during the winter.

In the autumn, Father announced, 'I want you to pull some beet.'

So I was given a beet hook or 'tailer', as it was known. He accompanied me to the best strip. 'Show me how you are going to do it,' was the instruction.

I had never been shown the method, which was to work three rows at a time, grasping the beet leaves. You pull it up, swing it to the right-hand side, and chop the top just below the crown. You then formed rows of beet of convenient width to collect with horse and tumbril. I was sworn at for not knowing the method. 'I thought you might have learned that over at Foxes,' was the acid comment.

Bullock feeding was quite a pleasant job. The mangolds were clamped near the barn. You cleaned the dirt off and tidied up the tops at the clamp, brought them into the barn and cut them up in a manually turned beet cutter. A bed of chaff was laid out on the floor, and the sliced beet thrown onto it. Linseed cake and barley meal was scattered over next and it was turned over with a shovel, put into metal bushel skeps, carried into the yard and tipped into the mangers. In the afternoons, light was provided by a hurricane lantern which cast long shadows. The scent of the food, the warmth of the muck and the calmness of the animals was very pleasant.

Pigs formed part of the smallholding scene. Their food was mixed up in a square iron water tank. Middlings and water was prepared after each feed for the following one. In hot weather it fermented slightly and I doubt if this was really very good for the animals. Father always had a 'swill pail' standing near the door of the kitchen, into which went apple and other vegetable peelings, odd bits of bread and the rinsings of beer jugs. This was taken in the morning and shared out among the sows. There were not many hours in the day when things were going smoothly. Father insisted that every animal was well fed, and this sometimes resulted in a visit from the vet. If a sow or bullock had to have a 'draught' of medicine – injections were not used as much then as now – the place was in uproar.

Joseph would summon help from whoever happened to be near and holler and upset the whole show, and the animals especially. When pigs were fattened and sent to Colchester Market loading them up often proved to be a real pantomime. We took them in our lorry with the high sides put on and a proper long tailboard for the animals to walk up. Pigs didn't seem to like to leave their home. If they did not run up into the lorry first time they would not budge. When things were going awry, Father got madder and madder and almost frothed at the mouth. He swore and tore, and if I got near him he would tell me, 'Git out of the b— way!' I wasn't helping, so why didn't I do this or that...? Mother would occasionally walk down to see what was happening and be told to bugger off. 'B— women never were any good.' Once a sow was loaded up by putting a bushel skip over its head and as it backed away was guided up into the lorry. It was really quite a funny sight but no one dared laugh. We always had a dog or two around; usually a fox terrier numbered among them. What wonderful ratters they were! One old mongrel dog was rather disregarded and lived in an open-ended barrel. One piece of the other end was missing, so that when it was fed its tail would stick out through the hole. 'Whoever saw a barrel wagging its tail?' said someone.

The threshed straw stacks stood where the elevator had directed them and were only slowly consumed into the stockyards. On one occasion a hen was observed to fly down infrequently for a feed. Eventually, someone went aloft on a ladder and reported, 'There's a whole lot of chicks up there.' He came down to get a container and we counted 23 lovely little chicks. Just went to show what nature could achieve without any help from us. We were most upset on one occasion when a hen was discovered with her feet securely stuck in about 2" of tar in a bucket, dead.

We had a 3 ton forward control Morris Commercial. It had a six cylinder side valve engine, and during the harvest we used it to cart the corn. I became a fair hand at loading with sheaves and we carted several acres at Shore Farm for Len Robinson. I had a go at driving sometimes, and after jerking forward and spoiling a load was only allowed to drive it empty.

Trouble was brewing. One of Father's men left his employment to work elsewhere, so I was advised, 'Now you know what you've got to do, boy.'

I had to go into the coal trade. I bought a cap and bib and brace overalls, and in the autumn of 1939 I began. I was introduced to a No. 6 shovel and kitchen nuts and cobbles. There were complaints that it took longer to load the lorry. The professional average was 1 cwt. per minute; it took six shovelfuls.

Toward the end of the last one, with deft movements one could drop just enough nuts into the bag, held by the driver, to cause the bob weight on the scales to rise. I didn't think that I should have been expected to do what the strong fellow who had just left could do. He could lift 12 stone of corn off the ground onto a lorry unaided. It was not a very happy time for me. We used to have about twenty ½ cwt. bags of coal and about fifteen bags of split chestnut logs on the lorry to a total of about 3 tons. For a start I only carried the halves and the wood. Cousin Albert was the driver, and he laughed at me in my cap. I got mad and threw it onto the railway and never wore it again. We had no waterproof clothing, and when it rained we made a shoulder pad of several thicknesses of Hessian to soak up the water. After heavy rain, the base of the coal sacks were dripping black water. This soon found its way down your back.

Coal arrived in wooden wagons containing between 7 and 9 tons. Factors' names were painted on the wagons: Albert Usher, Coote & Warner, Thomas Moy and Rose Smith were frequently seen. They had button doors, and the floors were about as level as a brick rubble yard. They were shocking things to work a shovel on. This made the job harder and more difficult and I cursed every day, when two or more wagons stood in the siding. We had to unload their contents loose and take it up to the yard and shovel it out again. 'Do a hundred shovelfuls without standing up' was the challenge. Fair stocks of coal were held, and sometimes we had to throw the coal up several feet from the lorry floor when the bays were filling up. One day, toward the conclusion of emptying a wagon, I stood on the end of a loose floorboard, which tipped and hit my shoulder and covered me with dust – bare head and all. I hated it more each day.

My attitude toward the job was not helping my relationship with Father. We were delivering in Wix on day and I walked over to the offices of G Paskell and Sons and saw Roger. I asked, 'Please, Mr Paskell, do you need any carpenters?'

'Well,' he replied, 'we don't need any carpenters at the moment, but I'll take you on as a sawyer.'

I said I'd let him know. When I got home that night I told Mother.

'I hope you will not go,' said she. 'I have enough to put up with from your father now, and this will only make matter worse.'

I knew she was right, and my heart sank another notch. I never said a word about it to Father.

Now and then we would be asked to move someone's furniture from one house to another. We would have the high sides on the lorry with iron straps across the top. A sheet would be put over if it was a wet day.

I recall one moving job in the village. Albert and I arrived at Chapel Cottages at about 8 a.m. The elderly husband and wife were seated at the breakfast table. Nothing had been packed in preparation for the move, so we went upstairs to make a start, and what a job we had! We had to fold up sheets and feather beds, there were two on one bed, and dismantled the bed frames – but not before we emptied the chamber pots into a pail!

I was entrusted to carry some of the items downstairs. As I went through the living room, what I was carrying collided with the canary's cage hanging above the breakfast table and dislodged it from its hook – crash! It went all over the over cluttered table. The two occupants were still in the same chairs; I think the scene is better imagined than described. After this off-putting episode they arose, and began to help by telling us they wanted what we had just put on the lorry to put something in. Later on the old gent was trying to move a chest of drawers and took the drawers out. He took them to the top of the stairs one at a time and tipped the contents down to the bottom. There was a heap of clothes, small pictures and sundry items of all kinds. We asked him what he had done this for. He made no reply. By midday, when we were loading the second load, we told ourselves that there couldn't be much more now. However, we were then reminded of the 'outside stuff': a small hen house, six hens, wire netting, ten railway sleepers and several bundles of faggots. What a day's work for about a pound note!

On another occasion we were involved in another furniture-moving operation. Barny Payne, who lived in Chapel Cottages, had lost his brother. Now this old lad had lived on his own at Bradfield in an old thatched bungalow. We went off at the appointed time. Berny came also. He didn't know what he would do with the contents of the bungalow. Grass was growing profusely on its roof. Inside were the bare essentials for existing on one's own. Even then I had an eye for antiques. Over the fireplace were two powder horns and a muzzle-loading gun. I soon found out that our client did not wish to part with them. 'You're asking for the most valuable item in the house!' he told me. He was sure there was money in the house. 'I'm damned if I know where he kept it,' said he, coming increasingly frustrated. There was a large feather bed, and he looked it over.

'Come on, let's get this into the garden,' said Berny. We rolled it up and did as he asked. He produced his knife and slit the cover from end to end. He was soon engulfed in a cloud of feathers. It was quite amusing, although he didn't think so, for after about half an hour, there were a lot of feathers but no money – not a penny. We packed most of the items he thought he needed on the lorry and brought them back to Wrabness, and his house became rather lumbered up, as his wife said during the process.

Another memorable day's moving was when we had to take the contents of a grocer's shop from Dovercourt to Wrabness. This included vats made of slate with about 3/4" thick sides. They were about 4' long, and were used to pickle bacon in. They must have weighed about 3 cwt. each. I had to do my bit in lifting them onto the lorry. Little wonder we had worn joints in later life! There were dozens of jars of sweets put on at back, and I was delighted that the lorry cab was full of people, and I came the short journey home in with them eating as many as possible, and pocketing a few a well.

There were rumblings in the news of the activities of Adolf Hitler, and in September war with Germany was declared. We were issued with gas masks and Air Raid Precautions booklets. We were warned not to allow any lights to show after darkness fell, and although our house was still lit with oil lamps and candles and was in a state of semi-blackout anyway, it was still necessary to put up shutters to all the windows. I made some from old pieces of lino on wooden frames and made them fix tight with turn buttons. There was an air raid warning within the first few days, after tea. We sat round the table with long faces. Mother turned down the lamp wicks and made the surroundings nice and gloomy. Father was the most pessimistic man that ever there was. I think his memories of the previous conflict were still very fresh in his mind. The All Clear sounded without any mishaps. For several months everything carried on fairly normally. On the rounds we found that some ladies would be indoors with the doors locked. Some would be worried to the extreme and talk in short sentences of brothers, sons, and fathers lost only twenty-one or so years ago. Some men who were reservists were being called up for war service, and according to age, the lads were having to register with the possibility of being called up.

We used to haul sugar beet to the Ipswich beet sugar factory. These were loaded by hand and we started work at 6.30 a.m. on some days. When we were busy with coal, we would take in a load of beet and deliver coal afterward, and try to be finished by 1 p.m. in order to get another load out after noon. Four tons of beet were thrown on that old lorry, and we used to eat our breakfast on the way home, not stopping at all. I had the disadvantage of not being able to see in the dark. One dark morning with a torch lying on the 'running board' of the lorry, I struggled with a beet fork, managing to knock the torch off its perch, and needless to say it wouldn't light up again. I made a fresh start and threw a forkful of beet, as I estimated, onto the lorry buck – but it wasn't on course and the beet hit the side window of the lorry and smashed it. You would have thought I had killed someone. 'No wages for you this week, me boy!'

'I couldn't see,' I protested.

We had a sack hung at the window for a day or two, until someone produced a piece of ¼" plywood with an oval hole covered with a piece of celluloid. This was fixed to the winding mechanism and was a good substitute. 'There – p'raps you'll break that one!' said someone.

In the early 1940s coal was becoming more difficult to obtain, and cousin Albert was called up for Army Service. I was fifteen years old, and not able to drive the lorry in practice or legally. Father had never learned to drive. What were we going to do? Drivers were not very plentiful in our locality. Wallace Marshall as mentioned before. Wallace offered his services; he could drive but wasn't very keen on humping the sacks. I was getting stronger and was carrying 1 cwt. sacks most of the time. Was I to be expected to do all the rotten work? 'He'll be an old man before he's a young one,' my ma said to Father.

On the Monday of each week we delivered coal to Stones Green. On the last Monday that Albert was with us he took his chickens in two crates to Thorpe Market on top of the coal sacks. When we got to the council houses, the nearest point to Thorpe, we proceeded from there. I never go to Thorpe without thinking of that day. My world was as black as the coal. My heart was in my boots. Wallace turned up the next morning. He carried a home-made canvas bag with three pints of his brew of beer. We loaded up, after a fashion, and went off to Great Oakley to deliver it. This village was a difficult one to negotiate. There were narrow streets, and a lot of customers had their coal tipped in a cupboard in the living room next to the fireplace. Wallace was about four stone too heavy for nipping in and out of these establishments. He puffed and swore, and tipped coal onto hearth rugs and collided with oil lamp fittings hanging from ceilings. He had frequent swigs at his beer and when we reached the Maybush Inn, he went into the bar for another couple of pints. We somehow reached home again one and a half hours later than normally in doing this round.

Wallace had to make a rapid journey to the nearest lavatory at the station. We had to deliver more coal in the afternoon. He drove home to dinner in the lorry – something I had never done; I always used by cycle. He had two pints of his beverage for this part of the day, and was not very pleasant to be with and so we struggled on, day after day, and gradually the rounds got behind because of the extra time taken, and also supplied of coal were not arriving regularly. Wallace's mother had become ill, and one day he turned up very upset. He had been up all night and smelt of whisky. He should never have been allowed to drive. He complained that his mother had called for him all night and said he was 'b— well fed up with her.' He added, 'I told her that I was finished with her for all further eternity.' He chanted this over and over.

Before loading up that day we had to get our month's ration of petrol. We were allowed 5 gallons a week, and used to go to

Goslings at Manningtree. We had to make the journey specially, for we did not deliver that far out. On the journey Wallace muttered continuously and on the road along the Mistley Walls, which was reasonably straight and wide, he went across the white line and collided with a Brooks lorry coming in the opposite direction. This ripped part of the sides off both lorries. We pulled up and the drivers got out and confronted each other. The opposition said to me, 'This bloke's drunk.' I agreed. We exchanged a few words. I did not really know the procedure. We went on to fill the lorry tank and 2-gallon cans with petrol. The chap in charge said, 'You've got a rum fella here – he's bin drinking, ain't he?' I said I only wished I could drive.

On the way home Wallace continually chanted 'Old Mother bumps, belly bumps! Cock a leg, shake a leg!' Then he would come out with, 'That driver was comin' at me, b— sod! You're old dad will have to be told about this, John boy. That driver is a b— sod... Old Mother bumps,' etc.

The journey was only five miles but it seemed to take hours. When we arrived back in Wrabness, going down past Domine we passed a neighbour (whom Wallace didn't particularly like. He slowed down and shouted through the open window, 'Get out of the b— way, Old Mother guts, guts – greedy guts!'

When Father, who was awaiting us at the yard, saw the broken lorry back, he eyed Wallace up and down and he was visibly shaken.

'What did you say? Did you get the other chap's lorry number and name – and who did the motor belong to?'

I said, 'No, the other chap said he was drunk and I agreed with him.'

'Oh, my Christ,' said Father.

I was afterward told, in no uncertain terms, 'Never admit anything to a third party.

I cannot recall any sequel to this incident so perhaps all parties were 'satisfied out of court'. Wallace was persuaded to go home and sleep it off. He protested that he was all right and that Father was more drunk than he was. An argument ensued and I got on my bike and came home for a few hours until they sorted themselves out.

'I wish I was old enough to drive,' I told Mother. We were getting into a muddle with the coal rounds. The villages were not getting a regular call, and if customers had been left for two weeks they demanded two weeks' fuel, and this of course meant that a load went about half as far as before. So the effect was to make matters worse all the time. Sometimes Wallace would turn up for work, sometimes not. When he didn't we tried to use the horse and tumbril, which was slow and awkward. Father had heard of someone at Lawford who wanted a job, and this chap was to be seen cycling to see Father one Sunday. There was an empty house in the village and it was all arranged to go and move his furniture into it, and he would drive for us.

So Wallace, Father and I went off to collect. The house was one of the land settlement houses. We found the place and the prospective driver. He was about sixty years old and didn't look very active. We loaded about half the furniture into the lorry and various frictions were sparking off. Wallace considered that the new man 'Wasn't any b— good for what we wanted.' There was a good old argument, and Wallace started to take things out of the lorry and put them back into the house.

'Who's the governor around here?' protested the new man.

'I don't know who's governor,' said Wallace 'but I know you won't by any b— good, and we can do without your sort in our village.'

'If the people there are any of them like you, I don't want to know,' said the householder.

Father, who was not usually stumped for words, didn't know what to do next. Though he'd often be the first to shout and swear, he was subdued, and above the confusion said, 'For Christ's sake, shut up a minute. I think you had better stay here – I'm sorry for all this trouble.' He offered the man a £1 note for the upset. So the pieces were put back into the house and we set off home. At Lawford the King's Arms was in sight and the lorry was persuaded to stop. While therein, Wallace said he would carry on working for us and couldn't understand why Joseph had needed to even consider a new driver.

Derek Kidgell was of similar age to myself, and we were quite pally. We went out in the evenings off and on usually to the

Wheatsheaf. He went to work for a local haulage contractor who had several lorries, and some of the older models were in a dilapidated condition. The new recruits to driving were started off on them. Derek was driving 'No. 17' a vehicle that should have been on the scrap heap. It had no floorboards in the cab and the front wings flapped as it was being driven. He maintained that you could drive along the middle of the road until you saw another vehicle coming. The roads were not as congested as they are now, and 30 to 40 mph was about the average speed. If he was proceeding past where I happened to be delivering he would pull out the choke button/control and then turn the ignition key off and on. This resulted in a charge of unburnt petrol and air mixture being present in the silencer, which would be fired when the next lot of hot gases met it with a loud report. He revelled in this caper. It also appealed to yours truly. On one noteworthy occasion the charge of explosive mixture was rather large and it split the silencer. I did not consider it a lot of fun taking it off to get it repaired, sawing rusty bolts and being cursed by Father for wasting time. Poor Derek was soon called up and was taken into the Army Service Corps. He was killed in an accident when his vehicle turned over in rough terrain somewhere in a war zone, I think in North Africa.

In among all the troubles of the coal trade I was still spending any available time in the barn, where I was making a workshop. I even ventured into the realms of teaching woodwork to about five lads, who were several years younger than I. There were schemes afoot to create youth clubs, and through (I think) the Education Committee we were allowed a few basic tools. I encouraged the lads to make toy aeroplanes and railway engines in wood, but this activity was short lived for there was not sufficient room at the only bench I possessed. Father, needless to say, considered this as 'a b— waste of time'. He said, 'You will find out that once your name is written down they've got ye.'

However, Saturday afternoons and Sunday mornings were spent in the barn. I repaired cycles for the remaining lads of my age and various friends. We put new ball races into pedals, new brake blocks, repainted the bikes and generally had a lot of pleasure. We enjoyed the fruits of our labours by tearing around the villages as hard as our legs would go round. I used to get searing hot and go and get a glass of beer from the nearest pub. We would sometimes be several miles away from home at 9.30 p.m. on a summer evening and try to get to Wrabness Wheatsheaf by 10. The War Office was arranging the call-up of the older lads, and soon there were fewer than ever.

Dick Garret and Harold were working at one of the farms in the village, and this was a reserved occupation. Dick wanted me to rig him up another cycle. The one he rode was a very high-frame model. He had a smaller one in his garden. He asked, 'Could you make it up, John boy, so I can turn our for a ride?'

The poor old lad brought it down to me one Sunday morning. Father was going up to the village at about 11 a.m., and as he went out of the gate he found Dick huddled up in the ditch with the frame lying near by. He hollered for me. I came out of the barn and went to the gate and saw the catastrophe. We got into the ditch and tried to move him. This we did.

Dick was dead. We couldn't understand what had happened. Father hopped on his bike and went off to tell Dick's parents. In the meantime Flora came by in the milk van and saw the problem. When she arrived at Dimbols she reported the news, and the soldiers who had a searchlight on the meadow in front of the house came to Domine with a stretcher and put the body upon it and chased back to their site. When Father arrived at Mrs Garret's he found her there alone. Jim Garret had gone to Ipswich to work. Joseph, in his blunt way, simply said, 'Mrs Garret, we've found Dick in the ditch, and I think he's dead.'

The poor woman must have had the worst shock of her life. The post-mortem proved that he died through inhalation of vomit in an epileptic fit. I thought Father needn't have spoken so directly. Couldn't he have said, 'We've found Dick and he has had an accident'?

'Well, blast – I told her the truth, din't I?' was his equally outspoken answer.

There were short visitations by Nazi planes from time to time, and on a sunny day in July one of them dropped incendiary bombs across the village. One fell a few yards from the back of our house into some ripening barley.

'What the hell?' hollered Father.

'That was a near one for the house,' said I and thought briefly of what the result could have been. No one had had much fire drill, but between us we shovelled soil onto the spluttering bomb, and very little damage resulted. We reported the happening to the lads at the searchlight sight and two came and collected the tail fins, which was all that remained.

Father naturally had to have a go at them, and said, 'That een't any good you coming here after the buggers have gone. Blast – they're back in Germany by now! What's the use of gun sites if you don't fire at the sods? England wants to wake up!' he lectured.

The sergeant took little notice, but said that 'Hitler was going to try to burn up our crops by dropping isolated incendiary bombs in ripe cornfields.' There was no recurrence of this as far as I can recall.

In the ballast siding at the station there was a large piece of artillery mounted on a large rail truck. It appeared to be about 6" gun. There were several box trucks standing around and these were not moved when shunting was carried out, so we reckoned they contained ammunition. There was about a score of soldiers in attendance. Our wagons of coal, when we were lucky enough to have any, were placed just anywhere, and sometimes were inaccessible. We were labouring to move one with a pinch bar under the wheels one day, and as things were not going according to plan, Father launched a broadside at one of the lads in khaki: 'Great louts buggering about here! If I had my way you would all be over in France, keeping Hitler from comin' over here.'

He got a rapid reply, and found that the young gent was not a great lout and it was not his wish to be where he was. There were six gun sites around the village apart from the searchlight. They were positioned to protect the RN Mine Depot, which was a store for various types of mines used by the Navy. Explosive bombs did fall around us occasionally, and one fell behind the railway signalman's house and scored a direct hit on his air raid shelter. This was constructed of old rail sleepers. It was sheer luck that the occupants of the house, the Lofts family, were not sheltering in it at that time. I think someone had been ill, and therefore they stayed put in the house.

In the log of the Wix Fire Station there is an entry 24 February 1941: '1.15 p.m.: Mr Carrol phoned giving orders to repair bomb damage at Railway Cottages, Wrabness, as soon as possible in the morning.

Paskell's at Wix was the Auxiliary Station, and they would have carried out the repairs. Over the radio frequently we would have be chastised by the voice of Lord Haw-Haw, who would commence with, 'Germany calling, Germany calling', and pour out propaganda about the strength of his country and our weakness. There is another entry in the aforementioned log, which was probably written by Roger, which runs something like: 'Heard Haw-Haw. I would like him to know we've got a coffin here were keeping for Adolf with Paskell's compliments.'

To my dismay, Father would sometimes agree with old Haw-Haw, and a minor argument would ensue.

My visits to Foxes were curtailed to a great extent after I was engaged all day with humping. Mother and I still went over about once a week in the evenings, and one night we were scared out of our wits. Enemy aircraft were abroad, and tracer bullets were flying about, and we considered it rather foolish to always visit in the dark. About this time an explosive bomb was dropped in Temple Field opposite our barn, and damaged pantile roofs. During that night a piece of shrapnel came through the roof of the garage at the coal yard, went right through the lorry floor and dented the petrol tank. Tubular steel towers carrying steel cables stretched from end to end were erected across arable land with the intention of preventing enemy planes from landing. These were not the least help when preparing land for producing a crop or during harvest, for they were often placed from corner to corner of a field. 'Don't know what good they are,' said Father. 'If the Germans want to land over here that won't stop 'em.'

Gas masks were issued to everyone and we had to carry them at all times. I cycled to Dovercourt one Saturday afternoon, and three miles from home I discovered I'd left my gas mask at home. So I pedalled back home to collect it. Such things became part and parcel of living. We all had identity cards.

The registration numbers and letters became imprinted on one's memory. Ration books were issued, and one thing I remember very well was sweet rationing. I'd swap other items for sweet coupons – a bag of wood logs for a few precious squares of paper. A shopkeeper at Great Oakley obtained a supply of broken chocolate; it cost 5s a pound. I made frequent visits to this establishment; sometimes coupons were not required. The proprietor's wife whenever I went in called me her 'little chocolate drop'!

Wallace was still with us, drinking his usual quota of beer and doing his best to make me a driver. He taught me how to change gear down: 'To change down, rev up,' said he. Every time he did his best to achieve a change without grating the gears. Revving up was part of the double-declutching procedure. When the gear lever was pushed from top to neutral you let the clutch out and pressed the accelerator, pushed in the clutch pedal and engaged the next gear down. Changing from third to second was made slightly more difficult because you had to go 'through the gate'. I got the message eventually.

Driving a vehicle on a delivery round is a very good way to learn to drive. It involves a lot of gear changing and reversing into narrow gateways etc. Wallace said in the police driving test you had to reverse a car in the dark into a garage with a single torchlight at the far end as the only guide to aim at. If he hadn't drunk so much beer, hadn't smoked so much (he smoked Churchman's Counter Shag rolled into cigarettes, which included the dog-ends mixed in), and had washed more frequently and thoroughly, he wouldn't have been too bad. He was very honest with money. We had a leather pocket bag apiece with about £2 float in change and a couple of 10s notes. He insisted on having this counted out in front of Father before we set off on the morning round. When a credit sale was made, he would have this written on the left hand side of 'The Book'; when a payment was made for a debt for goods delivered previously, this was recorded on the right-hand side. By deducting the left-hand total from the value of the goods taken out, after adjustments for any returns, then the right-hand total was added, and the resulting figure should be the amount in the 'till'. Practice and theory did not always work out. Father began to see where the money was coming from and where it was going to. Sometimes there was a discrepancy of a few shillings 'Had we been to the pub?' He had never before worked out the toings and froing in this way before.

The winter of 1940 was cold, snowy, icy and cruel. Some of the hills around us are steep and long. They became sheets of ice. There was no salt spread by the Local Authority then. We tried to use chains, which were not made to fit lorry wheels. They were just a long lengths that were wrapped round the tyres, through the holes in the dished part and secured by a hook. It was not long before the hooks came undone and caught on mudguards, effectively ripping them and straightening out the hook. Everyone needed more coal than they got. We were harassed by customers who were out of coal. Frequently toward the end of the day we would have 4 or 5 cwt. of coal and deliver 1/2 cwt. each to needy folk who had no other means of cooking or heating. I am not sure when fuel was rationed, or rather, a 'maximum quantity that could be supplied' to a householder was specified by the Ministry of Fuel and Power. This was 34 cwt. per year for most of the war years. Customers had to be registered with a coal merchant and for special cases, i.e. illness, or if they cooked by coal. The Local Fuel Overseer, Mr Kemball of Kelar's Tye, Elmstead, would grant a licence for an extra 5 or 10 cwt. per year. The maximum amount was not an entitlement but an amount to be expected only 'if the merchant had sufficient stocks'. But of course, if Mrs X had victoriously done battle with the LFO and obtained a licence for extra', she expected it and that was that. The fact that we had not received our weekly allocation of 15 tons for several weeks, it did not concern her: 'Where's me coal? I've got a Mother here – she's eighty and must have a fire. I'll bet you've got a fire in your house!'

I have a coal price list dated 8th May 1940 for the rural District of Tendring. It lists the following:

Seven varieties and qualities of coal with –
Wallsend at 62s per ton, 3s 2½d per cwt.
down to Kitchen Nuts at 50s per ton, 2s 6½d per cwt.
1st Qual. anthracite at 90s 11d per ton, 4s 8d per cwt.
Coalite at 60s per ton, 3s 7½d per cwt
Coke at 52s 4d per ton, 2s 8½d per cwt.

The prices were not very different from these in 1918. Then, one ton of coal cost £2 according to some old delivery tickets I have. I think our profit was about 15s per ton in 1940. This was gross, and out of this had to come short weight of wagons, turn of scale and some slack from fuel taken into stock. Wallace received around 50s per week, and I got around £2. Farm wages were 30s per week, approximately. Our wages were not too bad. I saved some of mine, and when I got a chance to go to Dovercourt, which was not very often because there was too much work to do, I would buy more tools. Saunders had a good ironmongery shop in the High Street, opposite Woolworths store. I still use several of these tools today. I would go and buy old pieces of furniture from David's, e.g. circular mahogany tables and pine cupboards. I bought a large cabinet, used possibly in a chemist's and used it as a tool store. He came to see me a few days later and wanted to buy it back. 'Give you a profit,' said David, but I didn't sell it back. I learned quite a bit about the construction of various joints and carpentry methods by pulling things to pieces.

Somewhere about the summer of 1940, Mr Nevard, a coal merchant of Little Oakley, was in dire trouble with supplies. He bought his coal from Hill, the coal merchant in Harwich, as he needed it. He did not have a very big yard and had very little stock. He was worried to death. 'Them owd wimmen keep mobbin',' he complained. Father had an agreement with Mr Nevard to buy his round for a ton of coal. We delivered this, and the two gents shook hands on the deal. No document apart from the delivery ticket changed hands. A handshake was a bond between fellows and was looked upon as a deal clinched. Father reminded me that we should have to work to pay off the new purchase. £2 10s was several hours' work. The remainder of the load taken to Little Oakley was to be delivered to the new customers. Most of them had to be satisfied with 1/2 cwt. apart from the two better-class folk who lived in better-class houses, who were deemed to be entitled to 2 cwt. a piece. When someone who had seen us delivering to Mr Nevard's customers and to his house wrote to the LFO, it caused us another battle of words; we duly received an enquiry via the Enforcement Officer, who was keeping a eye on us. He was quite a decent fellow and understood what had happened, but pointed out this was against the rules. A letter followed from the LFO, rapping our knuckles and reminding us of the provision of the Act, 'which allowed 15 cwt. to be delivered from May to October, except where a licence had been issued'.

'Oh, bugger Old Kemball!' said Joseph.

I was often at the wrong end of arguments. The one that defeated me was customers wanting to pay next time round. As we were not delivering very frequently, an amount of 5 cwt. would bring a bill which was often not paid for several weeks or months – and sometimes not at all. Some customers were artful, and if one was, as I was, a bit easy-going, the previous bill was not mentioned by the customer, and I was hesitant to remind him or her that the paperwork got lost in an array of roughly written carbon copies. Joseph tore into the state of debts at intervals when something else had upset the show. I was often in a state of not knowing what to do next, for apart from any other reason I was not yet sixteen years old.

Steam coal was supplied to farmers for threshing with traction engines. It was also used in many farmhouse fireplaces. It was not very nice stuff to handle. When loading up one would pull a large piece out of the rail wagon and put it onto the platform of the scales, then add other pieces to make up the 1 cwt. Sometimes the little stack would collapse before weighing was accomplished, and general swearing, and mutterings would result. Each cwt. was chalked up thus, IIII, to make five. It was simple to see how much you had on board. It was hard, back-breaking work. I'm certain boys of sixteen years today would not do this work. I wouldn't expect them to.

I made friends with Percy Smith, the blacksmith at the crossroads (this was named White Cross on an old map), who plied his trade at the old smithy where Archibald Paskell had worked for many years before. Percy was one of the old school of farriers and smiths, and one of the best. His workmanship was excellent. With the wartime government supporting farming he was getting more work, and would often be working in the shop with the light of two hanging oil lamps and his fire after tea. He was glad of the work. In the 1930s he said he didn't owe anyone any money, but he hadn't got any.

Blacksmith's shop; Percy Smith

'Some farmers would ask, "How much to lay a gang of harrows?" I would quote my price and they would say they could get them done cheaper elsewhere." Sometimes implements were worn down too far before they were brought to me, and the extra labour would be the downfall of the estimate.'

He had been a smith in the 1914–1918 war. 'Before you were accepted you had to pass an exam. We had to shoe a horse, do test pieces of fire welding, and do test pieces of simple design like these.' He showed me the pieces tucked away in a drawer; they were about 3" x 1¼" x ¼" thick. 'These were sawn and filed to fit, and the test by the inspector was to hold them up to the light and if there was any showing through the joint you did not pass. I had a chap on the next forge in the long shed, where there were about twenty forges, who was not very sure of himself. I told him to keep doing his best and I helped him along. The inspectors were pacing along all the time, but I got him through by passing bits to and fro when they were at the far end.'

I have two old accounts of work by his hands for Father in 1929 and 1954:

10th Oct	2 shoes to cob	3s 0d
	fitting new axle key and	
	collar to furrow wheel	3s 3d
	2 shoes to cob	3s 6d
6th Nov	Fitting 2 new plates & bolts	
	to cart shaft	4s 0d
9th Nov	Fitting new pins to van wheel	9d
16th Nov	2 shoes removed cob	1s 8d
17th Nov	2 shoes removed cob	3s 0d
27th Nov	New hook and link to seal,	
	and hook and link to throat band	2s 3d
29th Nov	2 shoes & 1 nailed cob	3s 10d
1st Dec	2 shoes cob	3s 0d
5th Dec	4 staples & nails	8d
13th Dec	2 shoes cob	3s 6d
14th Dec	Horse shoes nailed	1s 6d
18th Dec	2 new hard chisels	3s 3d

Paid to P Smith with thanks Jan 1929

The expense of shoes for the cob seems considerable, but he was used on the road on the coal van and kicked his shoes out quickly.

The account for 1954 is for 12 months and is lengthy, so I will extract some of the most interesting items:

4th Jan	4 Shoes	£1 4s
30th June	Bramble scythe ground	2s 9d
4th Aug	1 waterloo rub	1s 9d
4th Aug	Scythe cranked and ground	2s 0d
15th Sep	120 teeth re-sharpened and repairs to 8 harrows	£5 4s
20th Oct	New set of chains eye bolts and draw eyes and links, fitting up iron whippletree for harrows	£3 15s
17th Dec	Fitting new draw irons & stay & new bolts for tumbril coupling	£1 16s

The total was £16 8s 9d. The item of 120 teeth to harrows is worth mentioning, for this did not work out at 1 shilling a tooth, and the 'New set of chains' were supplied by us, and the 'Iron whippletree' was from the tripods put across the fields with strong stranded wire across the top, to prevent gliders landing in the event of German invasion. It's interesting to observe that the eight harrows and the whippletree were introduced to use with a standard Fordson tractor, and the four shoes in January were the last we needed.

However, back to 1940. There was an ancient lathe in one corner of the old shop. It had a bed about 8' long of two timbers of 5" x 3" dimensions. It had a long foot treadle driving a heavy cogwheel that had been shod with a piece of cart tyre. There would have been room for four feet on the treadle. It was used by Archibald Paskell for turning cartwheels, naves, etc. Father was one whose foot was helping to work the aforesaid one day when there was a small grindstone being whizzed between centres. He was near the tailstock and undid the screw, with the result of course the grindstone became detached and flailed around before the operator's eyes.

'I like you, Joe, but I don't like your nasty way,' Father was told by the venerable Archibald.

I will add a few notes on the method of holding wood for turning. To begin, to anyone not knowing anything about the lathe, it is practically the same as a potter's wheel but working horizontally. Shaping the wood is achieved with gouges and skew-sharpened chisels. One method of securing the wood to be turned is by driving it onto a couple of spikes fixed to the pulley shaft or mandrel.

Another way is with a carrier fixed round the wood by a set screw and a tail engaged with a slot in a faceplate. The latter method was the one used on the old machine at Percy's. There was a large wooden box, with about a score of these in a variety of sizes, capable of holding work from 2" to 14" in diameter. I showed a lot of interest in this lovely old and primitive machine – Would Mr Smith sell it? I went down one evening, walked by moonlight, and asked him.

'No, I shan't sell it,' he said, 'you can have it for nothing.'

I was delighted. I only needed the top pieces, headstock, tailstock and tool rest. I couldn't see how we could get the large woodwork out of its corner. I built a bed to accept the top gear upon it. I used a Morris motor wheel for a flywheel and part of a sewing machine for the treadle to drive it. I spent hours adapting the mandrel to drive work between centres, and to make a faceplate to attach flatwork to, for example when turning bowls and bases etc. It eventually worked very well and I made handles for beet toppers, chisels, candlesticks and handles for scythes. These were made from sallow.

I seem to recall these were called thole woods. I approached our Smith with a view to selling him some, and made a sample pair, complete with a hole through the centre. They could be purchased by him for 6d each, so I didn't make a lot of money, but it was good fun. I've spent many evenings in the barn by the light of a hurricane lantern treadling that old gadget. (Bernard used to call them his 'curious gadjicks'.)

There were mice for company, and an occasional rat scuttling about. One evening I was treadling away and the work jumped out, probably because I dug in too deeply with the gouge, and knocked the lantern over on the bench at the back. The paraffin spilt and I nearly had a fire – the chips and dust were nice and dry.

In the confusion the torch fell onto the floor and I had to hunt about to find it among bits of wood dust cobwebs – and mice. I didn't get a lot of encouragement from Father, but we had an ancient Smyth corn drill which I took to pieces and repaired. This included turning a wooden handle for the winding mechanism on the box. This was spoken of as 'a very good job, boy'.

Back to the smith's shop. We supplied him and other blacksmiths in the area with coal called 'smithy peas' for their forges. This was semi-coking variety. The colliery supplying this, which we had always aimed at, was Barrow. Previously to the war there was no difficulty in obtaining the quality asked for, and without fail, Father would always ask for about a 7-ton wagon, and one would arrive with 8 or 9 tons aboard. But in the 1940s it was not a very important item from the Ministry of Fuel and Power's viewpoint. Our stocks of 'peas' had run out and we pressed for a further wagon. One did eventually turn up with the label 'BARROW COLLIERY' upon it. But the quality of the contents was not up to the standard required. 'It never saw the sky over Barrow,' remarked Percy.

The trouble with poor quality coal for forge work was, and I guess still is, that when pieces of shale or slate are subjected to fierce heat they clinker up and spoil the fire; when the fire was being blown up with bellows to white heat and impurities were present, the work being shaped or welded would not come out clean.

False links were items needed on harness and tumbril chains, and for lengthening short pieces of chain these were a link with one end split to allow a solid link to pass through. I requested two of these of Percy once and when he was shaping, bending the split portions, it appeared to me that they would become welded together. 'It's false links we want,' said I.

Percy continued without looking up or saying anything and very shortly two perfect items were being cooled in the water trough and thrown on the floor at my feet. 'There you are – false is what you've got!' said he, with a look of an artist who just completed a satisfying picture.

One day I was chatting with him and he picked up a harrow tooth and said, 'This is the shape of things to come, I suppose.'

The tooth was a 1/2" coach bolt with the tooth acetylene welded to its head. Percy's were all formed from one piece of iron. 'But,' he continued, 'the strength of work is the decay of trade.'

I concluded that there may have been a feeling of defeat in his mind. Our ancient self-binder was giving trouble one harvest and we asked Percy if he would come and look it over. I watched and assisted him to pull parts of it to pieces, and we sorted out how many new spares would be needed. So off to Joslin's at Colchester I went, and with the help of their many lists and catalogues ordered the bits. These were delivered in due course. So I started to poke around the old contraption and found where the items fitted, and hey presto – we had a nearly new binder.

Subsequently I called at the smithy and Percy asked me, 'Did you ever get the parts for the binder?'

'Oh, yes,' said I, 'and I've put it all together.'

'Oh, have you?' said he. He stopped blowing the fire and came over and confronted me and said, 'Well, the next time you want me to come to Domine Farm to look at a machine, or anything else for that matter, I shan't come! You were glad of my help, weren't you?'

'Oh yes, yes,' said I, moving back a little.

'I suppose you thought you'd save some money, doing it yourself? Well, next time you can get on with it!' he continued.

I was very crestfallen and said, 'I'm sorry... Will you still do work for us?'

'Yes, I'll do work down here, but I'm not running about after you, Mr John, if that's your game!'

There was little more to be said. I told Father about this little episode, and he said, 'Serves you right. I guessed that's what he'd say and I can't blame him.'

I did not worry too much about this. It just taught me not to be too clever. I could see Percy's point of view. I continued to call in either for a chat or with a job and we got on nearly as well as we had previously, but I wasn't quite so sure of myself. He would sometimes tell a few yarns of years ago. He worked for a time at Wix at Tuckwell's forge somewhere near the crossroads. A certain old woman, whose name escapes me, who used to smoke a pipe, would go into the shop and pester the men for a bit of baccy.

Percy was ready for this one day. He had been to the 'hinus' (hen house) and picked up a dry dropping which he crumbed up with a little tobacco and put it aside for later. When she came on the next mission her pipe was readily filled and lit. She puffed her way out of the shop. When she again turned up, on the scrounge, there were no remarks about the flavour of the previous smoke. So someone asked her, 'How was yar larst pipeful – smoke all right, did it?'

'Why, yis, bless you,' she replied, 'that smoked a treat!'

I have a very dog-eared account book which was given me by Roger Paskel, and was I'm sure the book kept by his Uncle Arch. It refers to the years 1913–19. Here we see that on 22nd January 1913, Mrs Robinson of Shore Farm was charged for:

2 Shoes	1s 4d
2 Shoes, 2 removed	2s 0d
New eye & Key and rep	
crotch to cultivator wheel	2s 6d
Mending scraper	4d
Laying coulter	1s 0d
New coulter clasp	3s 0d
New bottom to wagon skid	1s 9d
1 Shoe pony	8d
2 New couplings to trace	2s 4d
2 false links	3d
2 shoes, 2 removed cripple horse	6s 6d

For Mr Tucker of Home Farm, Ramsey:

4 shoes	2s 8d
June 1913: Shepherds Crook	2s 0d
Water Bath, soldered	9d
Shoe steeled, pony	1s 0d
New axle key & collar and stalk laid	3s 6d
New end to scraper to plough wheel,	
2 mattocks laid & steeled.	3s 6d
New grass nail to scythe	6d
New screwed end & Nut and	
funnel to turnip cutter	1s 4d
Ironing up whippletree and	
2 new whippletrees	10s 0d

Dec 1913:

1½ doz. frost nails

2 shoes & screwed holes 2 shoes (Nag) 2 screwed holes, new breast & new land side, new bottom to plough, new scythe complete

3 latches 3 keeps 3 ketches

For J Calver, Post Office, Wrabness:

New set plates, knives and bolts, and repair to root cutter £1
Remove shoe & redress foot of lame horse.

Rev. Miller, The Rectory:

Sharpen 72 teeth to harrows
Soldering kettle
1 pint of oil
Oven peel repaired
Candlestick soldered

There are the usual run-of-mill items, and for January 1913 there are 18 entries, many more than the other customers, for Goddard had many more acres, and appears to have paid very promptly. On Primrose Hill was the Postman's Hut, which presumably was for the rest period due to whoever was cycling round with the mail. It was probably very welcome in the winter time, and when it was raining hard. It appears someone lost the key, for the blacksmith has an entry on 13th January 1913:

The Post Master, Manningtree:
Bursting door open at Hut at Wrabness
Fixing new lock and fitting and repair
door at hut at Wrabness   3s 0d

There is repeated reference to Stockholm Tar through the book. The book consists of many pages and in its entirety has work of this nature.

The smith's work in addition to shoeing work involved many other tasks. A little explanation of some of the names given to the items handled may be of help.

Laying coulter: Means hammer welding piece of steel to worn tip (Coulter was used in horse plough in form first cut of furrow)

New bottom to wagon skid: To skid was a iron shoe introduced under the real wheel of a wagon acting as a brake on hills.

Grass nail: 1/4" diameter piece of iron between scythe handle and blade.

Lath hammer: Tool used for cutting and nailing laths to studwork before plastering wall.

Landside: Was a piece of flat iron at side of plough opposite the breast.

I'm sure that the turnip cutter found its way to Domine, and we used in the barn for many year.

The horse was attached to whippletree harrows by the pummel tree. Also called 'double tree' in some parts of the country.

In another dog-eared book, entitled *The Horse Keeper's Handbook*, there are two recipes using Stockholm Tar, one using:

Refined Mutton Tallow   1 lb.
Stockholm Tar   1/2 lb.
Soft soap   1/2 lb.
Linseed Oil   1/2 lb.

Melt together the Tallow and oil then add the soap and dissolve and lastly the Tar, mixing the whole together. This is a most beneficial dressing for Hoofs that have been much rasped and pared, removing all brittleness growing and expanding the hoof and is a very great measure preventing sand cracks, and a liquid Hoof Dressing with the omission of the Tallow is the same as above.

'Sand cracks' means a division or crack in the wall of the hoof. It usually appears on the inside quarter of the forefoot or on the front of the toe on the hind foot. The treatment was to remove the shoe and cut away the hoof below the crack, and to take the pressure from the crack, replace the shoe. Soak a pad in balsam of oil and bind over the affected part. In bad cases, clamps and rivets are necessary to hold the cracked hoof together.

The reference to 'laying' meant that the worn portion of the tooth or coulter or whatever would be drawn out by hammering and a new piece of mild steel would be welded on by heating two portions to bright red and uniting the hammer blows. The smith would recognise when the colour was right through experience.

'Ironing up pummeltree' means making a collar of iron to fix round the ends and thereby strengthening same. The whippletree was the wooden bar fixed behind the drag chains either side of the horse. When two horses were used, the whippletree was hooked onto the ends of the pummel tree and this to the plough or harrows.

The mattock which was a pick with flat ends, one at right angles to the other, used for cutting tree roots; and trenching cuplons would refer to couplings. 'Furrel' was a ferrule, an iron or brass band, often a piece of brass or steel pipe of small diameter, put on the end of a handle where the tool, a file, chisel or screwdriver entered it. The 'New Grass Nail' was a piece of 1/4" round rod, flattened at one end, with a hole for a screw or nail for fixing to the scythe handle, and a hook at the other end to fix into a hole in the blade.

Percy showed me how to fix up and hang a scythe to suit the workman. You put the end of the handle or stick under your right armpit and the bottom 'thole wood' would be fixed where your hand was. The upper thole was fixed a forearm's length from the first one. The end of the blade that fixed to the stick often had to be heated and set down to suit the hand or rather the height of the user. When he, holding the two tholes, put forward his right leg, his boot toe should touch the tip of the blade. The 'bail' was a device either similar to a wooden rake only with three long teeth, or simply a curved piece of chestnut or similar tied to the stick, and when used for cutting corn the bail laid the cut corn in a neat row.

In the smith's shop lurked other odds and ends. There was a very long and heavy muzzle-loading gun of large bore. The butt had stood so long upon the damp floor that the bottom couple of inches had rotted away. What would be now described as an eighteenth-century chair with curved back and arms, which was where it was because it was for 'the lame and or lazy', stood in among all sorts and shapes of lengths of iron. Hung on its back was a waistcoat, the front of which was of a beautiful green material, and was once surely owned by an aristocrat. Nearby was a drilling machine covered in dust with what seemed to be a dozen gear wheels. The drills were pre-high-speed steel twist drills, and simply flattened at the business end and ground to cut. It had no chuck; the drills had shanks all the same size with a flat and a set screw registered on it. Percy had a quite modern drill and later a threading machine. The old drill was a collector's item. Behind the forge and its huge bellows were bottles of wine; some Percy had made and some he had not. Sometimes one of these would be broached and the world looked a little rosier.

On Primrose Hill, in the old thatched cottages, lived Mrs Pitches and her son, Ernest. He was not exactly sound mentally. He walked his dog round the village every day. Some folk, whom he approved of, he would stand and talk to; if he disliked anyone would hustle away, muttering. He frequently would be in Percy's shop, working the bellows, and never spoke to anyone. His mother was almost always dressed in black but was a cheerful creature: 'I don't care if it snows,' she would say. When Ernest told you a little news he would say, 'Keep it dark! Keep it dark!'

The Smithy was not just a place of work; it was a meeting place for men of the village. The smell of burning hooves when shoeing, the fierce glow of the hearth... Its closing was the end of an era, and left a great gap that was never filled.

Wallace was still driving when it suited him, until the January of 1942. I was very occupied in these days and my visits to Foxes were not as frequent as they had been. However, on one occasion when I was there and Cecil said, 'I reckon Tater Marshall's a-getting tired of his job by now.' I said he wasn't too unhappy. It so happened that he wasn't far out. A few days later Wallace said he thought I should be driving and he had had enough of the 'bloody coal trade – and of most of the customers!' With the prolonged winter, work on the land was at a standstill, and Father had been speaking to our neighbour, Edgar Garnham. He agreed that we could hire one of his men to drive for us. Percy, Flora's brother, came along within a few days, and what a difference he made. He was strong and willing and we began to get on with the job. The weather was cold and had its usual problems – when we were stuck with a long carry where the lorry could not be got to on an unmade road, for example.

Five cwt. had to be delivered. We would each take 1 cwt. on opposite shoulders, and carry a 1/2 cwt. between us on the unoccupied arms. This operation accomplished twice would amount to the 5 cwt. He encouraged me to drive more, and I began to get fairly good at handling the old bus. We set ourselves time limits and would weight up 60 cwt. in an hour. We had a few leg-pulls; on 1st April we pulled up outside the smith's shop and Percy said, 'Smithy wants to see you.' So in I went. Oh dear, what a fool!

Sometimes when we were following one another and had to go through a gate, whoever was first through would pull the gate closed just in front of the other; but all this was short-lived, and when the weather improved my mate had to go back to farming.

There was no one around to help us at all, so Father had to forget about pigs and horses and come on the coal rounds. He had never been out on the lorry to any extent and was surprised there were so many customers, and at their attitudes towards us. I was driving regularly now and applied for a licence to drive and was granted one on the 22nd July 1941, aged 16½. Father seemed to enjoy the experience, and could see some of the problems with rationing and with customers' inability to pay, for sometimes genuine reasons.

He was suffering with hip trouble and we took on Geoffrey Peck, who lived in Ramsey. He was around sixty years of age and really not up to the strenuous work of handling coal. He didn't stay with us very long, but long enough to get his name in the paper. In Great Oakley one morning a lady who was not on our register came to our loaded lorry and tearfully said she had a junior member of her family ill, and she had no fire and no coal. Geoffrey said, 'I'll soon alter that.' He took a cwt. to her house. One of our customers living next door wrote to the LFO telling him of this, and this resulted in the Enforcement Officer seeking us out. He confronted us some days later and after several swear words extracted a signed statement from Geoffrey, countersigned by me. So in due course off we had to go the Mistley Court held at the Police Station, and were both fined £1 for the offence – Geoffrey for committing, and I for aiding and abetting.

We did not offer him any compensation for his misfortune and this added to the friction. He was rather obstructive with customers, and some complaints reached Father's ears. One day Geoffrey and Uncle Ted had a skirmish after an argument, and Geoffrey was asked to leave.

I was taking more interest in running the business, and a friend loaned me a book entitled *Rational Bookkeeping*, and I taught myself the old double entry systems. I brought some account books in half calf binding and when Father saw the price he complained. I was sorting out the week's takings and spendings once, and it didn't balance. I asked Joseph if he had taken cash, and how much.

'Huh! If I want some money, I shall take it. You and your books! David Marshall used to say if you keep books you've never got any money. He kept all his accounts – as you call 'em – in his head!'

It was not very long before the Inland Revenue wanted more precise details of our goings-on. We had to employ an auditor. Through recommendation, we asked David Bennett to officiate. He thought I had done well to learn as much as I had. I had done a reconciliation statement between bank and books, and got praise. But not from Father, for he maintained that without all these figures the tax man would not have known half as much as they did, and we wouldn't have had to pay as much tax. I said to Mr Bennett that I didn't consider we were making a lot of headway in money terms. He looked through some recent figures and said, 'But you and your father can draw £8 per week!'

There was supposed to be an advantage in making the business a partnership. And with little ceremony, it became JW Calver & Son. We both had authority to sign cheques with the other's knowledge. Neither of us took advantage of this, probably because we knew there was very little money in balance.

Great Oakley was an interesting village. It was almost self-supporting. There was a bakery owned and run by FJ Baxter, next to the bakery and Tom Ball's blacksmith shop. Essex House was a grocery shop owned in the 1940s by a Mr Eastaugh. These people used to deliver groceries to the surrounding district and we were among their customers. They managed to deliver all through the war years and had to stop in the 1960s, through economic pressure. In fact it was owned by two different people in the latter years. Along the main street a little further and standing back from the road was Swan Yard, and at one time a pub, The Swan, stood here. Then next to this was the post office and a saddlery and harness repair shop. Billy Blowers was postmaster for about sixty years. He was barely 5' tall and was a Methodist lay preacher and used to stand on a stool in the pulpit. The story was that once he was saying, 'For a little time thou shalt see me, and for a little time thou shalt not see me,' and promptly fell of the stool. He was deaf, and made a continuous nasal noise a kind of humming, that came out as 'new, new new' noise. At the time of Chapel anniversaries he did his best to rehearse a certain hymn and would keep up the dirge all day long.

Mr Barker was the saddler, and in addition to harness repairing he cut hair and repaired shoes. Opposite him there was a wheelwright's shop owned by Philip Smith, who lived at Malting Farm and was also the undertaker. The farm was a dairy and customers came to collect their milk in jugs.

Just before Malting Farm was Ted Chester's pub and general store, named The Maybush Inn. You could buy boots, overalls, wool and working clothes here. On one occasion when we called with coal and a half-pint and our cheese sandwiches, our venerable landlord addressed us: 'Hello, Calver, what have you got for me today – flyaway or hellfire jack?' He had his leg horizontally placed on a chair. He was suffering from gout.

'Have you got something wrong with your foot?' I asked.

'Well, you can see it ain't anything wrong with my head!' he replied acidly.

Access to the yard behind the pub was through two large wooden doors. They had seen their best days and did not swing on their hinges very well, in fact they had gouged out a deep furrow in the ground by being opened with some difficulty for several years. He had chalked upon them in large letters:

John E Calver, driver of coal lorry, 1945

LIFT THESE GATES DO NOT DRAG THEM.

In the yard stood a carrier's horse-drawn van. It was laid out inside with racks and shelves and in nice flowing lettering said, Millinery Silks cotton Etc. On the headboard and on the outside was boldly signwritten 'Mitchell's Service Van'. It was in reasonable condition, but over the years gradually fell to pieces. There were two ends of a Victorian bed in one of the sheds, and I offered him 10s for them.

'What the hell are you talking about? I don't know what things are coming to! They are worth £1 of anybody's money,' he retorted. So I left them. Several years later he sold them to me for...£1.

On another occasion his wheelbarrow stood under the bar window bearing the caption, 'Don't lend your barrow, look what happened to mine'. It had a broken shaft.

There were two other grocery shops, one selling hardware and a milliner, RW Hooks, kept the garage and looked after the district with a motor coach service. He ran regular services to Colchester and Ipswich and was carrier also. In the garage there was a magneto fixed to the bench coupled to and driven by a hand grinder, and used very successfully to test spark plugs. I went in there one day to borrow a spanner.

'Yes, you can have it – come back in a few minutes, we've got to find it.'

So I took a few more bags of coal to someone and I returned. I picked up the spanner and yow! – it was alive – one of the lads had wired it to the mag and gave it a whirl just at the right moment! All the chaps working there were very good mates, and one always looked forward to going there.

The provender mill was run by HG Overend. The brick round house of the old windmill stood in front of the building that was the mill proper. The round house still contained the massive crosstrees and the struts supporting what was left of the huge post that had supported the buck of the windmill. This old landmark was burned out in July 1948. At the back of the mill was a tall brick chimney that served the steam raising equipment. This was redundant, and the motive power was electricity! We sometimes took a few bags of barley to be ground into meal and oats to crush for feeding the bullocks. I've mentioned Mr Baxter, the baker, and he was a first-class one. We supplied him with coal and he of course was allowed extra coal for the baking. This was sent under licence, and on the first wagon received was a label with the words 'Quasi domestic'. This unusual term was alien to Father, and to me for a matter, although I suggested it was not for domestic use. The dictionary would have told us: 'A prefix implying appearance without reality, sort of.' We just bagged it up and delivered it as we would have done any other wagon, but customers badly needed coal and got in touch with us. We had no telephone and contact was made through Aunt Grace at the post office.

'Oh, bugger old Baxter,' said Joseph. 'He'll have to wait – we're short.'

So FJ had a word with the Fuel Overseer, who told him we had or would have a wagon of coal for bakery use. Oh dear, what a to-do!

Father cursed, and so did the baker. We finished up going to Ardleigh Station and picked up 2 tons from Moy's yard. This was picked up off their ground stock. It was dusty and not good quality – 'It's a waste of your time and my money,' was the remark from our customer. He wasn't far out!

Queen Street was a very narrow road and there was just room to get the lorry through. Everyone who lived there had their coal brought through the front door and mostly tipped into a cupboard next to the fireplace, or in one or two cases it was carried through the house and tipped at the back. One elderly lady had hers tipped into a shed with a corrugated iron roof. She was in there one day discussing with Joseph the lack of coal and the inability of Calver to remedy the matter, and I lobbed a lump of coal onto the top of the roof from next door. It made a lovely clatter. The lady jumped out of her skin. My customer saw my action and abruptly told me that she couldn't spare any of her coal ration to make people laugh!

In some cases, when you got behind a house there were numerous back yards and small gardens, linen lines and sheds. It was quite easy to tip coal into the wrong coal house, for there didn't seem to be any boundary that fitted any pattern. In a few cases someone would be registered with us and have their mother living with them and register the other with another merchant, thus getting 'two rations'. This causes arguments between neighbours and letters to the LFO. I was beginning my education. I soon learned that politics were taboo. You must agree with everyone. I did my best to say the right thing. When someone's relatives had died it was very difficult because I probably did not know them. If I said, 'We've all got to come to it,' the answer may have been 'Well, he was my father.' If I said, 'She was a pleasant person,' perhaps the reply was, 'You didn't know her.'

Once I asked a lady, 'How old are you?'

The look she gave me made me draw back a step. 'You never ask a lady her age!' she replied.

E Keeble farmed at Great Oakley Hall, and I have heard it said that during the early years of the century he employed fifty men. I recall we carted 6 tons of fertiliser from Wrabness Station to his farm and the governor was poking his stick into his men's ribs and backs to hustle them up while unloading at the farm. A few years after the time encompassing my story, a Welsh miner and his wife came to live in Queen Street. His name was Ezra Edge. He was very much left of centre politically, and when I heard some of his previous life I could see why.

He told me, 'The mine owners treated us like dirt. Where we sometimes needed four pit props we were allowed three, roof falls occurred and men were injured. I have been present at a post mortem and seen a miner's lungs cut through with a saw; they were packed full of stone dust. There was no compensation. I became a trade unionist from the beginning.

There was not a lot that I could say; his wife was stabbing sausages with a very sharp fork. On one occasion a General Election was in the offing. I did not argue with them a lot but they knew I was not a socialist. The good lady said, 'I shall pray to God tonight to give you a little sense before next week and tell you to vote Labour!'

On our next visit she said, 'Did you have any sense given you?'

I replied, 'I was on the phone to heaven recently and was told to please myself, and that God had leanings to the Right!'

The ensuing looks and verbal onslaught were enough to upset your system for a few minutes. It was quite understandable that the old wounds were never healed, and I could see why trade unions came about.

Ezra toured the village canvassing for the Labour Party.

In those days there were always several children around the villages. They were a bit of a nuisance climbing up on the lorry, interfering with empty sacks and taking pieces of coal from sack to sack. The fun for them was the ride between houses. Great Oakley was one of the worst villages for this. We were at Sparrows Corner one afternoon and unloaded. 'Give us a ride – give us a ride!' they chanted.

'Okay, hop on,' said I. We took on about six or eight and we came home through to the Soils bridge and there stopped. 'There you are,' said I, 'now walk home.'

'Rotten old sod!' and suchlike were the retorts, and off they had to go, trudging back about a mile. This did have the effect of stopping their capers to some extent.

Stones Green was one of the little hamlets that hadn't changed for centuries. The first call was Mr Finch at Kiln House. There were the remains of a brick kiln behind the house but it was very overgrown with elder and nettles. The boundary wall was constructed of peg tiles laid in batches of four and bonded like bricks, and various sizes of land drainpipes were put in at intervals and capped with large semicircular bricks. In the old shed where we tipped the coal was a model boat about 24" long. I asked the old gent if he would sell it. 'Well, yes,' he replied. 'How much?'

'I reckon tha's worth £2,' I told him.

I bought it to find that the hull tacked over the ribs was cardboard, which of course went soggy soon after it was put in water: that was another write-off.

At the general store and post office lived the Goldsworthy family. Miss Rose looked after this little establishment. Rationing did not go down very well. She wasn't used to coupons, and was usually harassed by some problem. Her sister had been married and her brother was a bachelor. There seemed a lot of friction within the house, especially regarding the coal supply, for they were not used to being short of coal.

In a lath and daub house called 'Willow Cottage' lived three tenants. This place was in a bad state of repair. Mrs Morgan lived at one end. She was a large lady and had several in her family. 'I wish my old man could win the football – my poor little kids are a gooin' about with their shoes done up with self-binder.' She meant string. The house had no sink inside, and a table stood outside the back of the house with an enamel bowl on top and a bucket of water beneath. A small piece of soap on a saucer, a scrubbing brush and a flannel completed the scene. In winter the flannel was frozen if it was not taken in at nightfall. In the middle let lived 'Shrimp' Budds, one of the labouring chaps. Old Shrimp used to holler. Sometimes he would visit the Black Boy, and if Father was there (which he frequently was), Shrimp would shout, 'Hello Joe, what you gooin' to hev?' and get excited.

The landlord, Chas Boggis, would decline to serve him, assuming he had been on the booze, but Father would pour oil on troubled waters and tell Chas, 'It's about time you knew him – he's as sound as a bell.'

One day I called on him and he was very distressed. 'I can't howd me water, mate. Tell Joe, won't ye, tell he I shan't be about there much longer.' He was soon to be found in Tendring Hospital, and did not survive many days.

At the other end of the cottage lived Mr Piddock. He was an old sailor and kept himself and his crumbling house in spotless condition. He frowned if I spilled any coal on the floor when tipping it in his cupboard next to the kitchen range. This was one of those where 1/2 cwt. were essential, for the door was only 15" wide. I'm not sure if these folk had their own well. If not, they would have had to fetch water from the communal well at Well Cottage, a distance of about 50 yards. This ancient apparatus had a windlass and chain permanently affixed to the bucket, and you filled your bucket from this. On toward Great Oakley was Rose Cottage (there were several of these in the village). It had an enormous thickness of thatch – must have been 2' at the back, where we found the coal house, which was protected by the overhang of the thatch. The lavatory was nearby. It was one of the few left that had a large brick-lined pit covered on the outside by a lid of weatherboards. No one had to ask what it was that ponged in the hot weather.

Further on we found Brook Cottage, which was on a corner of the road and by the brook that flowed from near Houbridge Hall, where there was a lake or pond. Brook Cottage was flooded sometimes after very heavy rain. Up the little hill you gazed upon a large thatched house which was named the Barn Houses, pronounced 'Housen'. In fact it had been a barn in the earlier part of its life. There were three or four tenements. The first one we called on was Mr Hynard. He was a wistful old chap, short and fat. He lived there with his daughter; she was rather unbalanced. She used to walk to the well across the road for a bucket of water with her frock tucked into her bloomers, to the amusement of onlookers. The old lad was large and whiskered, and during cold windy weather he would poke his head round the half-opened door when I had shot his coal ration into a part of the back of the house used as a coal cellar, and holler, 'How much am I owin'?' I wasn't sure what it was that he was trying to say. 'Why, how much is your bloody coal? This cowd weather had gone right through me and bin klinced the other side.'

The centre tenement, which actually was part of one of the midstry, i.e. the portion of the old barn that is a kind of large porch attached to the main part of the barn, lived Bert Howard. He was a thatcher by trade and had several tools. I traded half a bag of coal for one or two small wooden planes. He had fixed a piece of a magnet into a handle and demonstrated using it with a nail held at right angles. As a hammer it worked very well (I recently bought the modern equivalent for tacking upholstery). 'Tha's like living in a wire nettin' house – I'm baked a one side and frooz tuther,' he said. He once offered me a piece of apple pie. It had a very thick crust; I declined the offer. 'That won't poison you,' he said, feeling a bit put out. He said of his father, 'He used to put his religion back in its box on a Sunday evenin' when he packed his best suit away.'

I enquired about how he managed to survive. 'I git an owd pigeon and a rabbit now and agin,' he said. He survived until about 1976, when I heard of his death at Tendring Hospital aged 90 plus.

A few more yards towards Great Oakley was a brick cottage occupied by the Stannard family. One of their number used to deliver religious tracts around the area. They had their coal put in a cupboard next to the fireplace. The walls in the living room were covered in pictures of relatives and various scenes from the Scriptures, sepia landscapes and moonlit churches with snow around. I counted thirty on one side of the room once.

Back towards Wix abided two maiden sisters who earned their living by taking in laundry. They carried the water they required in pails from a well quite a distance from their house and boiled linen in a copper in the 'backuss' (back house). The clean items were ironed with the old box iron, the bits of which were heated in the large cooking range fire. Coal was as essential to them as to the baker. Slate in it was a bane, for they needed a bright fire to keep these pieces of iron hot. Their hands were lily white and the skin was wrinkled by the constant immersion in water. Their finished product – 'as white as the driven snow' – was despatched in cases with a leather strap around them and collect by RW Hooks. Without doubt it was a hard-won living, all on a piecework basis, of a set sum per garment or sheet. They had a licence for extra coal and were allowed 5 cwt. per month in addition to the usual three. We were usually owing them several cwt., for we often hadn't got this amount to supply. Frequently we had to quote the conditions: 'The extra amount granted you by this licence can only be supplied if your merchant has sufficient stock.' We were being offered an occasional wagon of opencast coal. This was a new source of supply and very unreliable. Some of it was slatey and hard. The two ladies just described were the recipients of some of this once or twice. 'We want kitchen nuts like we used to get when Mr Harvey was on the lorry,' I was told. So I felt that they thought most of the problems were of my making. I ventured to say that there was a war on, but the remark did not seem to make any difference.

Tom Balls was the blacksmith at the old shop near the bakery. Next to the shop was the house occupied by his mother a short lady and very pleasant. I think his father owned the shop before

Tom came to be the smith. The children (or some of them) used to run through the shop on their way to school, in the little door and out of the traverse door. 'Hello Tom!' they called on their little bit of enjoyment. Tom was short and stocky. Shoeing horses always seemed to be difficult and hard for him. I'm sure he did not ever charge enough for his labours. He'd say, 'I'll pay you, John, as soon as I get some of me bills in. Some on 'em don't seem to come in very quick.'

He had a very up-to-date drilling machine driven through flat belts by an electric motor. 'I come back from dinner the other day and old so-and-so was using it. I shall have to put a shilling on his bill for the use of it, I doubt, wouldn't you? Well, I shall have to think about it. I can't stick it.' He would always have time for a few friendly words. 'Time is money,' someone told him once. 'Well, there must be five minutes,' said Tom. If the weather was snowy and perishing he would 'slide off for a cup of tea' and down to the marshes with his gun.

We proceed through Great Oakley, turn left at Sparrows Corner and then pas the Soils Cottages, turn right, and at Salt Water Bridge there was a cottage that was subject to flooding when the stream overflowed. The stream was tidal many years before, and ran into the Stour and obviously the water was salty up to that point. Mill Pond Farm was nearby where the water accumulated to turn the stones of the water-mill that stood further toward Ramsey. This is clearly shown on Chapman & André's map of 1777. Ernie Overmoss was the owner of the cottage, which he had bought for probably £100 or so. He would repair it and then sell at a profit. He was carpenter, bricklayer, plasterer. When he needed to read he took spectacles off and turned them back to front. He was wanting wood to build a glasshouse. He had a number of metal doors with the top glass missing and intended to put a sash within this oblong. He had some willow logs cut down a year or two before and asked me to take them to Paskells to be ripped up. I queried the value of willow for this job. 'It will last as long as I will.'

I did as he requested, and eventually brought it back, converted. Next time round he was to be found in his workshop in among the orchard trees, making up the frames, all by hand –

how I envied him, with his feet covered in wood shavings! This construction lasted many years and it was well made. I talked to him at length about building and he mentioned the brick kiln across the field. We went over there one day with snow underfoot and there arrayed before my eyes were red bricks with patterns cast on them, and cornice and corner ones – just what I needed. So I put some into a bag and lugged them to the lorry – and I knew I'd got them by the time I got there. The newly formed ranks of the Home Guard were using the old place for target practice and it was soon broken to pieces. Upon arrival home I put my prizes out of sight on a shelf in a shed at the coal yard, to find a few days later that the wormy old shelf had collapsed and half the bricks were spoiled.

Further up the hill at the Rectory lived the Rev. Cecil Redgrave. He was as poor as a church mouse. He cycled everywhere; a car was out of the question. The Rectory is a lovely Georgian house with a well staircase. While delivering to him one day we found him confined to bed, and he called me up to see him. I climbed the stair. He barely had the necessities of life. The house was as cold as a fridge. There was a candlestick on a chair beside the bed. There was no carpet on the floor, not even a mat beside the bed, but scattered all around the chair there were hundreds of spent matches. In later years he would play the piano to us. A little interlude on a summer day was nice. 'The Bees' Wedding' was a favourite of his, and he was quite accomplished. He had few friends. Among his enemies was Wallace, and he compared him to the Rector of Stiffkey, about whom Wallace was well versed. When the Rev. appeared in the village on his cycle, sometimes wearing a wellington on one foot and a soft slipper on the other. Wallace would chant, 'Davidson – will not – Lyon – Rose Ellis – anymore!' According to him these names were associated with the case of the misunderstood Rector of Stiffkey and were thus arranged for maximum impact. I see that in one of our ledgers of 1942–43 we delivered him 2 cwt. of coal per 14 days at a cost of 3s 4d per cwt. A cheque on 29th December for £2 10s left him owing us a balance of 12s 5d. It was 5th April before he managed to pay us a further £2 5s. To survive in a large house with 1 cwt. of coal per week during cold weather in these days would be unthinkable. Central heating in the 1940s was for the wealthy. I knew of two residences in the area with such a luxury, although I doubt if the owners could obtain anything like enough fuel to run them.

Down the Back Road lived the brothers Marchant – Dozey and Ted. One of them worked at Goddard's at Poplar Hall and walked across the fields by footpath every morning and back at evenings. I'm not sure which was which, but one of them had an unfortunate appearance. His face was long and he looked a bit like a horse. The house they lived in was behind some others, and I think at one time their sister had a small shop there. When one or other of them ran out of bread or some other commodity there was no sharing. The lucky one would eat whatever he had and his brother had to go hungry. When one of them died sitting upright in a high-backed chair, the other did not realise his brother was dead, and he stayed in that position for several days until someone intervened.

Around this time we were very short of coal bags. The Jute Control, Dundee, were not very helpful, and allowed us fifteen new bags each year.

I heard of some second-hand ones at Thorpe-le-Soken, and one day called at the gent's house who knew of them and we went off to look at them. The vendor nearly jumped for joy when I offered him £4 for them. My informant would have like to have been thought of as a friend of the vendor's daughter. He suggested we should have some tea. Whoever was assisting me I cannot quite recall; he and I were black with coal dust, but we sat around the kitchen rather awkwardly and drank tea under the protesting looks of the lady. When we arrived home I had a good look at the bags. They were absolute rubbish, not one of them was any good. They had been patched over patches and 'pussed up', as Father called it.

'You want to wake up, mate, buying muck like that,' he observed. He didn't ask how much I paid for them; I'd have told a lie if he had.

Some cottages had a fry pan hanging outside on the weatherboards. They were not washed out and had a lump of fat adhering to the wall with drips running down from it where it hung. In some cottages you couldn't find room to put the change on the table, for it was so full up with items used to support the needs of the family. The bath used at the weekend and the smaller ones used for washday were hung on any convenient nail on sheds or the back of the cottage. One had its coal store next to the lavatory in the same 'back house'. The loo's door had a broken hinge and it hung askew partly across the corner where the coal was stored, making the job more difficult. In the summertime one didn't stay in there any longer than absolutely necessary. 'Old Partner' Rush was a dealer and a little on the artful side. I liked the look of a brass-bound coal box that stood in an outhouse. Was it for sale?

'Why, yes, Johnny, I should think so,' said he with expectation. 'How much?' said I.

'How much durst you give, Johnny?' he taunted.

I suppose this had the desired effect, for I reacted in a way that this phrase was a challenge. 'Three pounds,' I ventured. 'Well, yes, that's very fair,' said he.

Later he offered me a revolver and two cartridges. 'They're little dears,' said he. It was a .45 by Pryse of London, and in good order. This was never used, for I attempted to convert it to take 9mm garden gun cartridges and of course failed. Eventually I took it to the police station during one of the amnesties that were organised a few years back. (In 1994 I sold the coal box for £80.)

At Wrabness, there arrived another schemer by the name of Fred Lane. His game was similar to that of Overmass, and he bought the old Thatch Cottage in Main Road for £75. This is now named Malkins Coat (it should be 'cote'), as this was its name way back in 1656 when a manorial survey was carried out. He was an engineer by trade, but was equally proficient as a carpenter, bricklayer etc. He was an expert faker. He opened up two fireplaces in that ancient place and, having a collection of ancient wooden brackets and panels etc., he made these look even older and more genuine that they really were. I visited him frequently; in fact I should think I was a pest. He took me into his confidence and demonstrated some of his methods. He said, 'Precast concrete blocks and sections are going to be the building materials and methods of the future.' He had made moulds to produce different sizes and patterns of blocks, some for walls, some for window sills, and a very large and difficult one for making a hollow section for building a chimney. This, when full of semi-dry cement, would have to be turned over and lifted off. He had rigged up a device in a frame to effect both these operations. He also excelled in making small decorative lozenge, hexagonal, round and diamond shapes in cement from moulds. Some were florets; Chinese lions, and grotesque images would form some of the collection. These would be planted into wet plaster in between studwork and on outside walls.

I fell in love with the whole idea. He gave me a few books; among the more interesting ones were *Lord Bacon's Essays* and *From the Earth to the Moon* by Jules Verne. The former was the first classic to come into my hands and its contents seemed to be very deep and I felt I was in distinguished company. Fred also owned two motor cars; one was a Singer, probably about 8hp. I could have bought them for £5, each but Father didn't think I was ready for a car. I guess she was thinking I would spend too much time travelling away from work (in it); perhaps it was a blessing in disguise, for one of them was bought by a neighbour who managed to get it on the road after a lot of work. It had a rather unpleasant habit of jumping sideways when driven over 25 mph.

In our 'front room' was a Victorian semicircular throated cast iron fireplace. I fancied building a brick front and hearth and pulled out the rather monstrous old thing. Now this is where the bricks were to be used that I salvaged from Great Oakley. On its front on either side are displayed two 6" square red bricks with a pattern of leaves. Fred made me the keystone in red coloured cement and put a fleur-de-lys upon its front. I had sufficient cornice bricks to make the mantelshelf. It was lovely fun, and it's still steadily burning coal and wood to keep us warn on cold winter nights.

Farming was now being looked upon through different eyes. This has happened many times for the past few hundred years when a country is at war. Many small farms had become run-down. Fertiliser use was not understood by the majority of older farmers. Muck was the usual method of feeding crops. Lime, or chalk, as it was known then, was rarely used, and not at all by Uncle Bernard.

The old lore of 'Lime and lime with no manure, makes farmer rich but his son poor', may have persisted. The War Agricultural Committees were 'poking their noses into whatever was going on, 'and reclaiming dormant acres to grow crops to feed a nation suffering from shortages of food. 'Bloody old C and another article jist outa college has been here looking about,' said Cecil.

The eventual result of these perusals was a directive that several loads of chalk were needed at Foxes Farms for unproductive acres. 'I een't a-goin to have that dam stuff about here,' said Uncle Bernard in conversation with Father.

'You want to go along with what they say for a start, Bunny,' said the latter.

'No, that I shan't – never! Why, where that chalk come from there een't nothing grow at all!'

A lorry load of the splendid stuff was delivered to the farm. Bernard addressed the driver with the following definite ultimatum. 'If you bring any more of that bloody stuff here I shall shoot you!'

It was said with malice and the driver was not going to risk the possibility of Berny carrying out the threat.

The gents from the 'War Ag', as it became known, called and tried to reason with him – but to no avail. There is not doubt that this organisation did an enormous amount of good work. Thousands of acres of derelict land were brought back to production. Small armies of men were engaged on cutting hedges, clearing ditches and clearing scrub and small trees from neglected fields. The price of wheat per ton in 1934 was £4 16s 8d. In 1939 it was £5, and in 1941 was £14 13s 4d. How anyone could make a living in the 1930s in agriculture is a mystery; there was no money to put back to build up the business.

Quite what powers were given to the War Ag that enabled it to turn a family out of their farm and not only the farm but out of their house as well is still beyond me, but this is what they did. Poor old Aunt Lily sat near the kitchen range trying to make a little butter in a screw-topped jar by shaking the cream it contained. She was distraught; she had developed cataracts in both eyes and was living in a twilight world. The ulcerated legs had not healed. Her clothes were drabber than ever. Cecil was in a state of remorse and in a cloud of stunned silence. They were all beside themselves. This was the death knell to an old farming family. 'They can't do it. They can't turn us out of our house, can they?' my poor old aunt managed in such a sorry tone. Mother was in a state of disbelief; she didn't know what things were coming to. One end of Spring Cottage was to be their home for the next few years. Where they would have gone to if they had not owned that small place I've no idea. Of the documents that were drawn up to effect their removal, I've equally no idea.

Horses were harnessed and coupled to wagons, and between them the furniture and chattels were moved to the new abode. There was much more than could be comfortably accommodated and it was just stood round the walls barely leaving room for the table and chairs. Bernard assembled a rough shed of corrugated iron at the end of the triangular garden, where he spent some of the daylight hours. He even had the old lathe installed at the back. The Titan tractor was towed up to the Firs and soon broken up for scrap. Other items were stored at Butlers Farm. What happened to the horses and cows I've forgotten – probably taken to the sale yard.

Foxes Farm was hired to LT Hinnel, 'who was making a good job of farming' – and to pile the agony on even more, a family of gypsies were soon occupying the house. What use the husband was as a farm labourer was questionable. He made pegs from the plentiful willows around. His wife produced a second child, and its cradle was an orange box lined with a curtain. Father remarked in no uncertain terms to the new tenant that 'the unthatched corn stacks that had green corn growing upon their roofs were a disgrace, and he'd never seen this at Foxes before'. In an ironic way Bernard had a kind of new-found independence, for he was paid a rent for Foxes and there were a few £1 notes to be seen at Spring Cottage. I delivered the meagre coal allowance at intervals, and Bernard supplemented this with the 'daily ration of wood' – hand sawn, of course.

Along with the furniture that went to the cottage was an Edwardian compactum that could not be housed because of its size, and it was stored in the shed. I was attracted to its pleasantly carved door panels. It also had a little sentimental attachment, for within its confines the various cartridges, some of which I used to borrow, were stored. One day I asked Bernard if he would sell it.

'How much will you give me?' said he.

'Fifteen pounds!' I replied.

'You're a gentleman, Jack,' said a surprised uncle.

It was really worth about a couple of pounds. It lay around in its damp shed for several years and suffered. When I collected it was not really any use at all; in fact, forty years later I've still part of it in the barn, unused. However, the money helped to provide him with a few pints of beer to pass away the days.

Butlers Farm, mentioned in the Manorial Survey of 1656 as 'A messuage and tenement with appurtenances seven and twenty acres. Three acres of meadow and three acres of woodland called Butlers' had been farmed by Uncle Lewis' and was in fact owned by him through the inheritance in his father's will. He scraped up a living there working very hard. I recall him losing pigs with an attack of swine fever in the 1930s, and coming to see Father. 'Makes you wonder what the hell to do, Joe,' said he.

Butlers Farm is an interesting holding, there is a long slate roofed bullock yard with a walkway where the stockman could feed the stock with ease. The farmhouse is brick with a thatched roof at the southern end, on a building called a bungalow, but this was originally a private chapel. It has small Gothic windows. Lewis was a good chap and worked hard for the village and the church. Church fêtes were his high spot and he would have a tin of sweets and a trail of children following, who would be rewarded by a handful thrown at random. At the Rectory, the Rev. Wade Evans had a housekeeper who was a lady about whom little was known. In some way she pressed her affections upon him, for he had lost his wife several years before, and was in need of someone's looking after. This resulted in him getting married in 1936.

'I'll never call her Auntie,' said I to my Ma.

The results of the attachment are perhaps best left out of this little story. He was undoubtedly in poor health, for in the cold winter of 1940 he died from blood poisoning in hospital just a few days after a blackthorn pricked his forearm while cutting a hedge. His new wife inherited the estate, and Cecil eventually hired it from her. He managed to farm it by pressing a neighbour into cultivating and planting it for him. Corn was still being cut with self-binder stacked and threshed.

He ordered a ton of steam coal and we delivered it. It was to be thrown through a small door in the brick wall behind the bullock yard. I threw a large lump and hit the door frame and loosened it. A few lumps later it received another knock and out came some bricks. Cecil was around and hollered, 'What sort of bloody game do you call this? I shall take the damage off your bill – in fact I may never pay you!'

I protested that he shouldn't have needed the coal put into such a stupid place. Why couldn't he have had it put in a heap in the stack yard like other farmers did?

He replied, 'I don't want the engine driver fillin' his tender off my heap when he leaves here.'

There was a shortage of beer at the local pubs, and this caused a lot of bad language. At the commencement of harvest, Cecil said, 'I was up at 4.30 this mornin' and started cuttin' round [with scythe] at half six. The sun was glarin' in me eyes, I was sweatin' hot by 8 – and no beer! Why – what the hell are they doin' to us? They want corn for bread and malt for beer. We're growin' it – and can't have a drink! I don't know what things are coming to! Your father used to brew – what's the matter with him?'

I replied, 'I don't think he can get a licence now.'

This did not do anything to alleviate the situation.

Butlers in later years

Rufus Fisher, the only son of Edward Oswold, living at Butlers Farm was on his way home from getting his food from town. I mentioned all the bad happenings in the lane from the Main Road (Butlers Lane). To elaborate, Uncle Lewis died tragically with blood poisoning. Dick Garratt came to grief and there were several other tragic happenings over several years.

Rufus said, 'Well, I reckon it's all due to Grandfather Fisher turning gypsies off the field where the bungalows now stand, and one of their number put a curse on either him or the field – or perhaps both. Rufus then went on at length to tell me that it was our great-grandfather who had a dust-up with the gypsies. He found one of their number in the barn at the Firs and fired a pistol at him. 'The bullet was in one of the beams,' he declared.

'It is now?' I asked.

'Well, I een't sure now,' he answered, looking at his boots. 'There's a spot in the orchard that haunted – there's a lot of spirits down that lane – they fair do throw ye sometimes,' he continued. 'When we were threshin' at the Firs, the engine driver couldn't get enough lock on his steering and he asked my father to pull the wheels round. Father shouldn't have done it. There was a hot coal shot out of the chimney and hit the back of his hand. It was a long time healing up, and the soot was under the skin until his dying day. There was another occasion when we borrowed a chap from the Hall for threshin' corn. The buckle on the pitcher belt cut his head – badly – but it didn't cut through his hat.'

Rufus lives in a fair amount of seclusion, with no services at all. His well is in the back yard. The last time I looked down it, it had plants growing from the side and they would have brushed the sides of the bucket on its way to the water. He slept under sacks. Rats kept him company. Candles were his source of light. And in the recent cold spell, he had to request a supply of them. (He saves £2000 per year as a minimum from his harvest.) He collects newspapers from the train and knows more about the goings-on in the world than most of us.

He was well to the fore in the 1930s when wireless sets were being made at home. He understood the theory and could map out a chassis plan from memory. In more recent times he and an assistant rigged up a wire arrangement and jammed radio receivers in the near vicinity.

Michael Everett, my nephew, tells me (1987):

'I went to see him, and in the window where a pane was broken was a picture of an old gent with a beard. 'Who is this?' I enquired.

'Rufus replied, "Tha's grandfather, he's doin' the only thing he's ever done fore me – keeping out some draught. Never was any good; might have had a big estate and riches – thousands of pounds."'

Michael continued, 'He's got a rat trap near the back door and I've seen two rats in it recently. One door has a broken hinge. I mentioned this. "Well," Rufus replied, "if anyone tried to break in the door will fall over 'em. That'll be one to me. Rats? Yes, yes, I heard one the other night and kept right still."

Many years back Edward told me, 'We had a lot of flies – hundreds on 'em. We had some cyanide, and sprinkled it on a newspaper on the table. They fell whenever they passed over it.'

(1988) I met Rufus at Dovercourt. 'How are you?' I enquired.

'Fell down and hurt me knee and ribs,' he answered. 'Everything has gone wrong since they came over [this referred to relatives from Africa]. Little things have gone wrong all the time. Tha's the spirits from that old gypsy. The spirits come over strong on her.' [This lady was a cousin's wife visiting from Africa.] Rufus went on, 'I wish I could escape.'

The house is now a listed building.

During the 1939–45 war, Rufus was seldom seen in daylight. He used to walk or sometimes ride a cycle up and down the lane in order to exercise and amuse himself. His father used to do all the fetching and carrying. They had a large garden and grew strawberries. The orchard at Butlers had some reasonable fruit trees and the produce from these two areas was taken to Harwich to sell to a greengrocer, by bus or on the train. The goods were transported from home by a two-wheeled sack barrow, with large wheels. Bernard had made this many years back. He fashioned the shafts from willow. The wheels were iron, around the rims a rubber strip was fixed by rivets through holes drilled by a breast drill. I think Berny enjoyed drilling holes through iron. 'You've got to give it all you've got, Jack,' said he. 'This is the dragon barrow. Somebody'll git tired pushin' it, then they can drag it – hee hee!'

So Edward trundled this to and fro with no assistance from his son. Rufus was doing a little work on the straw stack while threshing one day, and Cecil said, 'Tha's the most valuable stack o' straw I ever known.' Apparently Rufus had a tin in his pocket with about £200 in it. Some of their surplus money was buried in a biscuit tin under the shade of an apple tree. Panic prevailed when they dug frantically to recover it. 'Din't make a plan, ye see,' said Edward. 'When we took it to the bank they said it was a bit mouldy.'

Rufus was asked by Joseph whether he would assist with threshing at Domine once. 'No, I've got a headache,' he told Father.

'I'll hope you'll keep it,' said Joe.

Rufus did very little work, and always shunned meeting anyone. He told me of his method of strengthening his stomach muscles. 'I lay on the floor with a pair of heavy boots on and lift my legs up and down, and as I progress put weights on the boots and my muscles are as tough as iron.'

He demonstrated by slapping his belly, and it was tough and hard. Back to the garden, I said once, 'This is like the Garden of Eden.'

'Yes,' he replied, 'but there are a lot of serpents in it.'

Quite how he escaped being called up during the 1939–45 war has always been a mystery. But this he achieved. I never thought that he would have claimed exemption, for this holding was of small acreage. During the winter of 1991 his outbuildings were demolished. The lovely garden wall was also taken down. Who in their right mind would have had this done? It ran east to west, and was a lovely shelter.

I saw him plodding from Manningtree to Mistley one day in early summer and stopped my vehicle. 'Do you want a lift home?' I asked.

'No, no, I've got a ticket through to Harwich,' he replied.

'How are you?' said I.

'Don't get a lot of happiness now – shan't, now I'm nearly eighty,' he said, looking at the path.

So I left him to proceed wearing his usual wellington boots and BR overcoat. He had been involved with some seemingly ugly people, I'm thinking.

On Wednesday 29th May 1991, at about 12 noon, we heard the sirens of police cars and an ambulance. We were just off to the Cliff Hotel to celebrate our forthcoming Ruby Wedding. We went round by the station and saw these vehicles at the bottom of Station Hill. We returned home at about 3.30 p.m., and at 5 p.m. there was a police presence at Domine.

The lady inspector and a constable asked if I was who I am,

232

and said Rufus had been knocked down by a freight train and killed. Could I identify the body (at a hospital)? This was a real shock, and we did not recover for 48 hours or so.

So on Monday 3rd June, Donald Fisher and I went off to the Colchester General Hospital to view Rufus's mortal remains. There was only his face visible, of course. He had left a will and appointed an executor, which was a great relief to me. The solicitor told me that I would have a copy in due course. So on 13th June, he was buried in the newly formed piece of the graveyard at the church. Quite a simple funeral. I said to the Rector that Rufus viewed the Bible as a 'work of fiction'.

Keith Fisher was interested in what he was likely to get out of the estate. One of our number, who was an executor, said, 'I'm afraid you'll be disappointed. Large sums of money have been parted with, and we don't know quite where they have gone.'

The bank has closed his account. So we, or some of us, chatted and were told that Rufus had been carrying a bag of papers, among which was his birth certificate, that he had two .410 guns in a sack on his back and cartridges in his pockets. It seems he was looking for a safe place. He was being hounded. The family members retired to the Firs for a light refreshment (the weather was cold and wet), so the ancestral home was visited once again. Seventy years earlier, his grandfather's funeral wake took place in the same house.

On 25th September I attended the inquest at Chelmsford, and learned the details of Rufus's death from the driver of the train.

'I saw a person going across the line and sounded the hooter. The person began to hurry, the horn sounded again, and the person tried to hurry but fell over, right in the path of the train. He made no attempt to get up, perhaps he hit his head. I shut my eyes; there was nothing I could do.'

I gave my evidence saying what I knew of Rufus's health, hearing and sight, all of which seemed reasonably good. So there we are; there is little more to say, apart from, 'He trudged along with head bent.' Once again I must mention the tragic happenings in this part of the village. If Rufus could say anything, I know he would reiterate the story of the gypsy! There was conjecture later about his death that with the harassment he had, it may have been intentional.

I was talking to Bill Porter recently about Rufus and Butlers. He said that he used to deliver the newspapers there on a Saturday, and his arrival was observed from a distance. On his getting to the front door, Rufus's hand would be visible through the opening with the correct amount of money, and Bill would put the paper in its place, and the hand was withdrawn very quickly.

He also said that one harvest time he and another lad helped load the wagons with sheaves and unload at the stack etc., and he went off home with a 10s note, which of course he was well pleased with. Such was the strict upbringing that his whole family had that his father went off to Butlers Farm to make sure that he actually had received that amount of cash.

We sold Rufus a standard Fordson Tractor around the late 1950s, and he did try to do some work on his land. Michael, who was born nearby around 1943, went to work on the land, and spent a lot of his spare time at Butlers Farm. Rufus and he got on quite well. Guns were always in evidence, and many bullfinches were shot as they pecked the buds of fruit trees. They would nail up a plastic fertiliser bag and fire a shot at it, a certain distance away, and see the spread of shot. Several experiments of this nature with various shot sizes etc. would be carried out. This would assist them when after rabbits, and so on. Michael said when discussing life and death, 'If there is life after death, 'I'll let you know somehow.' Michael said recently that a barn owl made a nest in a building but was probably scared away with the sound of gunfire. He added that some time after Rufus's death he was down at the farm and the barn owl was seen in the twilight. He was surprised and said, 'That's Rufus returned!'

According to the members of the Manningtree History Society in 1997, Butlers Farm house was a hall type of manor house and dated from about 1450.

Butlers Farm, circa 1920

Chapter Eight: The War Ends

We all plodded on and put up with rationing and bombs, and in the summer of 1944 the flying bomb menace was with us. On some days we got little sleep and stood under the apple trees watching these devilish things going toward London. Some were low, and one hit a tree near Davidson Farm at Wix. One fell and exploded behind the Wheatsheaf at Wrabness. It shook old Ships Farm house to bits. Uncle Bernard lived just over the road at Spring Cottage, with Cecil and Lily. Bernard went round to see what had happened to the occupants. They were very frightened and had cuts on faces and hands from flying glass. The old house had to be demolished after this. Spring Cottage suffered. Its roof was badly damaged and the windows blown in. Aunt Lily was in bed, covered with broken glass, and dared not move. Cecil, who slept in a chair downstairs, went to her assistance and carefully cleared up the devastation. The house had to be re-roofed and fitted with new windows. While this was being done Lily managed to walk down the fields, passing her old home every evening, to spend the night at Domine. She would struggle back next morning. 'I must get back to see to Cecil's breakfast and put the milk bottles out,' she would say.

One morning she fell over in a muddy gateway and had the greatest difficulty in getting to her feet. She called for help but of course there was not one within earshot. This was the end of her journeying, and within a week or two the house repairs were complete.

The war in Europe come to an end in 1945, and there were celebrations in every village and town. I was in the Wheatsheaf Inn one evening around this time; I must confess to having been seen in this establishment quite frequently. The place as full of all sorts and conditions of men, soldiers included. Some of them were very tired of Winston, and of being in khaki. Cecil was around. 'What's the matter with these buggers?' said he.

I said that many of them were not Conservatives, and that we'd have a Labour Government before long. He swore to someone and about someone else, and I noticed a glass upside down on the counter. 'Cool it,' said I and quietly put the glass the right way up.

Another visitor to the 'Sheaf was Paddy Store. He had been a villager and a friend of Father's. He had gone to work in docklands in London as a young man; he was large and tough.

The end of the war was sufficient reason to return. He had a pocketful of money and spent it on whoever was within earshot of the bar. I've never seen anyone drink longer and harder. Even Father was having to ease up. 'You'll spend all you money, Paddy,' he said.

'I know where there's some more growing, Joe, so drink up.'

The 'Sheaf was a very popular pub in those days. It was often packed full of customers and you had to elbow your way to the bar. Harry Weeks came from Ipswich and played the piano, and we sang all the popular songs of the day. I think I knew all the words, especially to 'L-l-l-like you very much', 'Russian Rose' and 'Run, Rabbit, Run'.

Some of the soldiers knew some bawdy old numbers and one or two of them were very good entertainers. My ma did not like my activities during this time. She said one day, 'I lost your father to the pub – I hope I will not lose you as well.'

On one memorable occasion someone set fire to a vase of pampas grass in the crowded saloon. It caused a fright and could have been disastrous but was quickly smothered. The landlord, who did his war service in the Navy, was a pleasant fellow; his name was Cyril Pett, known as 'Pat'.

His wife's name was Claire. I made a high bar stool for them and repaired a piano stool. The bar stool had a square top cut from a circular mahogany table. I confessed to someone I didn't know what kind of wood it was. The seat of the piano stool was padded and it lay on the bench for a few days and one of the cats peed on it and of course it smelt awful. I didn't know quite what to do; I think I put some disinfectant on it. Someone said it wouldn't be noticed because the scents already there in the pub would mix all right...

There was a Polish Army Captain called Captain George, who was often in the Saloon. He was a very well-mannered chap and very well groomed. I do not know where he was stationed. He said, 'Ve shall not be in fear of zee Germans in the future after see war. The Russians will be the aggressors! You know where I cam from there voss a visky distillery. There voss zeese large vats vith liquor in. There voss also zee rats, zee rats they seet on zee side of vat they deep their tails in and leek them, and they after a time fall off drunk. Zee problem voss that sometimes they fall in the vat and they have to be fished out with a spoon on a long steek.'

Vic Chaplin, who I think lived in Mistley, was usually around. He rode an ancient motorcycle with a box sidecar. He used to be the gardener at the 'Sheaf and the place was a credit to him. I've seen him standing against the wall in the bar, asleep – only briefly, of course – but he was really work-worn.

I was in the saloon one evening with a pal, and a lady who lived nearby was encouraging us to go back to her house. She had a bottle of rum, and my pal was becoming very interested. She went off outside and he was about to follow. 'For goodness' sake, don't get involved with her,' I advised.

He thought I was chicken, and he hesitated, so she looked back in the pub. 'For Christ's sake, wake up, or I'll find someone else!' she said; but we stayed in the pub. She said to me one evening at the counter, when buying cigarettes, accompanied by a soldier friend, 'We shall have to smoke these bloody things tonight, but it won't last many nights.'

In July 1948, Aunt Lily passed away. Mother was heartbroken. She felt she had lost her mother, I'm sure. She gathered some pink roses from near the front door of Spring Cottage and put a little note: 'These are flowers from her garden which she loved so much.'

Mother had been unable to see much of her for some time. She was suffering with varicose vein trouble and could not get over to see her, for we had no car yet.

It was all very sad; the family was breaking up. A Sunday or so later, Cecil came down to see her and me. He was in a 'state' (his word for turmoil), for Lily had not made a will. 'There's her legacy from the old chap's will, and I want it... There's several things of hers I want,' he told me, in no uncertain terms. 'You'll heta make out a will and forge her signature and leave everything to me.'

'I can't do that!' I protested.

'Why, o' course you can…you must!' He then went through all the remnants of the family – nephews, nieces – who would benefit if I didn't.

Mother was not knowing what to say. This dialogue took place outside the barn here, and Father appeared to supervise my feeding the pigs and made a remark about why were we talking out here. Mother said, 'We must talk.'

Cecil said that what we had to say was our business, and walked away. He beckoned me and I obliged and he said close to my ear, 'Now then, you know what I said – don't let me down.'

After much deliberation I did put certain words onto paper, but when it came to a signature it was abhorrent and I threw it into the fire. Cecil came to see me and looked a bit savage. 'You're a fool!' he said, and swore about the state of the family.

'Did you really think I would carry out your request?' I ventured. 'Would *you* forge someone's signature – especially a dear old aunt I've known for all these years?'

He considered this and simmered down a little. 'Well, no, I didn't think you would,' he admitted.

Within a few days he hired C Pett to drive him to Colchester to see their solicitor – Page and Co., 60 North Hill. He used to call it 'Hill 60'. This was announced with an excited shout and had some association with numbers given to locations during the Boer War that he had read about. He and his brother Edward would sometimes become involved in an agitated discussion about some campaign of war time. Hanging in the cottage was a picture of the massed armies ranging over hill and dales, with captions describing the various advances at different times of battle. I never really knew what war this referred to. I think there must have been some relative involved with hostilities in the past.

However, Cecil was at Colchester. Someone at the solicitors called him a 'twister'. Quite what transpired I did not venture to ascertain. There did not appear to be any noticeable difference in the way of life at Spring Cottage. The two brothers lived in the same way as they had done for years, separately to a great extent.

It's worth taking a look at the life at Domine in the 1940s and 1950s. We were then growing a variety of crops – mangolds, sugar beet, peas, wheat, barley and oats, and occasionally an acre of two was undersown with clover and grass, the latter and oats for feed for the horses. We had only about 18 acres, and the acreage of each crop was between 2 and 5 acres. Sugar beet was 2 to 2½, as we were only contracted to grow a small amount.

In these early post-war days we had not chemical control of weeds or cereal disease. Horsepower was becoming very difficult; we never really had a good pair of horses. We had an ancient Smyth's drill. I took this old machine to pieces and repaired it. We were all set to drill some wheat, and Ted was horseman. Suddenly the horses took fright and tore off on the first bout of the headland. They came back to the buildings and stopped. The speed of revolutions had undone my efforts and broken the tines in the box and it was useless. We had the humiliation of picking up the bags of seed positioned on the headland. 'I'll sell this bloody place or set fire to it. That's what I'll do!' said Father. 'I'll get a gun and shoot myself...bloody place!' he fumed. 'Ought to have had my arse kicked just before I gave the last bid!'

He was often going to set fire to the place. On one occasion, a fire of hedge brashings set the dry sides of a muck hill alight. 'Come on, for Christ's sake, put it out!' I laughed. 'Whoever heard of a muck hill afire?' I said.

'That's right,' retorted Father, 'you laugh – it's no laughin' matter. Get it *out!*'

A little later I ventured, 'You talk about burning the place...but when we do get a good fire going, you get into a panic... You'll never set fire to anything!'

One day we were near the road gate and a car stopped. The driver asked the way to the shore. Father said in his usual direct way, 'You go down here over the bridge near the school, down past the church, turn right near the depot, and when you git there go and drown yourself.' The driver looked a bit puzzled and pointed a finger at his head and slowly made his way to the river.

Soon after the war we had to have new horse hoe. This was a two-wheeled machined pulled by one horse with a frame to which was fixed hoes that the person walking behind guided up the rows of beet by holding two long handles. This came from Joslin's at Colchester, and was very smart in blue and red paint. Bernard was talking to Father in the 'Sheaf one day in the spring, and over a pint or two Bernard was persuaded into coming to help with using the hoe. While he was thus engaged, I said sarcastically, 'The hoes ain't very sharp, Uncle.'

'A jamb is worse than a cut,' he said, without any hesitation.

About this time we had to have another horse. One of our two old lads had to go. Uncle Ted was working here for a few hours a day. He and Father had talked with the shepherd who worked at the Hall. The shepherd was the kind of chap who could do almost anything, according to what we heard in the Public bar. We had an unwanted bitch, and he was asked to come and shoot it. The shepherd, using our .410 gun, took aim and fired. He hit the dog in the stomach. He leapt to restrain it. 'It moved, it moved!' he yelled. 'I haven't got another cartridge – go and get one.'

I raced indoors and got one. He then had a second attempt at close range. It was barbaric; this sickened me and I felt like treating him in the same way. Why he was so well thought of was a mystery to me. However, there was a Horse Sale at Ipswich Market and I could hardly believe it, but Father gave Ted and the shepherd a signed open cheque, and off they went to the sale. They returned in high spirits later in the afternoon. 'We've got a horse – a bloody good 'un,' they said. The animal turned up by ET Mills' lorry soon after. He was like an elephant. He was nothing less than a doctored stallion!

Along Church Road at 'Selaw' lived W Gay and Edna. I became very friendly with them. In the early days of the war there were moves afoot to create youth clubs, and Walter formed one. We met in the village hut, once a week, and the highlight of the evening was a Brains Trust. He was the leader and appointed two other on the panel. I asked as many questions as possible, many of them on practical ways of doing work and hobbies. One I recall was, 'What is the pressure in pounds per square inch exerted on a piece of iron by a ball-peen hammer, considering the hammer to be wielded by a normal person?' I think the answer was, 'It depends on how hard you hit it!'

My father was utterly against the idea of youth clubs and

considered they were the first step to a kind of Hitler Youth organisation.

I made Walter and Edna a bookcase and a needlework box on legs and they were quite pleased with my efforts. Walter was pro-Russian and talked at length of communism. He was an engineer working at the RN Depot. He made me a faceplate for my lathe. He gave me HG Wells' *Short History of the World* for Christmas in 1942. They moved soon after this to Trimley near Felixstowe, and about ten days after the new horse arrived I went on the train to stay with them for a weekend. We cycled to Bawdsey and they made me very welcome. Edna even went to the trouble to put me in the Blue Bedroom, as this was my favourite colour at the time. I came home on the Sunday evening off the 5.30 train and as I walked up the road to the house my distraught mother met me. 'You'll never believe what a weekend I've had! That horse…your father took him out to water and it grabbed him the shoulder with its teeth, and he's in a dreadful mood.'

After a few days things quietened down and I had to phone Joe Porter at Marks Tey, and he sent a lorry to collect the monster. Of course Joseph lost money on the deal, but for once this was not my fault.

Uncle Ted Calver farmed at Clays Farm, Wix. It was about 50 acres, I believe. He had a small herd of cows and sold milk around Wrabness, and also probably to a small extent in Wix. He was a rough diamond. His house was a couple of hundred yards from the farm. It was a First World War army hut converted to live in with brick chimney stack, and partitioned off into various rooms, one of which was a small dairy; this was to the north-west of the structure. The roof was felt, and I could never think that the dairy was cool during hot weather. Ted was a bit arrogant and just a little sulky. On occasions he would, with the company of another, drink too much home-made wine and spend the night in the barn, and was not up very early to start the milking the cows. The barn was built on the Dutch principal with an iron frame. He was enterprising enough to have an Amanco stationary engine to driver a chaff cutter, and feed chopper to cut mangolds for feed. He was a decent chap to work with, and was quite good with horses. He had a motor vehicle in the late 1920s for milk deliveries, which was quite upmarket for those days. In the 1940s when the 'War Ag' were exhorting every farmer to improve his output, pressure was being put on him. He quickly sold his holding to a neighbour, and as can be seen in these notes came to help Joseph.

Horsepower was becoming very difficult, as one can imagine. We had one remaining, and Ted was getting older and Father less capable. Ralph Porter started work with us in 1944 and was to be given an 'apprenticeship' in farming and the coal trade. Soon after Ralph started work here Father, Ralph and I were engaged in harvesting at Sextons field, and did not want to stop long for tea. We went to Aunt Grace's and she produced cheese and bread and cakes. 'These cakes are stale,' she said. There were about a dozen; I tucked in, to the rejoinder from her, 'There's nothing wasted where a pig is kept.' Ralph sat in amazement to see all the food and it disappearing so quickly, for rationing was beginning to bite. 'Goodbye, cake gut has got you,' was another remark I was to hear. Aunt Grace, in that rather dull old shop, always produced food. 'There were two families evacuated from London who could not afford butter, so they had margarine and left the butter for "under the counter" customers,' she told me.

In the early 1940s there was a little hullabaloo in the post office area. There resided in Mistley an ancient aunt of Joseph, Ted and Grace – I think a sister of their father. She lived in a house full of Victoriana, and was seemingly deteriorating in health. Flora's sister, who was postwoman, went with Grace to 'do a little tidying up'. The pair of them came back to Wrabness with fleas upon their persons. Grace said, 'Dirty old woman, I'm bumped all over!' Her method of removing the fleas was to stand on opened newspapers on the floor and shake them out of her clothes. How she dealt with them after that I've no idea. She quarrelled with the ugly tempered old lady, and Ted's wife saw an opportunity to 'get in' and took over from Grace. There was a lot of aggravation; Ted spent a night or two there and was bitten by those fleas. On his way over to Domine by cycle, he stopped at various acquaintances and undid his fly buttons to show whoever was looking the numerous red bumps on his upper thighs. Laughter ensued, especially from our blacksmith, when Ted called at the shop. There was a quantity of old furniture which went to Ted's house, and a certain amount of money. Joseph said he didn't care about the money, the house or the bloody old woman…

A year or two later we bought our first tractor a blue standard Fordson. This was second-hand. These were difficult to start. This one had blocked supply tap from the tank to the engine and many swear works were uttered over it until Percy, who was the pastmaster at controlling these things, told us the reason. We purchased an old Ransome trailed plough, and Ralph managed to teach himself to plough with it. We were having difficulty harvesting peas. These were cut before they were quite ripe and collected and stacked when dry. We tried cutting them with out-of-date pea makes (a long hook on a long handle). We tried the scythe, and things were troublesome. Once again at the pub, Bernard said, 'You want that old clipper under them.' He had a 'Deering Ideal' grass clipper which the Fishers had bought in 1917. It had a long pole on for horse pulling and had to be adapted for the tractor. Bernard was once again in his element removing the long pole, providing and fixing a short one, and 'ironing it up' for coupling to the tractor. We started to cut the peas which were laid down the field, and could only be cut coming up.

Each swathe when cut was forked away to make a pathway for the next journey. 'We had to slip after them' was the expression. Whether there was an obstruction or a hole I don't recall, but suddenly the pole snapped.

'Well, I'm buggered,' said Bernard. 'What a bloody fool, just look at that knot! I should hev known better than to have put a bolt in there.'

As you may have gathered, the bolt was put through a shaky part. So we started to look for a substitute. Bernard was to be seen making off on his cycle, and went up to the 'Sheaf. Next day we had rigged up the old machine and – where was Bernard? Joseph went off to the same destination to return in due course with the news that Bernard was sitting in his usual chair and 'wouldn't say a word'. He sulked for the next day and when he came back the peas were cut. 'Mended the old thing then, Jack?' was his brief remark.

Black grass was always one of the worst problems. We found sometimes ploughing in the early spring killed one lot of this pest. It was meant to survive, for it always was ripe before the crop of corn, and when cutting corn with the self-binder the grass seed was flailed out to plant itself again. With the fattening of bullocks and rearing pigs, all straw was returned to the land as muck. Fertiliser from the bag was gradually introduced, mostly through the recommendation of neighbouring farmers more open to change than we were. Spreading this was a problem, as we had no mechanical spreader. On one occasion sulphate of ammonia was taken onto the field in the usual bags. It was tipped out at stepped intervals, similar to laying out muck and spread with a shovel. The concentration, especially where the bag was tipped, prevented growth. 'There you are,' said Ted, 'I told you this stuff weren't any good...neither are tractors! An owd hoss muck the land as it goo along...tractors don't!'

We eventually bought a Massy plate and flicker distributor. This was used up until 1977 with a few repairs, and was a very accurate, albeit slow, machine. It had wooden bearings on flicker, and worm drive shaft. These were a bit of fun to make and fit for yours truly.

Breeds of wheat then did not produce crops remotely resembling what we have come to expect in the 1980s. I think 'Bersee' was a name frequently met within those days, giving about 12–15 sacks per acre. Sacks of 4 bushels weighing 18 stone i.e. about 30–35 cwt. per acre. Spratt Archer barley gave us about 30 cwt. per acre. Sugar beet in good years produced 15 tons. Cappele wheat was upon the scene in the 1950s, and in 1955 I recorded in red ink 'The Cappele wheat threshed out at 20 sacks per acre'.

In 1946 the weather was wet and a piece of barley was laid flat. We cut it with the Deering clipper loose and carted it like hay. We had an enormous stack, and it was difficult to stamp it solid. When we threshed it in the spring of 1947, after the notorious bad winter (of which more later), we caught 136 rats. We had the obligatory wire netting round the stack and machine. We all joined in the killing with sticks, and our poor old dog, Spider, almost died of exhaustion. She laid up in her kennel all the following day, but survived. These beastly vermin were gathered up and taken into the field in the wheelbarrow – in fact I had to make two journeys – and buried in a mass grave.

Peas produced from 1 ton to 35 cwt. per acre. The breed was Harrison Glory. On one occasion when threshing, due to a probable maladjustment of the concave on the drum, the resulting product was split peas.

'They're too hard,' said Stan Fenner, who was in charge of L Hinnel's threshing set.

'Stop, stop!' ordered Joseph.

Spanners were manipulated to attempt an alteration. 'Can't open it any further. This settin' was all right when we were at Bill Kirkwood's.' So off went the machinery, with little improvement.

Beecham's foods did not really want to buy them. 'You're under contract,' said Father.

'You had a contract with us,' they announced. However, in the end they did buy them – at a reduced price. This fact was stated to Master Hinnel, but despite discussions, this account had to be settled in full buy us.

I must mention Joe Porter of Marks Tey again. Father and I went via Pat's car to buy yearling steers. We were shown five and agreed to have them. 'Can't pay you straight away,' said Father.

'What do you mean?' said the dealer. 'Every time I come to your place ye got a stack of corn standin' there, got money everywhere! Corse you can pay me!'

The purchase arrived and were installed in the bullock yard, and soon after we found that there was an odd one which the others would not allow to feed. So up we went to the phone box to tell the vendor. 'What do you mean, boy? O' course they're a batch – never heard such a yarn!'

'I'm to ask you to come and pick that one up.'

After a long discourse he agreed and collected the animal.

If he had need to write a cheque, he would produce his cheque book, and with a quick sweep of the tongue across its face would moisten it and write in the details with an indelible pencil. Someone told me he would kill a duck by simply holding its head between his first and second fingers throwing it away from him and twisting its head at the same time and its neck was broken. He would always be seen at Colchester in Jacklyn's Restaurant at midday and without fail would have a large bag of bread rolls, bought elsewhere beforehand. No one of the staff said anything about this, he was just accepted.

Father was a stickler for time, especially in the mornings. I wasn't very cooperative. 'You're a proper Fisher, you'll work at night, but the mornings – no bloody fear!' he levelled at me in bad moments.

Feeding livestock was to be accomplished at the same time each day, come hell or high water. Ralph called at the farm to start his day carrying buckets of meal and water to the various sows and pigs, and feeding the bullocks with food mixed up the previous day. This was shovelled into bushel skeps and swung onto the shoulder and carried into the yard and tipped into the mangers that were hung on chains from the beams. Father would be there supervising. If an animal was not eating as he considered it should do he became upset and angry. One foggy Christmas Eve we had about twelve fat pigs in one sty. When I arrived home at about 5 p.m. I was met with, 'One o' them pigs won't eat.' So I had to phone Mr Crawford, the vet at Ardleigh. He came in the evening in a fog that was thickening.

I took a hurricane lantern to the sty. 'Which one is it?' asked he. Father did not know. They all looked all right. 'Why didn't you mark it?' said the vet. Joseph was rather crestfallen and had to admit he should have done.

Colchester Market on Saturday mornings was a highlight that was indulged in every few weeks. If pigs were sent to auction a visit was imperative.

When Father was able to get around without difficulty he would go upon the train. He would dress himself up – 'like a retired squire' the signalman said one day. I disliked the cattle market with steers, cows, and fat bullocks, with pieces chopped out of their ears and blood running in the gutters. It was a very busy place with some burly-looking chap ringing a bell for all he was worth. The bell was hinged to a wooden post that moved to and fro with each clang. By 11.30, Father would retire to the Market Tavern and it would be full of old characters. Some of them dealers, some dressed like fellows from the Wild West, with a roll of notes stuffed down shirt fronts. Among their number would be a horse slaughterer with trousers covered with all sorts of unmentionable materials; they literally would have stood alone. If I went in for a drink I felt like an alien, and soon drank up and went out. Later, our visits were made by hiring Pat's old Morris car. It was Cecil, Vic Chaplin, Joseph and I – most of the time they would be on the booze. I was using most of my time perusing the exhibits in the Castle Museum, Holytrees House or the Minories. I usually bought a new tool of some kind either from Barnetts at the market off one of the ironmongers that were numerous at that time. On one occasion in the lorry park at the market, a quarrel was in progress between two men. Others present quickly formed a ring and a fight ensued. It didn't last long. The fellow who lost was employed by Joe Porter, or one of his sons. He also lost his job. 'A bloke who can't defend himself ain't any good to me,' said his employer.

The journey home with our boozy gang was noisy. Pat who had also had a drink was a quiet chap but joined in the banter; Cecil would make much of a particular barmaid who had tickled his imagination. Encouraged by Vic, Cecil commanded Pat to call at the 'Sheaf. This was really not necessary, for it was the first house in the village we came to. So round the back we went at about four o'clock in the afternoon, and more beer was purchased. 'Tha's your turn to pay, Jo Calver,' said Cecil.

'No, it ain't. I'll toss you,' said Father.

The dice would be taken from their hiding place and shaken. 'One count seven,' said someone. 'Best out a three, shall us?'

So each participant would toss three dice three times and total the dots; the lowest scorer paid. Cecil was wicked, frequently, and would challenge someone's score if he was losing. While Pat, who was drawn into the school, was concentrating, Cecil would stealthily remove his pen from his top jacket pocket. There was another set of five dice. These had Ace, King, Queen, Jack, ten, nine, upon their six sides and were shaken three times and if one got high 'cards' you left them on the counter, and aimed to match them with the next toss. Now and then one would toss out five Aces or Kings first time. There would be a lot of excitement from Cecil if he was on a winning streak. If you looked away for a second when he was tossing he would flick a dice over to his advantage.

After feeding the stock from 7 a.m. to about 7.30, Ralph cycled up to the coal yard to help with loading coal. In the afternoon sometimes we would be loading up for the following day; he would be kept on the shovel until the last minute, to the mounting fury of Joseph. I'm not sure of the exact date, but around this time we employed young Bill Morsley. He was about seventeen years of age and we taught him to drive the lorry, and as soon as he had accomplished this he left our employment for a job at Brooks' in Mistley. He was a boisterous lad and quite a good worker, but cheeky to customers. One rather obstinate lady, proceed to come from her back door to see me. Bill had delivered her allowance of coal and she considered the amount was insufficient. As she walked along the path he banged the empty dusty coal bag on the wall just in front of her, smothering her with dust. He did not care a damn. I think that he and I hold the record for eating cakes. During one day we ate three dozen cakes. We bought them from Baxter's calling there three times and getting a dozen each time.

Kenneth Lee was also a budding worker. As a young teenager he came and helped us shovelling. Bill treated him shockingly. Ken was tied up with rope lying around the goods shed at the station and hoisted up on the crane inside the shed and left there for ten minutes or more. I was supposed to be in charge but my intervention made little difference to the hilarity. On one occasion while acting about Bill's hobnail boots were driven up the shins of our long-suffering lad, with really nasty results, and he didn't shed a tear. We had only one horse now, and he was getting stiff through not being worked. Ken was delegated to exercise him and he came and rode him a mile or two fairly frequently. But the old hoss was deteriorating. The slaughter man was sent for. Horse slaughterers were a rough breed. Their trousers were covered with dried blood and muck. 'Send you a foot back in half an hour, governor,' said he. Joseph just walked away; it was the end of an era.

Ken worked for us for a year or two when he left school. He was here fordering the pigs one day. We had about eight decent five score specimens. Somehow, almost unbelievably, the two-tine fork he was using slipped from his grasp, turning its points upward, and one prong entered the neck of one of the pigs and within a few minutes it lay dead. Father hollered and people began to run about. 'It can be bled and we can eat it,' he directed. I knew nothing about butchering pigs and cared less and, amid many moans and such remarks as, 'I know I don't know nothin', I've seen pigs killed bled and salted afore you were born.' We had to dig another grave, and Ken said some time later, 'I don't know who felt worse – the pig or me!'

My diary for 6th April 1948 reads: 'Builders arrived to repair Domine farmhouse today.' Part of the front was in danger of collapse. There had been a hole in the wall under the window upstairs for years; water seepage down the side of the dormer window was the cause. One thing led to another. The workmen extracted several armfuls of dried grass from under the tiles that the sparrows had retaken in over the past twenty decades. Eaves were not blocked up when the old place was built. The weatherboards had rotted in many places allowing mice free access, and on one or two occasions a rat. The entry on 16th April reads: 'They pulled the kitchen roof off today – the devil of a mess with the wind from the east, very cold.' The intention was to plaster over the weatherboards on expanded metal laths.

This was unobtainable, so we agreed to have wooden laths to be nailed on and plaster applied to it. Hory (Horace) Smith, our blacksmith's brother, was the lime plaster labourer. He had a large bed of hot lime and sand with water put in the centre, and he worked it up into trowelling consistency with a long-handled scraper. This had to be made on the previous day and looked like hard work. When one coat of this had been applied to the laths, a coat of Portland cement was spread, and after this was set, the final coat of lime was applied, and pebbles were thrown into its surface to complete the 'stone-dashed' finish. The wooden lath method, viewed in retrospect, was not wholly satisfactory. In several places it has had to be replaced with metal lathing.

The diary entry for 16th March is: 'Rat shooting in the barn.' The wooden plates holding the studwork of the barn had been hollowed out by these creatures, they had formed tunnels and lived hidden from view within. They also had a haven under the old wooden threshing floor, still remaining. This was the full length from the midstry to the large doors where the wagons were admitted with their loads of corn sheaves many years ago. It had an interesting floor: pine boards of 2½" x 6", with a groove ploughed on each edge and a metal strip about 3/4" x 3/16" inserted as a loose tongue. They were laid on oak tree trunks flattened on two sides. This was all revealed when we removed it and put concrete down in later years. Father told me he helped to thresh here when a lad in the early years of the century. They had a 'horse work' in the yard which drove a small thresher in the barn. The afore mentioned was a long wooden arm fixed to a bevel gear driving a bevel pinion upon an iron shaft that supplied the power for the thresher. The horse was tethered to the pole and walked round and round all the time work continued. On the thresher the feeder or operator held the ears of the sheaf in the machine while its beaters flailed off the corn and chaff. The straw was collected by other assistants and loaded into a wagon and stacked elsewhere.

Back to the rats: they had everything in their favour when we had horses. Oats were tipped out on the floor and covered with sheets of corrugated iron, a perfect spot for the rats. Pigs food was stored in Hessian bags and their contents mixed with water in a tub or tank. I think we had a drove of rats, for we caught them in gin traps and wire traps. I used the 9mm garden gun after dark. I had a cycle lamp with the bulb adjusted to show a spotlight. I held this under the gun the spot trained on a target during the spring and through to the autumn I shot seventy-eight of these beasts. One night Joseph accompanied me, we had a torch apiece and a stick. There was a tool cupboard on the bench with a space behind. Father hustled his stick at the left-hand side and I struck away at the right. These horrible creatures just tumbled out, and I flailed away like a maniac and killed twelve. Several escaped. The activity continued into the next year. Between July, August and September seventy-two more were destroyed. We set gin traps all over the place, and most mornings one or two rats would be hanging by a foot, to be struck with a stick. If caught in a wire trap they were dropped into a tank of water to drown. One was found in a gin and its front incisor teeth were like a sabretooth tiger. One could only imagine that it was unable to eat for a considerable time and its teeth had grown through not being used.

Chapter Nine: Courting

Now this little story seems to be getting a bit ahead of itself. A reader may think to him or herself the writer does not mention the state through which most of us males and females seem to go. I refer to what was then called 'courting' or 'falling in love'. So here are a few details.

There were little flurries from the early days. Back to the journeys to school on the train, when Chrissy wrote in my diary, 'I'll get in the train every day with you and we'll have a private talk.'

Needless to say she did not keep her word. Conspirators were always around to intervene, even if she had tried to delight my passions. On one occasion I found myself in a promising situation. We had to walk from the school to the train at Parkeston Station. There were bushes and undergrowth in places, and I had a little bit of fun under their cover with another promising young lady. She said, 'We'll get in the same compartment.' We did, but just as the train was starting, Dick jumped in and said, 'I'll spoil your fun for you, Calver.'

Betty was Welsh and just as pretty as Chris. I had a carrier on my cycle and she liked to ride home from the station to Primrose Hill. In the cold winter of 1940, when we had left school, this virile young man walked from his warm house over snow and ice to Primrose Hill to see her. I carried a torch and had long gauntlet gloves with zip fasteners. We had arranged to meet, and I stood around the corner of her house for some time, not daring to knock on the door. I gave up after about thirty minutes. Walking home I called in at the blacksmith's where our smith was working hard at 8.30 in the evening. 'You're dressed up to kill tonight, John boy,' said he.

'Oh, just out for a walk,' I answered.

I only met Betty infrequently and one evening when we had been to the 'Sheaf she said, 'We could get married and live with

Kate.' (Kate was her sister.) We were about sixteen years old then. I was quite alarmed and did not see her many times after this. I visited Percy one day, and whoever was with me told him I was going to get married. 'Oh-ah!' chuckled he. 'Who to? Old Maud Britton?'

The latter lady was a poor old spinster who lived nearby on Primrose Hill. Betty eventually married an American serviceman and went to the USA – but at least she did stay there.

June was very friendly. She wandered past the gate through the lane one fine evening. I just happened to be in the vicinity and we had no sooner exchanged a few pleasantries when along came her father. He announced that she was late and was expected home half an hour ago. He gave her a hefty box of the ears. I never really found out if he disliked me, but she did not cross my path after this. Perhaps the position of the area on the map has a black mark. It did not seem to be favoured by cupid. In the wall of the old cart shed a few yards from gate, there is a hole. A hole – so what? I hear you say. There are many holes, but this one was whittled by someone's 'shetnoife'. Along side cut into the boards is what can only be the outline of a sailing boat and a plough cut while a father sat waiting. My father told me the purpose of the hole. It was strategically placed to allow the occupier of Domine Farm to keep an eye on one of his daughters doing a spot of courting on the stile on the footpath to Foxes. His patience was rewarded, so the story went, for a certain young stag was observed with the young lady. Father proceed over the road to address the young gent in no uncertain terms: 'You leave she alone – I'll take care o' she!'

I saw Flora off and on in the early years of the war. I used to cycle down to Lower House with some of the off the ration chocolate for her now and then. Aunt Grace was still managing the post office and the shop, and we had some of our groceries or rather rations from her. Now she was one of Britain's 'nation of shopkeepers', and Joseph, as I've mentioned before expected cheese and other essentials over the amount we were allowed. So on Saturday evening I would go and collect whatever was available. As the war years went along, Flora and her mother had moved into Hope Cottages, a couple of doors away, and I would call sometimes with a small offering of butter or cheese or tea, and our friendship increased. I made a few oddments in wood: a pair of turned candlesticks, a jewel box, a rolling pin, and tea tray, and we went walking occasionally around the village and to the picture house at Dovercourt. We discovered a shared liking for classical music, poetry and country walks and ways.

We found goose pimples appearing on our arms when thrilled by a lovely piece of music. We wrote short poems to each other. These are now extinct, perhaps for better committed to memory. These few lines come forth from Flora:

> The lane was long and narrow,
> The hedges rather high
> The yellow noon was shining down
> From a cloudless sky.
>
> The air was sweet as honey
> And hardly a sound was heard
> But one little sound that we noticed
> Was the call of a little seabird.
>
> At the end of the lane we just lingered
> For a wonderful sight we could see:
> The tide was just turning and whispered,
> Please remember a good night for me.

One verse from my repertoire is all that comes to mind:

> I've often thought, and thought at length,
> Of a life of a different kind –
> But when I wondered with whom I would share it
> A question mark came to my mind.

I think it's as well there is no more of that around!

Near the PO lived Mr Miller, nicknamed 'Bronco', a romantic who was very much the poet. He lived in a fantasy world. He would collect a 1/2 cwt. of smithy nuts from the yard because it was a few coppers cheaper than a delivery of the usual kitchen nuts. He would hope to talk to me of the poets when we were loading a lorry. One of the more forward assistants would chip in with,

> 'The boy stood on the burning deck
> His hands were covered with blisters.
> The fire had burned his trousers off
> So he had to wear his sister's.'

Much to the dismay of our poetic old lad.

Walking home from seeing Flora in the evenings in the late spring and hearing the liquid notes of the nightingale coming from the ballast pit at the station was thrilling. I found a sonnet by Milton that says it all. Here are the first eight lines only:

> O, nightingale, that on your bloomy spray
> Warblest at eve, when all the woods are still,
> Thou with fresh hope the lover's heart dost fill,
> While the jolly hours lead on propitious May.
> Thy liquid notes that close the eye of day,
> First heard before the shallow cuckoo's bill,
> Portend success in love; O, if Jove's will
> Have link'd that amorous power to thy soft lay...

And 'Song on May Morning':

> Now the bright morning star, day's harbinger,
> Comes dancing from the east, and leads with her
> The flow'ry May, who from her green lap throws
> The yellow cowslip, and the pale primrose.
> Hail, bounteous May, that dost inspire
> Mirth, and youth, and warm desire;
> Wood and groves are of thy dressing,
> Hill and dale doth boast thy blessing.
> Thus we salute thee with our early song
> And welcome thee, and wish thee long.

I knew little of Keats or Gray or Coleridge. Bronco had a much thumbed copy of *A Golden Treasury*, which to my delight his long-suffering wife gave me after his death. While he was still with us he was walking past the farm one Sunday morning swinging his walking stick with great gusto, as was his custom. He stopped to have a chat as I was watering the horse in his trough near the well. I think Father was getting impatient, so to cut our conversation short, I said to our poet, 'Write me a poem about the oak tree.' Within a week or so he produced the following:

> 'Twas Sunday morn when I met John –
> How can a lover tell?
> John said to me, 'Write verse upon
> Yon oak beside the well.'
> Consign this to the wind that blows
> Kiss Flo but never tell
> The story of the oak that grows
> Beside my Jonnie's well.
>
> Beside my Jonnie's well one night
> (Where maybe some may spoon)
> I wrote my verse, drunk all right,
> 'Neath owl and laughing moon.
> Wherever I go, wherever I be
> Or look in fire of coke
> My thoughts do go unerring by
> To shades of Jonnie's oak.
>
> Over the uplands and over the lea
> Out where the curlew cries
> An impulse seems to hurry me
> Till the oak stands in my eyes.
> Until the oak stands in my eyes,
> Till I feel fit to choke
> Through dwelling on the enemies
> Besetting Jonnie's oak.
>
> Those ghostly waving arms I see
> A gale-rocked antlered head

That groans and signs and creaks to me –
For leaf, the wild gale shed.
High in the oak the sparrows chat,
The owl flies hooting o'er
The habitat of rodents that
Adore the silent how.

In net and cot are spiders licking
Jaws for flies that climb
On oak where beetles cease not clicking
Tick in clock-like rhyme.
Phut! fell the nut from acorn cup
To soil of fertility
Thus from the nut the butt shot up
Into the old oak tree.

Caws from the oak, then a gun smokes
Jim crow falls from the tree –
Chokes then croaks for dress cold folks
Flying o'er blue, blue sea.
Now I must go where roses grow
In yonder secret dell
Having a face the nudists know
And sing my songs to Nell.

(1948)

His wife's name was Nell!

Flora and I continued to meet. I used to sometimes cycle up to her home and should not have been on the road; I could never see in the dark.

I had an acetylene gas lamp which gave a good light sometimes, but they were prone to flooding with a slight turn of the water valve. A warden once said I was showing too much light. I took little notice; I obtained a new double-cell battery-type lamp and fixed it on the left-hand fork of the cycle and soon collided with someone's paled fence and bent it into my front spokes. If I got as far as the bottom of the hill below Dimbols without incident I could not avoid going into the deep ditch, and sometimes twisted my handlebars and had to try and straighten them by standing astride the front wheel and grasping them to twist them back.

I gave up this caper soon after going into the ditch one evening and losing my spectacles. I crept back to the friend's house, feeling my way along the grass verge with my foot. Fortunately I was within about 15–20 yards from the friend's house. With his assistance the specs were soon located, hanging on the hedge. I simply walked around in the winter evening. At Hope Cottages I was aware of the difficulties Flora was having with her soldier friend, and of course must admit to feeling elation when she told me that their relationship was ended. I watched these – to me – dramatic days, and was really very unhappy when I knew he was coming home. I was building a glasshouse at the time. I said to my mother when things were seeming to go wrong, 'I wish I'd never got to know Flora. It would have been easier.'

However, from my point of view things had gone in my favour. Our friendship ripened. We walked arm in arm, and one magic moment we kissed, I'm not quite sure where or when, probably in the sheds up at the coal yard! I didn't propose. I just said, 'We'll have to get married.' The idea was that having the house at Domine repaired, we could live in half of it.

I spent some time doing a few cosmetic jobs. We had a black kitchen range fitted into the old chimney breast. I put in a large sink – but where was the water to go? We simply had to have a cesspool, and under great duress and fault-finding from Joseph, this was put in. We still were using water from the well at the farm buildings, pulled up the roadway in a 20-gallon water barrow. We did not have electricity for many years to come.

Flora came to tea some Sundays and we talked of getting married, but her mother was not well and demanding quite a lot of attention. So we just waited. But we did become engaged. I went to a little trouble to make the affair a surprise. I cut a piece of cardboard into a gauge to obtain the right ring size. Upon reflection, Flora did not choose the design she would have liked, but at the jeweller's the one that I thought would be nice was described as a lover's knot with a solitary diamond. We went off on a stroll along the shore on a lovely evening in June.

'You are going to have to wait until we get down there,' I said.

'It was the longest walk I've ever had,' said my lover.

So we were about halfway round, and I gave in and it did just about fit. So we were a further step along the marital road.

Flora's sister married N Cottee in 1949 and went to live in the living quarters of the shop owned by his sister at the top of Station Hill. This seemed a bit of a pill for Flora. Her turn did not seem to be any nearer.

I started keeping a diary in 1945 and quite a large percentage of the entries relate to what the climate was doing to us – or for us. On 5th September 1946, the entry read:

The harvest has been dreadful, today we loaded up the lorry with sheaves before dinner, left it on the field, heavy rain during dinner and it was set in the mud.

('Set' of course meaning bogged down.)

The details of the winter of 1946–47 that were recorded with a fair amount of detail.

The weather during most of the first three weeks of January was reasonable, but to quote:

Thursday 23rd: It became bitterly cold with north-east wind and snow fell on 24th and 25th. Sunday 26th was the worst day I ever remember resulting in dreadful drifts. Temperature down to 22 degrees F during the weekend.

Tuesday 28th: Snow falling all day. The road to Little Oakley is a mass of drifts. Everyone is on foot as it is impossible to cycle.

Coal was the main means of heating, and in many cases cooking. It was still rationed to 34 cwt. per year with, as I've mentioned before, licences for additional supplies. Customers were often desperate, especially when illness was encountered. Central heating was non-existent in the country areas. Rail deliveries of coal were unreliable; we sometimes had a small wagon of opencast coal, which was in some cases dreadful quality, and we got no thanks for it.

No salt was applied in these days; chains and ropes were wound round the tyres of vehicles to obtain grip. This method was of very limited help, for a rope did not last for many miles and chains broke loose.

19th to 21st February: Heavy snow. Temp down to 18 degrees F. Drifts level with lorry floor. German prisoners of war digging out the Great Oakley road from Wix. They dug passing places, otherwise single track.

5th March: Conditions were as bad as in January, temperature down to minus 4 degrees F, i.e. 36 degrees of frost. AA report roads worst in living memory.

13th March: This is the seventh week of the dreadful weather. Snow going, with floods in many areas. Fenn country in great difficulties and a distress fund has been opened.

The foregoing is much abridged, for weather notes are a trifle boring. How we survived as we did is now a mystery. We did not hear about hypothermia then. Probably the news was censored; Flora and I were walking out some evening and there was really no one around, scarcely a vehicle to be seen. There were cases of water pipes being frozen 12" to 18" underground, and we didn't have antifreeze in radiators and engines. We had a muff on the lorry which had a roll-up blind; this was rolled down when going off on a journey, and put back when one arrived at the destination. This worked quote well providing that you remembered the ritual. On occasions we forgot to roll it down and the water soon boiled. Paraffin lamps were lit and hung under the bonnet and then covered with a layer of about eight old sacks. Mostly this method got us through the trauma. On one cold morning our lamps were found to be gone out and the side of the engine block, which was covered with a plate of galvanised iron with about twenty hexagonal studs holding it, had a large bulge. The engine was frozen up! The starting handle was engaged and we actually stood on it to move it. After much effort the engine fired and we ran it for a few minutes and stopped for a similar time, to thaw it out.

20th March 1947: We threshed the loose barley today. 35 combs of best (not malting quality) approx 15 seconds. We killed a record number of rats – 131 – 28 small and 103 fully grown – I filled the barrow and had a mass grave in the field. The 'loose barley' was from about five acres of very badly laid barley which we had to cut with the grass clipper, and carted and stacked as one would a haystack from the 1946 harvest.

In September 1949 I joined the Parish Council. For some unknown reason I had attended meetings as a member of the public for the past year or so as an interested observer. It may have been in my blood for (as you may have read previously) both my grandfathers had been members of the Council in the early years of the century, but not for any length of time. Father was quite pleased that I had joined, and I must say that in no way did he encourage me to do so, and by October 1967 I was in the hot seat. There were those on the Council with a political bias to the Left, and it was a stormy period. Into 1952 we had £110 from money raised during war efforts in the village coffers. It was to be spent on providing a playing field. A public meeting had been called; about twenty people were present.

The proposal was that the money should be spent on repairing the village hall, which was becoming dilapidated. When it came to a vote, I soon learned that one had to call for a vote on the amendment first. Anyhow, it went the way of the village hall. Any person who had put in money for the original idea had the chance to have their money refunded. Hardly anyone asked for this; it was just as well, for nowhere could anyone find any details of how much individuals had put forward.

A diary entry reads: 'I did not enjoy this meeting much.'

Jumping several years, in May 1955 we read:

Problems with Parish Clerk. Deficit of £35 in the funds. He cleared off and we had difficulty getting Council books and accounts back.

On 17th:

Found his address. Cheque followed, and I took over the Parish Clerk's job.

One particular Council member was of great assistance in the above episode. We had to go to the clerk's house, and his wife, who I felt rather sorry for, could not tell us much about her husband's whereabouts. We called on her on two occasions during the troublesome week. One of our members said during a special meeting that he knew a CID man, and he would soon find our elusive clerk. Other members, I among them, thought otherwise. 'We don't want him to lose his job,' said someone.

The amount of money doesn't appear to be a lot today, but then it was quite a sizeable sum. 'I'm glad you didn't go to the police. Don't be in too much hurry,' my auditor advised.

Now Andrew Mitchell was a capital fellow. He was helping Cecil to farm Butlers, helping us in various ways, advising frequently and helping with village charities and events. We organised a whist drive to support to Cancer Research, and I knew little about running a drive. Andrew came along with raffle prizes and one of his farmer friends. After the raffle was drawn, they held an auction of prizes they had won. They bid against each other and we sent £20 to the fund.

The diary comes to hand again.

3rd February 1950: Father has got to the two-stick stage, and manages to get to the barn. Everything has been going fairly smoothly of late. The ten pigs are looking well and the calves are now worth what we paid for them, says Joseph.

I think they had been here about a month. On 23rd February we find:

Quite a good day. Heavy shower at 12 noon for about 15 minutes was the only bad spot. Today is Election day, quite a great day too. Ancient and Modern appeared in our village. W Garnham was round with his 'Victoria' (horse-drawn carriage) with Syd Carslake as 'footman' in the morning and Roger Paskell in the afternoon. They did quite a trade and came for Father and Mother, with Uncle Edward already inside, at about 3 p.m. to take them to the Polling Station. This offered great amusement for everyone concerned. The great result I eagerly awaited, as upon this day I have no doubt a great deal depends.

Uncle Edward [Fisher] came round in the evening and election results started coming through at 11 p.m. on the old 'battery wireless'. Each time the music was interrupted our eyes lit up and sank as the various candidates were elected. He went home at midnight when the score was Labour 7, Conservatives 6. Mother and I went to bed at 1.45 a.m. and the score was Labour 21, Conservatives 13.

The next morning: Hopes of our win are slender this morning as our party is somewhere like 23 behind. At dinner time hopes went up with a bang as almost every result was a Conservative win... The state of the parties on 25th February was a Labour majority of 10.

28th February: Threshing oats: caught 17 rats with the aid of Spider [our dog] and Andrew's dog. Later in the day I went to Colchester to get my new glasses after waiting since last July.

31st March: The wind is east and cold. Father is still in bed, and has gout in both feet in one knee, and his right elbow is almost useless, so things are not too good at Domine again. I have been finishing the roof of the drill and tractor shed today, as we are out of coal and nearly every other kind of fuel.

No one ever had gout any worse than my father. He must have had a reserve of uric acid that was building up for three parts of the year, and in the springtime it filtered down to his feet etc. and brought him the most appalling misery. Gout swells up joints and the inflammation in them is intense. The colour was brilliant red, and it's no exaggeration to say that you could feel the heat from the affected part an inch or two away. Father's temper was absolutely shocking. He did not want food, couldn't have any of his beloved beer, and found fault with everything and everyone around.

Dr Beckett would call and suggest colchicum, derived from the autumn crocus, which would give one 'violent diarrhoea'. 'So you want me to spend all bloody day in the sh—house!' Father bellowed.

'Well,' replied the doctor, 'it would drive it out of your system.'

Usually some tablets were prescribed, but with little benefit. My mother took all the knocks and was very demoralised. When Father eventually was able to come downstairs it was upon his bottom and he sat around with leg or legs up level on a stool. 'Can't have a glass of beer…what a bloody life!' he complained.

Within a day or two the entry tells us, 'On scythe today, trying to make the lawn look better.'

We had never owned a grass mower of any kind, and scythes and hooks were used, with a stick with an oblique branched end to pull long grass to you. In 1987 I still use both of these implements and in some awkward corners they cannot be bettered.

On 24th April, we had no coal and spent the morning 'docking, with the wind north-west and very cold. Snow has fallen in various parts of the country.'

I dread to think of the irregularity of the coal deliveries. For as I said before, a day lost could not be made up. By 26th May we see that: 'The weather had been lousy. This last week or two…temperature rarely over 45 degrees… Barley behind Gatehouse has laid a bit…sugar beet…finished chopping and yesterday and continued horse hoeing today.

'The mangolds are not so good but we hand hoed the thistles today. The little greenhouse was finished.' This was bought for £5 as a wreck and I had a lot of pleasure rebuilding it; the diary reads: 'I killed the cucumber plants by putting fresh stable manure in.' The ammonia was too much for them. On 29th May, Whit Monday, petrol being off ration from Saturday 27th, pre-war scenes were the case at many holiday resorts.

Over all the war years we stored a 1935 Ford Popular car, one of those costing £100. This was for sale, and I fancied it and bought it for £100.

It was a four-door model. Joseph did not praise me, but when he wanted to go to Ipswich Market it conveyed him and brother Ted there and back. The price was a source of argument; £100 was a lot of money, he reminded me, when a large account for coal purchases arrived. Not very long before this, about two years,

I think, we had to buy a new lorry and went to the bank manager's office. The gent on the opposite side of the desk inquired about our assets. The farm was not worth a great deal, and the coal we had in stock was worth several hundred pounds. 'But you might not put the money in the bank,' said he. We were allowed a 'fluctuating overdraft', and didn't overdraw by many pounds. How different today, when the moneylenders are falling over themselves to loan you money!

Our new lorry was a Morris normal control, 3 ton capacity. It was powered by a 4 cylinder side valve engine and was a slow slogger. But it had a problem; we could not keep the batteries charged. Several times it was in the garage with a view of finding why. All that it needed was a new voltage regulator, and why no one could find this simple fault was beyond me. The difficulties if we ever used it after dark were sickening, and we had to keep the engine running fast when standing. This was achieved by placing a piece of 'fishplate' (for joining railway lines) on the accelerator.

Father was still insisting on going to the 'Sheaf as often as possible. When he was capable, he used to ride his cycle and most days would make every effort to get a pint. Jack Tillett, who was a rigger in the Navy in his young days, and a perfect hand stitcher, made Father a triangular canvas bag to hang in the frame of his bike to enable him to carry home three pints of draught beer in his own screw top bottles, safely locked away within.

It was quite a performance when the bottles had to be washed. They had to be treated with hot water and drained for some time. At one period he would take a few potatoes or swedes to a customer just down the road to get a shilling or two to spend at the pub. One unwelcome memory is of an occasion he took a tumble when getting off his bike by catching his foot in the goods on the carrier when dismounting. This resulted in a dislocated shoulder. Andrew Mitchell took him to the hospital for x-rays. 'I'm so sorry to waste your time,' I proffered.

'I'm at your disposal,' he replied.

Father was in a lot of pain and was upset for several weeks. As usual, Mother suffered trying to see to his needs and pacify his bad humour. I said, 'Why does he have to mess around with these little lots of stuff for these people?'

I was within earshot of Joseph. 'I knew that wouldn't be right for you!' he hollered.

Dr Beckett did his best to encourage him to lose weight. Diet sheets were introduced; we were encouraged to understand carbohydrates and protein. 'Eat a bucket of greens – beer is concentrated carbohydrate,' advised the doctor.

'Gits on your bloody wick,' complained Joseph.

Our valiant doctor was well known for visiting his patients at very late hours. One winter's evening at about 10.15, Father considered he had waited long enough for his supper. Looking at his watch drawn from his waistcoat pocket, he announced: 'He won't come now,' and made his way to the cupboard for a few dry biscuits. 'Git us a bit of cheese,' was the request to Mother or me; and he settled down to enjoy it with his glass of beer from the screw top bottle. Hardly had a draught of his elixir of life got past his Adam's apple, when in walked Dr Beckett. He stopped at the door to the living room and said, 'Of all the damned old fools!'

Poor Joseph – he looked savage and flustered and murmured 'Oh my Christ!'

In 1950, Aunt Grace suffered a stroke, and within a week she had died. People were in those days still dying in their own homes; someone who usually lived 'just down the road' would come and sit through the long nights with a member of the family to watch over the unfortunate person in the last throes of life. After her death, the post office was run for a time by her two children, Albert and Joyce. There was a red lacquer long-case clock that had stood for probably the previous sixty years in the living room of 'Paravia'. The dear old thing had been made in Colchester by Nathaniel Hedge in, I discovered by a visit to the reference library, about 1765.

It was taken in lieu of a debt owing to Grandfather, so Joseph told me. As a youngster I admired the artistry of the lacquer work with strange buildings, stairways, figures and birds. To my surprise and delight I was told by my cousins, 'Mother said you were to have the clock.'

So it was duly delivered and installed in what was to be our living room. The movement was almost in a state of collapse and the wood a bit dilapidated. It did function, but not very well. In addition, I received (before someone threw them into the dustbin), the sextant and telescope that had been used by our great-grandfather.

In the kitchen at the west end of the old house, Father became fond of using the telescope perched on the window sill with the window open, to watch the cows coming out onto the meadow on a farm over the river in Suffolk, probably in Stutton. Such was the magnification of the old instrument.

I was still going to see Flora, and now and then managed to run out in the car, go to the cinema and still go for walks. Since we were engaged, which seemed a long way away now, Flora's mother did not give me a very good welcome. In fact sometimes she would not speak. Flora bought me a signet ring which I've worn for all the years since, and her ma frowned on such things. The old lady was not so well now, and Flora was having a bad time looking after her. Between work at Dimbols and sleepness nights, the poor girl was losing weight. Pressure was becoming intolerable. She had spoken of leaving work at Dimbols, and I said we could do with a little help at Domine. My mother had to go to hospital for an operation on her varicose veins. So Flora said to her employer on a Friday, 'I've been thinking things over and I'd like to give my notice in. I would stay on until you get somebody.'

'What's all this about?' said Madam.

Flora told her of her intentions and next day went to work as usual. She went into the cellar to get some fruit to cook. Madam followed her down and asked her, 'What are you going to do then? Have you made up your mind?'

Flora said the situation was the same as it was yesterday. The retort was, 'You can take a minute's notice if you like.' Poor Flora was shattered. When the time came to noon, her money – £2 19s 11d – was on the table in the kitchen along with her stamp card! No week's money in lieu of notice – nothing. What wonderful gratitude for fifteen and a half years' of hard and rotten work!

Flora came round to Domine to tell us of the recent happenings straight from Dimbols. Mother could not believe the story. Flora quite naturally was in tears. This was the scene when I turned up. I think I said, 'Don't worry too much.' I had said previously we would pay her for working here, and now must implement my promise. So Flora had more time to do all the menial tasks that were her lot. Reginald Waterson, who lodged at Dimbols, and of whom we shall hear more later on, called at Flora's house and pleaded with her to return to her employment there. She refused rather emphatically.

'Would you come back for my sake?' he pleaded.

'No, not even for you,' my girl replied.

She came here to Domine when she could, and did try to get a little order into the place, for Mother had not been able to keep abreast of the domestic duties. Washing clothes was a difficult area for various reasons. No boiling was done, because there was nowhere to boil it. The kitchen copper had never been used for this purpose, just for brewing beer, and this was now out of the realm of possibility for Father. Incidentally, he didn't seem to have many friends calling on Sunday mornings since the home-brewed had dried up. I had made an attempt to make a sort of wash house in a portable shed, with a portable copper fuelled by coal or wood, of course; but the pan had seen better days and I bought a tin of paint that was according to the label capable of replacing the enamel. It was a false hope and nearly choked me in the process of application. It is rather difficult to describe the untidy state into which we had now sunk. No decorating had been done for ages. Mother had just managed to cook meals, wash up and sit around.

'Where is the washing line?' asked Flora.

It consisted of a piece of line about 10' long strung between two apple trees where there was little breeze and little sun. Mother was taken into hospital in November, and Flora came and cooked a midday meal. The cupboard near the kitchen range contained odds and ends, among which were condiments which stood just inside the door. Flora and her sister were asked by Father to clean it out. A tin of peppermints which had been used for that purpose for ages just inside the door. The scent of its contents pervaded the confines of the cupboard. It was strange, really, that it contained so many useless items. There was a smaller door beneath. This contained old shoes and empty bottles upon the mouldy brick floor.

I think the girls took most of the items out and didn't know what to do with them. When Father was consulted, he retorted, 'I don't care what you do with that b— rubbish!'

Of course, in such situations one always throws something away that is most useful. The cupboards were scrubbed out and the most likely usable items returned. 'Can't find anything in there now,' complained Joseph. Did some of the items get put onto the dustcart? Was there a dustcart then?

Mother came back from hospital after about fourteen days. She was rested, at least, and the legs were improved. Flora continued to assist her. They got on very well together. However, Flora was not earning much money under these circumstances. Her savings were becoming depleted. In 1951 her own mother's health was deteriorating and at the end of March she had a stroke and was nursed at home for the last few days by Flora and their neighbours.

It was a 24-hour vigil and she got little sleep. The old lady died on 4th April, aged 72. I spent that night at Hope Cottage. The two ladies helping 'set about' cleaning and laying out the body. I use those two words literally for within minutes of her last breath they were going about the job. I wondered why there was not a moment's quiet for reflection. Her husband was buried at Blakenham, but to bury her there seemed out of the question. So our village churchyard it was to be.

The funeral took place within the next week. It was a very unsettled wet spring, and it thundered while we were travelling to the church. 'She was always afraid of thunder,' said someone.

So Hope Cottage had to be scrubbed from top to bottom and the tenancy terminated. The contents were distributed to one or two members of the family. Several pieces were despatched here. Among interesting items were the 1/2 gallon barge teapot and six country elmwood chairs, which we still use. Flora went to live for the next two months with Daisy and Noel and their firstborn, Lynda.

Within days of Flora leaving Hope Cottage, the landlords pulled down ceilings and took out the kitchen range and generally improved the place. Why scrub it? Flora was left wondering why she had asked for a new lock for the front door ages back, and it was never fitted. At last we could marry. It was with a feeling of relief and excitement that we decided on the 2nd June. Flora was really short of money, and I gave her a small amount for survival.

The part of Domine that we were destined to live in had, as I mentioned, had some small improvements. The living room was one of the latter pieces to be attached to the east end and had weatherboard on the north side, and the kitchen was the last piece of the hotchpotch to be added. So we had weatherboard on one side of our kitchen, matchboarding on the ceiling, and of course a brick floor.

Over the years there had been no rainwater gutter along the back of the kitchen, and in consequence subsidence had taken place. I had previously fixed one and led the water into a large tank, which of course overflowed, and did not help at all. In the days before the kitchen was built on, whoever lived there simply had one up and one down. But it did have a boarded floor, albeit with a pronounced hump along in the centre. There were no air vents and are none now. It is still exactly as it was. It may be rotten here and there but it's come this far. This room was the nerve centre. It had a roll-top desk and the deed box turned on end that served on a safe (still does). We put a square of linoleum on the floor and the surplus items from Hope Cottage were put in there. Flora scrubbed the brick floor. 'Now we'll scrape the walls,' said I. We did a lot of cleaning up and just about made it habitable. Flora blackleaded the range. Food was to be stored in the cupboard under the stairs were mice got into the cornflakes.

I had the old Ford car serviced at Crawley's garage at Dovercourt, so as to be sure that it would take us to Pitsea, where Flora's sister-in-law lived, where we were always promised a honeymoon. I recall us two going down the Eastern National Bus to collect it, It was not ready so we went for a walk along Fronks Road; everywhere there was the blossoms of May. It was very romantic. I ordered a wedding cake at Baxter's at Great Oakley. It had three tiers and very lacy decorations when I collected it. I found it very fragile and some pieces broke off. Where were we to hold the reception?

Not at Domine. We didn't consider it much. Joyce was living at the post office. Whether I suggested it or whether she did, I don't recall, but it was decided to hold the festivities there. Daisy, who was just across the way was not very pleased. 'You could come over here...'

We had to have the banns called, and we went to see the Parson, Rev. Wade Evans. We knocked on the back door of the Rectory, stated our needs and were asked into the dirty old back kitchen. 'I hope you are not contemplating a divorce,' he said bluntly.

I replied, after the surprise had disappeared, 'No, I hadn't thought anything about that.'

'Well,' he rejoined, 'a lot of people do have that thought in mind these days.'

So we progressed toward the day. On that June morning, I was rubbing the shoots off potatoes, to cook up for the pigs, in the copper house at the barn. Father was present and kept me at it until the last minute. I had a blue suit complete with waistcoat ready for the occasion. It had been carefully kept in a drawer, brushed now and then, for about three years, in readiness. I just about got into it. The parents were making an effort to look smart. My ma was pleased to think we had got this far. She wore a nice dress and little blue hat. She was seldom dressed up these days.

Joyce's husband, Stanley, was our best man. He also provided the transport in his Standard car. Brother Percy gave Flora away. Before we got quite this far, I had to go to the Rectory and cancel the two hymns we had asked for. Flora said she couldn't bear to hear the organ. I called at Daisy's. Flora answered the door, and I announced my reason. Daisy came upon the scene and was most put out. 'You shouldn't have seen her this morning – you've spoiled it now!' she said, with a little venom.

Flora emerged from the door to receive bunches of flowers and other presents. She said, 'Pity it isn't raining,' to one of the bearers.

'Why?' someone said.

'There wouldn't be so many onlookers then,' said she, slightly acidly, I suspect.

There were several people at the church. It was a really lovely sunny day. Flora kept me waiting a few minutes past 12 noon. She had a turquoise dress with black trim and cream rosebuds as a bouquet. We spoke to each other as she came up to the step of the chancel. When I said 'I will', Joseph uttered, 'Tha's done it...'

The fee – I hadn't thought about money! Stanley paid the 7s 6d and I don't know if I ever repaid him. Lynda was soon with us, when we had our photos taken. She had become very fond of Flora for some time, and especially since she had lodged at Daisy's. We returned to the PO to a very informal gathering – a few drinks, and of course cutting the splendid feathery cake.

'Speech! Speech!' some of the gathering demanded. I simply thanked everyone without many adornments. We were to take the parents back to Domine and then go off to Pitsea. The car refused to start. Couldn't understand it. It was all right. 'Thought you had it looked at,' said Joseph.

It transpired that Basil had removed the rotor arm from the distributor. Father was getting bad-tempered, and when he learned of the reason for the delay, addressed the gathering by saying, 'I reckon tha's b— rotten!'

This outburst put a definite gloom over the party. Mother was embarrassed. Flora was not very keen to ride in the same motor as he. We had several telegrams. One was from the postman from Manningtree, who we knew very well. It stated:

REPORT SITUATION AT MIDNIGHT, DEPTH, LENGTH BREATH, WEIGHT, ANCHOR HGW 414.

The number was that off the Morris PO van, which fact escaped us for several days. I make no comment.

The presents we received numbered about sixteen. They included a jam dish, cake stand, tablecloth, two cruets, cheese dish, and so on. Not as prestigious as presents these days, with list produced beforehand and sometimes items upon them costing hundreds of pounds. No one had a lot of money in 1951 – well, not around us, anyway.

So we eventually left for a week. Mother did not look forward to a week alone with Joseph. We were about five miles into the journey when the dynamo of the car stopped charging. We found a phone box and rang our garage; the proprietor suggested a garage in the back streets of Colchester. So we found this, told the one man in charge of all things our story, and a new dynamo was fitted. While this was being done we went and had some tea in Jacklyn's Restaurant in the High Street. Would anyone notice that we were just married? There were pieces of confetti around. So we paid another bill (for the car) and went off to 56 Manor Avenue, Pitsea.

We were met with much love and enthusiasm. They had another cake for us, and we had another party. We were impressed by the prefab with its bathroom and small but quite convenient kitchen. We went out in the car sightseeing and had to go to Billericay to get special ration cards for the week, for many things were still rationed. Believe it or not I had to buy a wooden rebate plane for 10s at a tool shop. I had to draw a cheque for £5 at a local bank and pay for a phone call to our bank to confirm that the account was valid. No fear of running into debt then! I don't recall what the balance was, but not a great deal, I fear.

Another milestone was reached on 2nd June that must be mentioned. This was that David Porter started work for us. He had left his employment at Andrew's at Priory Farm. Andrew took a dim view of this and considered that I should have spoken to him of David's intention. I was rather sorry about this, but said he would have left in any case.

We had two letters from Mother while we were away; one was dated 5th June:

> *It seems very quiet here without you. All the stock are all right, the heifer is better thanks. Ralph and David are getting on all right. They were unloading coke yesterday and delivering some today... Dad is not too bad today, in good spirits, but will be glad to see you back when your time is up. Mr Randall and Mr Munson called yesterday and wished you all the best. [These gents were travellers for Coote & Warren, Coal Factors.] By the way, if you should happen to see any khaki drill trousers in your travels, perhaps you will get some as your working trousers are wearing up.*
>
> *With love etc.*
>
> *PS: Just had a bread and cheese dinner! Has Flora any message for the butcher on Friday?*

And a further letter written on 7th:

Glad you have been getting about a bit, there's nothing like it when you are young. Don't tell us you've lost weight after being married such a short time!

Letters cost 2½d postage. Then we read: 'When you return home on Saturday will you call at Joslins? If you are soon enough to bring four 'L' hoes – two right, two left, please.'

(These were for the hoe to go through the sugar beet. This was the horse hoe; the frame with the hoes had been adapted to work with the tractor.)

The letter concluded: 'PS: Muggins (Father's self-styled nickname) says he is a bit grumpy today. Roll on Saturday.'

We were never to be far away from work. When we returned up at Domine on that Saturday, Joseph was present with Ralph Porter feeding the pigs and we were met with, 'There's the hell of a bloody mess in them sugar beet!'

Not a word about whether we were well or anything about anything. I don't recall any time when he mentioned our getting married or about the past or the future.

So we began life in this small apartment. The black kitchen range was a problem from the beginning when the wind was blowing from north-east or north-west. We bought two tilley pressure lamps and found that they leaked paraffin. That was why they were standing on a wooden tray when I collected them. So I got new washers and improved them.

There's no mention of when in the diary, but we did have calor gas fitted. This comprised of a light in each room a gas ring, a boiling copper and a gas iron. The only snag with this was that the propane froze up in the severe weather, for the bottles were stored outside, so we brought them into the kitchen and improved the situation, but increased the fire hazard. We still had candlelight in the bedroom.

Life at Domine was now quite different, I of course came home from work and went into my own back door. 'We miss you coming in,' said Father. Mother did not really want to let go of me. She came from her end the house to ours via the communicating door with small offerings of food, which of

275

course were not appreciated by either of us. Flora heard my father's outburst and bad language, and on one occasion said she didn't think it very nice and told him so.

'If you don't like it, you can bloody well clear out!' was his summing-up.

She got involved in the day-to-day business of the household chores; among these were feeding the chickens in the afternoon. Joseph would be standing in the kitchen awaiting the egg count. 'How many have we got today, Flora, mate?'

'Sixteen.'

'What the hell's the matter with them? I'll sell the buggers, if they don't buck up.'

Eggs were collected weekly by the egg packing station and paid for the following week. He said he could make a profit from his chickens, and gradually built up several pound notes in a empty tobacco tin. How did he achieve this? Their feed was taken from the pig food bags, and that subsidised his account, for he did not put any money back.

He had his chair back to the south-facing window. On his right hand was a table with a battery-operated wireless, his notebook, ready reckoner, ashtray and tobacco. For a year or two he had a canary in a cage on top of the radio; the poor thing died prematurely from nicotine poisoning. Each week Jack Austin came from Thorpe-le-Soken with a freshly charged accumulator – for 6d, can you believe?

Chapter Ten: The Fifties

In 1951 Mother had a little break at Hatfield at her sister Adelaide's, at their terraced house over the tiny confectionary and tobacconist's store run by son, Ted.

We went there in the Ford on 29th August and on 1st September we returned to collect her. Father came and we had to have a meal at midday. I think there were rissoles on the menu, 'Had enough of these bloody things when I was in the Army,' said he.

We passed huge circular stacks of wheat (sheaves) this pleased Joseph. 'Now that's what I call a stack, John boy!'

According to my diary the harvest was a problem. For 30th August I read, 'Wet harvest – slow' … '15th September: 'Barley still to cart' … 3rd November: 'Sold Barley 160s per qr (£8)' … but not quite so good in March 1952: 'Barley down to 135s (£6 15s)' … and at end of that month: 'Stuck in snowdrifts near Primrose Hall, walked home across fields to get tractor to pull us out.' A further entry reads: '120 tons of fuel in stock. "This weather don't suit me as I am." Quoting Joseph; it was always right for everybody else but not him!

I was finding David Porter a very willing and honest chap. He liked a glass or two of beer, had a wonderful sense of humour and liked nothing better than an evening in the pub at a darts match and a sing-song. I began to occasionally go to these, but never really took to the idea, for one night in the fog we all left in a coach, about, thirty folk in all, to go to the Wig and Fidgett pub…and got hopelessly lost! Before long I arranged for David a driving test, which we he passed without difficulty.

In 1952, on 12th September, Uncle Bernard died. 'He sort of slid down onto the floor,' said Cecil, with quite a degree of shock. He had had heart attack. His mortal remains were taken to Foxes. The house was vacant then, and there in the emptiness of the old farmhouse in his coffin he lay. Mother, Flora, Cecil and I went in

Porter brothers combining barley

Ralph with last horse, 1951

Cutting corn with self binder. John at the back, Joseph standing, Ralph on tractor

Our last stack of wheat, circa 1960

– 'Just touch his old whiskers once more,' said Cecil, with much feeling. It was a strange sentiment, recollecting all the disagreeable things that had been said in the past.

We walked round the house and a bunch of sweet William flower seeds were hanging to harvest on the end of the brick oven (Bernard had been over to the garden at Foxes, off and on.) Mother touched the little bundle. 'He shouldn't have died,' she managed to say.

The funeral was on 16th September. Cecil, to whom credit was due, I suppose, was most insistent that grave stones should be put to all his family's graves. He chose a sheaf of corn as an emblem of decoration on Bernard's. 'Resting where no shadows fall' is inscribed on his stone. Rufus said once of Cecil, 'He's a sentimentalist and a materialist – a rare combination.'

Cecil was now the remaining occupant of half of Spring Cottage; Aunt Rosie and husband, Johnnie, still lived next door. I called with deliveries of coal on the rounds and now began to 'go down' to see them more frequently. Now of course Foxes Farm could be sold, and all the legacies from their father's will of 1921 settled. So Cecil had to go the Page and Co. on 'Hill 60' at Colchester.

Foxes – of about 60 acres – and three other small fields were auctioned in the September of 1953. Andrew had rented, for £180, Foxes until Michaelmas 1952, and bought it for £4000. There were two other lots: a portion of land at the Firs, and two small fields further down the Harwich Road, which were bought by Rufus and Frank Fisher for a further £1399. The details of all the income and expenditure cover four large sheets of paper. Cecil with his crafty wisdom – or perhaps it was just fair business – demanded that interest be paid on all the legacies to those of the family remaining alive. These were Adelaide, Rosie, Edward and Lydia.

The details in Mother's case were:

Balance of legacy of £200, £160
Interest on £200 (the legacy in the first instance) from 10th May 1928 to 18th February 1953, when £40 was paid on account:
(24 years, 284 days) £198 4s 6d.

Interest on £160 from 18th February to 28th September 1953, £3 17s 10s and the final distribution.
Lydia received a further £457 1s 3d.
Income tax was charged, and amounted to £90 19s 1d.

This was interest at 9s in the pound, and Cecil's portion; it is interesting to note that it reveals a 'Balance of legacy of £300 due to Miss Lily Fisher, deceased, under the will of etc. and payable to Cecil Fisher under Miss Fishers will' So he managed to contrive that her estate came to him without my help, as mentioned earlier. He also of course had his share and the same amount in the final distribution as did Mother. Rosanna received similar sums; and when the cheque finally arrived, husband John came to our house clearing his throat with little nervous jerks, and expected me to give him the cash there and them. I suggested that they should pay in into a deposit account at Lloyds Bank, and as soon as possible I took him to Dovercourt and did the necessary. It enabled him to go and draw a sum at any time. For once in their lives they were rich; she was 81 and he 80, I think, in 1953, and when the whisky bottle was getting low I imagine another quickly took its place.

My diary appears non-existent from December 1953 to 1955, and those years must be committed to memory, as is a great deal of the foregoing. The last weeks of 1953 and first several weeks of 1954 are imprinted on Flora's brain and mine, for one night in November at about one o'clock in the early hours Father hollered out. We were aroused and entered their living room, to find Mother lying on the floor. She had been sick and could not move. 'You've had a stroke,' I said. She was usually last to go upstairs to bed. Father woke to find she had not arrived. He complained considerable about this fact, but it would have made little difference.

Somehow we got her onto the old couch. They go by the name of 'chaise' in these enlightened days. She could speak with a deal of difficulty but was paralysed, down her left-hand side. We brought the iron frame single bed downstairs the next day and she was made more comfortable. Flora should have been a nurse. She took on looking after her. Nurse Ginger, the District Nurse, came in regularly and was a great help with advice and practical help. Dr Beckett called weekly and dispensed medication, with little effect. Mother was not moved out of bed. I think education in dealing with paralysis was not as advanced as it now is.

She had not control over her bodily functions and it usually happened that the nurse would come and tidy her up, and had just drawn off in her Morris Minor when Mother would 'wet the bed'. We had a rubber sheet covered by a drawer sheet. These were washed constantly and were difficult to dry and air quickly enough to keep a supply on hand. Her appetite was almost non-existent; steamed plaice was often cooked and we tried to feed her with a spoon. Flora had to have some help and company, and Aunt Rose, Ted's wife from Wix, was engaged. 'Black-eyed Susan', Joseph had named her many years ago. We paid her for her trouble; she was quite a good companion to Flora. I had to collect her from Wix each day and take her back in the evening. I was in the process of changing cars, and brought an Austin A40 van. We eventually had windows put in the sides and a seat that folded down to floor level. This was a great improvement on the Ford. It would carry half a ton and was frequently used to convey coal etc. to odd orders. It was a difficult job to get sacks on one's back from such a low floor. 'Want to use it to make it pay for itself,' said Joseph. The lights on this were a great improvement on the 6 volt system of the old Ford, and made the evening journey to Wix easier. Quite what happened to the coal business during those weeks is best not discussed; there were many people kept waiting, I suspect.

Father was able to get around a bit, and did try to help in rather a clumsy way, but during the latter weeks of his wife's illness he took to his bed with gout. He made little effort to help himself or us. Mother gradually got worse and in February 1954, the doctor called and took me aside and said, 'She is deteriorating.' He thought that to save further distress and anxiety he should give an injection to end it all. I had to agree. 'I would do the same for my own mother,' he said. So within a few minutes he had administered the dose into a vein and the effect was instant. A change came upon her face and that was the end.

It didn't affect me a lot just then. I did not regret what the doctor had done. I do not now. I told Father she had died but I don't think I told him exactly what had happed. Flora and I were both present at his bedside. He shook his head in the nervous way he had when under stress and shook us both by the hand in order, I suppose, to establish a new bond between us. It was a strange moment.

Rose stayed here that night and slept with Flora; I spent the night in the double bed with Father. The noisy old alarm clock was clanking away.

I never slept a wink. Syd Lawrence, the undertaker for Roger Paskell, was summoned and we said we would like Mother left in the house. The room was cleared enough to accommodate her coffin. Someone brought an Airwick air freshener; I never quite knew why. That stinking thing... we would not have one near us afterwards. Father did manage to get downstairs on the funeral day, but he could not come to church. Albert stayed here with him. We chose a spot on the cold north side of the church near Joseph's parents' grave. There were several people around. Dear May Stone from Mistley, a lifelong friend of Mother's, came, and on that dreadful walk around the grave dropped a bunch of snowdrops into the grave. I shall never forget that moment. I was absolutely heartbroken.

As I write these words I'm not far off tears.

I'm not sure quite when the money came from the family estate, but Mother never knew much about it. I doubt if she really understood anything. There was about £470. This was transferred to Joseph with a fair amount of trouble, as there was no will. He had to go to a solicitor and swear an affidavit. He had to repeat the various words after the solicitor. 'This is my affidavit' was pronounced as 'happy David' by Father, who was getting more exasperated every second. We invested the money in a deposit account at Lloyds, and the small interest was quite pleasing to behold. I told our man, David, of Father's pronunciation and it just about amused him to the extreme.

So life went on relentlessly. Father came into meals in our end of the house. He mellowed a bit and was reasonable toward Flora most of the time. At breakfast he would perhaps want a boiled egg.

Flora would time its progress, but he would say, 'There's no need to time it, I'll do it.' He would count the seconds to himself, and when its allotted time was up he'd say, 'Right tha's done now.'

It was not often a reliable method, but he really could not complain if it was not done exactly to his desire. His taste for good food hadn't waned. He liked all the things that were bad for him but usually had his own way. Sundays were a day of problems. He would want to be taken up to the Wheatsheaf at 12 noon looking like a retired squire, usually with a small buttonhole flower, and in early spring violets were his speciality. I would go back for him at about 1.15 p.m. and he would just have one or two for the road and we would arrive back home at close on two o'clock, when the dinner was past its best, to the aggravation of us two. He would eat quite heartily and then go off to sleep in his usual chair and wake up in a most sullen and aggressive mood at about 4 p.m. Pigs had to be fed, and usually there was some problem with a sty door that needed a nail to keep it from falling to pieces or a pig that needed something we had not got, like a needle full of the elixir of life. Often frustration brought forth, 'I'll bet a bloody shilling if I could get about things would be different about here,' from his store of demoralising sentences.

Flora with her very willing ways soon became involved with the occupants of Spring Cottage. 'Little Johnnie' Gardiner would come round announcing his presence by clearing his throat and say, 'The missus want to see you, particular.' He would go off on his cycle, which he mounted by a step fixed to the left-hand side of the rear wheel. Someone once called him 'Johnnie Spring', for he would sort of spring up from the step and forward onto the saddle. Flora would comply and cycle down to their humble abode and there would be something needed from Dovercourt, or she would act as chiropodist. This was a daunting task. The toenails of Roseanna had grown into grotesque shapes. On one big toe the nail had grown round under the toe. Flora took one of my small hacksaws to effect its removal. In their house, fleas were present. John would sit near the kitchen range and when one appeared on him within catching distance he would try to catch it between thumb and finger and throw it into the fire. This wasn't a very good method. They had a couple of cats, and of course they had their share of fleas. John would have a cat on his lap and with its claws penetrating his trousers and a few flea bites round his neck to make the picture complete.

How this old couple survived over the years has always been something of a mystery to me, for John never had regular work. But they seemed to always have good food and fresh vegetables from the garden. Rosie would not appreciate our visits if she had just served up their midday meal. Flora would sometimes get to see them at about 3 p.m. They were not orientated by the clock, as was the pattern of the Fisher family, and they would be just about to sit down to whatever had been cooked – often dumplings and stew. There were problems with something alien in their bed, and the attention of the local authority was needed. How this came about I've no idea now, but their bed was dusted with something like Keating's Powder. It resembled a flour bag afterward. Why the house didn't catch fire is remarkable, for through the winter nights Rosie would carry a lighted oil lamp up the tiny winding staircase. The idea was to warm the bedroom. The staircase was in fact a spiral made of wedge-shaped threads around a post. There was nothing unusual or unique about it; many cottages had this type of stair which was really a space-saving method.

Doctor Beckett had to call and see her about a leg problem, and his attention was drawn to a warty growth on her nose and he said she would have to attend hospital for treatment on it. Rosie was very reluctant to agree to this but eventually she gave in. Doc wrote a letter and an appointment was made. Flora went on her cycle to Spring Cottage to accompany her to hospital in an ambulance. The dear old lady had opened the letter and complained that she could not read it. Flora looked at the written word and said to disguise the rather difficult situation, 'His writing is unreadable.'

'Yis, that is,' replied Rose.

The letter read: 'Dear Mr? At last I have persuaded this old trout to come and see you...' The hospital people were not amused, and asked who opened the letter. The reprimand given to her had little effect. She had to make twelve journeys to complete the treatment. Flora managed to accompany her on eleven of them. The treatment was effective.

On the old brick oven that jutted out at the back of the cottage grew a large wallflower plant that was perpetual. I think I've discovered why. The wallflower is a member of the brassica family and lime-loving. The mortar used in the eighteenth century was, of course, hot lime (unslaked) and sand.

In the front window of their abode there were always geraniums and in the winter the old aunt would place newspapers between them and the glass 'to keep them warm'. Uncle Edward once said she gave him ajar or home-made jams. 'It was very nice, very tasty, but we found a piece of mutton bone in it!' On 8th February 1957 it was their fiftieth wedding anniversary. The diary entry records, 'They walked to church and then home to Wix where they lived in deep snow.' I hope my composition is a little better now.

Uncle John was suffering and became ill. Pneumonia developed and on 28th October 1957, aged 84, he died. Flora went to see Rosie before the funeral to find her trying to shorten an old black coat. She had started stitching, turning up about 6" and had got about two-thirds of the way round and hadn't gathered in the flare so the turn had tapered off to nil.

Flora had to undo all her stitches and do the job properly. He was buried a short distance from the south door of the church in the 'old part' of the graveyard. One very amusing incident Flora experienced went as follows.

The undertaker's bill for his funeral had been received by Rose, and in her whimpering tone she said, 'I don't know how I'm going to get this to Wix. If Johnnie was here he could take it down on his bike.'

Flora consoled her by saying that I could take it some time. 'Yis, yis,' she replied, in her sorrowful way.

Somewhere around now we were looking for a house to house David, who was thinking of marriage. Hope Cottage, Station Road, had become available, and it was purchased for £600. It was one of the terrace row built by Grandfather. It was a constant source of trouble from then on, but it did keep our man working for us.

David married Janwt Morsley in November 1958 and set up home there (at Hope Cottage).

What may be worth a mention is that when we purchased it, it was occupied by other tenants so we had to go through the unpleasant performance of giving them notice to quit. The faces were not looking at us with much favour. But the husband was a policeman working for the railway company, and he soon afterwards told us that by showing the notice to the employers, they quickly found a house for him and family near the station where he worked. 'You did me a good turn, 'cos the new place is better than this one,' he remarked.

Life chuntered along and the diary does not tell us much in very great detail; we had not enough coal at times. David and I were getting along well. Father and I went to a farm sale at Bradfield Hall. He wanted a tumbril which had been adapted to be hauled by a tractor. His was the last bid; where was I when this happened? I had got into the house, where some items were being auctioned. I brought for 2s 6d the frame of a folding fire screen. It was mahogany. I eventually filled it with fabric and it is still in use. This was my first acquisition at an auction.

The wheels of the tumbril had been painted and puttied; they were on the rotten side and didn't last very long. I was pleased with my day, especially when I found that David had had the initiative to take a load of coal out in the afternoon without instruction. Somewhere around this time we had a stock of not very popular opencast coal in stock. So I took the law into my own hands had a sale – 3 cwt. for £1. It sold like hot cakes, no complaints about the quality. 'Could we have some more?' was the request from most customers. Strange things you encounter among the general public! The diary continues: 'threshing corn' still seems to figure in the entries. '26th April: Threshing wheat, 49 sacks, 10 rats.' … '26th July: Hailstorm ruined crops in some areas.' … '27th August: Shocking harvest weather, wheat laid.' And on 1st January 1957: 'Petrol rationed and many firms face shutdown.' This was in response to the Suez emergency.

23rd January: Threshing machine arrived. We are shorthanded and there's a lot of bad language. 87 sacks Barley – about 17 per acre (34 cwt.), 5 rats.

19th February: More threshing – 68 sacks wheat, 22 rats. Spider the dog got most of them, nearly collapsed.

She was completely exhausted, for most of them were caught in the ditch of water behind the stack. She laid up all next day and did recover.

John Macaulay bought and came to Poplar Hall in 1943. Dimbols Farm was sold in 1952, and he bought this too. Soon after he employed a farm foreman who was to live at Dimbols. He was a Scot, married to a Scottish lass, Nancy. We became friendly with them through meetings at the Wheatsheaf. He drank whisky and was very noisy. Flora and I and he and his wife even went to dancing lessons in Dovercourt, for a few times. He could tango very well, and Flora took to it like a duck to water. Nancy and I didn't. I soon got tired of this. Around 23rd December not many years on, we were to meet at Dimbols in the evening. Flora and I went up there and Nancy was alone. He had gone off with several cockerels that he'd fattened for the festive season. When he eventually returned he was practically blind drunk. He was abusive, and eventually fell down in the kitchen and hit his head on an uneven flagstone. We tried to get him to bed and he lolled about saying, 'Bugger the Pope and his paraffin lamp' … 'Good old Dimbols,' etc. Flora was just about sick of all this and we returned home cold sober. After this episode we had little more to do with them.

Cecil, as I trust the reader will realise, lived next door to Rosie. He was afflicted by a rodent ulcer on the lower lid of his right eye. It appeared as a black mole. Dr Beckett had repeatedly told him of the dangers, and he was eventually pressed into going to hospital. We see that on 30th April 1957, he was off to Roehampton Hospital. He had an operation and a skin graft taken from under his left arm and was in great discomfort. I became more involved with him, and when taking Father to the 'Sheaf on Sundays I went to see him while Joseph stayed his usual time.

Cecil started to drink more whisky and I took him a bottle from the pub fairly regularly. I began to find out more about him. His complaints of his stay in the hospital were lengthy and vitriolic. 'The grub wasn't fit to eat. There were coloured nurses, working there [of course], Black 'Navie' nurses. You could shove a banana up their snouts.' There was news of a certain doctor having died. His name escapes me. 'Died,' said Cecil, 'he worn't no b— good or he would have saved hisself – call hisself a doctor!'

The doctors and surgeons told Cecil they couldn't guarantee a cure, for the roots of the ulcer had started their journey to the side of his face. He was always ready to blame someone else, and Dr Beckett was, according to him, the reason for his not going to hospital before. Exactly how he arrived at this conclusion escapes me.

I started to call and see him in the evenings occasionally. His living conditions were very rough and dirty. His table was the one used at Foxes and still had the same brown American cloth on it, and all the items used in the course of whatever food he consumed were left upon it and not washed up very often, if at all. He used the old kitchen range for heat and cooking. I did my best to keep him in kindling wood, and on one occasion he left a handful of sticks lying on top of the stove to dry out and they caught fire. Another happening, more serious, was when the wooden beam or lintel spanning the chimney breast caught fire. It must have smouldered for days and burned through the wooden surround, and as the hole so caused became larger allowed air in and it began to burn briskly. There was an old stirrup pump which actually worked and he managed to extinguish it. This lintel had to be pulled down and concrete replacement put in.

Next to the fireplace were two cupboards, one top, one bottom. The top one was a kind of food store cluttered up with old crockery and other indefinable items. Flora took a joint of lamb to him one day. 'Put it in there,' he commanded. She did so, and it sort of disappeared to the back of the cavernous depths, sliding over the crocks. He liked food flavoured with all the proper herbs. We got him a chicken on one occasion and promised to get the various items for stuffing but failed to do so. On the next visit he was most annoyed. 'Have you eaten it, then?' I asked.

'Et it? Of course I've et it – cleared it up in two meals… Wasn't any damn good without flavouring…nothin' in it!' he retorted.

There were several cats around; he was always fond of cats. They spent most of their time in the house, and under the many items crowded into his room they emptied their bowels. Nurse

Ginger, the District Nurse, called regularly and I think through her the RSPCA demanded their removal. Cecil was in a rage about this and cursed all authority, but a plywood tea chest with a piece of wire netting covering the top was brought, and the cats – I think there were six – were put in. Cecil said, 'twixt rage and sorrow, 'Bloody sods! Poor old tom looked up at me and I know he would have said, "Don't send me away, don't send me away," – if he could!'

His affliction was not improving. The roots, if that is what they were, had not been completely removed. He swore – about women – for he was convinced that his problem had been brought about by a sexual association with someone (unnamed) many years ago.

'When I was ploughin', I got my cock out at the end of every furrow, 'cos I thought there was suffin' amiss,' he confided in me in a quiet tone one evening.

He was wearing a shield over his eye now and presented a rather ominous appearance. He was not totally confined to the house and used to cycle to Butlers Farm to see what Andrew Mitchell was doing for him, for he had been talked into cultivating, planting and harvesting the crops there. Cecil frequently called at the 'Sheaf as usual, at all times of the day, to drown his sorrows. On one occasion he called in to see Andrew at the Priory Farm, probably to argue over a price charged, and his wife placed a large round fruitcake on the table and cut two portions. My charming relative during the discussion helped himself to the cake and ate piece after piece and left very little. Andrew's wife was really very annoyed about this for it showed his greedy nature to the extreme.

More of his strange ways are evident in what is to follow. One evening he was finding fault with Andrew once again, and said, 'Write this down – have you got your pen?'

I had, and proceeded to place in a sort of bill the following:

7 harrows, borrowed and unreturned, now worn up at 13s 6d	£4 16s 6d
Side rake in working order, borrowed	£3 10s
7 holes wilfully torn in new stack cloth, 9 tags torn off only used once by me,	

cost £26 when new	£6
Damage to grass mower cutting weeds round fields, broken sections and fingers and running with no oil	£1 12s 6d
10 acres potatoes, land fouled, application of excessive weedkiller in wheat to kill charlock which would not have been needed if you had kept crop clean	£30
£20 received for 10 acres of potatoes, this should have been £50	£0

'Now send that to Mitchell without delay,' was my instruction. I called on him again within a few days and he asked, 'Did you send that on to him?'

I replied, without any apology, 'No, and I'm not going to, you can send it if you like. He's looking after your interests – what a way to behave toward him!'

That put the cat among the pigeons, and he told me just what he thought of me and went on to say that Joe Calver never had been any good. His temper cooled and in a week or two he thought out another way to try to extract a settlement of £1 11s 3d from Brooks at Mistley. I wrote another letter explaining that through an oversight when barley was sold to them the small sum had been paid to his brother by mistake. This letter was written and ready to be sent but was not, for it is still intact in my records. I think he really did not know what he was concocting in the confusion of his life. He had to visit Colchester Hospital in May 1958 and I took him on the appointed day.

'Want to git there afore time, I want to go in the Hospital Arms and have a drink or two afore I go to the butchers,' he told me in no uncertain terms before the day.

His request was complied with, and in our A40 van we set off. He was soon off to the pub, which of course opened at 10.30, and I said, 'Your appointment is at 10.45.'

'Oh, sod them! You go and tell them I'm here'. So I once again tried to help. The system within the hospital was, as is often the case, running late. I persuaded Cecil to come to keep the appointment, within reason. So under protest he came out of the pub. The waiting room was fairly full, and rather hot. He said in a low tone, 'Goo and turn that thing off,' pointing to the radiator. 'I'm not interfering with that,' I protested. He scowled and eventually he got up and, standing with his back to it, attempted to turn the knob. This proved harder that he anticipated and he returned to his seat. When he had been seen by whoever it was, he was not at all pleased. There was not a lot of hope of him being rid of the malady. He complained that Dr Beckett was the reason for his dilemma, that he took no action in the beginning. I didn't get involved in this discussion.

He then wanted to do some shopping. I said it would not be easy, for he would have to walk from the car park.

'Why the hell can't we shop from the car like we used to?' he complained.

We did manage to stop reasonably near to Chas Browns on the outskirts. He brought a box of candles. A box of candles – so what? But this was no ordinary box: there were literally hundreds of them. 'Why did you by all those?' I asked.

'Well, I did a deal with 'em,' he replied.

In due course he found that within the depths of the box a considerable number of them were stuck together and misshapen and not a very good buy after all. However, back to the journey home. Soon after we got moving again he wound his side window down and shouted at pedestrians sentences such as, 'You're a b—fool!' and 'Get out of the way, you sap!' and, 'Your hat's on crooked!' and so on. In a way it was really quite hilarious and I laughed at his antics. We eventually approached Wrabness and the 'Sheaf came into view. 'Stop here!' he commanded.

'I'm not waiting for you,' I retorted. So I dropped him at about 3.30 and delivered his candles at Spring Cottage. When he walked that short journey, I've no idea but he probably had a few pints and went home to sleep it off.

I continued to visit him on Sundays and sometimes in the evenings. He wanted me to write him a will, and after several discussions, I put pen to paper:

'This is the last will and testament, etc. I give and bequeath…'

The provision of a tombstone at the place of burial was to be included. I was to have £50. I knew enough to say that if I was a beneficiary I couldn't witness the document. He was quite impressed by my way with words, which was nothing very wonderful, but he was lost when attempting writing. It did not get as far as being signed, for each time I met him there were items to be altered, or someone who would have less or nothing at all. I had to re-write it. 'Put it in at the bottom,' he would say.

I said that codicils were rather difficult. 'What's a cod-I-what?' he queried I think eventually he did get a signature, but I did not ever see it.

When visiting him during dark evenings I used to pause before opening the old door with the brown paint cracked and flaking. The odour when I first entered – with a lungful of fresh air – was oppressive, but after a few minutes not very noticeable. He had an old American wall clock ticking off and on when he managed to wind it. Bernard had bought it off David Marshal for 1s. I fancied it and pestered him to sell it.

'How much will you give me?'

'A couple of quid.'

'What! That might make a lot of money up in London!'

'Yes, but you'll have to get it up there. Two pound ten.'

'Oh, well, all right, you twister!'

He also possessed a metal pestle and mortar and a silver-plated tankard, which with persuasion I bought from him.

Hanging on a door in the back part of the old show was Bernard's old tool bag. On looking into it I found odds and ends of spanners and an odd chisel and a tap wrench. No, he wouldn't sell them. So I must confess that I pinched this one item. He would never use it, and I didn't feel very guilty.

It was about 17" long, so I popped it outside the back door and when leaving tripped round to collect it and drove off down the lane and home.

On 18th March he was seventy years of age and I went to see him. 'Come and celebrate,' he had said. He kept a clean glass for me, or at least one he did not use. We had a drink or two of whisky.

'Who shall we drink to?' he said.

I was a bit lost to suggest what. I couldn't see that we could drink to his future, and dare not consider my own. Then I jumped in with, 'Let's drink to the success of farming!'

'Why, yes. To the success of farming!' he shouted. He was at times quite entertaining and yarned about years ago, of horses and the chaps who used them. As the time went by the surroundings seemed more acceptable, with a strange cosiness. The conversation got around to his father (the 'old chap'). He got angry about the run-down state of their farming, and why he left the Firs to Frank and spent money on the old Titan, and so on.

I went into the house on another day; the door was never locked. He was asleep on the old couch, completely swathed in dirty blankets.

I quietly withdrew. He would become very angry if woken up. Nurse Ginger still called frequently. One day she called at Domine and came to ask Flora, 'Could you come down to Mr Fisher's with me? I'm a bit nervous of him. Don't tell him I called for you... Say you were coming, and I'd just happened to catch you up on the way.'

Flora said she would and off they went in her car. Nurse had a couple of clean shirts, which she offered Cecil. He flew into a rage. He did not believe the story of the ladies meeting. It was all arranged. He did not want her shirts, nor her.

Flora came in for some abuse; they didn't stay very long.

He continued to suffer and became more difficult. In October 1959, the entry in my diary reads: 'Cecil very bad, trying time with him and Aunt Rose.' The old lady was becoming very frail. One Sunday on a visit Cecil said, 'Go and see Rosie – she een't a mucha. Tell her she want to make a will. You can do it and leave everything to me.'

So with trepidation I ventured to see her. I said something to the above effect. She said, 'Yis, yis, I'd like to leave everything to you.'

I said, 'I don't really want anything – what about Cecil?'

'No, no!' she replied. 'I want you to have it'.

So I returned next door and told Cecil the outcome of the visit. Cecil was not at all pleased.

'Well, she won't know what you write down,' he said with hand gestures. 'Make it out and git her to sign it.'

I once again complained at his ruthlessness.

'Well, blast!' he hollered. 'You can do it – what the hell's wrong with you?'

I felt I'd been here before a few years ago. In December of that year she had to go into St Mary's Hospital in Colchester. Flora went with her in the ambulance. Cecil could not see whey she had to go to 'that godforsaken hole' (it never did have a very good name locally).

Dr Beckett diagnosed pneumonia. Cecil didn't agree – what did he know? Flora went to see her by bus. The authorities had cut her hair into a bob and she had been bathed and was in a cot. In January 1960, I took her brother to see her. He threatened to seek out someone to have a go at. 'There was no need for her to have gone there,' he declared. She could not say much, and what she did was not very coherent. He attempted to talk about wills, to no satisfaction. On the 10th March she passed away, aged 88. I must say if she had pneumonia it was a long time taking her off.

Thus went the eldest of a family. She had the simplest of lives, of food and of environment, and really appeared to suffer very little. So once again I was involved with a solicitor to sort out her estate. Cecil was savage because I did not sort out a will before. He had to buy the house and contents. Oh dear, what a to-do. He offered £100, and to save further squabbles, I had to say all right. The four remaining relatives, including me, shared a few pounds after expenses were paid. 'What the hell do you want any money for?' Cecil said.

'Oh no, I don't want anything, according to you,' I retorted.

He continued to drink more whisky, to deteriorate and become more impossible. I still visited him regularly and delivered him coal when we were serving the locality. In among the coal there were frequently pieces of wood of a suitable length for use as kindling. They were probably off pit props, I imagined. I used to keep them aside to use and on one occasion took him a bag. On the next visit, I said in jest, 'Half a crown for the wood, then?'

He stared at me and said, 'What – what, charge me for that rubbish? It made my hands black – what a fool you are! I never did come across such a tight bugger!'

He would pay me when he felt like it, as he always had done. There were small disagreements about when the last bill had been paid and the items were carefully scrutinised. I kept accurate accounts, for everyone's benefit. He had a bank account, and when ever a statement was lying about he carefully cut out the column showing the balances, so that no one had any knowledge of his wealth.

On the 8th January 1961, I wrote: 'C in a very rough state, clipped his whiskers with difficulty.' The shocking truth was that by now the disease had eaten his right ear auricle away, and the state of the raw wound had to be seen to be believed. The dressing of it was not carried out regularly. He asked me to get turpentine to apply to it. 'I've never heard of such a thing,' I retorted.

'They used to put it on hosses' sore places,' said he. He was afflicted by chronic constipation, for his diet was not very balanced.

On one occasion he made the most awful noises, calling out about the pain he was suffering. 'Don't let it hurt me! Don't let it hurt me!' he hollered. To whom he called, I couldn't imagine.

Toward the end of January, Flora went to see him. Upon entering the house his temper was apparent. He accused her of stealing clothes from Aunt Rose's. 'You've taken some waistcoats that were Johnnie's, and other things. Bring back everything you took.'

Flora was shattered. She had not been into the house next door at all, since the old lady had died. 'What would I want his waistcoats for, or anything else, for that matter?' she asked.

'Why, your sister have got a boy, een't she? I 'spect you'd give them to her!' he retorted. His temper rose and he brandished a carving knife.

'What do mean by talking to me like this? After all we have done for you!' she said.

'You! What the hell have you done for me – any of you?' he roared.

Poor Flora! She backed out of the door and got away on her cycle as fast as her legs would go. He called abuse from the door as she disappeared. She was in a state of shock for several days and was scared that he would come over the fields and confront her. Father and I were reassuring her that he would not. In fact he was not capable of doing so.

On the following Sunday, the 29th, I took Joseph to the pub and collected a bottle for this unfortunate uncle as usual. He was quite subdued at first. 'Weather has been rough upcountry,' he said. After a few 'pleasantries' I tackled him about the affair of a few days before. We had a stand-up shouting match. I of course stood up for Flora. I grabbed the whisky. 'Are you going to pay for this?' I asked.

'No, I'm not paying you for it, I shall never pay you for anything. I shall cut you out of the will. Calvers never were any b— good. I curse ye... I curse ye!' he yelled. 'And all your possessions!'

On the doorstep I told him to go to hell... I never saw him again. I know who called on him; someone may have felt sorry for him or perhaps though they might have had a reward. Uncle Edward called round several times, asking me to go back, but all in vain. In early May he was taken to St Mary's Hospital at Colchester. 'They are killing him with drugs,' said Rufus.

On 8th June he passed on; I did not go to his funeral. Eventually his affairs were settled. I did not get involved. His cottage was left to his old girlfriend, and several years later she told me that he was sorry for what had happened between us two. The several wills were a source of trouble: 'Too many pens were used,' said Rufus. I submitted my account for the coal he'd had to the solicitor, and of course was paid. His bank balance was intestate, and was shared between the few remaining cousins. I received £27, with which I bought a typewriter, a new one... It was never trouble-free. Was the curse the reason? I doubt it. He had reached the age of 72.

'He hadn't anything else wrong with him and might have lived till he was ninety,' said Rufus.

By 17th December 1961, Rufus's father was very ill. I went to see him in Dovercourt Hospital. There was a severe frost, I remember. Rufus was there and stayed the night. I think he had to have a bath before being allowed to, but his father survived until 15th July 1964, and on the 20th I recorded: 'Uncle Edward's funeral today, quite a hot day. He was interred in his mother's grave. Part of the coffin was still visible after 70 years. He was 83.'

So the saga of the Fishers is more or less ended. (I am writing this in 1989.) Ted, who went to Africa in the 1940s, died last year, and one of his sons has settled in this country from there and lives in Kent. He has a son, so the name will carry on – but not in Wrabness, I doubt.

There was still a mortgage of £600 outstanding on Domine. Our auditor advised do not worry about it; interest was 4½ per cent. 'The money is best left in your business,' he told us. I'm not sure when, but somewhere around 1956, the body to whom we owed the money called in the debt. There was rather a lot of soul-searching for a day or two. A body, aptly named, The Loyal Orwell Lodge, Independent Order of Odd-Fellows, was approached. By arrangement, two of their members came to inspect the property to see if it, and we, were a good risk. The appearance of these gents was distinctly odd. One had a trilby hat and heavy grey trousers, at 'half mast'. The second showed great importance in a bowler hat and cords. With the wisdom of hindsight, Joseph led them along the back of our house, 'Because', he said afterwards, 'tha's made of brick – want to show somethin' that don't look as if that a-gooen' to fall down.'

The two strangers appeared to like the look of what they had seen and made a few sounds to one and the other. 'Yes, we think it is a safe risk, Mr Calver.'

They gave a glance at the farm buildings and off they went in their old Morris 8. The arrangement was soon implemented. The interest rate was 5 per cent, and we carried on for several years.

Referring to the diary again:

29th September: Charles Balham giving up as sidesman and bell ringer at the Church after 25 years and this was Harvest Festival and was the last service to be conducted by Rev. Wade Evans.

And then on 24th November: 'C. Balham died in harness a few days ago.' In fact he collapsed and fell upon the gang of harrows with a heart attack. It was at the end of the bout, his horses stood there as if in reverence, until someone saw what had happened. He worked at Wrabness Hall.

10th December: Frosty morning, bullock blown.

11th December: Up until 11.45 last night sorting last minute coal orders – must be an easier way of earning a living. £8 14s collected in tips this year.

I have no record of dates, but somewhere around this time Wallace was to be seen at work converting his brick-built wash house at the near of his cottage in Main Road into a sort of rudimentary dwelling. I said to him in the nicest possible way, "What are you up to, then?'

'Mind your own business… There is a lot of people who want to know what I'm doing.' He cemented the floor, fixed a small stove into the chimney opening, upon which he was to burn gas coke and boil his food. He arranged ventilation by lifting a pantile up an inch or so. There was a dilapidated sofa upon which he sat, and also dozed. When all was done he sold his house and was able to drink as much whisky as he could carry. He did not use water a lot, but to be independent he and someone went through the performance of trying to divine water, and they eventually dug a well to the rear of his establishment. He claimed to have interrupted the stream below, which supplied our well at the farm. 'That's about b— right,' said Father. But of course this was not the case, and our well did not suffer a shortage of water. The plot that Wallace's was on extended northward into our establishment and several years after the above alteration in his living arrangements he was thinking of selling a portion.

Ralph used to have a piece of garden within Wallace's boundary, and he said one day, 'I should go and see him, if you want to buy a bit.'

It was on 7th May 1964. The little piece of land was about half an acre, and we agreed a price of £75. 'I want cash in hand, an' no messing about,' said an unwashed Wallace. So I put the wheels into motion, and on the 11th of the month my diary reads: 'Went with Wallace to solicitors today.' The details were set down on the various pieces of paper and old deeds produced. I passed a bundle of cash for the solicitor, which he checked, and handed it to Wallace. He, without delay, arose from his seat and said, 'Thank you, don't worry about taking me home, I'll look after myself.'

I think he spent several hours in the Queen's Hotel. I wasn't sorry he elected to come home without my assistance. He had ridden in my van and was rather noticeable by the stale odour on the way down to town. After the purchase, Ralph spent several days with tractor and rope pulling out the trees from our new acquisition. Wallace was around and watched, and when the site was getting cleaned up we had to put a post and wire boundary in. The position had been more or less determined for: 'Drive a post in 2' from my well,' said he. This we did, and that was that. He did occasionally come down here; one day he brought two rooted cuttings of a sweet gooseberry. He walked into the garden and saw Flora. He said, 'Good morning, Mrs Calver… I'll plant these for you, you'll have golden drops for as long as you want them.'

He planted them just where he thought best. They were a nice fruit, but picking gooseberries is not one of my specialities, neither was pruning them so they gradually died off. I took a couple of cuttings, which grew quite nicely, but they never had a sign of fruit. Perhaps they were not happy there. He used in earlier days to dig up and mince horseradish root, steep it in vinegar and sell in jars. It was very strong. Toffee was also another speciality. The demise of this old lad with obscure but quite kindly ways will be reported later on.

In the late 1950s the Village Hall was beginning to need repair. There was a small amount of money lying in the TSB from the war efforts, and there was a section of the Parish Council wishing to spend this on buying a piece of land to the west of the hall to make into a playing field.

J Garnham and me thought it would be better spent on repairs to the south end of the hall. One of the 'Labour' members wanted to compulsorily purchase the land. A good old discussion – often heated – took place, and it was decided to support our proposal. The member resigned.

We needed more money, and a fête was held on the Rectory lawn, and cash was raised but how much I've no idea. The WI ladies always provided the refreshments, and the Village Hall Committee members did all they could to help as time went on I made some portable side shows and they are still being used forty years later.

A local builder was engaged to build a new addition to the hall.

For 8th February 1958, I read: 'Peter Eves, shopkeeper, Bob Hales, railway porter and gardener, and Herb Lawrence, have all died recently. They were all village residents.' The two latter very much so; Herb ('Hub' was the vernacular) was a real countryman. I knew him as working at the RN Depot and living in 'The Cottage' in Ash Street. He would take a few acres of sugar beet chopping to earn a bit of extra cash. 'The missus wanted some new false teeth. She said she could not afford 'em. I said we'll soon alter that.'

He used to use the Black Boy for a pint. 'I'll just goo in and see if my name is in the "Deaths" [in the local newspaper]. If it een't I can have a pint.' Ironically, he collapsed and died within sight of the pub. Bob had often helped Father, and Ralph and I stood there in reverence with heads bared as the hearse went past Domine.

The harvest of 1958 was one on which I wrote regular notes in the diary. We had a number of wet days in late July and the first week in August.

On this holding crops were 6 acres cappele wheat, 6½ acres Proctor barley, 2 acres sugar beet and 4 acres peas.

The traved wheat, was inspected frequently, and we even turned all the sheaves one sunny morning. The peas were thrashed by tractor and drum and were damp. We tipped them out onto the barn floor and they were turned over with shovels. They had to be taken to a neighbour's farm and dried. We took 38 cwt. (approx.) and returned with 31 cwt. – 7¾ cwt. per acre! The wheat stack was thrashed in March 1959. Most of the bottom five or so layings of sheaves had rotted 'round the bends' so we had to open out a beet pulp bag, gather up all the short stuff bring the four corners together, push a prong of a pitch fork through and hoist it up onto the drum. The result was 8 tons 3 cwt. of musty wheat. It was 38 cwt. per acre.

We were still catching rats. In 1959, I read: '5th January: Cold north-east wind, threshing wheat, caught 17 rats.' And on 11th: 'Temp down to 22 degrees, everything frozen up.'

On 4th February: '977 pound worth of tin wheels and purchase tax arrived today in the shape of a new lorry.' This was the point where the coal business became a two-lorry one. Father viewed the new purchase, and we started off well with, 'That ain't worth half that.'

So we were now able to put more effort into deliveries, and keep the rail wagons cleared, but it also meant that we were having to work alone, i.e. one person to each lorry.

I was trying to improve the coal yard floor, smoothing out its undulations. Chalk was one of the old methods. This was laid and run down with lorry wheels and eventually became solid. These methods did not suit me, and I wanted to lay concrete, but Father was adamant. The old methods were all right. He even went as far as to get up to the coal yard (I can't recall how) with Ralph, and direct him to put down shingle, of which there must have been a heap, and spread coal dust on it. This just about made me mad. 'How the hell are we going to shovel on that? We'll have shingle in the bags and get all manner of complaints,' I complained.

'One way of selling some slack,' retorted Joseph.

We had the telephone on by now, and I made some enquiries at Alresford Ready Mixed concrete. We had to tell them the area of thickness intended and they would supply. We had several pieces of 4" x 2" timber around and proceeded to lay this level. So I took the law into *my* own hands and ordered a load.

The diary records on 23rd July: 'Very hot laid 5½ cubic yards of cement today nearly KO.' The trouble was someone had miscalculated and we hadn't enough of the area prepared and had to quickly get more ready, and of course all the time this was being done the surplus was 'going off'. We got home to tea at about 7.30 p.m. very weary and thirsty.

24th July: Driest year since 1921.

1st August: Cutting wheat.

7th August: Carting wheat, finished stack on the 8th. (This was to be the last stack of corn at Domine.)

20th August (written in red ink): Combining – Gate House field 84 cwt. (2 acres). (Andrew came and did the job for us and this was 2 tons per acre. A complete breakthrough.)

6th January 1960: Snow and drifts. Coal trade brisk, stocks low.

9th March: Drilling spring wheat but rain stopped progress.

22nd April: Spider the dog, 13½ years, put to sleep today.

This old family pet had spent most of her years in a kennel under the old Bramley tree on a bag of straw. The opening of the kennel faced north-east with little shelter. Why she was never put in pup by some stray male member of the canine breed is a mystery. She would walk down with Father to the barn; he would not be aware of her presence and would bellow, 'Here – where are you?' etc. when she was near his boots. I recall the vet coming on that day at lunch time. 'There is nothing we can do for her, bury her in the garden,' said he. I could not eat my dinner that day.

Father insisted on going to the coal yard on Saturday afternoons if at all possible, and on 14th May we were 'removing the root of the walnut tree to extend the coal yard.' We sold the trunk for I think £5 and spent much sweat and labour digging out the root. His visit was one of disbelief. Some of the old pigsties were also gone. 'What the hell are you doing? Buggered if I know!' But he got over it. 'I 'spect you'll get your money back someday,' he said, simmering down a bit.

In 1959 we were still cutting corn with the self-binder, and the harvest began with my getting the scythe into action. I proceeded to 'cut round, going down the hill from here on barley. I noticed the red Massey combine harvester of our neighbour and me going into a two-acre field below Dimbols at the same time. In a matter of one hour that piece of corn was cut and threshed; my progress was a swathe of loose barley just about to the bottom of the hill. I think I said to Father, 'I should think it's about time we had a different system.'

The previous year had been troublesome around harvest and we had R Fenn's combine to cut some barley, and Father could at last see the benefits. So we perused the paper and there was a second-hand Allis Chalmer combine for sale at Elmswell. Andrew Mitchell was asked to assist. He took me over there and we agreed a price. This was in August. 'Right in the middle of the season,' said he, 'wrong time to buy.'

This orange-painted machine arrived on a lorry. This type of combine had its engine attached which simply drove the machine and it had to be towed by a tractor. The attached engine was in effect an Allis Chalmer tractor engine without wheels. It started on petrol and ran on TVO (tractor vaporising oil, or paraffin). It was quite an adventure; we hitched it up and started up the engine with its crank. There was a small piece of barley undersown with clover; the date was 31st August. The knife of the combine was a blunt as a stick and wouldn't cut butter. So we phoned the seller and someone came and put a set of new sections on, that is the knife section. They actually cut the crop, and we had another attempt. The cut corn was dropped out on moving elevator canvas, but it did not feed easily into the drum but went in in 'lumps'.

The beater bars were rubber-covered, and when we got into a reasonable piece of corn it made quite a good job of threshing. We then had to think of storing it, and we built a high shed at the back of the barn. As I write these notes, that very shed a month ago was blow down the field in the awful storm on 25th January 1990.

It was a semi-permanent construction of long chestnut posts, softwood rafters etc. and corrugated iron, that most useful of covering material for people who think that way.

The weather was wet in the autumn. Ralph spent most of one morning getting the machine into its house; we had the grey Ferguson petrol tractor then and as good as they were, they had no weight and reversing was difficult. The date by then was 28th October.

The diary reads for various dates in that month as follows:

Heavy rain, no winter corn drilled, 12 months average rain by 20th. To Strandlands with coal to Captain Classey, very wet and difficult journey.

22nd: Forecast – rain; flat tyre on van, to work on cycle, load of coal on own, soaking wet by 12 noon.

24th: To Wickham Bishops to L Hinnel's to buy two gilts.

L Hinnel had farmed at Home Farm Ramsey very successfully and had sold up and moved to his new holding, where he was breeding Essex pigs. These were 'in pig' gilts, one of which would not suckle her litter and savaged them as soon as they were born.

We took them off her to bring them back later when she had hopefully settled down, but to no avail; they had to be destroyed. More anguish and gloom from Joseph.

In October 1960, Andrew left Priory Farm to farm at Elmstead Market. He had been a good all rounder and friend to us all. The remainder of 1960 was very wet: 'Sugar beet a problem' … '10,000 houses flooded in Wales and Devon' … 'December: a lousy morning with north-west wind sleet and rain.'

We had had the average year's rainfall by 20th October, and on 31st December: 'More rain this year than in the last 100 years.'

Joseph was still trying to carry on as he always did, an entry reads: 'Cutting chaff in barn.' This was with ancient chaff cutter driven by the Ferguson tractor. We were cutting up rough grass complete with brambles – a rotten job, very dusty.

One instance of leisure time may be worth a mention, though out of context, for Joseph was then alive. One New Year's eve, it was. Flora had to babysit at her sister's and Noel's to mind their two bairns. The two parents were at a party at the RN Depot, where at that time parties were held on these occasions with great success. At about 9 p.m. the conversation between father and son were something like.

John: 'Well, do you want to go to the pub?'

Joe: 'Don't know. Don't think I'll bother.' Half an hour later: ''Praps we'll goo up. Shan't stop late, though!'

So off we went. The night was quite good, dull and cold.

In the 'Sheaf, as it was affectionately known, were to be found a small selection of village worthies. Drinking commenced with small bottles and no one seemed to take the slightest notice of the clock. I mentioned to Joseph the fact that it was 11.30. 'Well,' he said, 'might as well stay and see it in now.' Tots of Scotch were being passed about. Darts did not find their mark. The shove-halfpenny discs were out of control. At midnight a little jollity took place, and two and a half hours later we arrived home!

I recall hanging a coat over a window so that if Flora was looking over towards Domine she would not see a light. Rather stupid, really, for she would have seen the motor headlights anyway. I've no ideal what work was achieved next day, but probably nearly as much as usual!

Chapter Eleven: The Sixties

Some of the more dramatic happening of 1961 have been recorded previously in these notes, but the lesser ones follow.

14th February: Sunny day temp 63 degrees, warmest February day for 100 years.

14th March: Threshing our last stack of wheat. (This was cappele and produced 19 sacks per acre, which if they were 4-bushel sacks must have been around 2 tons per acre.)

The pig trade was still being pursued by various means. Boar service usually presented a problem. On 9th October, I recorded going to 'Lower House Farm to collect boar'. This large beast caused us a chase around the fields between Domine and there. This was over most of Foxes Farm. When we eventually got him here and put him into a sty with a sow, he proceeded to break his way out of the confines and went back to Lower House. So the sow, which was probably not on heat at the moment of her meeting with the sire, within a day had 'gorn orf', and once more Father was not pleased. Some time around now, Harry Fisher at the Firs, who was very keen on pigs and had a few sows, was intending to buy a boar. He came to see us and Joseph though this was a wonderful idea. So off Harry went on a Saturday and bought a young animal, which he kept on the three-quarter-acre meadow near the Firs. We called him 'Quinton' and when he had made the journey down the lane a couple of times, he walked with us without any trouble. So for a year or two the procreation of pig meat was less troublesome. Of course, Mr Crawford, a veterinary of the old school, was requested.

One occasion springs to mind. During the mating procedure, certain encouragements were carried out by the male, with the result that one of his tusks tore the rectal area of the sow. To enable the vet to see to the repair, the sow had to be 'lined'. Someone made a slip knot in a rope and put it over the snout of the sow. This was not very easily carried out, for she usually was elusive. When one had the rope noose in place, with the utmost speed the loose end of the rope was thrown round a post and tied, with the pig pulling like a tug of war veteran. This was the normal method used to control an adult pig, and especially when a boar had to have his tusks filed down. 'Well, boy, I sin a owd boar's tusks took orf with a sharp blow with a hammer and sharp cold chisel with a lump of iron held on t'other side o' the tusk – they'd just fly orf...' So someone told me on one occasion. I've never witnessed this operation.

Howsomever, back to the sow, now pulling on the line. The vet had to stitch the anus of this unfortunate animal, and after about 36 hours the area was very inflamed. Joseph was very concerned, and I was the chosen person to cut the stitches and release the area from bondage. The sow was very relieved, Joseph was more so. I cursed pigs under my breath.

Electricity – we had been pressing for a supply, and on the 10th October, a person representing the Electricity Board called and told us that they would be supplying us with their product very soon. Next year, in fact.

We were still using Calor Gas and had lights around the house downstairs; upstairs it was still candles and torches. In fact, nothing happened for about 14 months. The eventual installation will be mentioned later.

In November, Old Fred Lungley, who was 74 years of age was here, working at pulling sugar beet. The old lad was stiff and 'rolled' as he walked. Father said if 'his legs felt like mine do he couldn't do the job'.

I rather think that Fred was in a worse state than Joseph. Fred was one of the old school of horsemen who would never give in, and had spent all his working life on the land. Before his retirement from regular work, he spent several years driving an International tractor with threshing drum and elevator working for R Fenn of Frating. This necessitated a long cycle journey to work, depending on where threshing was taking place.

The old lad died in the January of 1962.

On 1st January my diary reads: 'Temperature down to 19 degrees (F) last night, 2" of snow.'

Dr Beeching's reorganisation of the railways was beginning to be felt at Wrabness. 'On 17th January, goods shed being pulled down,' I recorded. There had been lots of rumours of impending gloom around the coal trade at that time.

The stationmaster asked numerous questions about how we could run the business without the station. In what now seems lack of foresight, I think we complained that the trade would suffer, for road- borne supplies were more plentiful. By August of that year I noted, 'Railmen removing the back road from station yard: rail chairs dated 1889.'

This was the rail where our coal was usually shunted into. One track remained, which ran through the goods shed. The Coal Merchants' Association, a body which was then countrywide, had a branch in this area and was known as the Colchester CMA. I attended meetings along with CM Simmons, coal merchant of Great Bentley. These were in the evenings, usually, and the question of Dr Beeching was high on the agenda. I recall occasionally they were held in the afternoon at Chelmsford. In the room where we were assembled the sun was shafting through the windows, and so dull was the dialogue that I drifted off into sleep, a fact which was mentioned at a subsequent meeting to all concerned. In out of meeting discussion with one and another, I was learning that an awful lot of fuel was being delivered by road into merchants' yards. I was influenced by one of the factors to try this, but when the first load was received here I've no record. One of the big snags was that a long-wheelbase lorry was used and the load was dragged out so very far from the heap, taking up so much more room. In April of that year we were 'pulling down old sheds at coal yard.'

Every spare hour was being used to improve the place, and with the help of a carpenter I and our chaps even built an office, with the usual corrugated iron roof. There was no electric light, for I just never thought it was needed. Instead I bought a 12v generator, second-hand of course, and with the help of another very willing young man, George Muir, fixed up a few bulbs around the garage, wired them up and set up the genny. He was having difficulty upgrading himself at his employment, needing experience in driving lorries, and helped us on Saturdays. If a lorry needed greasing or any odd repairs, George would be falling over himself to do it. On 29th December 1962, the diary tells me: 'Bitter north-east wind, blizzard 7.30 to 2 p.m.'

1st January 1963: Freezing this morning. David's second daughter arrived last night. David has hangover through a night on the booze. (This episode did nothing to help him, or us for the weather was cruel. He was ill for several days.)

3rd January: We had freezing rain, everything covered with ice. This was shocking the coal. Bags became icy coats of armour. We had to create a brazier to thaw them out before we could use them.

13th January: Temp down to 15 degrees F last night. Ice on water in well at the barn, first time I've seen this.

17th January: We had now the additional help of one Mick Smith who called one afternoon. 'Do you want any help, mate? he asked. He was heaven-sent; this was one of the best offers I ever had. He worked like a demon. With the snowdrifts almost impassable, he walked to work from Great Oakley on several occasions.

20th January: We are cut off at Domine except on foot.

We travelled to the coal yard on the Fergie. When we got there, there wasn't much progress, for snow continued to fall. Deliveries of milk and food were seriously slowed down. It was chaotic. But for once we were among the few coal merchants with ample supplies, for I wrote on the 24th that we had thirteen wagons of fuel in the station.

In putrid weather conditions such as this, delivery coal was a very difficult task. Pathways to customers' houses were frequently not cleared of snow. When continuous drifting occurred, paths soon were covered again. But many could have been made easier to negotiate. We did have the benefit of plastic gloves and thick plastic waistcoats which at least kept one from getting soaked.

This adverse weather continued, and on 4th March I wrote, 'Sunny day, first frost-free night for 10 weeks.' The frost had penetrated down 32" according to the newspaper. We had planted some winter barley the previous autumn, but this was now completely burned off, and on 25th April I recorded, 'Ploughing in barley re-drilled next day.' The variety was Proctor in the first instance and Rika in the second, which harvested at 33 cwt. per acre. Life at Domine was very difficult throughout these weeks. We had by now a Rayburn cooker fitted into the kitchen, where the kitchen range had stood. In spite of having a new chimney built, if the wind was unfavourable we still had down-draught problems. The Calor gas was usually frozen in the mornings. With no piped water as yet, we were still using water from the well at the barn, and when the snow blocked up our roadway we could not use the water barrow and had to resort to carrying a bucket in each hand and walking to and fro. When one has had to make use water sparingly one does not waste it. We had the great advance of a tap under the sink, bringing soft water from a 200-gallon tank at the back of the house, which was frozen of course.

Joseph was becoming increasingly pessimistic. Flora was working her fingers to the bone to try to look after us all. I did what I could when I was at home, but the nights were tiresome. We sat with him sometimes and couldn't keep our eyes open. He seemed to need company as much as anything. The entry for 15th October 1963 reads: 'Father in trouble, bladder not working. Doctor comes to relieve him.' In fact he was blown up like a pregnant mother. The result was about 1/2 gallon of fluid in a white enamel bucket.

Within two days he was taken to St Mary's Hospital in Colchester. The management said his heart was too weak to undergo an operation. We visited him when we could, but he did not converse very well. I think he knew there was not a lot of hope. On 31st December he was moved to Tendring Heath Hospital. His brother was quite sure that we shouldn't have allowed him to go there. 'What else could we do?' I asked.

He needed medical attention. We did not get a lot of thanks for what we had done. There were calls from the hospital and we went to see him, and he usually cheered up a bit.

In January 1964 we had a supply of water brought across the field, and on the 21st the EEB started wiring here, and on the 28th we switched on the electric light. I told Father we had this and his answer, 'Somethin' else for you to play with!' On the 7th March I recorded: 'He is in poor shape. He managed to say "Domine is yours."'

I don't remember my reply. The phone message at 8 a.m. next day was to tell us he had passed on. I recorded: 'The end of another era, and perhaps the beginning of fresh things to strive for.'

His mortal remains were brought back here and 'lay in state'. Ralph came in for a last look. He didn't remove his cap. 'Bad manners,' said Aunt Rose. The funeral is lost in my memory.

Notes

A few wise works from the wisdom of Joseph:

1) Lazy people take the most trouble.
2) This maxim I must teach, betwixt you and I, You never miss the water till the well run dry.
3) Patience is a virtue, find it where you can often in a woman, seldom in a man.
4) Don't keep your money tied up in a napkin.
5) The first loss is best (in dealing).
6) The bigger the boat the bigger the oars (in business).
7) Fire is a good servant but a bad master.

He was interred with Mother. The gravestone, now very neglected, was inscribed with a line from Gray's *Elegy*: 'Let not ambition mock their useful toil.'

Father said when his father died, 'He left me the wide world.' I thought the same had happened with me, for on the reckoning at the end of it all the estate didn't look very promising. I still had the mortgage of £600 to service or pay off. I decided to pay it off. The mortgagees agreed to accept an instalment of £100 per half-year. What a lovely lot they were those Oddfellows. Within the three years I had paid the debt, and on a day to be remembered I received the bundle of deeds and felt at last I was master of my own fate. Flora put away all the cooking items and we went off for a dinner to celebrate.

I had by June of 1964 taken on another full-time employee, with the thought that I would spend less time on the coal rounds. Norman was a very likeable lad, but didn't care. When he broke anything and if I could repair it he would say with a chuckle, 'You've made nearly as good a job of mending it as I did of breaking it.' So the idea didn't work and I continued to plod along with sacks of fuel.

Harvest note, 26th August 1964: 'Harvest delayed owing to weather conditions. No wheat on offer. Occasional samples of feed barley 17s to 17s 6d ex-farm.'

I have no date (to my discredit) of when the station closed.

In the 'Goods Received' book I made note of 'THE LAST WAGON', but this has been destroyed. We were offered Mistley and Harwich as an alternative. We chewed this over and spoke to Alan Smyth of Beaumonts of Ipswich. They had a mechanical grab working at their yard at Harwich, and agreed to handle our fuels. This was grabbed into a haulier's lorry and brought to Wrabness. So now it had to be all road-borne fuel. We were now getting an improved round pattern, being able to get both lorries on deliveries all the time, and with no rail wagons to clear, to avoid demurrage, I began to see the advantages. Saturday mornings were always busy, and on one such, a long-wheelbase lorry with about 7 tons of Phurmacite on board had difficulty gaining access to the yard drove up onto the grass verge and dropped into the ditch. What did we have to do? Unload it into one of our lorries and shovel it out again. Who was going to do it? David's round was all sorted out and on the lorry. So I and assistants dug away on this load of ovoids, which was of course sloping away from our vehicle, making the job more difficult. The load of fuel that I was due to take out that morning had to be delivered in the afternoon. Not a lot of time off! Half the customers were out. So many delivery notes to be written, making double bookwork.

Harwich Station was under threat of closure. The haulier engaged couldn't believe it. CM Simmons was getting very involved with a very unapproachable Railway Board. He offered to establish a railhead at Great Bentley Station. The powers that there were gave a target of 10,000 tons per year as a minimum to be handled from there. They would then keep it open. So our valiant Mark chased around several of the local merchants, including myself.

The Simmons family had been very involved in selling coal and other solid fuels since about 1860, and are in fact in 1991 still carrying on.

Mark's grandfather was an old slave driver, and he has told me that as a boy he was sent into the orchard to pick up stones into a wheelbarrow. When he had found enough to fill it to a predetermined line, the old gent would scatter them around again and Mark had to gather them up again.

When he was holding coal bags to be filled, and the attendance officer came from the school to see where the young lad was. The older members would whisk him out of sight and drop him into the hutch where the oats were stored for the horse – or perhaps it was the mule, for they owned one of those tiresome animals at one time. All these preparatory years, if they can be so called, had made Mark into a very tough character, and in retrospect, I'm sure had I known of him twenty years before I did, I would have made more profit, for his selling prices were a long way ahead of mine. I was always in competition with other local merchants, and at a disadvantage. I could never quite come to terms with the fact that while we were driving to Great Oakley to wherever, a merchant in Dovercourt would have sold 2 or 3 tons down a 'street full of chimney pots'.

CM Simmons gathered a considerable tonnage and purchased a Fordson 4000 tractor with a fore-loading shovel that held about 5 cwt. of coal and was of a size that would go through a rail wagon door. The only hand work needed was to trim out the corners of the truck. The fuel was tipped into a local contractor's tipper and delivered to the particular merchant whose name was upon the wagon label. This, as is very apparent to anyone who has ever handled fuel, created a large amount of smalls and slack. Mark had now purchased a hopper holding about 15 cwt., where the fuel handled slid down by gravity into the sack which was standing on the platform of the scales, weighed and put onto your vehicle. At Great Bentley, the clearing of wagons became an urgent necessity.

Having seen the advantages of a tractor with a shovel, I very soon got on the phone and organised a shovel to fix onto our Ferguson 20 Tractor. We also acquired a brand new hopper and a sack lifter. This latter was an excellent tool. It was powered by a small petrol engine and hydraulic pump lifting the full sack, and when removed, its platform returned to the floor. There was a facility to insert a screen into the hopper and this would clean up your fuel to good standards, but of course slack soon built up to rather worrying proportions. The amount of hand work was suddenly dispensed with, and the turnaround of lorries speeded up. With the time saved unloading wagons we began to increase our tonnage by giving a better service.

The small Fergie Tractor was soon found to be not powerful enough or heavy enough, for with the loaded bucket up aloft the machine was very unstable. So we purchased a S/G Fergie diesel, a four-cylinder model which had much more power, but was a trial to start from cold. We had an aerosol can of Instant Start, which was an ether mixture which one sprayed into to air intake. Too much of this would lock the engine. So life was not completely free of trouble!

There is little reference to leisure time in my story. There was always too much to do. The Coal Merchants' Association was still active concerning the station closures. The larger factors were being talked into, or talking themselves into, creating receiving centres, which were being referred to as 'concentrations'. Two were created at Colchester, one by Moy's and the other by the Co-op situated at the Hythe. Mark was very opposed to these, for he could see the end of his railhead at Great Bentley. The various local CMAs were holding Dinner Dances around the counties. The first one I attended was at the Red Lion Hotel, Colchester. The Chairman then was Mr R Dorrington. It was held on 24th April 1963.

The menu was:

Vegetable Soup
Fillet of Sole Bonne Femme
Roast & Croquette Potatoes
Runner Beans
Peach Melba
Coffee

There were four toasts:

1) Her Majesty the Queen
2) The Borough of Colchester
3) The ladies, guest and visitors
4) The Colchester & District Coal Merchants' Association.

The response to the last one was made by CM Simmons. The Toastmaster was none other than myself – not wearing a red coat, though. All that I said was what was written on the programme or menu or whatever it is called.

Someone afterward kindly said that they could read anyway.

There was a kind of obligation to attend dinners, and other activities in the district. We went as far afield as Lowestoft and Bishop's Stortford.

One memorable occasion involved being taken to St Ives, Huntingdon, to have lunch with the directors of Coat & Warren, factors, from whom we had purchased fuel for many years. Geo Copley was the local rep. He lived at Diss, and I drove there and he drove us to St Ives. There was another merchant in the company. The object of the exercise was, as I learned quite quickly, to sell us something. I was offered extended credit from a really charming fellow. The office of the firm was commodious but not very modern; the clerks and so on working there had high desks which they stood behind and seemed to rush about from other points back and forth. There was not a lot of thoughts of comfort. Factors in those days did an enormous amount of business. I had to say that my yard was full of fuel, and despite the offers couldn't really purchase anything additionally to what we normally bought. However, this did not prevent our party being taken a few miles to Holywell to the Ferry Boat Inn. The red building was built in 1068. To read from the folder, which I kept:

English patriot Hereward the Wake crossed by the ferry at the Inn when he was fleeing from William the Conqueror. The ferry always belonged to the Inn, so no doubt the owner brought him over. The water in those days came up to steps of the Inn. Today since the draining of the Fens it only rises at flood times.

The lunch was a very good one. The Stilton was coasted down the table. This was the first time I had tasted Sauternes; it was lovely. The bill for this fare was 17 guineas, I learned afterwards, which I thought was a small fortune. It was a view of a new facet of the world, and a pleasant one. Our venerable host told me on parting that if ever he could be of any help I should contact him.

Other excursions followed. A coach load of merchants visited the Coalite works at Chesterfield, where coal was broken up and put into tubular retorts and partly burned to extract all the tars and chemicals. Away from the retorts were miles of pipes and storage tanks. 'They take all the valuable by-products and sell us the cinders,' said someone. When the process was completed the retorts were discharged into rail wagons and cooled down with copious amounts of water. If one of these wagons were weighed when really wet, and the water was lost in one's yard as in a dry spell, the weight loss was quite critical. I do wonder why we tried to sell so much of it. Of course in a wet season some did stay wet, but at the end of a stocking period when one tried to tally up losses of 7 per cent were common.

Another long coach journey took us to the West Country where the NCB manufactured 'Homefire'. In this process the raw material was coal slack, and some larger stuff ground up quite finely and heated to a certain critical temperature. At this point it was compressed in a hexagonal ram and if there was just enough 'stickiness' left the resultant piece of fuel would be firm and capable of being handled. It appeared that a high proportion did not come out satisfactorily, for there existed a large heap of broken pieces and slack. This was then used at a power station a few miles away. The resultant fuel is still in production (1990) and is excellent in every way I believe Dr Bronowski was the pioneer in this manufacture.

The CMA's unwritten rule was that the Chair should go round. There were one or two comings and goings. Then someone proposed J Calver, and I was installed for no less than three years, from 1964 to 1966, and as is often the case I got very tired of the job. Being rather easily persuaded, I had to resign my membership to escape. While I was holding office I had to preside at the dinners in Colchester. This of course involved me in making a speech. I remember typing one of these and made so many typing errors that it was of little use. A list of headings proved the best way. The responses to the 'Ladies, guests and visitors' was made by the President of the Coal Merchants' Federation. of Great Britain, a very honourable job – or so one would have thought from their appearance, and to some extent their aristocratic tones. I sat on one occasion next to Mrs Stobart, whose husband's job it was to respond. The dear lady was a big noise in the Women's Institute and talked to me at length in her best ladylike voice.

I didn't really have a meal at all, for couldn't very well reply to her with my mouth full.

Flora, who sat on my left, was observing the progress – or lack of it – and I said to her, 'Do you know, I don't know what the hell I've got to say.' She was worried sick. However, I was announced and after the toast I spoke for several minutes, and somehow it all went down very well. Upon the back of the menu appeared the name of Cyril Walker, who had the responsibility of providing the music for dancing. This was the part of the evening that I disliked, for I couldn't dance a step, for the Chairman was expected to start the dancing. I did with Flora attempt to, but hopelessly I fear. I'm afraid that the bar was the next move to calm my nerves. How many of us drove home in a state of mild or severe intoxication, I've no idea.

I did become slightly involved with the Concentration Depot at the Hythe. We were to be allowed 4 tons of Phurnacite per month, which could only be obtained from there. I argued that this could be allowed to accumulate to 12 tons for three months to come to Great Bentley. 'No' was the answer. So off two of us went to this establishment. The lorry was weighed in empty and was reversed up to hopper number whatever. One of us held a bag under the chute, and the other with a foot-operated pedal started the apparatus. The dial recorded the pounds in the bag but didn't begin to operate until about 100 were in the bag. So there was little time to stop it before there was in excess of 112 lb., which was then 1 cwt.

The order was that on 4 tons the allowance of 1/2 cwt. over

that amount was the maximum. Over that, the load had to be re-weighed. I think we went there three times, and on the last occasion the load was slightly over the maximum allowed. I stated emphatically that I was not going to re-weigh the load and got into the cab and drove away in a fury. I very soon told all concerned where to go too, and by various means obtained a load occasionally by road direct.

In 1965, I was still involved with our few acres. A couple of sows and a few chickens were the only livestock and the cropping picture was much as it had been for the previous years, with peas, wheat, barley and sugar beet. We had gone to the trouble of putting down a piece of concrete to store and load these latter, for Cappele wheat was becoming a good productive strain with 11 tons 5 cwt. from 6 acres. The income from crops this year £871, but with no knowledge of the expenses it is of little value to know this. I did spend some of it, much more than the profit, on a S/H Massey Harris 780 self-propelled combine. In May I went with Ralph to Elmswell, where this machine was for sale. There it stood with some fresh red paint here and there. It was powered by a diesel engine, had an electric lift to raise the cutter and header and was fitted with a large platform where one received the threshed corn into bags. About six could be packed on an extension. It had a wire screen within a cylinder, which was adjustable, exactly the same type as in the old threshing drum. This sorted the grain into firsts, seconds and thirds. It came without an instruction book. So we awaited its delivery, and when it came home we played with it, applied grease to the many nipples and tried to start the engine. Needless to say, two 6-volt batteries were below par. We altered the shed where the Allis was stored, and this relic was pushed onto a piece of available ground out of the way to be broken up.

By August the harvest looked forlorn. We had had 14" of rain and on the 10th I read that 'We started to combine barley but trouble soon overtook us', and 1st September: 'Fine day but combine not usable.' On the 7th: 'Worked to 8.30 p.m., wheat 18½ per cent moisture.' It was getting dark, and as we came up the field there were showers of sparks coming from the clutch housings. If there was ever an absolutely lousy buy this must have been the one. Whatever could go wrong just did. We frequently had the local blacksmith here.

We found later, when a well-versed mechanic from one of the main dealers was summoned, that the electrics were actually wired up wrongly.

In April of the next year we had to have the engine reconditioned and four new pistons were fitted. The cost of all this must have been quite prohibitive and our auditor probably said the coal business was subsidising the farm again. Another escapade we got involved in was buying a straw baler. This was advertised in Ipswich and at £60 looked quite okay, but it turned out about the same as the combine. We did do some work at Wrabness Hall using their tractors – until one of the lift arms got mixed up with the bolts in the flywheel of the baler, stripping them off.

My pigs lost money in 1965, so it states in the diary, and as a final footnote the rainfall was about 3" above normal through the year. But in October it was 2" below average, so helping the start for next year's crops on 7th: 'We were collecting coal from Great Bentley for stock, temperature up to 70 degrees – too hot for this work.' We must have been mad or looking for a job, for this involved us in bagging from their hoppers, bringing back here, putting a heavy plant from the back of the lorry onto the stockpile, humping the sacks over to tip into the hollows in the heap.

The rise in price of £1 per ton in October was the attraction. Three journeys were made per rail wagon, a round trip of 22 miles. Viewed in 1991, it seems a bit hopeless and unnecessary.

1st January 1966: Newspaper cutting: 'The small men who were voted into power in 1964' (This was the swing to Labour, which amounted to:

	Seats	Gains	Losses
Labour:	*317*	*61*	*5*
Conservative:	*303*	*5*	*60*
Liberals:	*7*	*3*	*2)*

'have brought the country to the lowest point it has ever occupied on the international scene – the very foundation of the Commonwealth has been shaken – 1966 would see the end of it as it had been known up to now.'

22nd February: 'We are getting nearer and nearer to conditions in a planned economy as you have in a Communist State' – head of CI. Considering the election was held in May, it did not seem to take long to upset everything.

The house was now mine to do whatever I like with. So I though that the main chimney needed looking over. It had two pots upon it, one badly cracked. There were in fact three flues, one from a bedroom not used. So we got the long thatching ladder and put it up to the chimney, and I had a look around. It was in a sorry state. I measured the size of the brick stack and commenced to make a frame to bolt around in order to fix a platform around to work off. We had bought six large crates, ex-RN Depot (used to transport magnetic mines). The 6" x 1½" planks of various hardwood were ideal for the purpose. Needless to say, the chimney was nowhere near square. One Saturday afternoon I tried to fix it around the old brickwork and got in a hopeless muddle. Help was needed; alterations were made and my brother-in-law, Noel, lent a hand. In April I began, and it was 4th June when I wrote: 'Crawled onto platform this afternoon.' I actually *crawled*, for this was the first time I'd ever been on scaffolding. I stood upright and held on. 'Going to have the pots off, then?' came the call from the garden. I inched my way back to the ladder, and came down. I had over the years topped up corn stacks that were almost as high as the present problem without any fear of falling.

With increasing confidence I progressed. The two pots were rolled down the ladder in a rope which was fixed to the top. I took off several courses of bricks and found the 'wiff' between, rotten for quite a long way down. So I made a mould with two pieces of multi-plywood and packed in cement and ballast. The brickwork became quite a bit of fun to put right. The work of bringing down debris and carrying up new materials was the hardest part. On 2nd July the platform was removed.

The interior of the west end of the house was my next goal. When it had been built, a small larder was created. In all the time I had lived here it was never used; in fact the door was rarely opened. It was damp and airless. There were odd pieces of old clothes and among them a lovely tablecloth with drawn thread and crochet work. Flora, to her credit, carefully washed and cosseted it and it is now a treasured possession. So the partition wall had to be removed. The amount of dust was considerable, so to minimise this I built a screen across the living room to make life a little more tolerable. The partition was the usual elm studwork with lath and plaster.

The studs were 2½" x 3", bearing the marks of the pit saw very clearly. Some were quite good, others rotting, for their bottom plate had no damp course; in fact none of the house had and in fact these are only small amounts now!

In the course of building the first cottage the carpenters were getting short of long pieces for the top plate, and made two common lap joints, one either side of the bedroom dormer window.

These needless to say attracted rot, for in bad weather a lot of water runs down the sides of dormers. This caused a nasty bulge on the front wall. It is still there for all to see. When the surveyor comes to appraise the old place one of these days, probably in my absence, he can rest assured that it hasn't moved for many years and I tell you for why. There were a number of large electric light poles in the vicinity for sale, and I bought four. These were taken to Roger's at Wix sawmill and ripped into square section to 5½" where possible. At the spot where the larder wall was taken out, I cut a hole through the ceiling, and with measuring equipment used several times and then a sharp handsaw, put a post up through the hole, bolted to the top plate and to the bottom plate. I then proceeded to put a bridging joist from it, suitably dovetailed in across the room, thus tying the walls together.

The floor joists were not nailed or joined above the previous wall, so I bored 1/4" hole through their ends and introduced 5" nails therein, making a strong job. Needless to say the old floorboards were removed before this, for they were wormed and rotten. In the process of my work I didn't find a nail any longer than 3". These were of course handmade of wrought iron and were probably quite expensive. There again, timber was sometimes in short supply, no doubt, for elm trees took 70 or more years to grown to dimensions needed to obtain large sizes of beams. Elm age-hardens and I defy anyone to drive a nail into it. Inspection of the staircase proved that the damp airless conditions below had caused it to suffer the same fate as the floor. So this was the next hurdle.

I wanted wood that would not be subject to attack by worm, and discussed this at Wix. Sapele was available and was suitable. I had never used this before. It was very dense and heavy. Did I want it cut to length and put through the thicknesser? I usually reckoned I could hand-plane and cut up most of my material, but said, 'Yes please,' to this question. I was glad that I did, for it 'plucked' badly when hand-worked. The old stairs had four 'winders' – usually there were three, the centre one called the kite. I think in this case it was to give a 'quick lift' to the rising, as room upstairs was restricted. It was also 3' wide. I followed the pattern of the old layout, and at the first step, which was literally a box, I placed a sealed jar with items relevant to the date, i.e. coins and newspaper cuttings: a time capsule. On 28th October 1967 I recorded, 'Finished the stairs today.' If I had had the chance and been born in 1725 instead of 200 years later, I would have enjoyed being a stair-caser and hand-railer, having tried to understand the complications of this noble profession from a book bearing this title.

The stairs I was building was about the only opportunity I would get. I could see possibilities for a short banister with turned spindles on the landing. I had seen some at an antique shop in Lavenham, so one fine afternoon Flora and I set off there and there they still were, walnut ones with reeding upon them. Theses were ideal. I recall that the proprietor's wife didn't know the price of the bundle of about 20 pieces. Her husband was not well and she went to inquire; he was past caring and said £10. The lady thought they were underpriced but she had to accept his figure. So I paid up, and we didn't even stop in among the lovely old oak-timbered buildings that always fascinated me to have a cup of tea. We drove home with my prize, planning how to use them. Flora thought it a dry old journey. I needed a matching newel post at the end, and had a Victorian bed end with huge side turnings. So I set to work to put reeding upon it by hand.

This old end had come from David Marshall's several years before. So I laboured on, in the evenings and at weekends, through cold weather when it was really not at all pleasant, for there was no heat on anywhere.

The walls all around the old larder and stairway were crumbling. They were red bricks laid on their sides nogged in between the stud work.

The bonding was pug or clay and plastered all over, studs as well, with lime plaster with cow hair to keep it together. So out most of them came, some of their own accord as hammering continued. I replaced them with portland cement with a galvanised nail tapped into the studs here and there. When rendering them I left some of the studs uncovered and put linseed oil on the exposed surface, which gave a nice honey colour to the old wood.

1st January, from *East Anglian Daily Times*: 'No, we don't like the look of 1967, especially as it will mean 365 days of continuous Labour Government.'

I must add that during the progress of this work during the winter of 1966–67 Flora had a bad attack of flu, in fact almost pneumonia, and I see on 9th January I wrote: 'Snow last night and bitter north wind. I am trying to run the business, cook a bit of food (mostly fish fingers, I seem to recall) and do a little nursing. Flora is not very well!'

I said I always wanted to be mixing up cement on the dining room floor, and now this was just what was happening. It was just like a builder's yard, and I did a little at a time through the winter.

We had had water laid on from the main road at sometime in 1965, and had a bathroom fitted into the west end kitchen, and with electricity and piped water life was a little easier.

Over the past few years I was always looking for tools and especially wood carving tools. They were something that seemed to attract me as much as anything ever did. I began to chop around with some of them and carved what looked to me to represent convolvulus leaves onto a spandrel-shaped piece of mahogany-type wood that was found in the huge crates that carried magnetic mines, which we bought from the RN Depot sale. The local paper seemed to want to advertise my activities, as can be seen. The spandrel/brackets amounted to three and are fixed in the corners where post meets beam in our old house. One of our customers said, 'I see you've got your picture in the paper, bent over a piece of wood!'

Tom Webb built me an extension to the wooden shed to create a garage for our A40 car. This was to become my new workshop eventually. Tom said on one occasion when I was up aloft shaping lead round a dormer window, 'He properly love it.'

Despite all the efforts of Mark, the railhead at Great Bentley closed in 1967 after operating for nearly three years, so we were all relying on road-borne fuel from now on.

Work in the house continued. I did pause to wonder who could have lived here when the cottage was first built. I imagined that they were a newly married couple and how thrilled they were to have a new home. But they may have been elderly and survived with difficulty. The snow that sometimes falls in February was driven by the same force of north-east wind then as now. There were no supermarkets full of tins, packets and bottles; no daily delivery of milk or newspapers.

Syd Gosling, now eighty plus, told me once that when his ancestors lived here various members of the family contributed 6d each per week to keep an elderly grandfather at home, rather than he was taken to 'Tendring Union'.

So in March, I look down the temporary partition and began to look at the old brick floor, which of course was laid onto the bare earth. With advice I decided on a parquet floor of oak blocks. We had the assistance of David and Ralph Porter to taken them out. There was a large pile of them. They are very hard, almost impossible to cut. Some were about 1½" thick, others tapered to one end. Maybe they had been walked on so many years and had became worn to this shape. They are a nice pink colour. I eventually built them into a wall, together with old reds, in the garden. 'The old priory ruins,' said Doc F B once.

The builders were in no hurry to start laying the new floor, so I put pencil to paper and sketched a new fireplace. I intended a four centred arch, and built it with old reds taken from old cottages demolished on Primrose Hill. I managed to fix a primitive panel above from old oak, and in May went off to Dunmow to purchase a fire basket. This was of cast iron and seemed to look well. But when we lit the paper and kindling the smoke was reluctant to go upwards, so I jacked it up with bricks to reduce the opening. Having found the height I cast out two concrete blocks, and the sight of a wood fire was recompense indeed.

In May 1968, I employed an electrician to wire up the three rooms and have the help of sockets and plugs. As the reader may conclude, all the work so far accomplished was done by hand, saws, planes and brace and bits.

In June the builders and floor layers showed up and about 6" of the soil and loam floor was dug out, a sheet of polythene put down, and a concrete floor laid. When this was dry, the block layers turned up and laid a herringbone pattern floor. There were problems, for the concrete was not to totally dry and the blocks moved about a bit. However, twenty-five years on it is all still there.

Our Friends at Dimbols, Peter and Yvonne, had spoken to us about having a holiday, and of all the places to visit, Paris was their goal. Flora was reluctant. 'Who will look after the cats?' she asked. I think there were six of them.

Dear old Ernie Paske had been here taking phone orders and doing a spot of bookkeeping and he would look after our home. Ernie was a gentleman's gentleman in his day and I trusted him absolutely. I gave him a purse containing some valuables and on returning home the first thing he gave me was the purse without a word.

Now from the diary:

On 29th August 1969, we four plus Elizabeth left there shores in their Morris car on the train ferry for Zeebrugge. That night was very rough, but we did not suffer much and had a breakfast of bacon, egg etc.

We set off through Belgium and arrived by autoroute in Paris at 3.30 p.m. It was raining. Peter and Yvonne went off to find a hotel. This was the Hotel Michelet de l'Odéon, about four floors above ground floor by lift to our rooms. This was in the Latin Quarter, where student riots had taken place the year before. Cobblestones had been ripped up an thrown at the gendarmes. I think that a lot of them were still missing, for it seemed a bit rough travelling. Breakfast of coffee and croissants.

By the Métro to the Flea Market: 'Hold on to your wallets and handbags,' Yvonne advised. There we brought pictures and tapestries. There were antiques, and some looked as if they had been taken from churches. 'You buy a Jesus?' someone asked.

We could only afford a meal in the evenings and took numerous tins of food. We bought bread and had a snack as noon. We were by the Métro again to the Arc de Triomphe and walked down the famous Champs-Élysées. Coffee was about 4s a cup on the pavement cafés. We were quite taken with all the wonderful buildings. On the parapets of some of the bridges (ponts) were large boxes fixed.

Various odd folk turned up with keys to unlock them and sell books and maps from them. I bought a volume of plates of pictures in the Louvre Museum.

1st September: we dined in a French café with sawdust on the floor. The large portion of undercooked steak almost made me feel ill; real spaghetti was served which was quite unapproachable.

Hard-up students were singing for their supper. Very odd collection of people of all nationalities. Today we went to the car to Chartres Cathedral. Wonderful medieval building with the stores from the Bible in stained glass all round. The intense smell of incense seemed too much for Flora and me, and we didn't stay in there very long. We all set off for Paris and clatter-clatter…the exhaust pipe was falling to bits! Peter had trouble with his back so I was destined to crawl under and see what to do. 'I didn't bring many tools, wanted to keep the weight down,' said he.

I had a pair of light-coloured trousers on. The tar on the roads of France is just as much like tar as in this country. There was a piece of wire and a pair of pliers. So a sort of repair was made which lasted us through the holiday.

2nd September: The traffic in Paris has to be seen to be believed. At pedestrian crossings on the second that the green light showed, the vehicles just leapt away. We went to the Louvre Museum and saw the Mona Lisa, with the guards and the moisture control. Outside we were moved quickly when a large heavy van pulled up and two guards with Sten-type guns at the ready jumped out. Another person stepped out with what we thought must be the wages for the people working there. At least they didn't wait to set what was going to happen. As the days passed we went to the Palace at Versailles, to Notre Dame, to the Palace at Fontainebleau, and went for lunch in the forest there. Our money was going. I record we paid 8s 6d for five bottles of lemonade. One very pleasant afternoon was spent 'under the bridges of Paris' on a pleasure boat. Manitas de Plata, a guitarist of note, entertained us (talking) at breakfast; we were getting tired of rolls, croissants and jam for breakfast.

We viewed the prison where Marie Antoinette was imprisoned and touched the guillotine blade reputed to have severed her head.

We left Paris at 8 a.m., and after getting lost in Kent through not having a good map arrived home at 10 p.m. (the white cliffs were really a welcome sight). So we went to the Cottee's to tell them of our homecoming, and I do not recall there was much interest in what we had to tell them. Lynda had left a note to say, 'The cats are all right but they have missed you.' I think we had about six of various sorts at that time.

Cats

So…it was back to work, which was about the same as usual, but before that let have some reminiscence about the cats.

I read somewhere of someone's opinion of the cat family and it was (in part): 'They are a jungly beast, usurping upon our hearths under a thin mask of civilisation. They make the night hideous, but be sure they will come home with the milk.'

Another few lines remembered were:

> I call my cat Anonymous
> He really is the sweetest puss
> The cutest and the neatest puss
> And always has been so.
> He never tells me were he goes
> But leads and shows his needs
> And sits with tail-wrapped toes.

Of course all these observations are correct, but with all their imperfections cats do a lot of good as well as harm. Father used to say, 'You don't know how much good a cat does.'

So I'll say, 'A cat has always lived here.'

When I was very young we had a longish-haired tabby named 'Toots'. I think Mother brought him here when she married. I wheeled him around in my pushchair as and when I was capable. I think he lived until he was 14. Sometimes male cats were castrated by a person used to the job, and of course without anaesthetic. A buskin was obtained, and the unfortunate animal held therein by another person by the hind legs and gripped between his legs. Needless to say there were many animals that were not dealt with, and consequently many unwanted kittens.

We've had many cats. One tabby in my teens is remembered through appearing back home after about ten days of absence with his back leg hanging, having been caught in a gin trap and in an awful state. The vet had to put him down.

When we were first married we had a tabby tom named Winkle. I taught him a few tricks. We rolled up different coloured silver papers and put them on the mantelshelf. By discouraging him from some colours, we got him to take a red one or silver, ignoring green. He walked his front feet along the edge while being held on my hand by his back feet. He would ride on my shoulder at any time. I erected a hoist by fixing a piece of board at the top of a broom handle. He would mount this when I held it and I pushed him up under the eves of the house at dusk to catch one of the sparrows roosting there. When I lowered the device and stood on one leg, bringing the other leg up horizontally, he would jump onto my thigh and down with his supper. If I collected a gun and proceeded to the barn he would follow if he saw me set off. We accepted a black and white kitten who was name Nips. As he grew up (like Winkle, he was not neutered), many fights ensured. I caught the pair of them on a broom once, locked together tooth and claw, and dropped them into a shallow water butt. They very quickly leapt out of there and this cooled their courage, I think there was a bit of Bernard here for I laughed heartily.

At Foxes at this time there was a 'mother cat', who frequently felt the boot of the fellow milking the house cow there. She found her way over here and Flora made her welcome. She had some Siamese in her make-up and was a lovely cat. So one day, as one would expect she brought across the footpath three kittens. There were accepted and became Titchy, Ging and Webb-Webb. The two first mentioned were female and of course produced kittens. Titchy had a black one which was to become the pet of Lynda. Ging had three lovely sandy ones which were all found homes, one being sent by rail to Southend, where it found much love. One awful experience was trying to drown kittens with two buckets of water. You put the little wretches into one bucket about half full and pushed the full one in on top trapping them in the bottom to drown. We had several rotten experiences with the disposal of kittens. One involved putting chloroform into a biscuit tin together with the poor little animals; they took several minutes to die. This was under the direction of the vet. Eventually, spaying and neutering was becoming the thing to do, and we had the younger ones dealt with.

One day in 1953 Joseph discovered a cat asleep under a bullock manger. It was in poor condition. A rat had just been caught in a gin in the barn and Father pulled out his pocket knife and cut the rat into pieces and threw it toward the cat. This was very acceptable to it, and thereafter the old lad stayed and caught many rodents. We called him 'BC' for barn cat. Father each day without fail took him a small allowance of bread and milk. BC survived for nine and a half years and we never knew how old he was. (One old customer in Stones Green said of cats to me, 'They bring love with them, they are always wanting something done for them.')

Mother cat was not spayed and some kittens arrived; one of these was a grey tabby and was in poor shape. The motherly instinct of Flora came into play and she fed this babe from a doll's milk bottle. 'Poor little sing,' we said and it was christened 'Sing'. She had to stay, of course, and was once discovered up in a high elm tree over at Foxes.

Harold, who was working there, volunteered to get her down. So off home we came and collected a ladder to gain access. She was wet and cold, and very soon had chest troubles. This grew worse and became pneumonia and along came the vet. This gent was one of what we thought to be something different. Cortizone was given to our pet and gradually she recovered. She ate nothing for days and one day Flora was pleased to report that this babe licked a piece of liver. So I find in the diary for 8th June 1974:

During the day we had to decide to have our precious little old Sing put to sleep. She was having much difficulty breathing and could not lie down because of this. So after 15 years we are without her. We both feel worse than when my father died. Things will never be the same again, for she was always there and expecting and receiving attention, but I suppose will have to put up with it. She has her resting place beneath the lilac tree. So now Luke is the only cat we have. Life should be easier, but I don't think it will be.

Reading this must seem to you rather a sentimental tale, but Flora had spent so much love and affection on this (and of course all cats), and we having no children perhaps shows the feeling within the story. Luke was a doctored tom, all black. He spent a greater part of his life in front of the Rayburn cooker, and grew into a solid lump of cat. His lungs gave up the fight through lack of exercise. His end came on 28th April 1980 at fourteen and a half years old. For a while we were without a cat. This situation did not last for very long – see muse on cats – verse three:

> And without a doubt that cat will come,
> (Last of a kindle, or starving stray).
> Home will be once again really home
> When the new unknown decides to say
> Soon to become an integral part
> Of my life, and the heart of my heart!

August 1980: The diary reveals:

A day or two back the black cat with the short tail that lives, or rather exists, next to the Village Hall was taking her four kittens for a walk, when I was taking Phineas the dog for his usual morning constitutional. The kittens showed little apprehension at seeing the dog, and one of them came over to see us. It seemed to say, 'Come and rescue us!'

I discussed the prospects on arriving home. We went off to the house where they lived (or rather survived). The family were very wild and unkempt. The kittens were nowhere to be seen. However, on the 20th we went to the house again with a box to collect two. One tabby was easily picked up, but a tabby and white was up a tree which I somehow clambered up and hauled her down. We put them in the 'backhouse' shed and they absolutely devoured milk and bread and meat. We looked in a little later and they had climbed aloft and were both in a plastic box on its side on the shelf.

The white one was to be called Pip and the tabby, Tammey. Pip on her first adventure outside dived into the periwinkle and came out with a mouse. She climbed trees like a rocket. Tam was rather less active and made friends with Phin – he has accepted the little cats completely. She eventually would lay on my back when I bent down to do gardening.

As time went on and they were taken to the veterinary to be spayed. Upon their return Tam was not bothered about resting a bit, but Pip did not accept her convalescence so well. However, the pair of them were hunting at all times, but were put into their bed at night with food of course. Again the diary: 'A certain gent named Friar Bartholomew wrote several hundred years ago that "the cat scratcheth and biteth and leapeth".'

These young ladies do all these things at the same time, and in the first days of their arrival here they licked upon the crumbs from the tablecloth shaken on the backyard. And so for a year or two we enjoyed them, but they would not keep within the boundary of our holding. Pip was to be seen up by the side of Brakey Grove, her white showing clearly. Flora would call her from our gate. She would come galloping home to be carried up to the house all 'lollopy' and relaxed.

One could not have expected them to keep off the road, for that was where they had to try to find food when they were tiny. So Tammy was nowhere to be seen one evening. Flora called her repeatedly. We searched next day and found her dead near Foxes Stile. So I stitched her into a blanket parcel and buried her in the garden.

On 30th July 1985, Rosemary telephoned Flora and sounded very distressed. Her cat had had kittens, and through her tears she said, there was one 'pretty little tabby – oh, do have her, she'll have to be put down.' Flora said, 'What do we do?' I said, 'Oh well, all right then.' So there soon arrived another blue-eyed bundle. She was named Tammy II. Her bedroom was the garden shed across the grass and to the call of 'food' etc. she would race into its safety without any trouble. She was not in need of cosseting and never did want to be cuddled. Pip hissed and behaved like a cat; Phin was fascinated. She (Tam) was shown the working of the cat flap and within a couple of trial runs used it like a veteran.

So life went along fairly smoothly (as far as cats were concerned) for a few weeks, and then at 6.15 on 23rd October, the doorbell rang and Mary M had driven up and said, 'I've just run over your cat.'

I was mortified. Flora came to the door. Poor Pip was laid on the passenger seat of the car. I carried her indoors (or perhaps it was Flora) and put her in the transport box, hoping to perhaps take her to the vet. She kicked a couple of times and that was the end. I closed her eyes and cried. I cursed motor cars. We both felt sorry for Mary, who offered to bring us a replacement kitten, but we declined. We spend the night half asleep, half awake. Flora said, 'She is dead, isn't she?' For an awful moment I thought, well, er... 'Oh yes, I'm sure she is,' I said.

I didn't feel I could face another cat burial next morning. But I had to, and another piece of blanket was wrapped around the old lifeless pet and quickly buried near the box hedge, where little disturbance would take place.

So we were left with one. She was spayed but not before having a love affair. She was 'in kit', and when this is the case the operation is more complicated and traumatic for the patient.

The next turmoil was in April 1986. Flora was concerned that Tam was nowhere to be seen and hunted for her. She found her in the shed near the barn in 'a distressed state'. I was doing work at Dovercourt for one of my clients and on arrival home was confronted with this dilemma. So we went off to Clacton with her to find she had a cracked pelvis. There was no treatment and we fetched her home in a day or so, and she convalesced in a box near the Rayburn cooker. She had a pan of sawdust for urinating etc. and began to eat more each day. As soon as she felt like it, out of doors she went. Motor cars and other machines were to be avoided by her.

We assumed something of this description was responsible for her injuries, so in 1992 she is still with us.

In March 1987 I recorded we have been feeding, off and on, a large black tomcat who had been courting Tammy. He 'couldn't understand why she ignored him'. Within a few days we found him with a rotten snare around his hips. With difficulty, we captured him and cut it away. These things should be banned. He became more docile and ate food like a vulture, and of course came indoors to take over one of the kitchen chairs.

When he was well fed, he would go, and we watched him going across the field in various directions many times. He was away three weeks at a time.

He had some amusing ways, but one bad disadvantage in that he had permanent enteritis. This was of course transmitted to Tam, and meant a further episode with the vet for her. Luckily, with his care it soon cleared up. Tom came and went until at the end of July 1991 he arrived here in a poor state. He had been fighting and had a septic joint on his left front leg and a swollen pad on the right. He was attended by many flies. So I'd been waiting for a good reason to bring about his end. One injection in the chest is all that it takes these days. I paid the £10 and brought him home to another burial.

There are odd memories that present themselves. The cat Toots would wait on the stile for my Ma and me when we went over to Foxes. Titchey would wait after dinner until Flora had finished eating and leap up onto her upper arm to go to sleep under her chin. Sing was affected by high-pitched notes, and liked the treble music played on the piano. On one occasion Mother cat (The one from Foxes) sat about in quiet misery. She could not seem to eat. I opened her mouth to find a head of grass across her palate. We had a handy canvas bag with drawstring into which she was put. Removal of the foreign body was easy. She was very grateful.

In March 1997 a large white tomcat visited us. He was very hungry and usually turned up about twilight time. In June he appeared with streaming eyes and was poorly by now. His tail had disappeared. So off to the veterinary we go. I suggested putting to sleep. 'He's quite a young cat – you like cats – we can get him through this,' said Ron Reeves; so an injection was administered. A week or so later fleas were given a jerk with organochloride rubbed into his coat on the skin (very dangerous stuff). In September we decided to have him castrated. This was duly done. Flora said, 'He'll say I did have a good job once and someone took it away from me!' The tail had a piece still attached about 2½" long. He could not keep himself clean, as this could not be moved up for his back bone as broken. So back to the vets for a further op, which has made life much better. In October 1998 he was indoors off and on and had really become an indolent heap. So Snow/Snowy had cost me:

£26
£34
£83.99
Total: £143.99.

Tammy is still with us, and spends rough days upstairs or anywhere she fancies. So in 1992 Tammy would fatten herself up from October onwards to survive with the winter. She eats small amounts frequently and catches a mouse fairly often, comes to the door to show us, want her supper and willingly goes into the backhouse shed, where her bed is a box up at eye level lined with an old pure wool blanket. As I write, she is asleep on her favourite chair. Should a stranger enter the room she is gone upstairs; if the door is open, I can say scarcely anyone had ever got to within three feet of her. Flora and I are the only people she knows and trusts. She is our cat!

Dogs

I mentioned way back of the demise of Spider, who was a small mongrel, rough-coated, white, who was usually just behind my father's boots on her journeys with him back and forth from house to barn. After her death we were without a dog until, on learning of Cairn terriers just down the road, decided to have a puppy. On 7th July 1974, we went along by arrangement and bought one. He was of noble parentage. He was to be called Phineas, abbreviated to 'Phin' or 'Phinny'. This breed is quite hardy and jolly. We took him around in the pickup and often went for walks with him to Dedham on the shore and in the Stour wood. Once in Dedham we were spoken to by a stranger who asked of his name, etc. She without doubt thought that Phineas was much better than Mandy, Pandy or Shandy, which names were usually planted upon dogs by their owners in those days. Dogs do keep you walking, and this is one of their virtues. They have other advantages, or so Flora always tells me. I walked him every morning up to the school bridge and back; this was about one mile.

Sometimes it was not fit for man or beast to be out, but on most occasions it was. He would leap into the roadside grass, and sometimes and a mole was his victim. So life went on until 12th April 1987, when he was showing signs of distress. He had of recent days become quite truculent. We could no longer pick him up, and on this day we didn't know what to do. So we phoned the vet at Clacton and took him there. The vet said our dog probably had this and that, and there wasn't a lot they could do; so the diary read: 'So we decided to have him put to sleep. I fingered his collar. "Leave his collar on," said I to the vet. Should we take him home to bury? Flora thought not. I couldn't face it. So we left him there standing on the rubber-topped table, just left him there and walked away. Afterward I was ashamed of myself.'

Life during the next few days were very different. Poor Flora! Phinny had been under her feet so very much. He had been waited on hand and foot, and was really very demanding latterly. 'No more dogs,' said Flora. We both immersed ourselves in work. I had to fix the panels I'd made to extend the reredos at the church – a job to be finished by Easter.

John H, who with his wife has kennels nearby, offered us another Cairn, but he was a couple of years old and we ducked having him. But at the kennels they also bred Yorkshire terriers and we decided in July 1988 to have a puppy. We went up there to talk about it and there were fifteen of these valiant little dogs rushing about in all directions. There was a litter due and we waited until September and went off to collect the little treasure.

The first night with this small hound was quite unforgettable. Flora tried to get him to sleep in a cardboard box. I had fixed a rebated piece of wood on the door-post and slipped a piece of ply into the slots. So we went off to bed and before we got to the top of the stairs he was at the bottom. Flora came down to try to repeat the idea, but the 10" barrier was no deterrent. He climbed over it and wanted to be with us. Inspection showed he was not clean round the rear end and Flora spent sometime cleaning him up. When this had been done she came to bed – with pup in arms – and he lay for what was left of the night snuggled up into her chin and, so she maintained, sobbed for some of the time. He was to be named 'Bobbie' and from the first time he was so addressed he was Bobbie. He was a little later having aggravation in his ears and the vet found he had mite in them. Poor little sod, we had to squirt lotion into them, and he didn't like that a bit. But this was pronounced 'A okay' eventually. So of course he ruled our lives. He sleeps on the bed, has chicken cooked to mix with his other food, does not like riding in the car, barks hysterically at planes and helicopters, at the phones ringing, and at people arriving to the door. He tears about with and after a ball, and plays with an orange to our great amusement. Flora would be lost without his companionship.

Over several years Margery Rouse, who after 1992 was living at Wimbourne House, Dovercourt, called in; she worked for a short period at Dimbols farm. She was a dog lover 100 per cent, and Bobbie was a very favourite one, rushing about the house.

By November 2000 our lives were beginning to change – drastically. Flora was losing her memory, and Bobbie, who had received a lot of my attention by way of washing trying to keep him free of fleas, had for some time been subject to internal wobbles. He would wake us up in the hours before sunrise and he had to find a piece of goose grass or cleavers and eat small bits of the end of the youngest, and this helped; but when it didn't we had to take him to the vet's. He was impossible in a motor car, and the journey there was enough to drive even a dog lover into swear words. 'Excess bacteria in the intestines' was the diagnosis, and a injection worked like a charm. But on about the 15th November, he was in awful trouble and had some 'evacuation of the intestines'. Our bedroom looked like a newsagent's on a bad day. I had to put newspapers down on the floor up against the walls and furniture. Bobbie sometimes missed the paper and my bare foot found the offending spot.

Back to the vet's, and the old hand who administered the injections had retired that very weekend. The young replacement, in spite of him having read previous treatments, did not use it, and supplied tablets – which were impossible, for Bobbie could not eat anything. By late afternoon he was so loose and continuously rushed outside, and I didn't know what to do. So I put newspapers on the workshop floor and shut him in there. So next day at 6.45 a.m. we ventured to look. He looked so pathetic, as if to say, 'How could you do this to me?' Diarrhoea was everywhere; the smell was sour and horrid. We carried him indoors and he was still being ill. We both agreed this could not continue. The vet's at Little Clacton, as it was Sunday, opened at 9.40. I rang John H, and he said he would take us; so he came and I put Bobbie into the basket. John's wife came to stay with Flora. It was all over very quickly.

After dinner we went to the workshop. I suggested we keep a piece of his hair. Flora said, 'I can see the piece I want.' So I cut it off and placed it behind a picture of him. The saddest part was when she kissed his little old head. I wrapped him into the towel that so many times we had used to wipe his feet. I stitched him into a bundle and cried like a child. Through my tears I blurted out, 'I didn't even give him any water overnight.' Then I dug a grave and hit tree roots which did not allow a very deep hole. But it was in a place where there would be a minimum of disturbance.

He was 12¼ years. Over those years he had dominated our lives, for approximately 4370 times he had slept on our bed. I didn't like this activity at all, especially when (as was usually the case) I was last to bed. He would growl and snarl and defy my entry. Flora said several times when we came home in the car, 'He will come back, won't he?' which was heartbreaking. I had a love-hate relationship, if anyone ever did.

Back to when he needed washing. He hated this operation. When we put the plug into the sink outlet he would hide under the most difficult chair there was to get him. Latterly, I would put his lead on at the first move. I wore a plastic apron, and if he caught sight of this beforehand we had the same performance. Fleas were subdued by using a flea control shampoo. We caught 40 on one occasion after washing and 30 on another time. Then eventually the veterinary chemist came up with a spray which, applied monthly, was excellent.

In July 2002, Tammy was continuing to live her life as usual until around June when she had become very choosy about her food. The mince I've cut up and frozen for her didn't suit; she couldn't jump onto a chair very well. She stopped going upstairs and became very thin. So I took her to the vets on 29th July, and it was soon over. Michael E came with me and dug her grave back home under the holly tree, where she had wandered through the 17 years she survived here. I shed a few tears but knew this day would come eventually. I miss her in the mornings and at night, when she would always be wanting attention. Grief is the penalty we pay for love.

She would follow me when walking Bobbie and stay waiting for us at the barn. When we returned she would like to have her neck rubbed by the rubber end to my walking stick. All the nostalgic things are very difficult to tolerate.

Now it is August 2002, and here I am without animals except for Snowy. He is as much of a pest as ever, leaping onto any elevated surface looking for food. He spends quite a lot of time in the shed but he does settle when I am sitting around. I am considering moving house when a new bungalow is built along Station Road, on the last fragment of land that remains of the field that my grandfather bought in 1891 or thereabouts.

It was not going to be possible to take him to the new address for it's just across the fields and he would have gone back. He had been in a fight and had a septic wound so another journey to the vets and another grave to dig.

Chapter Twelve: Antiques and Other Diversions

In 1968 we found the MOT tests on vehicles was becoming time-consuming and frustrating. We were, as for many years before, involved with Page & Scott at Colchester. What we had to do well before a test was due was to drive a truck up to Colchester and leave it there for a couple of hours while the lads gave it a preliminary survey. We'd come home and organise a date for the MOT test at Ipswich, drive back to Colchester for them to do whatever was needed to the vehicle, and they would get it to Ipswich etc. and then off back to Colchester to collect it – plus the account, which seemed to get larger by the day.

On a Monday I was involved on the first journey, and having two hours to spare, walked to the saleroom on East Hill. This was viewing day. I wandered in, and at the back among treasures not really on view was a large carved wooden picture frame. It was Chinese, as was the lovely needlework picture it contained. I didn't really study it closely and left a bid for £10. It was delivered here via a local carrier, the price £9. I started to admire its beauty.

There is a story in the frame, for at the bottom is carved a circular table with a scroll upon it. There are three Chinese figures around the table, each with the traditional broad hats on. At the top is a similar table with two vessels shown upon it. Originally three figures were behind, but one is broken off as it forms a large piece of the frame above. The sides are covered in incised carving representing birds, horses, people in robes, hatless, emerging from buildings. Every scrap of wood is decorated. The sizes of tools used must have been about the size of a darning needle. The needlework of the picture – of trees and birds – is almost beyond belief. There is not a stitch out of place. There are families of birds, cocks sparring around, ducks on the water. A bird of paradise sits on a rock, its tail sweeping down to the ground, two pheasants perch on a rock opposite, a silver stork struts nearby.

'The seals that you transcribe', the British Museum declares, 'give the names of the makers; The Lady Chen Chil'lan: Ch'en Wang: and Chinn-Lan.' The V & A, after looking at a photo of the picture, concludes:

> The panel probably made between 1850 and 1900. This meticulous type of embroidery is still being carried out in China today...it is in satin stitch executed in untwisted thread which gives a very glossy effect so characteristic of Chinese needlework.

I look at it mostly every day and see something that I'd missed before. So there was some good emanating from my cursed journey to Colchester.

Needlework is not one of my capabilities, but samplers were of interest. In the bottom of a drawer in Mother's bedroom I discovered one. Its border almost non-existent but enough of it remaining to show it was 'Wrought by Eliz Daniel Age 13 years, in 1772'. Its age and the quality of its execution was of considerable interest, and I put it in a frame behind glass. This shows a house and trees, the house looks quote a good Georgian type, and the motto reads, 'Beauty is a Flower that fadeth away, but virtue a jewel that never decay'. In due course I found other samplers; they mostly have a pious verse and the alphabet etc. They were in some cases done as part of the young lady's education, I guess. I'm reliably informed that some samplers have had the age or date picked out so as not to give away the age of the seamstress.

One gem, in its original oval frame, had just the following poem or verse upon it:

Against Pride

Let not gay clothing captivate your sight,
Shun tawdry ornament as vain as light;
Let modesty and taste your dress prepare
The external form demands a decent care.

Consult the fashion, but the medium know
Between the sloven vile, and flaunting beau.

Short is the triumph of the empty mind
Whole thoughts to rich attire are chief confined.

Study to wear the everlasting charm
That sickness cannot rob or age disarm.
The unchanging grace that virtue will bestow
Decay shall soon invade all else below.

Susannah Ling
Badingham

The border is a flowing stitchwork of small flowers and leaves. It is not dated, but is probably from the late Georgian era. I removed the wooden back, because a woodworm was visible. The back was actually a mortise and tenon panel of the thinnest wood. I replaced it completely with a piece of softwood of similar date. Perhaps this was wrong, in retrospect.

In 1992 there seems to be a revival of ladies doing sampler work.

I was becoming more and more interested in antiques. Here and there I was finding old pieces of furniture – sheds where we had to go through to tip fuel into odd corners. Sometimes there'd a broken chair or table. Mentioning odd corners, often fuel was tipped as far away from the house as possible, resulting in a long walk for the customer with a hod or two in his or her hands. Through some of the lanes around here there were still cottages using a kitchen range, and coal was still looked for by the older ladies still living in these dwellings. At one farm we used to tip the coal into what was at one time 'the backhouse'. This old house had a large brick oven and a large very early kitchen range. One bay had wide wooden shelves, and obviously bread etc. was stored in here years ago. There was a smaller bay nearby. The two customers living in the old house had husbands who were workers on the farm, and had their fuel tipped into these sections. At the larger one were relics of farming from over the years. There were old brashing hooks, hoes, a steelyard weighting balance, and a circular ebonised tray with a shell pattern in its centre. I asked if I could buy some of these items, starting with that tray. 'Take what you like,' said my customer. I offered to pay for the prize but was told, 'No, you're welcome.'

In the village I discovered a carved bedpost. This was mahogany and was eventually cut up and part used to make brackets for the mantelshelf over the kitchen range. Later, in an elderly customer's kitchen, I spied a circular table top. My enquiry led to her showing me the leaf in the shed at the back of the house. Further chat led to my going over the road and finding the complete frame in among the bushes near the tiny chapel.

Its castors were, of course, green with verdigris. The spindles and other steel parts were rusty beyond resurrection. The frame was happily just sliding rails and not controlled by a screw and handle. The legs were ugly, the sort that our Victorian ancestors would have covered up for modesty. All the bits were loaded onto the lorry and stored in the barn; 5 cwt. of coal paid the bill, under protest from my customer, as she said I could take it free of charge.

There were considerable finds at the Rectory. The Rev. was living in rather a muddle, and among several broken fallen-back chairs in the partly roofless shed, I found a large breakfast tip-up table on a tripod fees with reeded central column. It was, though, short of one of its feet. There were other items all over the place. I offered him a price which now escapes my memory, and I think with reservation he accepted.

The butler's tray, which I offered £8 for, did not come my way. He sold it for four times that amount, so he said, later on. These and other items were stored in the barn for the future.

On one occasion two chairs from the 1800s – mahogany, as one would expect – were standing outside the back of a customer's house. I enquired about them.

'Them old things? I'm asking the dustman to take them,' said the lady.

'I'll buy them, if you like,' said I, with hope. They were mine in exchange for two bags of Coalite.

I seem to recall this fuel was about 17s a bag in 1968. This may seem a poor price to the reader, but considering that Flora and I brought a perfect cylinder-top desk with cupboards under and satinwood fittings to drawers for £9 from an antique shop in Manningtree, you may have some idea of the difference in values twenty years later. In point of fact it was sold for £180 at some time in the 1980s.

One of my farmer acquaintances was moving from the sixteenth-century house his father had owned for many years. There were a few items for sale, and one of the best of them was a mahogany long-case clock of Scottish make. It was on top of a whole heap of broken furniture and was in need of repair. This along with hallstands, large side cabinets, brass fire irons, stair rods (5/8" diameter), a Victorian electromagnetic shock machine, and sundry broken chairs etc.

At the saleroom in Dovercourt I attended, I discovered a nice old needlework box, probably made on board a lightship, of teak with ivory or whalebone decorations, and old tea set and an early chest of drawers. This latter was of 1690–1710 vintage, of walnut veneer on a pine carcase. Someone said the top drawers were 'wonky'. I laughed this off. This item was mine for £16 (=10s). Truth to tell, I didn't know the possible date at the time that it was brought. Another interesting deal was some bedroom furniture surplus to a customer's needs: nice quality, but not valuable. The owner, who was deceased, had been a diamond settler in the 1920s. I purchased the pieces and was offered two urns from a shelf, that the vendor said contained the ashes of this gent. This did not appeal, but the furniture was brought to the barn.

Now I'm going back a year or two to about 1965. I was at the bottom of our field in the autumn and on the opposite side of the ditch two folk were talking. It was Peter and Bernard W. Now Bernard was a rotund fellow, probably about seventy years old. His hair was quite lush and wavy. Peter introduced him and I found he was interested in firearms. He was well acquainted with the 9mm garden gun, and had one which, with the adapted cartridge and very fine shot, was used to bring down butterflies. I had never heard of this, and during the next thirty minutes learned that he had bought and sold antiques for many years.

Flora and I were asked to Dimbols a little later on, and after tea Bernard entertained us with an amusing 'sketch' about a Jewish fellow who does not like eating melon 'because it made his ears vet', among other things. His knowledge of antiques and of the world in general was something else. One of my early acquisitions from him was a wooden figure, carved probably in lime, of a religious subject with an ermine cape and the head bent slightly forward, presumably blessing someone or somebody. Under its base a small piece of paper was fixed and upon it was written *Spanish, mid-1600s.* What a buy! I was fascinated. Soon after, Bernard found a plaster shelf and back piece to prove a perfect setting for it when hung in a corner.

I was finding a new life in becoming involved with old items, but I knew nothing of dates and the periods involved with them. On WH Smith's display in Colchester High Street, I discovered a Pelican Original, printed in 1955: *English Furniture Styles, 1500–1830*, by Ralph Fastnedge. It cost 10s 6d (52½p) and contained 310 pages of well-written information. I pawed and read and made notes and began to learn. The first chapter was called, 'The Period of Oak'. I really knew little oak furniture, in fact nothing about its decoration. When old Alfred Ham's ancient coffer came my way, I realised it was old and used it as a tool chest in the barn; but when I saw that it could have been made at anytime between two or three hundred years before, I started to treasure it. Now it's in our bedroom, full of blankets etc. and cleaned up and polished. Some of them had a box across one end (inside) with a lid for keeping a clothes brush and other small items in.

Bernard and I went to Wivenhoe at some time in this period where there was a real antique shop. There were pieces of furniture there I'd never seen before: nice chests of drawers, corner cupboards etc. and two court cupboards. These consist of a two-door cupboard at the bottom and a top one with canted front and two supporting pillars. The centre door at the top was a kind of secret one having hinges concealed. 'Now here is a good example of a court cupboard,' said Bernard. 'There are one or two restorations but basically this one is a good piece.'

So I paid £120 for it, loaded it into the pickup truck, and off we went home; but not before I'd made the acquaintance of the restorer working at the back of the shop. This was Jeff. I looked around at the lathe, the various woods and tools and the work he was doing, and can honestly say that he was the only chap I've ever envied. This was what I wanted to do.

I heard from someone, I've forgotten who, that at a shop in Colchester there was an oak bedhead. I made a few phone calls and took one of our lorries up there to collect it. It was in several pieces. Upon inspection, some were missing. The vendor sat in his shop of treasures. He was a bit pompous; at his small table there was a bottle of sherry and a wine glass. I mentioned the condition of my intended buy. 'Oh well,' said he, 'I can sell it to another buyer without rising from my chair.'

So I paid him (I have forgotten the figure) and home we came. This lovely old thing was the head of four-poster, unfortunately cut down at the base, with arcading in the back. It had been stored in a hayloft, for there was much evidence of grass seeds, and believe it or not there was still the perfume of powder within its dusty joints. At a considered estimate it dates from about the last quarter of the 1500s. Part of the arcading was absent.

I had noticed the collapse of an old timber house in one of the farm lanes, and calling nearby had a nose round. There were some of the floorboards sticking out of the ruins and I pinched a couple. They were as old as the bedhead. So with quite a bit of effort with a hand saw I sliced some 'thin bits', got busy with setting it out and carved as near a copy as possible. As I assembled it, I considered its installation in the bedroom, which was now in an almost a finished state.

I had covered the floor with 2' wide chipboard by now, so I arranged the joining up of the frames with woodscrews and carried the pieces up and fixed them all together back to the chimney breast. It looked dominant and unfriendly; Flora said something like, 'I've put up with lots of things, but I'm not living with *that*!'

So I took it into pieces again and since then it has adorned the stable bygones shed. I've never given up on the ideal of making it into a four-poster but the end posts have defeated the idea so far.

With Fastnedge's book at hand, I read in the chapter called, 'The Early Walnut Period, 1660–1690' as follows:

'This day the month ends…and all the world in a merry mood because of the kings coming.' Thus wrote Pepys at the end of May 1660.

This was of course the restoration of Charles II to the throne, about which I knew little or nothing. So I ferreted out many details of the periods of furniture through the following 250 years, and recorded them on paper. It was to become a voyage of discovery. One early find was the information that 'coarse dovetailing of drawers was taken through to the front and veneer covered it'. The grain of drawer bottoms ran from 'front to back, and not side to side', and this feature persisted 'throughout the first half of the eighteenth century'.

What a joy when I found this feature on the old chest of drawers bought for £16 10s. A similar one was bought from a shop in Ardleigh with double half-round moulding on the carcase: 'c. 1700 to 1720'.

One thrilling paragraph told me about Grindling Gibbons from John Evelyn's diary:

> This day (18th January 1672) I first acquainted his Majesty with that incomparable young man Gibbons whom I had lately met in an obscure place by meere accident as I was walking near a poor solitary thatched house in a field in our Parish (Deptford). I found him not in, but looking in at the window, I perceived him carving...I asked him, if I might enter. He opened the door civilly to me, and I saw him about such a work as for your curiosity of handling drawing and studious exactness I never had before seen in all my travels. I questioned him why he worked in such an obscure and lonesome place. He told me it was that he might apply himself to his profession without interruption.

The story goes on to say that the King was acquainted with the splendid work 'with festoons and flowers about' it. The King did not buy it, but GG was 'brought to the notice of Christopher Wren', who set him on a career followed with merited success for a space of fifty years.

The imagination attached to the thatched house and its being solitary appealed to me, for I had spent many hours along with tools and wood, doing carved work, but definitely nothing resembling wonderful stuff the like of GG. So I read on, and revelations of the Early Georgian Period of lacquer furniture were most instructive. Having acquired the lacquered long-case clock the descriptions were very near to my heart, for as I think I mentioned before I did attempt its restoration, and in fact what I achieved is still to be seen upon it now. The worst dilapidation was on the hood and its base, for the trunk was in reasonable condition. The pictures in the Chinese taste are as good as ever.

E Garnham sold Dimbols in 1953 (I think). He, his wife and one aunt and a lodger, R Watson, moved to Parham in Suffolk. Now RW was interested in antiques, and they became quite involved with buying and selling to a great extent to the USAAF personnel around. Flora was well acquainted with the family and I became a bit involved by telephone and bought about twenty metal boxes, each containing one year's publications of the *Connoisseur* dating from its early days about 1902. We stacked them in the house and whenever I could spare a few minutes I was perusing. What fun! In the early days one could have filled one's house with lovely oak furniture for a song. Often, it was quite late in the evening, Flora would have gone to bed and I would go through a few more copies. The legend of King Arthur was a bit of a mystery and seemed beyond my limited knowledge. There were frameable pictures of horses jumping fences, with hounds in attendance, horses pulling coaches and some just standing. I kept some of these and twenty-five years later they haven't yet been framed.

Reggie found me five warming pans minus handles. He supplied patterns for them and I turned up a couple and sold them on the coal round.

A few years later on, Flora and I went to Parham to see what there was to buy. 'The Church Farm' house was a large ancient place of two stores. There was evidence of a minstrels' gallery, so it was surely a house with the square hall and a fire on the floor in the centre. At a huge fireplace, where a log fire was burning upon a huge bed of ashes, there was the original chimney crane. It was so fascinating. In its early days the fire would not have been allowed to go out during the winter time. I could have filled my kettle and swung it over the embers and made tea, or with a cast iron boiler suspended with soup therein have ladled into my pewter plate its warming broth, and mused of what life was like 300 years ago. In reality of course life was not at all idyllic, for when one was ill, the horse was harnessed to get help; but it was nice to dream for a few minutes.

As time went on into the 1970s, Reggie restored long-case clock movements for us to perfection for around £10 each, can you believe. I asked him had he any boxes for sale. This meant tea caddies, needlework and trinket boxes etc. He produced about sixteen of various boxes for £30. I have had a lot of fun repairing and restoring these. He phoned one day and said an old cabinetmaker who had died had left a large number of brass furniture fittings. We went to their address, and found these were various handle back plates, some from the age of oak, through the Georgian period, and a few Victorian and French.

I bought them, of course. I spent several days sorting them and cleaning some of the worst with hydrochloric acid. I learned quite quickly that if this is used undiluted the fumes attacked one's throat, and also it produced reddening of brass making it look 'coppery'. I had this knowledge and diluted the acid with water, and both problems were partially solved; but I found the best place to use it was in the open air. Those handles were, to me, the equivalent of the contents of an ancient dig, and I eventually displayed some on the workshop walls, and they have been admired and discussed many times. But of course, as time went on, our friend had a stroke and his life changed quite drastically, for he didn't recover to any extent. He did manage to stagger around upon two walking sticks. Flora went for a short walk one day with him and she was upset to hear him say, 'I never thought I would come to this.' I did get the impression that when he could no longer contribute to the running of that large inconvenient house and to its financial success, he was looked upon through eyes as one would view a tree stump in a bank, rather in the way but difficult to obliterate.

We did go over occasionally after Reggie's death, and of course Gwendolene Garnham who was 'the wife' mentioned on a previous page, was the lady whom Flora worked for at Dimbols for 15½ years. There was very little affection for her from Flora, but one day she did get her wish, for we stayed to tea. 'I'd just like to have my feet under her table and have her wait on me for once,' said Flora.

I continued to thirst for knowledge of antiques. At about this time on the TV a programme called *Going for a Song* was being shown. That master of appraisal, Arthur Negus, was the star. The panel of experts discussed various old items and two other people, 'the guests', were invited to estimate the price of these objects would make at auction.

I think Sunday afternoons was the time appointed, and I sat glued to the box and with pen poised made lightning sketches of these items. Also there were notes on the subjects and the prices given; whether I ever referred to them afterward is doubtful, because the prices were quite astronomical – or so I considered them. However, it was great fun to do.

My favourite book was always at hand, and from its instruction I bought a chair of the post-Restoration period, i.e. after 1660, and another from a little later with a Dutch influence.

I learned of William Kent:	1685–1748
of Thomas Chippendale:	1718–79
of Robert Adam	1728–92
of Thos Sheraton:	1751–1806
of Thos Hope	1770–1831

and that T Chippendale compiled the *Director* in 1754, which was in fact a trade catalogue and cost £2 8s, a fair sum in those days. This work has been quoted and perused on many occasions since: 'the first pattern book to appear'. There is a rather sad account of a certain Adam Black. He wrote on Sheraton, who…

> lived in an obscure street, his house half shop, half dwelling house, and looked like a worn out Methodist Minister, with black threadbare coat. I took tea with them, there was little to make use of. My host seemed a good man. He had been a cabinetmaker, was now a publisher and taught drawing. And A Black was engaged in the most wretched work, writing a few articles and trying to put his shop in order, working among dirt, and bugs, was paid half a guinea, which I was half ashamed to take from the poor man.

Sheraton was in fact a designer, and published a work in four parts between 1791 and 1794, containing 113 plates. This was a very well composed account, for as I read later he served as a cabinetmaker and journeyman for several years in his earlier days. His drawing book, was influential for many pieces survived deriving from his patterns. His family were in reduced circumstances after his death. A further few words I've just seen (the various pages mentioning him are rather scattered) seem worth mentioning:

> Though I am thus employed, in racking my invention to design fine and pleasing cabinet work, I can be content to sit on a wooden bottom chair myself, provided I can but have common food and raiment where with to pass through life in peace.

The next main part of my favourite book is devoted to 'The Regency Period': 'About the year 1800 an effective new style was to be seen in Henry Holland's designs for furniture at South Hill, Bedford, and at Carlton House.' From another source:

> Historically, the Regency dates from the time when the illness of George III was so severe that he was unable to govern the country. This first happened in 1788 but he recovered within a few months. It was not until 1811 that the Act of Regency was passed, and the Prince of Wales took the title of Regent and assumed the royal powers held until his father's death in 1820. He then inherited the throne as George IV. So technically the Regency Period can be regarded as having started either in 1788 or 1811...There was a complete change of design at this time and furniture was plainly formed.

> There were fewer wood carvers in London and their numbers were decreasing.

I was quite familiar with chairs from this period, for as I may have recorded, Joseph and I bought four dining chairs with a rope-back rail in the back, reeded legs and turned roundels. However, at the time of purchase we had no idea of their age.

The foregoing extracts from the book do it no justice but serve to show, hopefully, the way I was heading. Many books have been published on the subject of antiques, and I've purchased several. My father said he could never learn anything from a book. But I have done.

In 1968, I see from books still kept that the year's turnover for Coal was £26,825; Coal wages £1568; Coal purchased £22,045.

From Farm: £1536. Petrol cost £334.

I drew £680 for survival and so on.

The figures look quite encouraging, perhaps, but I was growing very tired of the coal trade. I think the nett profits were about £1500 per year. David's joints were suffering a bit; he'd had seventeen years of the job, I'd had twenty-nine. I'd been to the doctor and then the hospital for x-rays on knees. 'They are showing signs of wear,' I was told.

Flora was still a long-suffering receiver of phone calls. There were overriding thoughts in my mind of giving it up. My friend Mark was mortified. 'You can't do that,' he told me. My auditor, my dear old friend Edward Turner, said, 'But it's bread and butter.'

I had been putting a few pounds aside out of the business and by 31st December 1968 had amassed £3475 15s which was in the Abbey National building society. The farm was sown to a rather changing pattern, for the 18 acres was about 2½ acres of sugar beet, which produced 52 tons 15 cwt. and came to £341; the remaining land grew 27 tons 11 cwt. of spring sown barley, which brought in £611.

The balances from the figures shown above was made up with sales of pigs, subsidies for various things, and some wheat still in stock at the beginning of the year. The profit made was not recorded, but probably most of it disappeared through the wages. The same crops were sown and harvested in the following year. In 1970 we planted a new strain of barley, which was Maris Otter, on 20th April – in ignorance, for this was winter barley and simply went yellow. It was swarming with aphids and was ploughed in in July. Otter was to become a wonderful malting sample and eventually I did get it sown in October, and got good results. The reason spring corn was grown here was usually we were too busy with the coal trade in the autumn to do the necessary land work.

I spent as much time as possible in the 10' x 8' shed. This was the workshop, and I was feeling more confident. I answered a situation vacant in the *East Anglian* for a wood turner at a cabinetmakers in Ipswich, saying I could work from home. They were sorry to dampen by enthusiasm but could not accept me on these terms. This was a setback.

In 1969 I was Chairman of the Parish Council. There had been rumours during the year of the Home Office taking over the RN Depot site here to build a prison. We had meetings, and it was decided to canvass the village to find what feeling there was against the idea. Support was very much against it. A public inquiry was asked for. After many months, one was to be held at the District Council Offices at Weeley. On 26th November 1969, the diary reports: '25th: Bad day of snow and strong north-west wind, very unpleasant. Customers were in need of fuel, the orders were coming in. The Parish Councillors were going to attend the inquiry and for my sins as Chair I had to represent.' The diary reads again: '26th: Weather better with sun. Spent a wasted day at Weeley. The whole day taken up with evidence for the Home Office in favour of a prison.'

So on the 27th we see: 'Weather fair forecast bad – spent from 10 a.m. to 2.45 at the inquiry on "the grill" for 25 minutes and got congratulated by W Garnham (Senior Councillor).'

The gent who grilled me was like Humpty Dumpty in appearance but his brain was not at all dim, for he did his level best to convince me the people of Wrabness did not have any idea of what having a prison in their midst would be like. There were benefits – jobs, and so on. One problem was that a local doctor had been sussing out some support for one. 'What about the poor prisoners?' said he. However, in the local paper it was reported that 'a prison was the prior need at the site, and most of the evidence against has been nebulous'. On the same date in 1970: 'The site is still untouched.'

I hadn't spoken to anyone in the trade regarding giving up the coal business, apart from the odd words as stated on previous page. However, on 8th September 1970, after lunch, I answered the phone, and the voice of one of the travellers from Thrutchleys coal merchants of Ipswich said, 'I heard that you may be wanting to sell your business.'

I couldn't believe what I was hearing. I said something like, 'Well, yes, could be…you had better come and see me.'

In the diary I wrote: 'You never know what's on the other end of a phone.'

Nothing much happened for a few weeks. It was 17th

November before I met the representative from Thutchleys, and by 24th I learned that they were in fact being taken over by Cawoods.

Diary entry: 'Meeting with Cawoods executive today, quite good progress.' By 1st December, the new heading was to be:

Cawoods Solid Fuels, trading formerly as JW Calver & Son Etc.

I agreed to stay on working for them to get the amalgamation off the ground. Thrutchleys owned the business at Harwich, which was originally Hills and then T Callaghan. The idea was to close this and run both from Wrabness. My two employees were rather taken aback. Would they get any redundancy payment? I feared not, because the new owners would continue to employ them. They came along to meet my two by now rather concerned chaps. Ralph, who visualised being put onto the lorry to do deliveries protested that he didn't know much about the rounds. David didn't think it would make much difference to him. So I made a deal with Cawoods. I measured up the coal yard and went off to see the solicitor. Cawoods' title was to run from 1891, the year my grandfather bought it. The total selling price was £3434. Debts owing to me were to be collected and paid up until 31st May; after then, back to me to pursue.

The stock of fuel in the yard was to be sold by them and I was to be paid 10s per ton over the price I bought it at. This worked out very well with no problems. I had to sign an agreement for three years not be concerned or take any part in the business of a coal merchant within a five-mile radius of the yard. (I said that they needn't worry on that point.)

So on 1st December 1970, I was no longer in control. At a meeting of the executives (there were three, I seem to recall), one of them said how much have we to pay you? I didn't answer. He perused the latest balance sheet and suggested £30 per week. I readily agreed.

One of the executives had drawn up a letter to be given to all customers. One line of it suggested that Cawoods would give as good if not better service than we had done. The elder gent read it and said, 'You can take that out!'

So, the yard at Harwich was to be cleared. I went down there for some reason and saw the rubbish that they were selling as fuel, and began to wonder what our customers would say. I went on a round or two with one of their lorry drivers to show him the ropes. What an experience! The coal trade was not a kid glove job, but we had a way of keeping a tidy yard, and empty bags on the lorry in a tidy heap tied on the journey the home. The cab of your lorry reasonably clean. The new crew were untidy, unscrupulous, and some were dishonest. One of them, quite an old hand, was a good worker and I said, 'I could have used a chap like you.'

'I should have robbed you, John!' said he, without any doubt at all. This was alien to me, for my lads, I'm quite sure, never robbed me of anything.

The new regime was tiresome. Every document seemed very unfamiliar and in most cases irrelevant. They had to be submitted in triplicate. This meant frequent journeys to Harwich with sheaves of paper and money. However, soon the manager from there came to Wrabness and the job was made easier. He was quite an easy fellow to get on with.

The office, such as it was, was not big enough, so the powers that be were considered. After discussions I was to enlarge it.

The control of loads in and out were becoming a problem to the Head Office at Ipswich. They were going to install a weighbridge. So without further ado a digger arrived and a large oblong hole was excavated. Bricks arrived, and cement and sand. Then a bricklayer came along and lined the pit with brick walls. Within about fourteen days the weigher was in working order, complete with large dial in a brand new wooden shed, which was about as strong as a cardboard box. So incoming loads were to be weighed in loaded, and out empty. The only problem was that it hadn't sufficient capacity for the incoming weight. So the ideal was to weigh the front end and then the rear, which seemed to confuse everyone, especially the lorry driver. Iron framed gates covered with heavy wire mesh were installed at the entrance. This caused the problem of a key first thing in the day. With all the precautions, there was nothing to stop a driver making out his list of fuel for a retail load and actually loading five or ten bags of a different and/or more expensive fuel, and pocketing the surplus cash. This played havoc with the amount of stock that should have been in the yard. After my time had expired, which was 31st March 1971, I was told of the disappearance of a bagged load of anthracite early one morning. Where it went to, was a mystery; the driver went missing also.

So the money for the various deals came in:

The stock in yard sold realised:	£2299
The business and equipment:	£3367
The debts collected:	£682
My Salary:	£389
Work for them (Materials)	£45

At the end of my period of employment, one of the executives asked me if I would like a permanent job with the company. I flatly refused, with a fist banged down on the desk top. 'No, thank you!'

The general store at the top of the Station Hill was owned and run by Audrey Harrison, her mother and family. She collected cash from customers who inscribed their names, as can be seen. We were presented with two very nice wine glasses and some wine. In 1993, what a difference in the village! Several of them are no more. But quite a number are.

The thank you card was worded:

Thank you for your thoughtfulness.
Cheers from all your Customers in the village.

In retrospect I probably could have asked for much more for the whole kettle of fish. Cawoods had a piece of land at Harwich which has probably been sold for a fortune. Flora took part in the ferrying of money and papers there, and I don't think we got any petrol money for it. But I guess I did extract a few odds and ends from there, some of which were panels which I made into doors for the garage attached to the workshop shed.

The figures above were probably, in those days (on a multiplier of ten, say), quite a useful sum of money. The debts collected were for the most part normal accounts of customers who paid quite regularly, but there were a few who were hurried into payment because there was a new name at the top of the bill head. I'm sure some of them would have never been settled, and of course some never were. Someone who had been in business for many years was talking about this aspect of his firm and said, 'We gave receipts to some of the customers with bad debts, for we considered that while they bought goods "one lot under the other" we were taking cash all the time.' I could see the point of view but did not get involved in so doing.

So now I had to think about this smallholding. The diary entry for 13th March 1971 reads: 'Did a bit of tractor work today,' and on the 14th (Sunday): 'Ploughed the beet headlands: good introduction to the job with deep ruts.' I had a reasonable tractor and modern corn drill which had been purchased at the sale at Primrose Hall when Miss Cross retired in 1965.

I had really done very little tractor driving. By the 27th, I was 'fertilising and cultivating for spring wheat,' and again on Sunday 28th: 'Cultivating from 9 a.m. to 1 p.m., nice to be out amongst the birds.' The next day: 'Drilling wheat, sunny day with cool east breeze.'

On 31st March: 'Without ceremony I am today relieved of my post as manager, but will have to finish the office at the yard.'

On 13th April: 'Have paid in the cheque for the business. So on we go, free to earn some more and call no man master.'

I see also I was growing 2½ acres of sugar beet, which were drilled by Bentley Contracts. These were of late being drilled 'to a stand', with pelleted seed, and germinated singly. They were still chopped out; I'd done very little of this tiresome job, but considered I best do it myself, and between the 11th and 18th May I must have finished them, according to the diary. Perhaps I did have someone to help – can't recall who, though.

Looking at the few details for the year I see that:

The Barley and Wheat brought £658 88
The Sugar Beet: £394 87
And the gross profit was £929
And the nett profit was £138
The Building Society interest was £209 in the June of 1971.

Looking at these figures in 1993, I do not quite know what to make of them. But of course we could always, draw a bit out, and now and then we did.

A friend called to see us one day and learned of our intentions. 'So you've opted out of the rat race then,' he said. I suppose that about summed it up.

In 1972, I enlisted the casual help of Michael, Flora's nephew. He had done quite a lot of farm work previously and was good at the job. I had a Huard two-furrow reversible plough, which was simply too heavy for the Ferguson 35. Michael made as good a job as he could with it but the reversing procedure was not hydraulic and relied on being lifted quite high up, and a lever when pulled should effect the turn, but it did not; so at the end of each furrow, one had to dismount and swing the thing round by hand. The Massey drill was excellent and a pleasure to use. Harvest was gathered with that rotten Massey 780 previously mentioned, but for several years we plodded on with 10 stones of barley per sack, which were stood on ex-WD tent bottoms to keep them off the floor to make the perfect home for mice. In 1972 Michael put in about 130 hours, for which 65p per hour was the wage; by 1976 this had risen to £1.20.

Problems arose one fine day when at the top of a cut with the combine. Its gearbox had a problem and it could not be moved. This was in 1975, so the old wreck was towed into the shed. We had managed 8 tons 13 cwt. to that point. I should have mentioned that now I was into 'monoculture' and the whole field was into Maris Otter barley. So what now? George Mitchell had helped with sugar beet in the past so I sent to see him. He agreed to come with a combine and trailers to carry the grain back to his store at Wix Abbey and to load it into the buyers' lorries. This was to prove a blessing, for the 10-stone sacks were originally dropped onto a hydraulic frame at the back of the buyer's lorry, and the driver had the unenviable task of grabbing the bottom corners of the sacks and dropping each one onto the progressing load. Many drivers developed spine and muscle strain with this method. The time had come to stop this altogether.

The next short-lived method was to send the sacks up to the top of the lorry using a petrol engine elevator to the driver standing on a wide board across the lorry sides. He had to catch hold of the sack, previously untied, and tip out the grain. Some chaps fell off into the lorries and bulk loading was the only sensible method to be used. It so happened that I even sold all those old Hessian bags to a firm in Ipswich for £33. In 1975 I had the old threshing floor removed from the barn and a concrete screed put in its place, so that the rats and mice had nowhere to hide under it now – and they probably mostly disappeared, for there was no corn in there anyway!

From then on George Mitchell did all the farm work, ploughing, flailing, planting, combining. It was the only sensible course.

The figures for the 1975 harvest were:

38 tons 5 cwt. barley at £67.
Total Expenses: £2563.56.
Gross profit: £1684.64.

For 1976:

40 tons 6 cwt. Otter barley at £87/Ton.
Total Expenses: £1064.50
Gross profit: £2471.88.

So it didn't look too bad.

In 1994 the figures were but:

38.08 tons Pipkin Barley at £126/Ton = £4775.26
Costings: £3561.10
Gross profit: £1214.16.

Season alone seems to govern yield nowadays. It is now sprayed five or six times and profits vary greatly.

There were a few problems with the system. George was not the most industrious chap. He kept his equipment in first-class mechanical conditions, but was not the first one to start fertilising or ploughing, and often was drilling corn well into December. On one memorable occasion, barley from here was in store at his farm and it was not looked at and did need drying, but this was not done. So it was collected in bulk, but of course was returned as unsuitable because of its 'nose' – without checking it, even. I picked up the bill for the haulage! However, after drying it made £152 per ton, and the gross margin was £2100. George continued until the 1987 harvest and announced he was giving up contract work. His farm had virtually disappeared after settling up the family's demands.

So I approached my neighbour R Macaulay, and he has so far (1995) been able to do the work for me. We are now all receiving an acreage payment from the European Union, via MAFF, and this seems to be keeping most farmers from going bankrupt; for the costs of running a farm, as can be seen below, have risen beyond belief.

1995 results:

40.8 tons of Pipkin Barley at £146 – £5929.07
Costings: £2732.59
Gross profit: £3196.48

Chapter Thirteen: Restoration Work

The workshop had no doors as yet, and as I mentioned, I had the panels from Harwich. These were very nicely constructed but only about 15" wide. I fixed then to cross members and had two centre opening doors eventually. This establishment had been the roof over Flora's car. She had been pleased to do 'meals on wheels' to the needy folk around, and sometimes helped with the 'trolley shop' at Tendring Hospital to supplement the needs of the elderly patients there. The car was an A40, which she was very fond of. It looked like we were taking a cut in income, so in 1971 my valiant partner said, 'I'll give it up.'

Upon inspection, the car was a rust box, and MOT tests were becoming more complicated. So it was sold.

We had the Cowley pickup with the gear change mounted on the steering column. This was a very useful motor, and was written down to £154 on the balance sheet; but it did good service until 1981, having covered 60,000 miles.

So the workshop was enclosed from the wind from the north-east. I had attempted a small repair with glue (nothing original in that, of course), but realised heat and a dry atmosphere were necessary. So my friend Mark found a rejected room heater, a solid fuel stove, and I set it in a chosen spot and then needed a chimney. So off we go to the local builders' yard to find short lengths of vitreous enamel pipe. Then a hole had to be cut in the corrugated roof, to allow the pipe through; not easy to make the job waterproof. There is a diary entry telling that 'I've started several jobs but not finishing many.' The fact that I was going to take up furniture restoration was becoming known around the district by word of mouth, I suppose, for I didn't advertise in the press or anyone's shop window. I guess one or two words to one or two people would have been enough.

We had a visit from one lady who had houses in Harwich, and these were let furnished. She had lots of 'lovely antiques that needed repair' etc. She turned up late with a sample. Of course tenants did not have the benefit of sumptuous mahogany chairs or a walnut chest of drawers. Oh dear, no; pine was the order of the day. It was stripped pine; some of it was dropped into a tank of caustic soda and if the paint was thick, left there for several days, then hosed down after. This sort of treatment played havoc with joints, and moving it was not kind to one's hands. I said I wasn't quite in business and stowed odd pieces in the barn.

Someone at Great Oakley had a really lovely Regency card table with brass ornaments on the pedestal. One of its four legs was broken. Thrown in at the deep end, I was. This was put into the queue that was beginning to form in the barn. The stable was also becoming home to some pieces in among the straw! I see by perusing that diary that 'Bernard Wilder and I went to Lavenham and Hadleigh – very interesting'. He used to come to Dimbols to stay a few days. A phone call would come our way and his aristocratic voice would say, 'Ah, is that the old faker?'

'Hello, Bernard, how are you?'

'Oh, not too bad…rubbing along fairly well.'

'Yes, good, good.'

'Ah, ah, I wonder if we could go on a little excursion?'

'Yes, I think so.'

'Ah, well, what do you think…about nine o'clock tomorrow?'

'Yes, all right… Where do you want to go?'

'Ah, well, well…could call at Evans, perhaps.'

'How's the antique trade, then?'

'Ah, oh, erm, nothing very wonderful. The prices are quite impossible. Er, er, I've erm, got a few items for you to look at. No obligation of course…'

'Yes, okay then, Bernard, see you tomorrow.'

So at the appointed hour he would walk from Dimbols, and his arrival was quite spectacular. He was quite large and had a wealth of wavy hair which was not grey. He was slightly bent and entered the door with a gentlemanly reluctance. He considered Flora was straight out of heaven.

'She has a kind heart,' I always say if a lady has a kind heart you can't go wrong. You have everything you want here, John. You don't have to worry about offending your neighbours. You can have the best of food. Ah, very, very nice.'

'Have you purchased anything of late?'

Looking at a book with the words 'Stock details' on the cover, by 1971 I see that I had bought quite a few items. Most journeys out had to have an antique shop somewhere accessible.

I think Flora sometimes got a little tired of trying to understand this new way of life, and the craze of many people to want to buy old items. Shops had multiplied over the past ten years and a sample from the stock book reads:

Cauffley Plate £3
Perfume Vase £2.50 (Imari)
2 Butter Pats £1.75
Cream Skimmer £2
Chinese Bowl £6
Chinese Tea Bowl £4.50
Earthenware Furniture Stands £3.50
Spode Oval Dish £1.75

So there was plenty to talk about with Bernard. After his preliminary chat, he would open his case upon the floor and say, 'Ah, ah, now, erm, erm… Of course, there is no obligation. Please say no if you don't want anything…but this is rather interesting…and this…'

So there appeared on this occasion a scarab beetle brooch, a silver ring with hinged lid (for aromatics, or to contain poison to tip into your enemy's drink), a couple of repoussé silver-plated buttons, with depiction of a huntsman with French hunting horn, and a cup and saucer described as Crown Derby wrapped carefully in his pyjama trousers! I bought all of these, and enjoyed the experience – with the exception of the trousers!

The interlude over, we waved Flora a fond adieu and off we went to the grey pickup. It was about 10 a.m. by the time we reached East Bergholt.

Lionel Evans had a shop full of antiques there. He was a showman, and would have sold you a stair carpet for your bungalow. He told a rare tale of visits to the Middle East to buy kelims and Persian rugs, and there were one or two lying about on the floor.

Bernard looked around and when the proprietor disappeared for a few minutes would beckon me to some dark corner to view an item whose value he hoped Lionel hadn't realised. But not a lot of luck here, for a price was plucked out of the air, and haggling resulted. The shop door opened, and in came a customer of a few days ago. Lionel was summoned.

'Now look here old chap, this is not good enough you must think I'm green, I've collected Bristol delft for years. This plate is not!'

A lengthy discussion then ensued. Bernard and I drifted into a small room adjoining, to find an artist at work copying a portrait. This was none other than the master faker in person – Tom Keating. He was absorbed in the job, and had overpainted his work with various colours. Bernard attempted conversation, but the artist was so far in the fantasy world for which he was to be renowned eventually on TV. He seemed emotionally absorbed at all times.

Bernard had several large portraits which if copied would have been financially beneficial, but the artist would only say a few words. I saw an old clock movement in the window. Closer inspection told me that it was Dutch with wooden frame and wooden arbours to the wheels; the price was £15. I backed off. Several weeks later the price had dropped to £11, so I purchased it. It was quite fascinating, but close scrutiny showed several parts were missing, particularly the escapement. In a friend's house some time later, I spotted a clock on the wall with a wooden-framed case etc. It was ticking away, quite loudly, the very same type of timepiece as mine. So thoughts of having something a trifle out of the ordinary were soon brushed away and the old junk is gathering dust upon a shelf in the workshop – eighteen years later! There were fragments of oak panels. The proprietor had salvaged some, which I bought and later wondered why; impulse buying, I think it's called.

So we travelled off to Hadleigh where The Shoulder of Mutton shop had all sorts of antiques for sale. Outside was a large butter churn for £8 and a real collection of old hand farm tools. My collection of such items was growing slowly. It was getting toward lunch time and my companion began to realise this: the Eight Bells was not far away. This hostelry was quite accommodating. They did meals that were quite reasonable. Bernard always appreciated 'civility, good bitter, simple food'. On occasions he would drool over the thought of feasts of duck, goose and good company.

I seem to remember going off to Ipswich on one occasion. He was in search of books, and we would have lost the last train home, if that had been our mode of transport.

Little antique shops in villages and towns were to be seen everywhere in the 1970s. Some were under the control of ladies, some of whom were dressed something like their mothers might have been. Some were Bohemian, some quite neat and smart. Some of them were knowledgeable, and quite a number were not. We found odd ones of the latter type, when a very nice old chest of drawers of about 1710 date, albeit with replaced feet, was for sale for £25. If one were allowed to inspect the back rooms of some of these establishments, all sorts of items appeared before one's eyes. On one occasion when we were allowed to drift around, three chairs were on show, priced £30 for the three. One was Georgian, of about 1760, design and fairly certainly genuine. They were to be sold as one lot, or so the lady said…but she was holding the fort while the proprietor was at an auction. Bernard talked her into accepting £18 for the one just described and she agreed. I paid for it and eventually repaired it. I made a frame for the seat, stuffed and covered it – and there it is, looking better each time my dear wife polishes it.

On another excursion we went toward Nayland to call at a Mr Wicks, who was of the same breed as Bernard. He resided in a large half-timbered house of medieval appearance. We arrived without arrangement, and the lady who answered the doorbell, which was rung by a pulling an iron handle, just peeped through the small opening that the security chain allowed and said, 'My. Wicks is not receiving any visitors.'

'What do you mean? I'm an old friend,' said Bernard.

'He's not well…not well at all,' replied the lady.

'But tell him it's Bernard Wilders – he knows me…he knows me!'

'No, I'm sorry, they are my instructions,' said she, and the door was closed.

Bernard was in a state of disbelief. 'That old woman ought to be ducked. Wicks' daughter is at the Ancient House bookshop; can we go there? I am not having this.' He was in a really foul mood.

My memory fails me as to what happened after that, but on another occasion we returned to this lovely old house, and within its walls we found an absolute emporium of old stuff. I bought two mahogany brackets made in the nineteenth century with heavy swirls of carving that 'looked as if it has been squeezed out of a tube'. These were eventually fixed in the top corners of a doorway in the house. Bernard purchased a nice model ship in a case, and was in a lot better mood than on the previous time. At Stoke by Nayland, there was a shop with 'Antiques and Things' displayed upon a board above the window. This was run by a charming lady and her male companion. Bernard and I called and the place was full of nice furniture. I bought a bowfront chest of drawers. It had two long and two short drawers, which were really deep, i.e. front to back, and the dark colour gave it a good appearance. It was getting on when we returned home with various prizes, and Bernard, when offered scones and jam for tea was soon carried away. We eventually unloaded the chest and it was wet with dew, but as I've often said, a light wash never did a piece of furniture any harm.

Back to Stoke, on the day mentioned we journeyed on to Nayland proper and there I found a small shop with a good stock of country items among them, butter prints. These little items were fascinating to me, for of course the carver's art is displayed in hollows. They are of varying quality and infinite in variety. Some have a thistle head or a cow, or a rose, etc. The really favourite one of the dozen or so that I have is a pheasant. It could be one of Bewick's engravings if it were flat.

Peter and Yvonne Brunning were going to visit Bernard Wilders down at Seaford in Sussex. This was in the autumn, and we set off at about 5 p.m. It was raining and blowing. Flora had the company of their daughter, Elizabeth, for the night. The journey was lousy. It was simply a black wet night, and the signposts were almost impossible to read, but we did eventually arrive. Bernard's house was a semi-detached largish chalet bungalow. He was extremely pleased to meet us. My eyes opened upon entry into the hallway. Two oak dresser bases, one with shelves, were bedecked with pewter plates and flagons, some of great antiquity. On the right hand was a lovely oak side table about 12' long. B had laid this for us with straw mats for plates and dishes. At one end was a high pile of sheet music. A court cupboard of small dimensions was at one end. Everything had a connection with the past. Stump-work pictures were hung over the fireplace. Maple-framed pictures abounded. A bottle of Claret – Medoc – was evident upon its coaster.

Yvonne was detailed to see to cooking several sausages and some potatoes. Large pieces of brown and white bread were produced, and when ready we sat down to rush seated chairs and wine was poured and it all went down well, It was a little bit like a medieval banquet and it has, as the reader will see, stayed in my memory. The eating of apples, raw, later rounded off the meal. After this I wandered around into the next room opposite, which was his library. The walls were covered with shelves full of books. Over the fireplace hung a genuine beheading axe, and a whaling harpoon. 'It's just another interest you know,' explained our host.

In a room to the left of the hallway he had his grand piano, and the piles of music were put to good use, for he could play very well. He claimed to be self-taught. All around the walls were largish portraits of noteworthy people in very ornate frames, some carved pine wood and gilded. My bedroom was small, with a dormer window and sparsely furnished, but with a comfortable bed. The walls carried several prints of the Cries of London. During the next day I was shown some of the items that he had for sale, and according to my stock book bought several. There was a tallboy with each of its seven drawers laid out with silver spoons and dressing table brushes and hand mirrors. My bank balance had to be given consideration, so I didn't say yes to all that we were offered.

We went off into Brighton and found the Lanes an interesting place. In one of the pubs nearby at lunch time, several queer-looking ladies and chaps were to be seen. These were the vendors from the shops. They were more like showbusiness folk, with emphasis on, 'Darling, do you know what I had offered me yesterday? … I just couldn't resist it, and of course the lady didn't have a clue as to its value.'

One shop had several curled paperwork boxes in its window. I had one of these delightful items but the price tags put me off. It's an exact science; in retrospect, I really should have gone in and had a deal.

We visited the Pavilion and enjoyed its extravagance. That anyone could have built such a place in England was extraordinary. So our little excursion was soon over. The car boot contained:

One gilt silk covered chair
3 panels of oak
2 blue and white oriental plates
Books; 3 bound *Chatterbox* for 1870 (nursery picture books)
Drawing room scrapbook, 1860
One 17 gallon milk churn, and
Various other items.

In October 1973, Reggie phoned from Parham one sunny day: 'I've a cannon – would you like it? Probably lost in the battle of Sole Bay. It's rather rusty.'

'How heavy is it?' I enquired.

'Well, I don't really know, but it's lying on a trolley… shouldn't be much trouble,' said he.

I've since discovered that the battle was fought in May 1672. Eventually we went over to Suffolk and with little difficulty pulled it into the pickup. It wasn't large – about 48" high with a bore of about 2". I say 'about', because its muzzle was rusted up with the effect of sea and sand.

Having got it home, I wondered what I'd bought it for. Flora thought I was silly to hump such things about. It was eventually seen by Bernard, who described it as a 'carronade' used at the stern of a man-of-war. He was visibly cock-a-hoop. 'Er, er, how much would you sell it for?'

'Well, I gave £50 for it.' (I foolishly told him the truth.)

'Will you take £5 profit?' he asked, rubbing his hands with anticipation.

I agreed. In the course of a day or two after Bernard had gone back to Seaford, a phone message conveyed the request, 'Can you make a carriage for the cannon, John?'

I chewed the request over and settled for a simple stand for the damned thing. Wheels were out of the question, especially considering the small profit. So in due course, BRS turned up and we loaded cannon and stand. I brought a heavy plank and perched on the back tailboard and tied a rope below, gave it one turn around the cannon, and the driver inside hauled while I helped down below. He wondered how he would get on unloading. I think I said, 'Well, it will come down without a lot of trouble.'

Bernard was well pleased with his purchase, and said that a fellow who helped him now and then actually picked the cannon up and held it above his head. I guess that it weighed 160 lb. So it was a little trouble to Bernard.

Some time later when cannons were still in the fore of Bernard's mind he rang me, having seen an auction taking place at a country house somewhere near Long Melford where two pieces of ordnance were to be sold. I asked of the auctioneers name and send for a catalogue for £2, and on view day Flora and I went for a ride – in the pickup of course.

We parked in between a Jaguar and a Bentley and said upon walking away, 'Fancy someone parking their old grey heap next to our Bentley!'

The house was full of family treasures, with a huge amount of Mason's Ironstone and many good pieces of furniture. Along one wall were about thirty years' worth of *Country Life* magazines. The cannons were standing on guard at the entrance gates and upon inquiry was told that the estimated price was about £600 apiece!

Of course they were mounted on their original carriages, all of cast iron, with wheels to match. So we ate our sandwiches and drank orangeade; the people sitting behind the Bentley had something much stronger to wash down their smoked salmon. There was a noticeable silence at the Seaford end of the phone when I told B of the day's escapade. 'Oh, oh dear me! Er, everything is becoming impossible,' he complained.

On one visit to Seaford, we found Bernard was becoming less capable. Flora came and we had bed and breakfast at a house a few blocks away. Lunch was not very easy; Flora and Yvonne had found his electric cooker oven rather neglected. Bernard was in the throes of having someone to clear out his garage, which was attached to the bungalow. A doorway had been cut through from it, a very narrow one of necessity. Bernard now had to succumb to a wheelchair, but he pushed it into the narrow door opening, and described what he was intending to achieve. He couldn't get the chair through, and even if he could have, there was a deep step down.

He pointed to nails driven into the walls and said, 'I shall hang a scythe over these other old tools, near the harness on that one at the end, etc.' At the back of the bungalow he had a shed access to which could only be gained by climbing four steps. He said to Peter and me, 'Can you please take these pieces of harness into the shed? I'll be able to get in there soon.'

We both knew he wouldn't – couldn't possibly. But of course didn't say a word, such was his optimism.

We had a Christmas card from him, and he wrote:

I hope you are both keeping well. Yvonne gives me good accounts and news of you – and that you, John, are happily busy with your repairs etc. Purchase of antiques nowadays is impossible except for the wealthy. I am contented with what I still possess. I am rubbing along pretty well, still in a wheelchair but quite able to cope in the house and hopefully make slow progress. If and when I am able to visit Wrabness again I will of course look you up. In the meantime I'll keep in touch. Have you had any luck with disposal of any of my bits and pieces? All the best for 1980. Excuse this very ordinary card, I had to rely on a neighbour for shopping and choice.

The pieces mentioned are beyond my description, as he now and again left items which I frequently found difficult to sell, for they were of little interest for most dealers and collectors. They are odd pieces that do not find a home. So Peter and Yvonne on their visits would ferry them back. Finally, as was often the case with humankind, hospital became necessary for him. He was some time in a nursing home, and he made the best of it all, in particular with the pianist who came to play periodically.

I had sight of the valuation for Probate, listing of course all his collection. The furniture list was like music to my ears, and also is recorded twenty-five items of statuary that were displayed in his garden at the rear of the house. These were not of great value: 'Just another interest, you know,' he would have said. He died in 1985. I was saddened. He was a fellow who I learned a lot from and I enjoyed his company. It's very true, and very obvious to me, that the quote 'It's who you know more than what you know' that gets one through life with an advantage.

The foregoing pages might appear to be the account of someone who's not very busy, but this was not the case. My services were constantly being sought. Cousin Don Fisher came to see me one evening in the early 1970s, worried about the condition of our grandfather's house. 'Could you come and look at it?' he asked. 'It's got to have something done to it, either repaired or pulled down.'

So I went along and I knew what I was going to say before I arrived 'Of course it can be repaired' I said. So Don arranged with a builder who had made a name for himself in the locality. The old roof was taken off and new timbers used to replace it. The old pantiles were replaced and a lot of renovation carried out. This old show was ancient, I had the pleasure of doing some work inside later when an inglenook fireplace had been uncovered. I filled in the front with old red brick and formed a small open fire grate opening in the centre. In the process of doing this I found wattle and daub behind, a section of which I managed to extract without breaking too much, and brought it home to display in the small museum that I was creating. The old oak rafters from the roof had been stacked outside. I had little deal and obtained about four. I mounted two pieces about 4' long into a piece of railway sleeper, and fixed the wattle between to show how it would have been used. It was probably 300 years old, but there were the holly or hazel wattles – wormy of course, but still tied to the crosspieces with strips of bark.

I was needing a table in our new room and could see possibility in the old timbers to make legs for one. So I scraped and planed and chamfered four from it. I used old pieces of elm from the bullock yard for the rails, and with a lot of hard hand work made mortises which had to have the holes bored with a metal cutting twist drill, for the wood was as hard as old bone. Roger Paskell, the builder at Wix, had some knotty oak boards that were not up to coffin making, so with a lot more planning and sawing, we had a 6' x 2' 6" table. The top is not really flat, and when we've used it for small parties I have been known to produce a few small wooden wedges to pass around to the guests to level up their plates! I look upon it as a 'Wrabness table' – such is the sentiment that I feel for this old cottage and its environs.

The owners of The Priory Farm were needing renovations to a fireplace. I went on a preliminary survey. Three fireplaces had occupied the large chimney recess, and the inglenook was visible through a heap of brick rubble. They wanted it as it was with breastsummer beam across the piers. They obtained one about 9 or 10" square. So I got busy with trowel and level and eventually it began to take shape. I made a cupboard door, panelled from old oak, to fill a corner and created a log store under it; a herringbone pattern hearth completed the job. It looked very authentic. A large fire basket was brought along, complete with iron poker, tongs and shovel locally made. All was fine until they lit a fire, and none of the smoke went up the chimney!

Various doors were opened in the room but with little effect. The folk were not too worried and eventually had to install a wood-burning stove, which did not look anything like a basket full of burning logs.

I had at various times made tripod wine tables, stools and carved old shapes and carted them around WI meetings in the hope of selling something; but to little avail. One noteworthy occasion was at Ardleigh. When I was going through this exercise, I showed a piece of acanthus leaf work and announced, 'There is no such thing as acanthus – it's just a name.'

Very soon one of the ladies present said, 'Oh yes there is, Mr C! You'd better do some homework!'

So there I was put right down. Among the items I was

showing were candlesticks. These took the form of a three-pointed leaf of ivy type, and a turned holder for the candle, for I think about £2; but although everyone said, 'How nice – you're a clever chap,' I brought everything home.

However there was a small glimmer of hope, for the folk at The Priory asked for three pedestal tables, two with 13" tops and one 18", the centres of each top inlaid with a piece of burr or 'cat's paw' to form a contrast to the mahogany from which they were made. The wood was all recycled, having been found in house clearances or from sheds etc. The first table I made was partly from a piece of mahogany that was used to cover a tank that held pig's food. Joseph could not imagine where it had disappeared to. I've turned up some old carbon copies or work done and in 1975: 16½ hours work cost the client £16.50. The job at The Priory took 104 hours and I charged £206; this was in 1978. Frequently I was told probably by people that I did not work for that I was not charging enough. I said to myself that if I put in 40 hours work I had earned £80. Some of the jobs on furniture took several hours to do, and when I thought of the value of the piece it seemed scarcely worth the time I was spending.

One of the lady clients who had tenants in houses at Harwich proved to be tiresome. Journeys such as:

'Collecting from and delivery to such and such, street in Harwich'	£1.50
Cut wardrobe into two sections, and install in No. 6, fix shelves and mirrors, tighten table top.'	£5.00
Credit one hour	£1.25
	£3.75

Looking back at those figures, I realise this was my way, and I haven't changed a lot. The accountant's figures are a bit of a puzzle. My takings for 1976 amounted to £1224. But there was that excellent organisation, the Abbey National, and in that year on £16,000, we received £1030 interest – which was, as the old miser said, 'a handy sum of money.'

Looking into old records, I received £237 from a young farmer who was now living at Burnt Ash Farm. The work I did for this sum had to be seen to be believed. Looking back I wonder why I did what I did. The house was brick and was originally two tenements. When I first went to see what was to done, I entered by the front door turned left and there was a room about 16' square open to the roof save for the bridging joist. All the floorboards and floor joints had been taken out. These were of elm and absolutely worm-eaten. They had been set into the brickwork and joined to the bridging by simple mortise and tenons. To add insult to injury, the bridging had dropped at one end by about 4". The owner had obtained about twenty oak replacements from a stable or similar, and they had taken on a nice dark colour, probably from ammonia fumes. They were about 4" x 2½" and heavy. I had to chamfer the bottom corners before fitting into the recesses and mortises. To support the dropped joist I fixed a large piece of oak to the wall under it, first inserting a slab beneath the joist. Having got all this together, I then had to get lengths of softwood cut at the mill at Paskell's cut on a long taper to level up the floor joist. Eventually the new floorboards were clamped and nailed. I'm sure I mentioned before that at Domine joists were not secured to BJs. This was the case at Burnt Ash. But I bored 1/4" holes through the M and T joints and drove 5" nails to tighten it all up. Then came skirting boards, which were a problem, for nothing was straight. After this, sir wanted two new windows in the newly formed bedroom. These he had made at Paskell's – sash with weights, of course. Someone made a mistake in measuring their width for when we went to fit them, they were about 3" too wide! The idea then was to take a cutting wheel up aloft to cut away the bricks on one side of the opening. So this young farmer suggested that I stand on a forklift with the electric cutter and slice away.

I refused, so he had to do it. He was a trial, and considered that if he got smothered in mud or brick dust or whatever I should do the same. Eventually these windows were fitted and the brickwork made good. After all this, insulation had to be fitted under the floorboards from the downstairs room and clad with plasterboard. He helped sometimes, and insisted that we wore protection masks over the nose and mouth, for fibreglass is very gritty stuff.

The other work at this house was more interesting. I fitted up a set of spindles at the landing of the backstairs, and made a gate to match to keep the children from falling down at night, and another £127 was collected to finalise the work. I made a necklace stand from a piece of the old elm for the lady of the house. This was a lathe job, and it was difficult to get enough worm-free wood even to do this. It was a simple goodwill gesture.

Given the foregoing, one may ask, 'When did you do any restoration work?'

The date of this work just mentioned was 1980, and I had been occupied now for about eight years. So here are a few jobs in detail:

Mrs OR June 1976:
Marry up your oval table to base supplied by me
Replace walnut veneer to top and make up and fit
Edge beading
Clean up and repair base legs as needed
Remove cross members from under top and refix

Cost of work	£10.00
Cost of base	£10.00
	£20.00

Mrs F, 1976:
To carving 'Emily Favell 1976' upon the
Front of small chest 15 letters at 25p   £3.75

Mrs MC, July 1976:
Davenport.
Make and fit new bun foot,
Make and fit 3 pediment stops,
Patch veneer & Polish up   £3.50

And so on. I was a journeyman, haulier, restorer, handyman, Some of the work was satisfying, some was not. Workshop work is what I like best. I doubt if any of the journeys were charged at anything like real cost. There was another path which followed on from my association with friend Judith. I was introduced to her mother who lived at a modern house in Manningtree. It overlooked the river. It had a large sitting room full of nice furniture, with some antique pieces. She had been used to a good lifestyle and wanted for nothing, but had suffered from some distress, having lost her husband. A man about the house was what she was needing. I very soon filled that requirement. Several repair jobs to furniture, curtains not hanging quite well, a name to be inscribed on a piece of wood and fixed outside, and so on. The house was in a very pleasing position and visits there were pleasant.

Mother had moved house several times, so I learned. She was being driven by J one day and a row of cottages, a terraced row of four, took her eye. Though some miles from this part of the country, they could be turned into a large house. This she did. I arrived there before all the work was finished. A new stairway had been installed, and spindles were needed. Could I turn them? I jibbed a bit. There were thirty required. However, as was my nature, I took them on. The builder supplied the material – quite good quality mahogany family wood. So the lathe was working overtime. I didn't fit them, but was involved in staining and polishing them. The house gradually was made liveable, complete with mahogany loo seats and gold finished bathroom equipment. It had carpets that were 2" thick, oil-fired central heating, eye-level cooker, doors with twelve bevelled glass panes. The curtains wouldn't have looked out of place in a palace, and there was a conservatory at the back.

So the dear lady moved in, complete with her two cats, Ding and Dong.

Over a year or two, Judith and I made many visits, and I even removed the roof from the garage and replaced it with corrugated iron. Now and then we went out to the town nearby for lunch, and came home looking 'bonny'. It made fixing a mortise lock a bit difficult! On one occasion the keys were lost, and I had to get in through a bedroom window. 'If ever you get into any financial trouble you must tell me,' she said to me on one occasion. Her stay was brief at this by now lovely old house. Her next move was into a bungalow much nearer here. I still got plenty of work from her here. I never knew quite why she moved around. I never asked any favours or asked any questions. This story illustrated once again, 'It's who you know'.

There are a few pages of details covering this short time that I'm not at liberty to write. There were a few bonuses from being involved with Judith Turberville. The quite well-to-do gent who came to buy Mummy's house in Manningtree came into the picture. He was a bachelor, and had very little furniture, so he was fair game for these antique dealers. He was given plenty of advice and soon had several pieces. There was a campaign bed. This had a very good quality mahogany head and foot with an iron framework of curved form over it, the ends of which fixed into holes in the ends of the head and foot. I became involved with putting it together, and made John Whaley's acquaintance. He and I got on very well. A piece of ceramic appeared, which was reputed to have been made by Palissy. How were we to hang it on a wall? So I made a back in mahogany and fashioned wooden hooks thus to hold the precious piece.

Two small pedestal tables on tripod feet were requested and made. Then came the pictures. Judith accompanied him to addresses I'd never heard of, and some were purchased. I'm sure the vendor saw them coming. One was reported to be 'The Blue Boy' by Gainsborough. I had the job of hanging these. It was a very pleasant period. The phone would ring: 'Ah, John, I've another picture, could you come and discuss where we should hang it?'

So off to Manningtree Flora and I went, usually on Saturdays, to have sherry and look at the boating activities from the first floor window. Positions were agreed, and next week I was back putting these splendid works on hooks. He had a liking for 'Blue Nun' wine, and I found I did too, so a bottle of this was sometimes left for me.

I supplied him with a large old compactum which was not easy to install, but this was not to his liking, so it had to come out, to be replaced by a modern chipboard plastic (Melamine) covered doors etc. The doors were warped and I ducked putting all this junk together, so someone else did; but they were never a success. I thought this was a retrograde move but knew better then to say so. The Jaguar car that was just able to get into the garage was another symbol of wealth. He came to see us a couple of times after dining at one of the village pubs. He had had several drinks and cooled off in our sitting room.

This all came to an end suddenly, for our friend collapsed and died of a heart attack in his bathroom. So that was that; most good things come to and end quicker than the bad.

The year 1974 was the date, so my records show, that we received our last delivery of groceries from Great Oakley. Times were changing – and rapidly. Essex House, Great Oakley, had been a grocery shop for many years, and on Mondays along came a motor car, the driver of which would take our order, and on Tuesday along would come the order. I think this must have been going on since the 1930s. Those old grocery shops were damp and not very hygienic and had been what they were for many years. In one of them I discovered a large warming pan. Hidden under some rubbish and also a iron deed box. I soon turned up a handle for the pan. The deed box had its heavy handles cut away from each end and I made a frame to stand it on and installed it on end as a safe, and it served its purpose quite well.

Looking through the by now many rough books of time spent on some of the clients' items, I came across one of the veterinary gent's name at the top of a few pages. Now this young fellow found out what I was up to and asked if I could repair this and that. A large portrait of a lady with respectable gilt frame was produced. 'This is for a client,' he said.

Someone at some time past either disliked the person so portrayed, or the way it was done, for it seemed to have been stabbed several times. My details of work done were:

Make up new frame for canvas
Repair canvas edges and holes
5 hours…   £10.00

When the time came for its collection, our vet paid me and then wrote out his own ticket for his client for £25. 'I'm not working for nothing,' said he.

On another occasion a bill was settled by presenting me with about 20 brass door knockers, ones with pixies, dogs and other strange items cast on them. I took exception to this method of settling an account. But there was no escape, so I carted them off to an antique shop, and the lady proprietor very kindly paid me on the purchase price she would have paid for them. Our unpopular gent breezed in one morning and said he had to fill a container with furniture for a friend in Holland, and brought various items. Of course there was a time limit on all these. I was getting a bit sore with all the hassle. Some pieces were not finished and he came and took them away; I think this was the parting of the ways.

There was another entrepreneur who always drove in style in a large car. In the early days I found him quite fair. If someone had a house to clear I would give the people concerned his phone number and I usually received a crisp note for my trouble. Jobs that came via him were the usual time-consuming affairs and I never became very rich from their execution. He would breeze in with tales of woe about how bad trade was. A large microscope turned up – and a cabinet that I adapted to accommodate the former. This involved fixing a shelf and making a drawer to fit beneath to hold the five magnifying barrels. This was all with very little room to spare. Can you believe it they were all slightly different sizes (i.e. in diameter) – and the whole thing was married up?

A real good quality bureau was quite a decent job, not being difficult. Could I deliver it to Harwich Quay at such a time, and load it onto one of the vessels on its way to Holland? I arranged help here to load it, and down to the quay we went. We humped in up a long gangplank (a stairway, actually). We put it on deck, and along came a customs official.

'Bring this down,' he commanded. So we did. 'Where is the paperwork?'

I said I had none. He couldn't believe this. So I went off to phone the owner. For once he was at home, and came to the rescue. The official looked in every nook and cranny of it, which was taking a long time, and the boat was soon casting off. I began to curse. A piece or two of paper passed between the parties, and we humped it back on board. 'Next time you're exporting, do it yourself!' I barked to the vendor.

In the barn later on he spied the breakfast table bought several years before that needed restoring. It was upside down, covered in sparrow droppings and dirt. 'Ah, what have we here?' said he.

'Not for sale,' said I.

'£100,' he followed with.

'No,' said I.

'£150,' he followed with.

'No,' said I.

We go to £250, and then he comes out with, 'I want some work for my restorer in Ipswich.'

This last remark did not amuse me! Bloody cheek, really. During the 1990s I restored it. All that it needed was a replacement of one leg of the tripod pedestal. This was a hand saw job to start with, using about 4" x 2¼" mahogany. It found its way to the saleroom and realised £800.

Further aggro was to come. This chap had a liking for musical instruments, and the old pub polyphone was being sought. There were a few about, realising around £3000 apiece. As time passed, he found someone who was capable of making them. This was no mean feat, for the mechanism consisted of a large perforated brass disc. At the cornice was a sunburst topped by a quite detailed piece of carving. No one seemed to want to make this. So I was asked, and did a sample which suited. This occupied four to five hours and I charged £15 for the job.

Six were made in all. On the collection of the last one he announced, 'I can get them made cheaper in Taiwan!'

The story sounds rather one-sided and I've picked out the worst of the bad bits. We did have some deals which were fair. But when one is, as far as possible, fair at all times, the unfair parts seem to show up.

There were a few Bohemian couples in the trade. One such lived in a large townhouse nearby and during the time I, or I should say we, were associated with them we got on quite well. The shop was a glorified junk shop. The lady seemed reasonable adept at a form of china restoration, and most of the ceramics in there were suffering from repair. One had to watch any purchase, for items were often married up. I did some work for them. Some items were rescued from dustbins and small boxes often had ashes in them. With the advent of plastic bin bags the folk were a bit downcast, as this source of merchandise would disappear. I bought several sets of brass fire irons from a neighbour and left them with our dealer to sell. I met him in the Dedham tea shop one day a month or so later. He had a roll of notes and peeled off several. The fire irons had done very well. Looking back at diaries, I see that in February 1981, 'I was asked to call at M's to collect another so-called antique.' 'Come in for a cup of coffee,' said our friend.

Flora and I picked our way through various items of metal and wood on the floor of the large gallery to the room that was the living quarters. The table was strewn with small items of jewellery and objets d'art (*obzhay dahr*) getting into boxes for the next fair. They had six cats, two Siamese that were being boarded, and among the other four was one 16 years of age and her daughter about 15. There is also a Burman which was really lovely. One of the Siamese pulled a towel off the rail of the Aga cooker and curled up on it. There was an old stove giving heat in the centre of the room, and around it at one time the other five cats were sitting. It was all rather cosy and pleasant.

Desks

One of my first encounters with a desk (apart from those in school) was the cumbersome old lidded box with sloping lid standing on four legs, which was in the lobby behind the post office in the 1930s. It contained very little of any importance, but was jammed full of old papers of previous transactions over the previous fifty years. The file of old receipts hung from the roof, which was a wooden disc with long wire with a hook, over which one hade to pierce the item to be kept. These were standard equipment and were fairly practical for large pieces, but smaller items were pretty inaccessible for they were jammed in tight at the centre. In my usual way of scheming I wanted to have a more accessible desk, and in the barn was a washstand base, minus marble top. There was a mahogany table top handy, and this was large enough to cover the frame of the washstand, and a piece left to make the ends. The fall was a further piece of mahogany and, can you believe it, my Aunt Grace gave me a pair of hinges, brand new, which were the type used for such a project! The problem of supporting the fall was overcome by a piece of wood which was simply stood upright under it, and lay around somewhere when not needed. I created a drawer for cash with curved 'floor' and compartments for the various coins. Our accountant said, when I mentioned the Heath Robinson support, 'I've seen many worse ideas that that.'

This probably served for a year or two before I bought a roll-top – correct term 'tambour' – bought at a sale at a house nearby, which I seem to recall is mentioned elsewhere in these notes. It was the nerve centre of the business for several years. It had the refinement of an automatic drawer-locking device, which worked when the tambour was open, being arranged to press down on a piece, allowing the iron hooks to clip off the back of the drawer. I used the desk until I sold the coal business and sold it to a friend cheaply, for I considered I'd spent too many hours sitting it fighting adversity.

At some time in the early 1960s, I saw a cylinder top desk (*bureau de cylindre*) in a shop in Manningtree. It was smart and good, with cupboards beneath. The price was £9, and it was a bargain. It was soon to be installed here. It wasn't used as a desk, but the four satinwood drawers were soon filled with all manner of trinkets, mostly useless. I recall Flora, who did not smoke cigarettes to any extent, decided to stop and a packet, partly empty, was put inside a pigeonhole and there remained. Sometimes she would produce it with pride when the question of using the foul weed arose. As time went on I was offered £180 for the desk, so it went on its way to the tangled web of the antique market. This illustrated inflation at work.

A friend nearby had just lost a relative and he asked if I could clear the house, but I was rather busy so I loaned him my pickup truck. There was a hand-worked drilling machine and an Edwardian sideboard which was pushed into a gap between two sheds. The weather was not helping its condition, so I accepted these items for the loan of the vehicle. The possibility or making the sideboard into a desk was immediate: it was 5' x 2' at the back. Its height was lowered, the carved panels in the doors removed and plain ones replaced them. I recessed the top to take a piece of skiver and it has served its purpose since very well.

Over the years some small dramatic spark must have been kindled within, from having spoken to Mrs Morgan occasionally when delivering fuel for the Aga. I thought I would like to assist with the WI Drama Group, which they were forming. My first efforts were not very spectacular. I see in a diary that one of the first rehearsals was in 1966. A number from the musical *Annie get your gun* was chosen by me, and there were so many words packed in and at a fast rate, and I couldn't sing very well anyway!

The village hall lacked a stage, the original had long since fallen to pieces, so we, that is the village committee, got together. I bought s/h plywood 8' x 4' sheets ex contractors, a good supply of 4½" x 2" timbers from a First World War Army hut, which was what our village hall was anyway, and sometimes with help and sometimes on my own, we soon had a good strong stage. Curtains were needed. These were someone else's responsibility; they had to be made fireproof. We hung them to be operated both together from one side – really quite upmarket.

Someone had a go at writing a pantomime. Back scenery was required, so I rigged up a rounded 2" x 2" across the stage. It was only 13' wide. I fixed Hessian to it, ran it a sort of trunnion and then with a few basic colours of emulsion paints soon had scenery. In addition to pantos we had a sort of Music Hall. I same into my own with a 4' square board mounted on feet covered with wall lining paper. I told the story of a fictitious countryman who lived in a cottage by illustrating the cottage and other rural items on the paper with a brush. Jokes were interwoven.

'Old Fred didn't know the difference between margarine and putty, 'cos on a warm day all his window panes fell out.' An illustration of a chicken caused 'This little owd hin says she's a battery chicken goin' into the barn for a re-charge.'

All this was original and caused a lot of laughter. The little concert party was really successful and we were asked to go to villages around to entertain, and did this with some slight difficulty. My pickup truck was much used.

It was not very pleasant or practical when rain was falling, for it was difficult to cover over the various projecting items in the truck. I've jumped ahead rather; I had to go at drag artistry and allowed niece Lynda to dress me up as the Carnival Queen with blonde wig, short skirt and plenty of lipstick. 'I'm Beryl Bean, the Carnival Queen' was the first line of the 'Odd ode'. This, along with other items, was due to take place in the Village Hall, and it did; but at the time here were electricity cuts and although we were prepared with a 12 volt battery and a car headlamp it did rather spoilt the effort.

Charles Penfold, the schoolmaster, was very keen to write pantomimes. He turned up with out-of-date stuff from the Tommy Handley era, and the jokes were mostly dead. He did, however, come along with the idea of 'Babes in the Wood' in 1982. He called in to see us every day just before lunch at 1 p.m. during his compiling of the script. A fresh page appeared every day, and he insisted on going over every word and line with me, and expected to be right all along. I rarely passed an opinion, for our lunch was on the table at one o'clock promptly, every day and the sooner he had gone the better. The winter of early January in 1982 was snowy, and on one rehearsal (he needed to be at every one) a heated discussion broke out between him and the producer, Jane. 'You've got the wrong one to act as Puck – it should be Janet,' said he very directly. Our producer told him that she was in charge and was changing parts around to experiment. The snow outside was wet and slushy, but out intrepid playwright stormed out of the Village Hall in low shoes to walk the mile home. His temper was cooled next day, for at 12.55 p.m., he announced, 'I am not coming to any more rehearsals.'

However, there were about 24 in the cast and several others involved. I was Dame Prudence, the Schoolmistress, and looking back at the many photos, I wouldn't recognise myself. It was enormous fun. The school 'children' – mostly over leaving age by several years – became naughty in the last showing and used a catapult to shift objects around the stage. Two bulbs were broken, and this was not very funny.

I watched Rolf Harris on TV with his third leg, and fancied having a go at copying this. So I got a broom handle, shaped a simple foot to the base, and practised in the house. Someone obtained the music and words for 'Jake the Peg'. With a pair of overalls and a spare leg from another old pair of stout straight cords, rehearsals at Robin Looser's house were organised. I never could make my legs and feet work to music, and didn't get on very well for several attempts. But I kept at it, and when the time came for the concert all went well. I like the old Music Hall number 'It's a Great Big Shame', and got away with this also. There are many photos of all the shows in my possession, which hopefully will be available if anyone considers they are needed!

Robin Looser was a keen photographer. He copied old village postcards onto slides and showed them in the old Village Hall to quite a sizeable audience. I know most of the scenes and narrated as we progressed. Several evenings were spent thus, with the proceeds going to the new building funds.

In 1975, one of the members of the Parish Council who had a strong voice and was to be heard in the church choir, said to me, 'We need a block of wood to elevate the Altar Cross, can you do something to help?'

So I dutifully had a look at what was needed and when I met with this chap said, 'I'll do better than a block, I'll make you one with some carving on it.'

I got to work and made a stand of five sides, two of them carved with oak leaves. The Rector of the time, Eric Hayman, was overjoyed, and it did look quite a good job. There was a short prayer of dedication, as follows, on 29th June 1975.

Priest: 'We receive into the keeping and care of the Parish Church of All Saints, Wrabness, this gift of a carved oak base for the Altar Cross on the Holy Table of this Church: the gift of Mr J Calver of this Church and Parish: craftsman in wood and creator of this work and labour of love. We dedicate this carved oak base to the Glory of God, and to the praise of all who work with their hands the Thing which is Good. In the name of the Father, and of the Son, and of the Holy Ghost. Amen.'

This was the beginning of quite a long association between myself and the Rev. Hayman. In fact he was always calling in to see us and had some new idea in the offing. He was very devout and believed every word contained in the Bible.

A remembrance book was presented to the church and I created a bookcase shelf for it and fixed it up. The reredos had two end panels made also; this was a benefaction from the Garnham family, and was a job for which I did receive payment,

Base for altar cross

Part of two panels; carving by J C

and was a nice thing to accomplish. The porch doors were a disgrace, so I did them up and gave them several coats of varnish for several years.

There was a redundant pew in the church which I made into a small table for the children's corner. The altar table had to be reduced in width, a hand sawing job. The old top was really hard oak. The vestry door needed ventilation holes which had to have a disguise in front.

The notice board needed struts, as the gales were pushing it over. This was also varnished and small repairs and so on. Since Rev. Hayman, there have been four incumbents and when they visit us, which they rarely do, I'll tell them I do not often attend church services, but I like to know the place is there for those who need it.

I joined the Wrabness Parish Council in 1949, and often wondered why I stayed there for about forty years. When the Queen's Jubilee came around in 1977, there was a debate about what should we do to celebrate the occasion. I had thought about this for a few weeks, and said to the assembly, 'I will do a history of the village and show it off in the barn.'

Several other ideas were around also. We would have sports and a parade round the village. Could there be a concert as well?

One of the councillors, to his credit, got to know of a project being carried out by the Records Office whereby old village documents were being repaired and put into good order. Some were mounted on silk. We had a steel deed box (circa 1900), with several bundles of ancient and dilapidated papers, which he was instrumental in sending to the office, and which they duly repaired extremely well. So this was the nucleus of my idea. The Records Office was completely helpful. They supplied sheets of transparent film which were to be placed over the books etc. to avoid, finger marks etc. But before this happened the barn had to be cleared and cleaned. I still had quite a lot of furniture in there. So with help we packed all of this into one end bay, and had the use of the centre and the west bay. I began to construct temporary tables using billiard table legs and thick hardboard for tops.

Lighting was non-existent. Robin Looser and some assistants wired six fluorescent tubes which were supplied by a 50-yard cable, the label of which read '3 amp, no earth'. These all worked quite well and proved a boon.

Flora was a hard-working member of the WI, and told the members of our escapade, and they were given some space to use. Photos of any interest were asked for and displayed. In spite of our request for their owners to write their names on the back, several did not and difficulties arose. In fact the very first complaint was, 'Where is the photo of my husband?'

This had arrived about ten minutes before, and couldn't possibly have been dealt with. I also managed a few bygones, which was the start of another project later on. One lady had a comprehensive collection of celebration-type mugs and plates, and I displayed these in a china cabinet. There was a small collection of Stone Age implements and old newspaper articles on display.

Flora and I became very weary of all the walking from the house to the barn with all the odds and ends, and occasionally passed one another without saying a word. I had two maps, about 30" square, mounted on hardboard. One was of old field names, and another of the village in 1939. Of course, in the days when we had house sparrows by the dozen (there is scarcely one to be seen in 1999), their droppings did not improve the details on the maps.

In 1911 when the village was due to celebrate the Coronation of King George V, my grandfather offered his meadow for use on the day. The parson at that time declined using his lawn for the purpose, because he would have no intoxicating liquor consumed. The day was a complete success, and E Fisher was well praised. Now it's a strange thing, but when I was involved with the activity on the previous page, I felt that he was behind me saying, 'Now come on, me boy, this is what you have to do!'

I felt that it was the thing to do, and I'm glad we did it. The celebrations were carried on for four days. There was a parade and some fancy dress all the way around the village. Flora and I drove our Morris pickup, which had a harmonium in the back. This I tried to play, but there were two piano accordions behind and it all clashed badly. Robin's family provided a film camera and recorded some of the proceedings which was shown in the village hall several times. There were sports on John G's front lawn, and a concert in the Village Hall, so one way and another we all did well. It was all very worth while.

But now, in retrospect considering the ups and downs of the Royals since that time, I would not get involved to this extent again.

There was soon a move afoot to build a new Village Hall. There was some opposition, especially from one of the trustees, who did not want to lose control or something similar. I was a member of the Village Hall Committee, and several meetings were called to discuss it. One member from each village organisation made up the membership, and it numbered about a dozen people. So every possible venue was explored to raise money.

In the late 1970s, we set up a charity shop in a vacant property in Dovercourt High Street, and about £600 was raised in a few hours. By August 1981 we had raised £9540, by December £10,343 and a year on £16,830 – and so on. One member was, by luck, the manager of the local TSB bank and he 'farmed' the money out and captured interest rates of 12 per cent and more. We had amassed about £30,000 by about 1983. At this time Margaret Thatcher, the Prime Minister, had institutes the Youth Training Scheme, which meant that the project's labour was paid for by the government.

We had sufficient money now to purchase the materials. Another member of the committee was an architect, who drew up the plans free of charge. Mr J Macaulay, the owner of the land adjacent to the old Village Hall, gave the land required also free of charge.

The demolition of the old hall – a First World War Army hut – was carried out by some of the lads who were enlisted on the YTS. I, among others, was sorry to see its demise.

Work then began, and F Graves from Bradfield was in charge of building the new hall. Later on, I did some work on the building, which amounted to putting in double glazed windows. It is difficult to mention other members of the committee who were all helping in various ways. Photos appear in various albums.

I was responsible for obtaining a brass plate with the opening date of the hall and Mr J Macaulay's name engraved upon it. It was fixed to a piece of floorboard from the old building. The memorial board, with all the names of the valiant fellows who took part in the Great War, was put upon the wall in the entrance. Later this was moved into the main building.

Chapter Fourteen: Changes

In the early part of 1983 to mid-1984, things in my life began to go wrong. Flora's favourite brother, Percy, died and her sister Daisy's husband passed away. Both were my best friends. Flora fell victim to a bad attach of shingles, which was awful. E Alaway was harassing me about his roadside boundary (which, although part of the deal I had with Wallace several years before, had nothing to do with me). The outcome of all this was that I was prescribed a course of anti-depressant tablets and was getting in an awful muddle. Driving my vehicle was not advised; in fact I really could not, or did not feel safe doing so. My workshop jobs were not being done as well as they should have been. Flora did not know what to do for the best. It was very strange, but if a friend of Flora took us out for a run out in their car, I began to feel a little more normal and didn't want to go back home.

In about mid-1984 I was beside myself and phoned my GP quite late in the day and told him of my feelings. 'You can go into Severalls Hospital if you like,' he told me.

I said I would, and late that night John H collected us and there I found myself among many strangers. Poor Flora was out of her mind with worry. 'In there with all those funny people,' she said.

That night I remember saying to a nurse, 'My wife and little old dog are at home and they will starve to death 'cos I've no money.'

She smiled and said, 'Things are not that bad, I'm sure.'

Actually, they were not, for we had building society accounts reasonably secure.

I was of course among fifteen or so males who were in for various states of trauma and depression. We trouped in for meals and had of course to eat what was offered, and no second helpings. We were allowed to walk around outside in the grounds. There was a modern church there, and one of the female nurses suggested I should accompany her to a service there one Sunday. There were about five people in the congregation, and I didn't feel it helped me.

My bedroom was as near to a prison cell as it could have been. The only window was high up and impossible to see out from. Someone at times during the night would open the door and shine a torchlight in. Prozac tablets were administered each morning. One's razor was given in and had to be returned immediately after use. The treatment prescribed early on was to put me to sleep for a week with an injection (I think this was the method), and I had one grotty meal at midday, but after the week was over didn't seem any different.

Flora and others came to see me and we (i.e. Flora and I) had to see a doctor off and on, but it didn't seem to make me see any light at the end of the tunnel. The other fellows were keen on watching TV, and there was a billiard table which I did have a go at, but I didn't know the snooker drill, never really having played or studied it.

One of the lads, who was schizophrenic, had a room stacked with books and he was in a mad state one morning. 'I've lost my Keats,' he said frequently. I had a small purse with a few coins and I used to telephone Flora sometimes. These few coins were so precious to me then. I asked her to bring a certain poetry book from home and I lent it to the fellow I just mentioned; he was ecstatic. I came home for a few days, but for some reason had to return to Severalls – I have completely forgotten why.

Upon returning I was not welcomed, but I settled in again and slept in a large room with about twelve or so beds; but my bed was the only one in there occupied. Then began a session of electroconvulsive therapy, which involved one being put out for a few minutes and a charge of electricity passed through one's brains. We were waiting in a long narrow room before treatment, both sexes being present, and one at a time were treated. One young lady was in an awful state of fear. I held her hand and tried to tell her that there was nothing to worry about; she tried to escape but could not. We were given hot tea and biscuits to recover.

On the radio many months later someone said that ECT was

similar to kicking a TV set when it didn't work. I am sure that it helped me. In the grounds was a building labelled 'Severalls Industries', and several folk were working there making blinds. I ventured in, and met the fellow in charge, a man with a mass of blond hair called Roger. He must be the best fellow I ever met there. He listened to my tale and found two circular tables that needed polishing. So glass paper and French polish were purchased, and I spent a few hours on them and he seemed quite pleased. He asked if I used veneer. I answered, 'Yes, sometimes.' Then he produced a box of 3/8" pins which I've found very useful in later days.

Flora and I once again had audience with the doctors, and somehow the story of the early parts of the bad patch that Winston Churchill called his 'black dog' came to be disclosed. 'Why didn't we know all this before?' we were asked. Flora was told, 'Your husband doesn't seem to be the sort of material to become to involved in this illness.'

So I was discharged. 'You may have to come back for re-appraisal,' someone said, but I never did.

Upon our arrival home, George Mitchell was doing farm work here, as he did for me then as a contractor. He welcomed me and said, 'What are we going to plant, John, for next year?'

'Let's have some more wheat,' I said with enthusiasm.

In those years wheat brought £100 per tonne. In 2002 it's about £60 per tonne.

So what now? The workshop didn't have a lot of work left over; I guess people had heard of my troubles. But we went for a walk, often a favourite one, in the Stour Wood, and opposite lived John H, a carpenter of good quality. He came to us and said, 'I know you are into furniture repairs and I was talking to an antique dealer in Thorpe who is needing items restored.'

My world seemed instantly brighter. I found his telephone number and we met, soon. He and his wife had a huge amount of furniture in dry accommodation, which is a great advantage.

So along came a Volvo car with various pieces for repair. The work was varied. The German customers came to their shop and were good customers. One item is 'extensive repairs to writing slope, new leather etc.' These were lovely little bits of cabinet-making, and looked smart when finished. Leather here is properly described as skiver, as actual hide would be too thick and is not really suitable. It could be purchased in the size required; there were eleven colours to choose from and 30 different tooling patterns for the borders. But the time spent on their restoration was sometimes much too long. Inside the better quality ones were secret drawers, and one wondered what they contained in past days: love letters, perhaps; what fun to have found one – but I never did. They had two inkwells, some with silver tops, but these were never left for me to find one. There must have been thousands lost or thrown away.

Having thoughts of the few bygones that I had on show in the farm buildings in 1977 at the Queen's Jubilee, I developed this gradually and the stable at Domine was in my ideas. This was, as such, already partly occupied by old pieces of farming gear. I bought several sheets of hardboard and cut them to size to fit between the old studwork. This was a slow job as no two studs were the same size, or exactly straight.

As I progressed, some of the items were hung up on nails and in spite of working in an awful muddle I began to think it was worthwhile. I put lime wash onto the hardboard and it began to look better all the time. Roger Paskell gave me an old treadle lathe that was used in S Ellis's, the carpenters and wheelwrights at Ramsey. I put a wide long table top along one side and covered this with woodwork tools, from many years ago. Large and heavy chisels for chopping mortise holes in cartwheel waves, draw knives, spokeshaves, wood-boring augers etc. We rarely went out without finding and buying something to fill the empty spaces. There was plenty to be bought. I discovered one of the largest butter churns at The Shoulder of Mutton in Hadleigh, it must have held 10 gallons. I can't imagine how much cream one needed to get going in its huge interior.

Another part of the farm buildings was an open fronted shed, longer than the stable. It had a lining on the rafters of wide boards and was obviously used to house cattle. This was to protect them from the winter winds, and of course once had doors, which had disappeared from sight and memory. So I bought several windows from a site where new ones were being installed, and with a glazed door, which was from the Ramsey bakery, filled in the opening. The walls were covered with hardboard and limewashed, like the stable. We gradually fitted the two benches with old smoothing irons, a German spirit iron, one that needed charcoal and the box type with the 'bit' inside. Teapots, dairy items, butter prints, milking stools and so on were added, with early vacuum cleaners and an early kitchen range, around which I made a mock-up of brickwork.

The intention was to have groups of people here to look around and raise money for charity. This latter idea brought very little, but did improve when Flora and a friend, Pat, served tea and scones from the front window of the house to folk who could not look around the garden. We were assured of the enjoyment from several letters received. This was in July 1994.

With the farm buildings 60–70 yards down a quite well maintained roadway, the journey to and from was beginning to be a bit difficult on foot, and I was using the car or the pickup truck to attend to the collection. As time went on it is almost difficult to admit but I was losing interest in it. When anyone did look around, I had to clean up and brush up around the items. They were covered with sheets of polythene but the sparrows, which are reported to be disappearing, certainly were not then. I had labels and descriptions attached to many pieces, which frequently needed reprinting. I was finding all this occupation rather tiresome.

There it remained really unattended for a couple of years. Our friends from Holland contacted us with a view to staying with us for a holiday. Flora was suffering with an arthritic knee and we had to say that we could not accommodate them. I spoke to the people at the Strangers Home at Bradfield Public House and they had room in the caravan and tent park. So the folk agreed to go there. However, I volunteered to show them around the bygones, so once again I was tidying again. Flora, who had been on a waiting list for a knee replacement joint for eleven months, was really suffering. I telephoned the hospital and used my powers of persuasion, and within a week or two she had premeds and we took her to Black Notley Hospital on 27th July 1996. This hospital was a bit dilapidated.

She came home nine days later. Visits by a therapist were not welcomed by her. I had to learn a small amount of cookery and waited on her as best I could, but I said she could have her kitchen back anytime. Climbing the stairs was never any better than previously. So with help, I brought our bedroom onto the ground floor. Someone said when you have to do that it's a 'downward step' – in more senses that one. The change was not understood by Flora, somehow. Nothing was where it used to be, of course, but it was very difficult for her to cope with.

Life churned along. I seemed to be spending a lot of time cutting grass with a ride-on mower and other push types. The vegetable garden was reduced in size and I was finding it very much harder to cope. Trees continued to grow; older ones blew over and had to be cut up. Open fires in the house were lovely in the winter, but all the effort required was not easy. I did still drive out, and our breaks were visits to Frinton or Walton and Dedham, which seemed minimal compared with some people's holidays, but a cup of tea and a couple of cakes were quite satisfactory. Flora often mentioned visits in her diary. I vividly recall the night of the hurricane in 1987! We came down from the bedroom and electricity had gone.

Flora lit candles and spent sometime cleaning brass. The noise of the gale was frightening, but she was occupied and didn't say much. We had two gas burners – emergency camping items – so we could have a hot drink. The willow tree had blown across the roadway so we couldn't get away by motor until some sawing was carried out. The old house was more or less undamaged. The barn had suffered. The oak tree nearby was over. When sawn into useable pieces it was found to be about 95 years old. Looking at diaries, we had frequent gales and lost power. Flora always occupied herself by knitting or cleaning something. In 1990 a terrific gale from due west demolished the brick chimney serving the Rayburn cooker. We were in the house. The crash was scary; I didn't have it rebuilt and bought a new electric cooker. This was a decision that was very difficult for Flora, and she got into severe difficulties with the various knobs.

She was among the founder members of the Wrabness Evergreen Club somewhere back in 1968. This was an organisation for the over-sixties. They met twice every month and she was a very keen member. They needed cakes and bread and butter. She took her turn with cakes, and when the lady who was responsible for the bread gave up Flora took over the job.

Newspapers were collected and stored at Wrabness Hall and sold to boost the funds. Flora was also a member of the WI, and took a very active part in the group of entertainers that Mrs Morgan began. They performed in the Village Hall, and when the time was deemed right took part in a performance at the Princess Theatre at Clacton, in which several amateur groups were involved. On another occasion one of the performers had to learn everyone's part, in case one was absent. Flora undertook this onerous task. It so happened that a motor cycle accident caused someone's absence, on the day of the performance. The lady producer said she would announce that Flora was standing in, and she said if you do I shall not take part. She carried out the job to perfection. Small poems were a frequent conquest. The one below was written in a diary while taking part in the function.

> Oh what an exhibition!
> It was such a splendid show –
> Nothing to pay admission
> People just walked to and fro.
> All club members were invited
> To show their considerable skill;
> A few said they didn't want to
> Quite a lot said, 'Oh, I will!'
> The labels were all tied on tightly
> To the items which they had all made
> Awaiting the turn of the judges
> Before being nicely displayed.
> There were babies' woollies and mittens
> Baby shawls as well
> Tablecloths and oven gloves
> And such a loo to sell.
> One grand old lady passed my stall
> And looked around to see –
> 'Had her cushion cover been sold?

It had some flowers on a sort of a tree –'
I was bold enough to ask her age
And soon came back the reply:
'I'll be 87 next birthday, that is if I don't die.'
I marvelled at her neatness, and how she could see to sew
Such a very tiny stitches, and so keen to have a go.
It's nice to just stand and listen
To what people had to say
Like, 'I've only just managed to get here,'
And, 'Oh, I've been here all day.'
It's fun being a club member,
Even if you only help with the teas,
So good luck to all the Older Folks Clubs –
We are proud of such people as these.

In one of my diaries I discovered the following: 'Our god-daughter called.' She had previously written telling of a friend had had a bad patch and was feeling depressed, and mentioned on a previous visit Flora had given both of them a bunch of pansies from the garden. The friend had pressed some of the petals and felt better each time she looked at them.

'Pansies for thoughts…'

I've told her on more than one occasion she was too good for this world.

Flora's friends were for ever. She had old school pals and I'm sure never had a cross word or a falling out.

I came back from the church having varnished the notice boards to be met by our dog, Bobbie. 'What are you doing out here?' said I. As we approached the open kitchen door, Flora said, 'Don't laugh – I'm on the floor.' She was sitting on the floor! I put my arms under her armpits and lugged her onto the chair nearby. I could not find anything broken and she seemed reasonable. At her sister's before this, we were just leaving and standing with our backs to the wall and she simply crumpled into a heap. There seemed no damage from this either. Our cooker was not working, so Pam cooked for us. Flora was very confused. I was trying to clear up the lane after the tractor sprayer carried mud outside, finding it difficult to use a shovel.

I've had to have a small operation on my left elbow, so that's another handicap. At the appointed time, the District Nurse came and removed the stitches from the offending spot. I mentioned slight memory loss etc. with Flora. She didn't elaborate, but I was beginning to wonder having read about problems in the newspaper. We went to Dovercourt by car and as we walked from the park, Flora said to me, 'Where are we? I don't know where I am…'

Now for the sad part of the story.

Alzheimer's disease

Extract from diary: Talked to District Nurse of my wife's strange changes in her memory. My first knowledge of the problem.

July 2000: Somewhere here we went to Dovercourt and she didn't know where she was. In a car park couldn't remember where the car was or the number.

5th September: Life becoming difficult with hallucinations. There is a third person in the house. I am John, and she asked where was John. 'I'm here.' 'No, the other one,' was her reply.

15th September: Flora very difficult – I am her brother.

26th September: Found her standing outside the back door with a walking stick and a bag with a dress. She was going to a cottage where she lived with her mother, who died 50 years ago.

28th September: She is sure she had seen Mrs Garnham in the garden. This was her previous employer. I'm at loss to know what to say.

30th September: Went to Village Hall to a picture exhibition where she met several friends, which seemed quite good.

1st October: Three tractors working in our field. Lot of activity. Flora was trying to get extra food to feed the drivers. She got plates on the table and was worried and unsettled. I should have taken her out in the car. 'Mother' again! I showed her the funeral bill but there was no logic.

6th October: Went to GP – first visit. He gave a few co-ordination tests, which she managed. No medication given.

7th October, p.m.: Several visitors, two of whom she hadn't seen for a time. Complete confusion. After teatime she went to sleep for one and a quarter hours. Upon waking, she didn't know where the bathroom was and I took her through the house. Came to slowly by 10 p.m.

8th October: By 10 a.m., 'I've got to go,' she said, I face her and say, 'Look at me – your mother is not there, she is dead!'

11th October: Lyn, her niece, came from Dovercourt for four hours, which had a good effect.

16th October: Flora in a muddle again: 'I must go' etc. She asked me when John was coming by.

17th October: A lovely sunny day. She said, 'What a lovely day' – repeated at least eight times during the day.

18th October: More confusion. Neighbour Pam came to sit around while I went to get petrol. Flora's sister, Daisy, came p.m. She simply says, 'Oh, she'll get over it.'

25th October: Lyn here again. Robert Macaulay brought two pheasants, one of which Flora plucked prepared and cooked. I buried the other. She needs watching all the way when using the cooker. Her sister did begin to realise Flora was not okay.

5th November: South-east gale with a vengeance, and of all days, sister and son turned up in evening in rainstorm. Flora was beside herself, trying to make tea and producing knitted items from the past to show. 'Oh, Flora, I've seen that before.'

9th October: Flora had conquered very (to me) intricate knitting patterns, but by now was losing the capability and was becoming unsettled.

10th November: Lyn came on the 10.30 bus and stayed until 3.45. We had lunch, and this gave me a few minutes to get out of the house. She did this fairly often. The effect on Flora was remarkable. Lyn had spent many happy hours here when young and had never had a cross word with us.

12th November: By 10.20 Flora wanted to go on the usual journey. She couldn't take in anything I said and wanted to ring the post office to see if Mother was there. Trevor, the postmaster and my cousin, abruptly told Flora that she wasn't.

15th November: We went to see Muriel and Ruth, and Muriel had reached 101 years; this made a change.

11th December: Flora was settled a bit, but two visitors who came off and on seemed to create confusion. Flora didn't seem to know them or what to do. She wanted to take them to Chapel Cottages where she used to live. I'm really stressed.

17th December: She has a coat on and says, 'I'm going to Mother's.' I locked the door. We went round to Chapel Cottages in the car. Flora lived there when the family came from Great Blakenham in 1927. She got out of the car and tapped on the door. 'Hello, Flora, come in.' (We knew the occupants quite well.) 'My mother is here, isn't she?'

We sat down for a few minutes; Valerie tried to reason. We went off and I delivered a few Christmas cards. When we got back home, both cold and demoralised. Flora was done for. Next day she did not recall anything about the day before.

20th December: We've had twelve visitors during the day and it's very tiring and confusing.

January 2001: We went to Mistley Walls and walked about 50 yards.

8th January: I noticed Flora's unease. 'Don't you dare go out without telling me!' said I, and went to the bathroom.

'I'm going,' she called.

'Wait!' I replied, but she was off on foot, with coat and walking stick.

I clattered out of the door to catch her up. She was heading for Chapel Cottages (where we went on 17th December). It was about 500 yards, and

Flora tapped on that door again and we went in. Valerie brought us home by car. 'Try to keep calm,' she said. Flora hadn't walked that far for many months since having her knee joint replacement in 1996. At 10 p.m. she said, 'I shall go to Dimbols tomorrow.' (Where she worked fifty years ago.)

11th January: Lyn here again; she seems to settle Flora completely.

15th January: Psychologists to assess Flora's medication. Flora is sure that her mother was now living with sister Daisy in the village. I suggested she telephone Daisy to ask where she lived now. This was done, and Flora was met with a rebuff and afterwards was in a complete muddle.

16th January: We got through breakfast and by 10 a.m., 'I must go,' said Flora. She seems to think her mother is there alone.

19th January: We went to friends near Dovercourt. Snow was falling. Flora seemed more compelled to want to go out the worse weather became. Lyn came and calmed things a bit.

22nd January: Flora insisted on going to Hope Cottage and strode out on her own. I got the car and followed her, picking her up about 100 yards down the hill. 'You don't think much of me or you wouldn't let me go alone!' We go round the back of the cottage and though there's no one there she is sure she could see her mother inside. I had difficulty getting her to come away. Went to Harbour Crescent next.

23rd January: I wrote a note to the people who lived at Hope cottage asking if they would write a note to Flora telling her that her ma wasn't here, which they did, and the lady actually put a passage on tape. She called with these items, but Flora didn't know what was going on. Total confusion.

26th January: I've developed a hernia had to go to see the GP. During all this time I frequently went out with Flora by car to sit and change the scene.

4th February: Pam comes here to see Flora most weeks for an hour or two – the only time I can get out of the house.

8th February: The Arecept drug being used but was withdrawn after a few weeks.

27th February: Our lives are becoming very traumatic. I was advised to lock the house doors. Flora most upset: 'You can't do this to me' etc.

4th March: Managed to go to Lyn's to lunch. Flora seemed quite good for an hour or two. Tendring Carers consulted, and by arrangement a lady came for two hours but Flora most upset and actually stuck her tongue out behind her back. Most unheard of for her.

5th March: I phoned Kim (the nurse) and said I couldn't take much more of this. Went to see GP and said the same. He thought I was heading for a breakdown, and more tablets prescribed. When in Manningtree that morning met some friends and had a cup of tea and Flora seemed settled. But at home Mother could be seen coming toward the house…

6th March: Phone rings and Kim said there is a bed and room at Michaelstow Hall Residential Home. Would I take it? I hadn't much choice and agreed. 'I'll come now,' she said. I said, 'Well, let's have a bit to eat.' So she said, 'Put some items in a case. I'll come at 2 p.m.' This she did, telling Flora that I wasn't well, and she would have to go away for a few days. We had some food and I had to pack this case – what to put in?

Flora was completely upset, thinking I was not well. She was whisked out of the house at about 2.15. 'I sat down and said I felt I had sent her to her grave. So I was alone. On my visit to the home, one of the carers said, 'You've probably saved her.'

The next day, after admission, nephew Michael recognised Flora walking to Dovercourt and couldn't believe his eyes. He stopped and spoke and two carers were behind with a car to collect her. They soon found out what they were up against. But she became institutionalised fairly quickly.

We had cleared away from lunch and I went into the kitchen looked around and came out again. The chair Flora sat in most of the time was of course vacant. The ensuing days and weeks were full of visions of where she was, what she had done, all thought the nearly fifty years of marriage. I was soon involved in a completely new and unfamiliar life.

I was advised by a senior lady at Michaelstow Hall not to go and see her for a few days. Lyn went on the second day and Flora said, 'Oh good, you've come to take me home.'

What does one say in such a situation like that? Lyn said that she had to say something like, 'I'm just going down to get something for you,' and simply not go back. 'That was the most awful thing I'd ever had to do, after all the lovely things Auntie had done for me; she had never let me down,' she said.

On my first visit to the home, the first question was, 'Has your wife a private income?'

I said she had a building society account. So I had to arrange her to sign a withdrawal slip, and £1500 per month disappeared from the account.

Then, 'Is your wife's visit respite or permanent?' I said the latter. 'Are you sure? You can wait and see.' I said from what I knew of the past year I was sure.

I would like to include here advice to anyone who is involved with a relative, or know anyone who is in Flora's condition, try to obtain Enduring Power of Attorney. I couldn't because if you mention Alzheimer's, whoever it is will not be of sound mind and cannot sign anything that important. I visited the CAB for various advice about joint accounts and solicitors, in connection with wills which we had written several years back. The toing and froing was quite a tiring affair. I visited the home, as mentioned in the 'diary'. I became passable at stitching name tags into Flora's clothes.

Flora was one of the loveliest girls there ever was. We were childhood sweethearts. Her mother was ill frequently in the 1940s. We married in June 1951 after her mother's death earlier that year. We came to live at Domine Farm. My mother, who died in 1954, got on extremely well with Flora. We both took an active part in village affairs and entertainment in Village Hall. She learned the dialogue in plays, and was a member of the WI. We always had our meals together and were very close. Family seemed not to happen; we had tests but there was some problem that I never really understood.

She always helped me and others in every way she could. Kim Evans said as she whisked Flora away, 'She might live twenty years,' words that are always ringing in my ears.

On 9th March, two days after Flora's admission to Michaelstow, I was summoned to see a psychoanalyst. A taxi collected me. The firm did a lot of collecting for the Colchester General Hospital. I can't recall whether or not I knew why I had to go. The caller said, 'We can't come onto your farm' – the foot-and-mouth epidemic was at its height. I sat in the workshop and waited until this vehicle, which could have carried six people, arrived at the road gate.

So I walked to the 'venue' and off to Colchester, and was interviewed by a Middle Eastern fellow. I questioned what this was all about. 'We thought you might kill your wife, and then yourself,' he told me. I guess it may have been the fact that I'd had a nervous breakdown seventeen years before. I answered many questions and left him without doubt that I wasn't that kind of person. I waited about an hour to be collected; other folk came and were interviewed (not in my presence).

11th March: Michaelstow needed more clothes. I scratched about the house. Carol, a nephew's wife, helped. Lyn had been to see Flora and told me she was in a double room. I saw her for the first time in complete confusion. The room was large with two single beds, a lavatory en suite and a washbasin. She had no idea where the loo was, in spite of my help. I managed to take her in the car and we to Lyn's to lunch.

20th March: Flora quite good a.m. New drug given.

21st March: Pam to see Flora.

23rd March: Flora's feet attended to (by a visiting chiropodist). She would not have this done at home. As time went on her feet were greatly improved by regular attention.

8th April: Took Flora to Harwich Harbour for half an hour. She couldn't understand why we went back to Michaelstow. I said, 'You wouldn't stay indoors, wanting to find your mother.' 'That was years ago,' she said.

13th April: I stayed with her three hours. She's very unhappy: Mother still predominates.

26th April: Flora had a fall (bruises).

6th May: Returned to Wrabness for lunch with Pam. We went to a church exhibition of wedding dresses. When the organ started to play, Flora couldn't stand it and we came home to Pam's. Difficult to explain why we went back to Michaelstow.

14th May: Flora's eightieth birthday; a few visitors.

16th May: We all had a family gathering at Lyn's.

24th May: Sister Daisy's birthday. Took Flora; going back very difficult.

5th June: At last she has a doctor. I take her to clinic to see him. She had water problem, really awful.

10th June: We've been married 50 years. I came back with her to John Hockley's for a little party. The ladies put on a nice little do. Flora didn't really know what it was all about.

13th August: Deteriorating… asleep so I came home.

2nd September: Flora has to be helped to eat. She had moved to Room 7 on the ground floor.

8th September: Flora had a mini-stroke – 1 aspirin a day.

15th September 2002: It's a strange life. Flora peeled an apple to eat. I took a tape; she seems to like piano music.

4th October: Flora between very good and poor. She seems happy with a snatch of taped music.

14th May 2003: She is 82 today. She seems to like to see Michael.

27th May: She has moved to Room 10 and has to be lifted by hoist and has a pneumatic mattress.

June: Flora in bed all the time.

July: Flora having all liquidised food; looks awful.

January 2004: Flora seems to have changed. She's brighter and tries to talk, and some things almost are understandable. She's thin – really skin and bone.

19th January: When one sees her we give a few pieces of crumbly chocolate or a piece of orange free of skin and come away without having said much to the carers or seniors. 'No change' is often the report. (The paragraph above is misleading as today she is in another world of sleep and non-movement.)

Domine, with all its neglected flower beds and overgrowth, was beginning to worry me. March 2001 was very wet and the barley was looking waterlogged. I was becoming quite depressed about it all. An elderly acquaintance living in the new flats at the home asked if I would like to see her home. So I did, and it was very smart. Several flats were served from a central hallway, and there is no garden or of course anywhere for a shed.

The rain continued and we had eight months of above-average rainfall to the end of May. Diary entry: 'There is a feeling of hopelessness around me in and outside Domine.'

'The barley produced a miserable 17 tons of poor quality grain. Worst harvest I've ever known.

'In October I went into local hospital and had the hernia operation. It rained throughout the night. Now I have a waterworks problem, and had to stay there nine days, waiting to see a prostate specialist. I'm catheterised now.'

This was the position for about fifteen weeks. Not a pleasant experience. These things block up and infections can be awful. However I had the prostate operation, and this was a success.

In January 2002, the Domine problems were always before my eyes, I did have a lot of help from relatives and friends. There were two Michaels who must be mentioned. Nephew ME and MM, a best friend who I had known and worked and traded with for thirty years. He supplied the transport for all those bygones to Diss Auctioneers, Suffolk.

Michael E did sterling work in clearing up all the overgrowth in Domine garden and around the farm buildings. He had huge bonfires with the rubbish. The barn contained heaps of redundant broken bits of furniture that might have been used, but never were, which were burned.

I had a young married couple who really wanted to buy the property. I had it valued and they offered a price very close to the top figure. The date for the changeover was 30th September 2003 and the day loomed large. I tried to think of moving as another adventure; it was in one sense, but it was quite sad. There were three bedrooms; two were used in latter days to store some of the items I had made which did not find a home. The prospective owners had lived in a flat in London and had little time to spare, but they were glad to accept a few pieces. I began to pack items of crockery in the spring. I found that the job went on and on.

I had laid up the Morris pickup truck for eighteen months. The MOT test was no problem – I got it back to work. ME & Son moved most of the furniture from Domine to the bungalow. They worked hard.

Later in the year, having seen an advert in the *East Anglian* for a regular sale of bygones and all sorts of items at Diss, with huge help from friends van loads of them was sold there. During 2003, three more loads were taken, and by now I had been involved in getting permission to build a bungalow on the last remaining plot of land from my grandfather's field. By March 2003 building had begun, and I had sold Domine. In March 2004 I settled in this smart modern establishment.

The area is very familiar, as I spent all those thirty-two long years in the coal business and in the beginning with the old post office. If I had have moved away ten years ago, I doubt if it would have altered the problems Flora has fallen victim to, but we never know what life has in store for us.

Following an article in a local magazine, her niece has written to the author with a tribute to her Aunt:

> Auntie Flora was like a second Mum to me. Having had no children of her own, she treated me like a daughter. I had a truly wonderful childhood, much of it spent at 'Domine Farm'. I would help Auntie feed the chickens and collect the eggs. She also let me pick up windfall apples, cut them in slices and climb in with the baby pigs to feed them.
>
> I had such fun. When she had Bantam chicks I was allowed to put them in her old shopping basket and bring them indoors for a while. One special highlight was to go looking for new kittens,

when one of Auntie's cats had given birth, in an old shed or the big barn. She even hand-reared one kitten with a doll's bottle. On old and wet days we would cook cheese scones and Scotch pancakes for Uncle John's tea.

We also had lots of adventures out to Dovercourt and even Colchester on the double-decker bus, as she did not drive in the early days. When she did get a car, a 'Baby Austin', she would let me turn the knob on the dashboard round the villages. I could go on for ever about all the kind things she had done for so many people during her life.

Alzheimer's is a wicked, evil disease which has taken my beautiful Auntie just out of my reach, but I still love her with all my heart, and thank goodness my memories will be with me always.

Barn Domine Farm

Printed in the United Kingdom
by Lightning Source UK Ltd.
106834UKS00001B/37-153